THE PRODUCTIVE GARDEN COMPANION

To you.

To you, beginning from exactly where you are: with a single pot on a sill, a small patch already full or only an idea you haven't quite named yet.

To you, arriving with whatever you carry: experience or uncertainty, weariness or wonder, a lifetime in gardens or none at all.

These pages are my way of walking beside you, offering what I've learned and loved, in the hope that they keep you in good company as you grow your own way.

From my home and garden in Daylesford, Victoria, I acknowledge the Dja Dja Wurrung people, the First Peoples and Traditional Owners of this Country. I pay my respects to Elders past and present, and I recognise the knowledge held by Djaara who have cared for this place for countless generations. I commit to listening, learning and acting in ways that care for soil, water and community in respectful relationship with Country.

A complete guide to growing for abundance and beauty in any space

THE PRODUCTIVE GARDEN COMPANION

NATASHA MORGAN

murdoch books
Sydney | London

Contents

INTRODUCTION

Why do I grow? Why do I design? Why do I keep coming back to green spaces? To be honest, I don't think I can fully explain this compulsion. But I know that it lives somewhere deep inside me.

From as far back as I can remember, I've always been drawn to gardens. Not in a tidy, goal-orientated way, but in the way a child is drawn to a patch of light, or the texture of a leaf, or the mystery of what might be hiding under the soil. It was never about achievement. It was about noticing. About being there. Absorbed. Curious.

Gardens were the first places I learned to trust my instincts. They became the places to which I kept returning through every season of my life because they let me be exactly who I am. They didn't ask me to perform, to explain or to prove myself. They merely invited me to pay attention. And, over the last decade, they have become my definition of living well.

For me, living well is about being in rhythm with the land. It's about community, creativity and connection. It's about making space for the things that matter most, and letting go of the rest.

Gardens are where that understanding has deepened most. As well as being places of productivity and design, they're where I've felt most like myself. Most steady. Most whole. Gardens have carried me through some of the hardest times of my life. They have reminded me what it feels like to be present and to find contentment in the rituals of daily tending. For me, living well looks like:

— designing spaces that nourish the people who use them
— growing food without chemicals, and preserving what's in season
— sharing knowledge through teaching, writing and conversation
— collaborating with others, not working in isolation
— finding solace and steadiness in the cycles of growth and rest
— noticing the first snow pea, the crunch of frost, the shape of a new leaf
— feeling rooted in who I am, not just what I achieve.

This book has grown from that place. Not as a manifesto or a manual, but as a companion. It's something you can return to, again and again, as you shape your own way of living well.

CREATING A REWARDING OASIS

I've always believed that a garden offers more than just what you can grow. It's a space that gives back to the land, to the people who tend it and to the rhythm of life itself. For me, it's never been just about cultivating plants. It's also about creating something generous and useful. Finding beauty in the everyday, easing off and letting the seasons guide what comes next.

This book brings together what I've learned across different chapters of my life, from designing large-scale landscapes and public gardens to building a life around growing, making and teaching. Some of those lessons came through formal

***Opposite page*_**Winter structure is part of the plan. Seed heads are left standing to catch light, hold form and keep the garden working for insects long after flowering has finished.

training and professional practice. Others were mastered while I was waist-deep in compost or as I watched the same garden bed change across a decade.

If there's a thread that runs through it all, then it's this: the most enduring gardens come from a relationship with place. Not from rules, trends or quick wins, but from taking the time to notice what's already there and shaping something thoughtful from that.

'If there's a thread that runs through it all, then it's this: the most enduring gardens come from a relationship with place.'

There's plenty in these pages about gardening and design. About soil, planting, preserving and making. Rest assured that you'll find all of the practical stuff here. But this isn't a how-to garden book in the conventional sense. It's a guide to help you think, feel, plan, grow and adapt so your space becomes not just productive, but truly yours. Whether you're beginning with bare soil or revisiting a garden you've tended for years, I'll walk alongside you as you:

- — get to know your space
- — clarify what matters most
- — shape your vision
- — work out the details
- — bring the garden to life
- — grow, maintain and adapt through the seasons.

We'll move between design thinking and hands-on know-how. We'll explore how the principles I've developed can apply across scales, from small backyards to larger productive plots, and how the values behind the design are just as important as the layout itself.

Throughout this book, you'll hear from others, too. I've included voices and case studies that reflect a shared ethos of seasonality, sustainability and beauty with purpose. One of those voices is that of Phyllida Steele-Wareham, who visited my current garden at Little Cottage on a Hill: 'The garden feels as though it's always been there. Natasha has layered it with intention and generosity, every space offering something to use, to admire, to pause in. Nothing is wasted, and yet nothing feels overworked. There's restraint, but also warmth. It's a place that makes you exhale.'

Phyllida's visit offered me a rare gift: the chance to see my garden through another gardener's eyes. Her words stayed with me, and they remind me why gardens matter. You'll find her full reflection in Chapter 8.

This book is an offering. A way to share what I've lived, tested, taught and returned to season after season. It's not about perfection; it's about building something meaningful, useful and yours. I've written this book to help you bring that same clarity to your space, whether it's a large backyard or a small courtyard, whether you're just beginning or need to see your garden with new eyes.

You don't need to have all the answers. You just need to begin. And this book is here to support that.

***Opposite page*_**Purple coneflower (*Echinacea purpurea*), ladybird, light, pause. There is beauty in almost every garden moment, if you pay attention. The garden is a shared space.

WHAT A PRODUCTIVE GARDEN MEANS TO ME

The word 'productive' is often used in gardening, and just as often misunderstood. It's usually tied to industry, output or how much we can do or grow in a day, but I've come to define it quite differently. For me, a productive garden is not about squeezing more in or working harder. It's about planting that is considered and seasonally responsive. About choosing to cultivate things that nourish both my life and the life around me.

My first sense of what productive could mean began at my *baka*'s table (*baka* is Serbian for grandmother). She would never let anyone arrive or leave unfed. 'Nataša, *jedi* [eat], you skinny same as rats!' she would say in her thick accent, before pulling out a bottle of something pickled or preserved from her cool cellar under the kitchen floor; abundance held in glass, and I later inherited those Fowlers Vacola jars and still use them to this day. That domestic alchemy of tucking abundance away taught me that a productive garden is generous, seasonal and made for sharing. Later in this book, you'll meet Nonna Carmella, whose pickled eggplants pressed the lesson deeper: that good food is simply what the garden offers and the hands honour. These experiences are the throughline: heritage, kitchen and garden folded together. They shaped my definition of productivity not as output but as a way of living, a rhythm you'll see echoed in the harvesting and preserving parts of this book.

A garden is productive not only because of what is grown there, but also because of how the space is used. My hybrid driveway and courtyard works as a place to gather, to share food and to turn the garden's offerings into time together.

Harvesting from the northern verge at Little Cottage on a Hill. Vegetables, herbs, flowers, fruits and perennials are planted here as a single, working whole. The verge is productive, beautiful and designed to give in more than one way.

Through writing this book, my understanding of 'productive' has expanded. Thanks to conversations with people across climates and disciplines, I've had the privilege of hearing perspectives that challenged and deepened my views. Designers such as Simone Bliss, who creates spaces for healing, and Mary Reynolds, whose work with rewilding speaks to gardens as habitat, have broadened my lens.

Yes, there are the obvious harvests: fruits and vegetables, of course. But, for me, a truly productive garden also offers herbs, medicinal plants, edimentals (see page 79) and aromatics that scent the air and calm the nervous system. It gives me ingredients to cook with, preserve and share. Plants to distil, to dry and to make into teas, tinctures or salves. Flowers that feed pollinators and brighten the kitchen table. Even clusters of fungi, self-seeded volunteers or mosses threading through the shaded edges of a bed are all part of it.

Some of the most meaningful yields aren't harvested in baskets. They're the knowing that I'm part of a system, and the clarity that comes from tending a bed through the seasons. They're the rituals that ground me.

'Some of the most meaningful yields aren't harvested in baskets. They're the knowing that I'm part of a system, and the clarity that comes from tending a bed through the seasons.'

When I created the garden at Oak & Monkey Puzzle, I wanted to grow armfuls of fragrant heritage roses with the classic 'old rose' scent, the kind that are almost impossible to find in a florist. The day I got to tick that off the list is one I still vividly remember. Filling a huge vase with fat, fragrant, saucer-sized blooms that I'd grown myself, creating a heady yet fleeting scent that filled the room in the best possible way – this is also productivity.

When I talk about a productive garden, I'm referring to a place that celebrates beauty as much as abundance. A space that gives something back, season after season. One that holds stories, rituals, and rhythms of tending and refining.

It doesn't need to be big. My current garden, Little Cottage on a Hill, is just 515 square metres (5545 square feet), and it's more productive than my 5-acre property ever was. It's not about scale, it's about responding to constraint. The smaller space asks more of and rewards mindful design. Because the dimensions are tighter and the thinking has to be sharper, the garden becomes more intentional in response. Every square metre has a purpose, and most plants are multifunctional, offering both structure and scent, food and beauty, shade and shelter. It's a garden that works with me and for me.

Sometimes, the most productive gesture is the one that sets something in motion: a bed prepared for someone else to plant. A system refined for the next season. A jar of seeds saved for hands not yet in the soil.

Productivity, to me, is the art of creating something generous. It's not about striving, metrics or even output. It's about living in rhythm with the land, and letting that rhythm shape what the garden becomes.

HOW TO USE THIS BOOK

This is not a gardening manual. It's a companion for those with any type or size of garden, from pots on a windowsill to a country acreage. It's something to return to across the seasons, as your garden shifts and your needs change. Some chapters are practical, while others are more reflective. There's no set order. Read the book in a way that suits your garden, your pace and your place in the year.

Throughout the book, you'll find QR codes linking to additional content: conversations, case studies and practical tools to support your gardening life. Some will take you to downloadable resources such as worksheets, templates, seasonal planning tools and checklists. These are ways to take what's on the page and bring it to life in your own space.

Woven through these chapters are the voices of thoughtful growers, makers and designers who have shaped the way I think about land, beauty, rhythm and resilience. Their words appear as sidebars, features or recordings linked via QR code. Each offers a window into another way of working with place and seasonality.

Whether you're creating a new garden, tending an existing one or reimagining what a productive space can be, this book will soon become a trusted friend supporting the way you grow, plan and live in rhythm with the seasons.

Garden beauty as mental nourishment

In *The Well-Gardened Mind*, psychiatrist and gardener Sue Stuart-Smith describes beauty as an important form of nourishment. The scent of a gardenia (*Gardenia* sp.). The cool shadow of a gum tree (*Eucalyptus* sp.) on a hot day. The shimmer of a pot marigold (*Calendula officinalis*) after rain. These experiences release dopamine and serotonin. They help us to feel hope, and to remain calm and focused. They awaken reward pathways in the brain, the same ones triggered by romantic love. And in places of hardship, such as trauma wards, refugee camps, prison gardens, it's flowers, not food, that people often reach for first. That's not sentimentality. It's survival.

Opposite page_Cutting Turkish sage (*Phlomis russeliana*) on the western verge at Little Cottage on a Hill. The purple flowers of another sage, *Salvia nemorosa* 'Ostfriesland', sit in the foreground, with Russian sage (*S. yangii*) threading through just behind them. Beauty, usefulness and the quiet mental nourishment of tending are all held in one moment.

PART -I- The garden and the self

1
MY JOURNEY

There are many ways a life can unfold. Sometimes it follows a straight line, but more often than not, it twists and turns, pulling you towards what you need. Mine has been the latter.

THE EARLY YEARS

For as long as I can remember, I've found that there is something grounding in tending plants and working with my hands. But, like many of us, I was raised with certain expectations to achieve professionally. And for a time, I did exactly that.

Careers counselling and a battery of aptitude and personality tests suggested that I should pursue architecture. I'd always drawn, always loved space and form, so despite my early doubts about the mathematics and engineering involved, I enrolled in an architecture degree straight out of high school. If I'd followed my instincts, then I would have undertaken a diploma in horticulture. But in my mother's eyes, gardening was a hobby, not a profession, and architecture felt like a more legitimate path.

I found architecture challenging. I was navigating a world that felt distant and ego-driven, and many of the architects teaching at the time seemed disillusioned, perhaps because they had turned to teaching as work had dried up in the recession. Then, during my studies, my stepsister was killed in the 9/11 terrorist attacks. The shock of this loss collided with my already shaky sense of belonging. I found myself deferring subjects, grieving deeply and questioning whether architecture was the right path. I turned to the garden; with the support of my Italian boyfriend and his family, I transformed more and more lawn of the home my boyfriend and I shared in Reservoir, Melbourne, into vegetable and herb beds, and the most incredible edible abundance.

It was then that I decided to take on landscape architecture as a double degree. From the moment I entered this new world, I felt at home. Suddenly, my architectural education made sense through the lens of land, systems and place. This discipline offered a grounded generosity and curiosity that I hadn't experienced in architecture.

Phil Edwards, my first design studio lecturer in landscape architecture at RMIT, helped me to secure a job that bridged architecture and landscape thinking: I joined the team working on the groundbreaking Council House 2 (CH 2) project with the City of Melbourne. My focus was on green architecture, soil and microbial activity in indoor plantings, facade greening and rooftop gardens. I didn't know it then, but I was beginning to map the space between architecture and ecology, form and system. That work planted something enduring in me: a belief that design isn't just about what we see, but about what supports it.

'That work planted something enduring in me: a belief that design isn't just about what we see, but about what supports it.'

One of the most significant teachers whom I encountered during that time was Dr Lee Ariav, a visiting academic from Israel. His belief in me was steady, genuine and deeply generous; he encouraged me to trust my instincts, reminding me that I knew more than I thought I did. He later became a kind of second supervisor during my final design thesis, and he often said the thing I most needed to hear: 'You already have the answers.'

My final thesis was formally supervised by Dr SueAnne Ware, who helped me stretch design ideas into new terrain. With her I explored possibilities; with Lee I found words, theory, grounding and confidence. That combination shaped how I work to this day.

I've often thought that the generosity of my lecturers is what seeded my own values of sharing and teaching. Those experiences are part of what fuels my desire to give back through my work. They also taught me something about how transformative belief can be.

Coincidentally, it was also during this time that I met the deeply charming and charismatic man who would become the father of my children. Despite the twelve-year age gap between us, we shared a love of design, and I was besotted with how he saw the world through landscape. At the time, I believed that we were building something together. I was desperately naive.

After graduating, I spent ten years teaching landscape architecture, while also working for Taylor Cullity Lethlean (TCL), one of the country's leading practices. One of my formative projects was the Australian Garden at the Royal Botanic Gardens Cranbourne, where over six years I helped to design and deliver Stage 2 of the 10-hectare (25-acre) site. That vast landscape was designed like a bespoke backyard: intimate, storied, grounded in how people would actually move through and inhabit the space. It was the rhythm of paths, the texture of materials underfoot, the way views opened and closed, the wiring of a structure to support an espaliered Wolgan snow gum (*Eucalyptus gregsoniana*). It was prototyping concrete to mimic the forest floor of Gondwana. These weren't just gestures, they were deeply considered moments, shaped through the lens of experience and storytelling. From the outside, I was thriving. But privately, something was starting to fray.

'From the outside, I was thriving. But privately, something was starting to fray.'

THE QUIET UNRAVELLING

At the same time as my professional life was expanding, my personal life was becoming more complex. I entered motherhood while still deep in project work, managing multi-million-dollar builds, running TCL's research arm, assisting the director with their PhD explorations and documentation, and teaching extensively. And yet, despite the competence I showed at work, I struggled profoundly in those early years of parenting.

I had built an incredible armature around myself – a structure that allowed me to function, succeed and avoid an unnamed discomfort – and I never left anything to chance. But when I had children, it soon became apparent that I was a highly anxious person. During my maternity leave, when I was unable to productively channel that anxiety into my work, I was left deeply exposed in the unpredictable terrain of motherhood.

I experienced postnatal depression after each of my two children was born. With my second child, I made the decision to hospitalise myself in a mother–baby psychiatric unit. I became a strange contradiction: I was able to manage a $15 million botanic garden, but I couldn't settle a baby to sleep.

THE SEARCH FOR SOMETHING MORE

At the time, we were living in a converted scout hall in inner-city Melbourne. I was still employed by TCL, raising two young children, and navigating early motherhood with all of its intensity and uncertainty. The demands were constant, and my relationship with my children's father became increasingly difficult.

Softly and steadily, I felt the pull of a different kind of life: one more closely tied to land, to seasons, to making. I craved immediacy in my creative endeavours. I found myself sketching ideas on the chalkboards attached to the walls at home, listing the things that brought me peace and inspiration: growing food, preserving, creating, teaching, design, beauty, community. I didn't yet understand how to weave them together, but I knew that I needed something different.

I began researching areas within 90 minutes of Melbourne, places with good rainfall, rich soil, agricultural diversity and a creative community. I mapped the 'sweet spots' in the quiet times between deadlines at work, inspired by my colleague and friend Joe, who shared my dreams of country living. And then one day, realestate.com.au sent me a notification: a former 1900s post office in Spargo Creek, near Daylesford, had come on the market.

The children's father and I visited one day in early 2013, under the pretence of 'keeping the country dream alive'. We both longed for a weekender that balanced out our inner-city life. Standing under the towering English oaks (*Quercus robur*) and a single monkey puzzle tree (*Araucaria araucana*), I felt something immediate: a sense of being called. It was as though the land itself had reached out. Although it

Opposite page_Motherhood in the in-between. Evening walks with Saffron and Oliver are special times.

was twice our budget and entirely impractical, it felt utterly right. So compelled, I sold my first home, which I had kept as my nest egg and retirement security, to make this happen.

The day before we got the keys, my partner was diagnosed with early-onset Parkinson's disease. It was a confronting time. I promised him, and myself, that I would do everything I could to support him. I stayed in the relationship far longer than I should have, driven by the need to one day tell my children, truthfully and without regret, that I had given all I could.

We never intended to move full-time to what became Oak & Monkey Puzzle. It was supposed to be a weekender, a place where I could begin to weave all of those chalkboard threads together. However, with the pull of country life – and weekends extending to late Sunday night, then Monday morning and beyond – by August 2014 we had sold our scout hall and relocated permanently.

BUILDING THE NEXT CHAPTER

In late 2015, I began developing my own business idea – Natasha Morgan – without showing a single person until I was ready. I didn't want advice or to be influenced. I needed this to be entirely mine, something no one could take from me. It was a full embodiment of my values: designing, making, growing, preserving and sharing. The business was not simply work; it was a reclamation of self.

With the help of talented friends, including Caitlin Perry and Tom Harper, photographer Lauren Bamford, stylist Stephanie Stamatis, and writer and publicist Amber Creswell Bell, I eventually launched my first website. A press release was sent out, and I held my first workshops in garden and floral design at the start of 2016. It still surprises me to this day that people came, and they kept coming. There was a resonance, perhaps because what I was building was not polished or manufactured. It was an honest invitation into the life I was learning to create.

In February 2016, I saw a message shared through a friend on Facebook: a call for someone to host a young woman from the United Kingdom who was travelling the world. Her name was Meg Travis, and she called herself 'Girl Friday'. The post listed all of these remarkable skills she had: baking, designing, making and more. She was the perfect generalist. Despite never having shared a home with someone outside a relationship, and a sense of unease in doing so, I said 'yes'.

Meg stayed for nearly three months. She stepped into my life just as I was embarking on my business, and she helped me to bring my early workshops to life. She also cooked, baked, helped to raise my children, and offered companionship and care. We didn't talk about the state of my relationship – she never really knew what was happening behind closed doors – but, in many ways, her presence was a kind of lifeline. The reassurance she gave me in spirit, in action, in belief and in generosity was something that I didn't know I needed.

Meg left in April 2016 to continue her year of travels, not long after helping to create the most beautiful celebration for my 40th birthday. She had planned the menu by hand in her travel notebook, something she always carried with her, and pulled together the kind of gathering that made everything feel possible again. It was joyful. There were friends and family, and for a few hours, I felt seen.

But in the week leading up to my birthday, someone said something to me that stuck: 'You're behaving as if you've got a whole lifetime ahead of you. What if you've only got tomorrow?' Until that point, I had convinced myself that I would stay in the relationship, that eventually, when my partner required full-time care, I would gently step away. That had been my plan: endure until I could exit without breaking the promise I had made to support him.

'You're behaving as if you've got a whole lifetime ahead of you. What if you've only got tomorrow?'

Meg's presence, her support, the steady rhythm of those months together shifted something in me. I had this business I was building, and this place in Spargo Creek where all of the pieces of my life finally felt like they could come together. And at the same time, I was trapped in a deeply destructive relationship.

By Mother's Day in May, I knew what I had to do. I shared with my children's father that the relationship was over. However, it wasn't a public ending, and life at home remained tangled and tense. I kept parenting, kept working, kept building the shape of a new life, all while still living inside the old one I was desperately trying to leave. The experiences that Meg and I shared, the joy we created together, helped me to believe that I could go out on my own. That what I was building was real. A few months later, the true unravelling began.

MY DARKEST MOMENTS

In September 2016, the relationship finally ended in previously unimaginable circumstances. What followed was a devastating two-and-a-half-year court process, a consuming and financially ruinous legal battle. It was only as things imploded that I began to understand what I had been living through. I had not named it at the time because I could not see it clearly from the inside, but I came to understand that I had been living in a relationship that had, over the course of eleven years, whittled me away slowly, incrementally and insidiously. The psychological impact was deeply profound.

During those years, from early 2017 to mid-2019, I was largely unable to work. My 'business' remained publicly visible, but behind the scenes I was barely functioning. The contrast was stark. 'You're living the dream,' people would say. And yet privately, I was living my worst nightmare.

The garden held me through that time. When I had no energy to work or create, I still had the soil, the light, the acts of care. I would stand under the stars, speaking silently to the universe, calling for the strength to keep going.

It was not until the court proceedings ended – and after years of therapy, time and deep healing – that I began to rebuild. My social-media audience, many of whom had followed from the very beginning, became a soft community during that time. I shared honestly but carefully, always walking the delicate line between vulnerability and protection.

'If I have soil, sun, water and fresh air, what more do I actually need?'

Covid stripped life back to essentials and sparked a decisive epiphany: 'If I have soil, sun, water and fresh air, what more do I actually need?' With that clarity, I could see that everything Oak & Monkey Puzzle had taught and held could live on a smaller and more intentional footprint, closer to my community and friendships in Daylesford and my children's schools and daily life. I wasn't turning my back so much as allowing a season to conclude. The garden had done its work and steadied me to the point that I could imagine something new.

And slowly, like the soil organisms doing their work unseen below the surface, a new system began to form, one that would hold me through the next season of my life.

FINDING LITTLE COTTAGE ON A HILL

The post-Covid real estate market was wild, and I missed out on several properties. Then one appeared: a small cottage near the Wombat Hill Botanic Gardens, perched on a hill with long south-west views, something I never had at Oak & Monkey Puzzle. The skyline held familiar silhouettes: western red cedars (*Thuja plicata*), Douglas firs (*Pseudotsuga menziesii*) and English oaks (*Quercus robur*). They were echoes of where I had been, but in a new form.

The property had wide verges, nearly 235 square metres (2530 square feet) of public frontage, sitting atop deep, volcanic soil. Thanks to recent council changes, nature-strip planting was now permitted. I could see the potential of the property immediately, both for growing and for continuing my work.

When I walked inside the house, with its white walls and dark floors, it instantly felt like home. My son stood beside me and whispered, 'This feels safe, Mum.' And that was enough.

Little Cottage on a Hill is not only my new home, but also a full synthesis of everything I've learned and continue to refine. It allows me to carry forwards the very best of nearly ten years at Oak & Monkey Puzzle in a distilled and intentional form, on a much smaller footprint. With 515 square metres (5545 square feet) inside the fence line, and two large verges beyond, I've been able to shoehorn an entire philosophy into a compact, deeply considered space.

What I'd once folded into the compost of hard seasons now feeds everything I grow, not just in the garden, but in how I live.

This is the place where I now write. One not of starting over, but of returning to myself, to my work, to the way I choose to live. This book, like my garden, is simply the next expression of that journey.

Opposite page_Little Cottage on a Hill. It is a small house, but it has wide verges, long views and room for a new kind of garden.

2
UNDERSTANDING SEASONALITY AND OBSERVATION

I've come to understand that seasonality is not a schedule. It's a way of being in a relationship with place. It's about noticing, and being willing to let the landscape lead.

READING THE LAND

Every garden I've ever created, from large public landscapes to my own backyard, has taught me that the real guide to timing is observation. The angle of light as it drops lower in autumn. The first flush of new buds swelling. The cockatoos returning to feed on spring's tender, sap-filled shoots as they push through the earth. The scent of soil after rain. The shift in insect activity as the temperature changes. These are the real seasonal markers.

The more I've leaned into observing these subtleties, the more grounded and confident my gardening has become. I no longer feel anxious about whether I've missed a planting window or whether I'm behind according to someone else's schedule. Instead, I watch what's happening in my space, right now. And I respond.

LEARNING TO SEE: A PERSONAL REFLECTION

'Observation is something I've had to relearn gradually through experience, and often purely by being present long enough for the landscape to start revealing itself.'

Observation is something I've had to relearn gradually through experience, and often purely by being present long enough for the landscape to start revealing itself.

One of the most formative moments in my understanding of observation came when I was a landscape architecture student, walking along part of the Lurujarri Trail near Broome with the Goolarabooloo People. We travelled on foot for days along the coast, sleeping in the dunes, moving kilometre after kilometre through Country.

In the early days, I noticed little beyond the obvious: the heat, the salt, the movement of the group, my sore feet and aching hips. But, bit by bit, something shifted. The further we walked, the quieter I became. By the third day, my vision had narrowed, and I began to see things I'd missed before. Small details emerged: tiny holes in tea-tree (*Melaleuca* sp.) trunks where native bees burrowed, subtle changes in the colour of the sea, patterns in the sand. There was a rhythm to what we were walking through, connections I couldn't have noticed unless my pace slowed enough to perceive them.

I was privileged to witness some of the ecological relationships that have been understood by First Nations people for generations, such as the connection between fish and bees: if you harvest honey, then you won't catch fish that day (it's a spiritual and ecological pattern recognised by the Goolarabooloo People: the environment itself won't allow the taking of both resources on the same day). These are not observations built in a season or two. They are the wisdom of thousands of years of careful noticing. I don't claim them. But being invited to witness them altered how I came to see place, and made me realise how much we can learn if we stay attentive.

That experience – as well as years spent living, growing and observing at Oak & Monkey Puzzle, and now here at Little Cottage on a Hill – shaped how I work with seasons today. Whether it's watching the first mushrooms emerge from under the fallen needles of a Monterey pine (*Pinus radiata*) after rain, or seeing the early signs of

summer's retreat, observation has become a peaceful ritual. (A caution: when foraging, particularly for mushrooms, seek expert guidance. Some wild species are highly toxic, so don't consume anything unless you're absolutely certain about the species.)

Over time, this practice of seasonal observation has extended far beyond my garden. It's become the rhythm I live by. My own life now aligns with these same cues: when to preserve, when to sow, when to rest. The garden has become my mentor in this. It has taught me to pay attention to the small shifts and to find a pace that isn't dictated by urgency, but by presence. Learning to live this way has become a non-negotiable.

Unique Indigenous knowledge

I want to acknowledge that the most sophisticated seasonal knowledge in Australia belongs to Indigenous communities that have read the land with extraordinary care over thousands of years. My own approach is shaped by my personal and professional journey. It's not intended to speak for those deeper knowledge systems, but to invite readers to begin their own practice of attention and respect for place.

CYCLES AND PATTERNS, NOT DATES

When you start observing your garden seasonally, you'll soon notice patterns that emerge year after year, not because a book told you they would, but because you've seen them for yourself. You'll recognise the early signs of a warm autumn or a late frost. You'll work out which plants respond first to lengthening daylight, or which vegetables bolt early when unexpected heat arrives. Over time, you'll begin to see what your garden offers back. Not all at once, but as a slow unfolding.

My friend Lily Langham, a sculptor and garden-maker, knows that it's time to plant brassicas (*Brassica* spp.) when the hawkmoths return. That sort of serene signal is the kind of rhythm this chapter is about.

You will also learn that not every year behaves the same way. In truth, we are gardening within increasingly variable seasons. Climate shifts, fluctuating rainfall patterns and temperature extremes all mean that strict calendars are becoming less useful with each passing year. Instead, observation is the most reliable tool we have.

This doesn't mean that you should abandon planning entirely. It means that planning with flexibility is key: holding a general seasonal rhythm, but allowing your garden to tell you when it's ready.

FOR EVERY PLACE, FOR EVERY CLIMATE

While my own experience has unfolded in regional Victoria, Australia, the principles hold anywhere. Whether you're gardening in a cool highland climate, a subtropical zone or somewhere entirely different, the invitation remains the same to learn to read your place.

In tropical climates, the cues might come from wet and dry cycles rather than four seasons. In the coldest alpine regions, the snow melt may signal planting time. In Mediterranean climates, the autumn break after a dry summer may be your most important seasonal marker. The patterns will differ, but the practice of observation remains universal. By leaning into your local rhythms, you build a confidence that no calendar can offer.

Opposite page_The view from Wombat Hill Botanic Gardens, looking north-west across Daylesford and Hepburn. From here I read the landscape in cycles and patterns, not dates.
Following spread_Little Cottage on a Hill, across the seasons.
Top left_Autumn.
Bottom left_Winter.
Top right_Spring.
Bottom right_Summer.

M.H.S. VIS.

Where to explore Indigenous seasonal calendars

The Bureau of Meteorology hosts Indigenous seasonal calendars and Indigenous Weather Knowledge pages, developed with communities across Australia. These resources show how seasons are understood differently across regions, guided by local plants, animals, weather patterns and time on Country. They are a strong starting point if you want to deepen your own observation practice and learn more about place-specific seasonal knowledge.

Seeing seasons differently

Tanya Loos is a nature writer and ecologist. Her local seasonal understanding has shaped my own thinking about time and rhythm in the garden. Based in the Wombat State Forest, close to where I live, Tanya draws on her deep ecological knowledge and daily field observations to share a local way of describing seasonal change, one that aligns more closely with the land itself. This way of reading seasons through local cues is not new, and sits alongside seasonal knowledge held by First Nations communities across Australia.

With that in mind, Tanya offers an alternative to the familiar four-season model: a six-season wheel of time specific to the Wombat State Forest and Victoria's southern foothills region. These are not fixed portions of a calendar, but responsive periods shaped by local environmental cues such as the arrival of certain bird species, flowering events, fungi emergence and insect shifts. For Tanya, this is what real seasonality looks like: grounded in place, sensed through observation and attuned to phenology (biological timing) rather than prediction.

In our conversation for this book, she shared her belief that everyone can begin noticing these signals in their own patch, whether the location is rural, suburban or urban. 'What birds arrive when the light changes?' she asks. 'What flower tells you it's time to sow, or to rest?'

To help you begin, Tanya has generously shared a version of her six-season circular calendar as a downloadable template. I invite you to use it as a prompt, not a rule, and to adapt it to your own region, place and patterns. Whether your climate has four or six seasons, or no named seasons at all, what matters is learning to look at and take in what you see.

OBSERVATION BELONGS TO EVERYONE

You don't need a huge backyard or a view across open paddocks to begin seeing your seasons. You don't even need a traditional garden. You simply have to start paying attention to what is already happening around you.

If you have a balcony, then begin with the light: how it moves through the day, how the temperature changes as the afternoon fades. Notice from which direction the wind most often comes. Feel the humidity shift after rain. Watch how your potted herbs respond after cooler nights.

If you're growing plants in containers on a small patio or in a courtyard, then pay attention to the first flush of growth after pruning. Observe how water drains after heavy rain, or how quickly pots dry out after a stretch of sun. Listen for the returning sound of birds in early spring, or the hushed stillness of late autumn evenings.

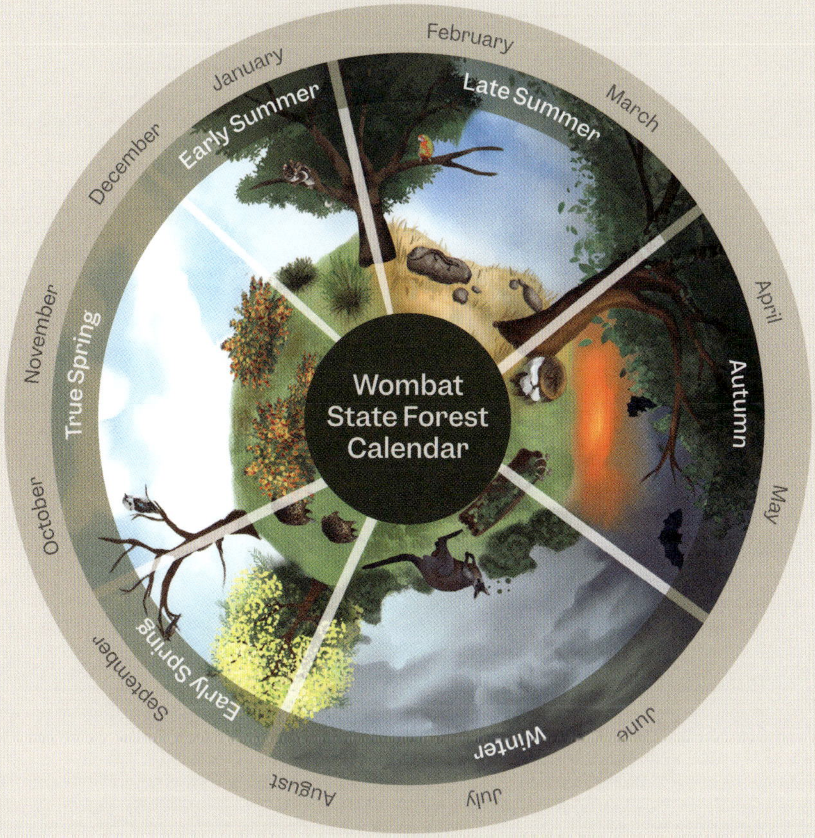

Tanya's Wombat State Forest circular calendar.

Scan to hear my full conversation with Tanya Loos, where we talk about seasonal cues, six local seasons and wildlife-friendly garden design.

Scan to see a downloadable circular calendar template that you can use for your own garden.

Even if you cultivate plants only on a single windowsill, you'll see patterns emerge when a plant leans towards light, when leaf tips brown from too much or too little care, when buds form in response to warmer days. What matters is not the scale, but the act of noticing.

Every garden is part of the same natural conversation, whether it's 5 hectares (12 acres), 5 square metres (55 square feet), or five pots. And observation isn't reserved for certain kinds of gardeners. It's available to anyone who is willing to pause, perceive and believe in what they see.

In many ways, this chapter offers the foundation for everything that follows. Because before we design, before we plan, before we plant, we watch and we learn. In doing so, we create not only more resilient and responsive gardens, but also a life anchored to the rhythms that matter most.

3
WORKING ACROSS SCALES

Everything in this book applies whether you're working with an acreage, a courtyard or a windowsill. Scale shapes decisions, but the design thinking remains constant, regardless of your garden's size.

SCALE SHARPENS CLARITY

Scale is an invitation to become clearer in your thinking. When you work within a large property, there's a kind of generosity available in the proportions. But even then, every part of the garden must fit together. When you work within a small space, the same principle applies. It simply becomes more visible.

No matter the size of your garden, people will understand the design through the human scale on the ground. The path width and where it leads your eye. The choice of material underfoot and what your hand touches as you move through a gate. The way planting meets gravel, timber, stone or lawn, and whether the junctions feel intentional. When those small decisions are resolved with consideration and consistency, the whole garden reads clearly. This was instilled in me early in my landscape architecture studies. One of my lecturers, Dr Lee Ariav, would often remind his students: 'Design lives in the details.' It became a mantra that, more than twenty years later, still shapes how I see space today.

Whether I'm walking through a 10-hectare (25-acre) landscape or tending a tiny garden plot, the principle holds. It might be the curve of a path as it gently draws you forwards. The crunch of gravel underfoot signalling arrival or transition. The way a step nestles perfectly into a slope, holding the fall of the land without force. The proportion of planting to open space. The rhythm between shade and light, shelter and exposure. The subtle way wind moves through a borrowed tree canopy, or how a water rill quietly reflects the colour of the sky above. Even the scent released when your sleeve brushes past rosemary (*Salvia rosmarinus*). It all builds the lived experience of place.

The Weird and Wonderful section of the Australian Garden (Stage 2) at the Royal Botanic Gardens Cranbourne. My years in the public realm taught me that big projects succeed or fail in the details.

An early photo of Melaleuca Spits, part of the Australian Garden (Stage 2) at the Royal Botanic Gardens Cranbourne. This public garden, which I worked on from 2005 to 2012, taught me precision at scale. It made every later garden feel possible, and quietly gave me permission to begin again.

MY OWN JOURNEY ACROSS SCALES

Before I made the move to full-time growing, making and teaching, much of my professional design life was spent inside larger projects, including the Australian Garden at the Royal Botanic Gardens Cranbourne. I worked on Stage 2 of that project over six years while part of the team at Taylor Cullity Lethlean (TCL), contributing to both design development and construction supervision. The planting design was led by Paul Thompson, while we at TCL focused on the spatial narratives, visitor journey and design principles, documentation and detailing.

This project, though 10 hectares (25 acres) in scale, demanded a design sensitivity not unlike that required for a backyard. From the spatial layout of paths and terraces down to the placement of individual plants, every decision was made with extraordinary attention to detail. Even at that scale, we were designing intimate moments, small pockets of experience and layers of planting that would shift across seasons and years.

Later, at Oak & Monkey Puzzle, my 5-acre property in Spargo Creek, I experienced scale again through a new lens. The landscape became a kind of canvas on which I painted areas, functions and activities. It was designed as a multifunctional series of spaces that could expand or contract depending on how they were being used. The planted beds, meadows and trees could nicely hold the four of us as a family, or 154 guests gathered for a Melbourne Food & Wine Festival Regional Longest Lunch, or for micro-weddings and workshops.

While there was the luxury of expansiveness, the small ways in which the space was experienced and inhabited were equally important and equally powerful. The intimacy of tea under the old apple tree (*Malus* sp.) carried the same design intentionality as the wide gravel circle prepared for large gatherings. Both lived within the same system of clarity and care.

And now, at Little Cottage on a Hill, I work within just 515 square metres (5545 square feet). Inside the property boundary lie the main house, gardens and workshop space. But beyond that, I've extended the productive capacity by transforming the verges: approximately 235 square metres (2530 square feet) of otherwise unused municipal space, now home to dense perennial planting, seasonal crops and borrowed views.

This deliberate downsizing means that every centimetre matters here. My boundary fences have become orchard walls, holding espaliered Huonville crab-apples (*Malus* sp.), pears (*Pyrus communis* 'Bonne de Maline' and *P. c.* 'Doyenné du Comice') and quinces (*Cydonia oblonga* 'Smyrna') across a 27-metre (89-foot) run. A collection of old copper boilers, once used for washing clothes, now overflows with thyme (*Thymus vulgaris*), French sorrel (*Rumex scutatus*) and sugar snap peas (*Pisum sativum*) climbing on handmade bamboo frames. The entire garden functions as a living demonstration that you don't need more space; you need intention, clarity and a willingness to begin.

START WHERE YOU ARE

I often remind my workshop participants: 'Start where you are. Use what you have. Do what you can.' It's a philosophy I first encountered through the permaculture-related teaching of Milkwood, and one that sits at the heart of this book. No one begins with perfect conditions. We have to work with what's at hand – small balcony, suburban courtyard, wide verge, long fence – and be clever with our design choices.

I've seen balcony gardeners harvesting enough herbs and greens for daily cooking. Suburban courtyards hosting espaliered orchards along sunny walls. Small pots of lemons (*Citrus × limon*) thriving on apartment ledges, giving their owners a full season of fruits. I've spied old bathtubs and stock troughs being used as thriving micro-gardens. The form doesn't matter, but the thinking does.

Above left _Oak & Monkey Puzzle kitchen garden beds in Spargo Creek, built for reach and wheelbarrow access.
Above right _Little Cottage on a Hill wicking beds in Daylesford, waterwise and built for vertical and horizontal productivity.

'Beauty, abundance and productivity are not reserved for certain gardens. They live in the way you work with your space.'

The principles don't change

Whether you're working with a pair of pots or a couple of hectares, the same design questions apply:

- What experience do you want this space to offer?
- What is the light doing across the seasons?
- How will water flow through or be captured by the space?
- What can the soil support, and how will you build its health?
- How will you move through and interact with this place every day?

The more you narrow your space, the more weight each decision carries, but that's not something to fear. In fact, it's often where the most beautiful and layered gardens emerge.

Everything that follows from here – the design thinking, the planning, the planting, the growing – can be adapted to gardens of any scale. My goal is not to prescribe a model, but to offer guiding principles that apply to all spaces, no matter your starting point.

Beauty, abundance and productivity are not reserved for certain gardens. They live in the way you work with your space. And you already have enough to begin.

Scale-savvy plant choices

Having a small garden doesn't necessarily limit your choice of plants. Simply embrace compact forms of standard species or train the growth of suitable trees and shrubs:

- **Dwarf:** A tree grown on (grafted onto) dwarfing rootstock. This results in a tree that is shorter and narrower than a standard tree, while producing normal-sized leaves and fruits.
- **Fastigiate:** These are naturally narrow, upright trees or shrubs that give height without width.
- **Espalier:** This involves training a tree flat against wires or a frame to create an orchard wall with minimal depth (see pages 250–2).
- **Cordon:** A single-stem tree grown vertically or on an angle along a wire for high yield in a narrow strip (see pages 250–2).
- **Fan:** A tree with branches trained to radiate like a fan against a frame to maximise light and access in shallow spaces (see page 253).
- **Step-over:** A knee-high, single-tier tree or shrub trained along a low wire, useful as an edible path edge (see page 253).

Note: Even with compact forms, you will need to choose an appropriate rootstock and commit to regular seasonal pruning to keep the plants within the bounds of your small space.

Here's a simple guide to accommodating your space constraints:

- no room for a full-sized tree → espalier, cordon, fan or step-over
- narrow bed width → fastigiate or columnar forms, single-stem cordons, berries on wires
- no ground at all → containers or wicking modules, climbers on arches and wall wires.

There are three big-to-small translation moves that you can make straight away:

1. full orchard to orchard wall using espaliers, cordons, fans or step-overs
2. large hedgerow to small edible hedge for structure and harvest
3. mature tree to deciduous climber on a light arbour for summer shade and winter sun.

4
DESIGNING YOUR PRODUCTIVE OASIS

To me, garden design is an act of generosity. It offers a framework for how you move, how you grow, how you gather and how you feel in a place.

CORE FRAMING

Core framing is the small set of ideas I return to so that any garden reads clearly and works in daily life. In thc sections that follow, I'll draw a line between design and decoration, show how structure and rhythm steady the eye and the body, explain why restraint brings clarity, and treat time as a design material. Think of these concepts as the calm space you can come back to when choices feel noisy.

Design versus decoration

It's easy to decorate. But design goes further. It creates a space that works across time and seasons, for people and place. This is the framework that allows you to inhabit your garden, not just look at it. When a garden is designed, it reveals itself slowly. It accommodates life.

For example, a garden designed for children shouldn't fight their instincts, it should welcome them. And it is often their instinct to create pathways where it makes sense to move. Design is about granting space for both what's needed and what's inevitable.

'It's easy to decorate. But design goes further. It creates a space that works across time and seasons, for people and place.'

Structure and rhythm

I like logic in a garden. That might mean using the same 20-millimetre (3/4-inch) gravel across different zones to create unity. Or repeating clipped English box (*Buxus sempervirens*) balls to hold visual rhythm through winter. Or balancing richly textured planting beds with a clean lawn edge. Even in small gardens, that rhythm gives us something to follow.

I also plant in drifts – sweeping lines or curves of the same species – because it helps the eye to rest. My friend Lily Langham, a garden designer, uses four or five plants in each of her drifts. Naturalistic planting designer Tim Pilgrim prefers eleven or thirteen plants. I cultivate drifts that respond to my space, but always stay true to the ideas of coherence and repetition.

The clarity of restraint

Like a child who mixes all of the paint colours together and ends up with brown, a garden with too many ideas becomes muddy. Legibility matters. Restraint creates breathing space. Even wild gardens benefit from structural devices: hedging, focal points and texture hierarchy.

In a larger rural garden, restraint is achieved by repeating a single hedging species to define 'rooms', carrying one gravel for paths and courts so movement reads clearly, or anchoring a long view with one strong focal element (a specimen tree or a simple seat on a gravel circle). Planting is held to a limited palette in broad drifts, so the eye can rest and the seasons do the storytelling rather than the plant list.

In a compact courtyard or verge, restraint might mean using one surface treatment from entry to seating (so the space feels bigger), installing a small grid of raised beds or slim vertical frames, or training a single climber with intent rather than having many competing species. A clean spade edge or low clipped form gives lush, mixed planting something to play against.

Designing for time

The gardens I design evolve with the seasons. I plant and prune with intention, leaving seed heads through winter for structure, for birds, for beauty. I work with what the garden offers over time. And I always think about the next layer: bulbs coming up through spent perennials, structure that carries across seasons, and how light changes as days lengthen or shorten.

An espaliered fruit-tree wall reads beautifully in every season. In winter, the trained framework becomes living architecture. In spring, blossoms turn it into a soft screen. In summer, foliage and fruits make a productive hedge. In autumn, the geometry is revealed again as leaves colour and fall. In smaller spaces, repeated evergreen forms hold the garden's bones through the quiet months while looser perennials weave in and out across the year.

THE WAY I APPROACH DESIGN

When people come to my workshops, they often arrive with a sharpened pencil, a clean sheet of paper and an overwhelming desire to get everything 'right'. But that's not how I teach design. I hand them a fat, black marker and rolls of tracing paper. Why? Because when you're holding something bold and imprecise, you can't get lost in perfectionism. You can't obsess over the detail too soon. You have to think more broadly about form, flow and feeling.

Western verge at Little Cottage on a Hill, Daylesford. Restraint in materiality – gravel, steel edging and lawn paths – allows the planting to carry the season.

We begin with a base plan, an aerial image or a sketched outline of what exists: house, fences, clothes line, trees, driveways. That's our ground truth. Then we build tracing-paper layers – sun and shadow, wind patterns, water movement, frost pockets, soil condition, privacy, views and noise – with one element per sheet. Layer by layer, the site begins to speak. You start to see connections. You notice the microclimates, the pinch points, the golden pockets.

And then I ask: 'How do you want to live in this space?' That one question changes everything. Where do you want to drink your morning tea? What window do you want to look out of and see movement from? What path do you want to walk along every day from your front door to your car, and what could meet you along the way?

'And then I ask: "How do you want to live in this space?" That question changes everything.'

Designing a productive oasis means planning for food, yes, but it also means allowing for experience. It means aligning your practical needs with your emotional ones. Your rhythms. Your pace.

It means designing spaces to be multifunctional. A path can become a place to pause. A verge garden can be both productive and decorative. A driveway can double as a courtyard. You don't need a separate space for every garden role. What matters is how the spaces relate to each other, how they work together and how they reflect your life.

At Oak & Monkey Puzzle, the design emerged from what the land told us. There was a clear sightline from the front door through the entry's window and out to the forest. That became an axis. The slope from the house to the tree line invited a series of terraces. The lower terrace became the kitchen garden and mudroom forecourt. The middle terrace, anchored by a beautiful old apple (*Malus* sp.) tree, was a place to catch your breath, a gravelled space for gatherings, stillness and views. The upper terrace was the flower garden, laid out in bold compartments like a bento box of blooms. The gravel between the garden beds was not just circulation, it was canvas. Each space served more than one role.

At Little Cottage on a Hill, the scale was smaller so the thinking had to deepen. I had just 515 square metres (5545 square feet) to work with, and most of that was house and studio. The verges – especially the wide, sun-soaked, western verge – became the garden. And the front driveway, originally a narrow strip beside a paling fence, was reimagined as a courtyard, an arrival space and an extension of my studio. Gravel to the edges. Climbing plants on mesh. A timber-and-wire fence that offered transparency and allowed the garden to feel expansive.

The tall, black-painted wicking beds on the northern verge created thermal mass, raised the crops closer to the sun and made tending the plants easier on the back. The planting across both verge gardens followed the same logic: rhythm, repetition, restraint. Big blocks of seasonal planting. English box (*Buxus sempervirens*) balls to hold the line. Trees with lifted canopies to allow movement beneath. And everything planted with structure in mind, so that when the ephemeral display fades, the bones remain.

These gardens are not complex, but they're layered in experience. What they offer is not just harvest, it's rhythm, it's memory, it's presence. They are spaces that hold life and allow for rest. In your garden, you don't need much. Just presence. And care.

BEGIN WITH A GARDEN DESIGN BRIEF

Given that design always starts with observation, the best place to start is to ask yourself: 'Why?' Long before you start sketching lines or placing paths, imagine the kind of life you want to live in your garden. Consider your wish list or your vision. Your emotional anchor.

In my own practice, this always comes first. Sometimes it begins with a Pinterest board, a folder of saved images, or a handmade mood board of magazine cuttings and written reflections. This is not to copy what others have done, but to get a sense of what draws me in. What moves me. What feels like home. Then come the words. I like to ask myself:

- What do I want this garden to offer me?
- How do I want to live here?
- What do I want to gather, create, share or feel?
- Who else will use this space, and how?

I invite you to ask yourself these same questions. You don't need to have the answers straight away. The act of asking is the beginning. However, once those questions start to take shape, pull them into a brief document that distils your vision and intentions in practical ways. It might include:

- **Primary purpose:** What is this garden for? Food, beauty, family life, sanctuary, sharing?
- **Emotional cues:** What do you want to feel here? Calm, joy, productivity, spaciousness, delight?
- **Core functions:** Do you need space for composting, preserving, a fire pit, a laundry, pets, kids?
- **Aesthetic direction:** What tones, shapes or materials do you gravitate towards? Loose and flowing? Sculptural and geometric?
- **Lifestyle rhythms:** Do you entertain outdoors? Garden in the mornings? Spend weekends preserving?
- **Non-negotiables:** What must be included? What do you want to avoid?

At Little Cottage on a Hill, my brief prioritised structure, restraint, access and generosity to the street. At Oak & Monkey Puzzle, it centred on rhythm, scale and gathering. In both gardens, the brief became the compass to which I returned again and again, especially when overwhelmed or tempted to add things that didn't belong.

A clear design brief won't solve every problem. But it will guide your decisions with confidence. And that, in a world of too much inspiration, is invaluable.

Scan to find a digital version of my garden design brief template to help guide your own garden brief.

Summer flowers gathered from the garden. It's a simple way of noticing what the season is offering and what I'm drawn to in colour, form and scent.

MAP YOUR SITE

Once you've clarified your vision, the next step is to ground it. This is where observation becomes practice.

Design isn't just about aesthetics. It's about working with what exists: the slope, the sun, the wind, the views, the privacy, the water flow, the soil. Reading your site is how you begin to shape a garden that is truly of its place.

I teach this using what I call trace-layer mapping.

Start with a base plan. You can use a printout from Google Earth, a hand-drawn site sketch or a scaled drawing if you have one. Mark the permanent or fixed features: house, sheds, fences, trees, driveways, tanks, utility zones, existing beds or structures. From there, the layering begins.

Use tracing paper to explore one site condition per sheet. (You could also use unwaxed baking paper.) Each layer helps to reveal patterns. I recommend starting with the following:

— sun and shadow (summer versus winter paths of light)
— wind direction and intensity (prevailing seasonal winds)
— drainage and water flow (where does water pool, run or dry quickly?)
— soil types and structure (where is it heavy clay versus light and loamy?)

Western verge and entry garden. A visually permeable fence line keeps sightlines open, and the paths and bed edges make the site easy to read.

— frost pockets or hot/dry spots
— existing vegetation (What's thriving? What's invasive?)
— access points and desire lines (paths you or others naturally take)
— views to frame, block or soften
— privacy and exposure (visual and acoustic)
— noise (road traffic, neighbours, wildlife)
— utilities and services (clothes lines, bins, gas meters, taps, septic lines).

This is slow, sensory work. It asks you to really notice. To return to the garden at different times of the day, across all seasons (if you have this time), and observe with fresh eyes (see below for a list of suggestions for looking deeper). You won't be able to do it in one afternoon. Let the place gradually reveal itself.

'Remember: your site is never a silent space; it's always speaking. Your job is to learn how to listen to it.'

Over time, the overlays will begin to speak, and you'll see overlaps. Maybe your sunniest spot is also the best-draining. That's gold. Or perhaps your privacy issue occurs in your windiest corner. Now you know that you can use planting or fencing there with layered purpose.

When you begin to work this way, your design becomes responsive. It stops being theoretical, and it comes to life. Remember: your site is never a silent space; it's always speaking. Your job is to learn how to listen to it.

Looking deeper

Site analysis isn't just about drawing, it's about noticing. The more time you spend in your space, the more clues it will offer you. Some arrive quickly. Others take a while. Here are a few suggestions to help you look more deeply:

- **Track the sun across the seasons:** Mark where the light reaches in both winter and summer. Which spots get full sun, have dappled light or stay shaded all day?
- **Watch for wind:** Which direction does it come from? How strong is it? Are there spots that feel exposed or protected?
- **Follow the water:** Where does rain pool or run? Are there slopes, dips or hard-packed areas where water never seems to soak in?
- **Notice the frost:** If you're in a cool or cold climate, pay attention to where frost lingers. At Little Cottage on a Hill, I use one small dip beside the driveway as my marker. If I see frost there, then I know it's been a cold night, even if the rest of the garden looks untouched.
- **Walk the ground:** Is your soil heavy and sticky when wet? Loose and crumbly? What areas feel compacted or dusty? You can often tell as much by walking as you can by digging.
- **Observe your slope:** Is your site flat or gently inclined? Does it fall away in certain directions? A slope can help to direct water, but it can also limit access to or create challenges for retaining water, so it's worth noting.
- **Check existing vegetation:** What's already growing well? Even weeds will tell you something about your soil. Some signal compaction, while others hint at drainage issues or acidity.
- **Look for microclimates**: Small, protected pockets, reflective surfaces and sheltered walls can create warmth. Nearby trees might cool things dramatically. You might find spots that allow tomatoes (*Solanum lycopersicum*) to ripen earlier, or protect lettuces (*Lactuca sativa*) so they don't bolt.

The more you observe, the more your site begins to reveal its logic. Keep a notebook if it helps. You don't need to catch everything straight away, but even small insights will help when it comes to making design decisions later.

Scan to discover my site mapping guide and checklist.

SKETCH, ITERATE, DISCOVER

Once you've layered your site and started to see the emerging patterns, it's time to explore possibilities.

I use the fat-marker method in all of my workshops. Why? Because when you have to draw thick and unapologetic lines, you're forced to think big. The process is more like creating a mud map – marking zones, movement, rough forms – rather than obsessing over where each specific plant might go.

'I use the fat-marker method in all of my workshops. Why? Because when you have to draw thick and unapologetic lines, you're forced to think big.'

At university, one of my design lecturers (thanks, SueAnne!) once asked us to do 100 sketches between classes. These were not final drawings, but different ways of reading the site. It was maddening at first. But by number 30 or 40, I was no longer trying to get it 'right'. I was experimenting. And sometimes, that's where the gold is.

In my workshops, I translate this into something that people can do in minutes. I hand out base plans (often of Little Cottage on a Hill), a few pieces of tracing paper and a thick, black marker. Then I say, 'You've got three minutes. Go.'

The looks of horror are consistent and completely understandable. But by the time they've done their third or fourth sketch, something has shifted. They've run out of safe ideas, the ones they've always imagined. That's when the magic happens. They say things like:

— 'What if I moved my main path to the other side?'
— 'What if I rotated the whole design?'
— 'What if I created a circular form instead of a grid?'

These breakthroughs don't come from planning, they come from doing, from sketching without fear, from people giving themselves permission to explore. I always ask participants to reflect afterwards:

— What surprised you?
— What worked better than expected?
— What patterns emerged across your sketches?
— Which ideas challenged your assumptions?

Then we take those concept sketches and place them on top of the site mappings. They start to see how a design fits: how it responds to sun, wind, slope, views. And how it might evolve.

Design is iterative. It's not about arriving at a perfect solution on the first go. It's about letting the land and your ideas meet in real time, over and over, until something clicks.

You can do this at your dining table or kitchen bench. All you need is tracing paper, a bold marker or pen and three minutes to sketch. Then repeat the process again and again. Sometimes, what comes out of that fourth or fifth drawing is the idea that changes everything. I suggest you do no fewer than ten sketches to ensure that you strike real gold!

***Right*_**Little Cottage on a Hill in winter.
Opposite page,
***Top left*_**Aerial base plan.
***Top right*_**List making.
***Centre right*_**Iterating sketches into a workable layout.
***Bottom left*_**Trace layer mapping.
***Bottom right*_**Observing the garden and imagining designs.

SKETCH CONCEPT #2 USING COUNCIL GUIDELINES
TO HILLS
UTILITIES

Thinking like a landscape architect

You don't need to be trained in landscape architecture to think like a designer. But there are a few principles I use in my own work that can help any gardener see their space with fresh eyes. These are some of the ways I think about space when I design:

- **Work in three dimensions, not two:** It's easy to design as if your garden is a flat plan. But real gardens have height, depth, structure and enclosure. Think about what rises, what overhangs, what recedes. Use trees, climbers, trellises and seating to shape space in every direction.
- **Consider sequences, not zones:** Don't just divide the garden into usage areas. Think about how someone moves through it. What do they pass? What do they glimpse first? Where do they halt? Where does one space open into another? These are the experiences that make a garden memorable.
- **Use layering to build complexity:** In planting, this means canopy, understorey and ground cover. In materials, it might mean gravel beside stone, clipped hedges alongside rambling perennials. Layering helps a small space feel generous, and a large space feel coherent.
- **Design for both view and use:** A garden should be beautiful when seen from the house, but also intuitive to walk through, easy to use and pleasurable to inhabit. Design with both perspectives in mind.
- **Let the site guide you:** Design isn't about imposing a plan on a space. It's about listening to the land. Use what's already there – sunlight, slope, trees, edges – as your cues.
- **Balance form with feeling:** Structure gives clarity. Rhythm gives grace. Restraint makes space for joy. But design isn't about control, it's about setting the stage for life to unfold.

When you think this way, your garden stops being a list of tasks or plant choices. It becomes a whole space. A considered, responsive, deeply personal environment.

***Top*_**Western verge nook. The gravel circle has been shaped as an outdoor room, with plants wrapping around the back of the seat, and a long westward view held in front. It is a place to pause. ***Above*_**The driveway courtyard. Designed for both movement and depth, it features Lebanese crabapple (*Malus trilobata*), clipped English box (*Buxus sempervirens*) and a black fence with mesh that supports silver vein creeper (*Parthenocissus henryana*) and *Clematis* 'Huldine'.

DESIGNING WITH MEMORY

At Little Cottage on a Hill, the gravel seating circle is anchored by a cypress slab bench milled from a tree that fell at Oak & Monkey Puzzle. It is a piece of one place held in the next.

Some parts of a garden aren't designed, they're remembered. There are features in my garden that exist not because they were planned, but because they hold something: a story, a feeling, a trace of experience that wanted to stay.

At Little Cottage on a Hill, there's a wide monolithic slab of wood milled from a 30-metre (100-foot) section of Monterey cypress (*Hesperocyparis macrocarpa*) that fell after a heavy snowstorm at Oak & Monkey Puzzle. It came down in the dark and trapped us on the property, traversing the entire entry garden and both sides of the teardrop-shaped driveway. After three hours of chainsawing and heavy winching, the SES (State Emergency Service) cut us free. I couldn't let the timber go. So I had it milled for 'one day', and now it sits at the centre of the western verge, angled just so, holding a moment that reshaped us. It's not just a seat; it's an anchor. And one that lets me enjoy the long view across Daylesford's rolling hills. One chapter brought into the next.

Design often begins with a gesture. A tree that must be kept. A line of sight that recalls a place you once stood. A rhythm that reminds you of somewhere loved. And, over time, these gestures become structure. They become memory held in form. When I work with others, I often ask:

— What are you holding on to?
— What do you want the garden to remember for you?

It might be a bench in a peaceful corner for your morning ritual. It might be a rose from your grandmother's garden. It might be a path that follows where your dog likes to run. Gardens are not just for growing things. They're for keeping things alive.

VISUAL AND OTHER SENSORY PROMPTS

'A good garden doesn't just function well, it speaks to us visually. It draws us in.'

A good garden doesn't just function well, it speaks to us visually. It draws us in. It moves the eye, holds the body, and balances complexity with calm. These prompts aren't rules, but reminders of what brings coherence, structure, beauty and legibility to the gardens I design:

- **Start with rhythm:** This gives a garden flow, both visually and spatially, and leads you forwards or holds you. It's the measured use of elements that help the eye to move through a space. Think rows of clipped balls, spaced evenly along a border. Or timber posts, spaced between plantings. Rhythm creates order without feeling rigid.
- **Use restraint in your plant palette:** Not every plant needs to be a hero. Too much variety can overwhelm a space. I like to repeat particular species in drifts, clusters or waves, sometimes in different parts of the garden, sometimes in the same bed. This creates unity. Grasses, perennials and clipped structural plants, such as English box (*Buxus sempervirens*), can all be utilised in this way.

- **Capitalise on contrast:** Your garden design doesn't have to be loud, it just has to be considered. A rich, woven perennial bed beside a clipped lawn. A black-painted fence that recedes and allows foliage to pop. A spade-cut edge against billowing textures. Simplicity in one zone allows complexity in another, and it provides definition.
- **Keep scale in mind:** At Little Cottage on a Hill, my raised wicking beds are 1 metre (3 feet) in height and framed in black. They anchor a narrow side space and bring structure to a tight footprint. Vertical climbers on mesh, clipped balls in gravel, and tall trees with high canopies all create depth without clutter.
- **Work in layers:** In planting, this means using plants of various heights and depths: trees, shrubs, perennials and ground covers. In materials, it might mean gravel paths beside garden beds, upright mesh against a solid wall. Layering provides interest across all seasons and helps a garden to feel generous, even if it's tiny.
- **Repeat key materials:** At both Oak & Monkey Puzzle and Little Cottage on a Hill, I used the same 20-millimetre (3/4-inch) crushed gravel for paths and courtyards. It feels firm underfoot, it doesn't track indoors, it compacts with time and wear, and it ties different parts of the garden together visually.
- **Get creative with gravelled areas:** They can be thresholds, gathering places and canvases. At both of my gardens, gravel offers space where furniture can be shifted, creates a feeling of respite or marks a transition between zones.
- **Define space with simplicity:** Use basic elements such as spade-cut edges, low hedging and open fencing to shape beds and paths. Structure creates clarity, and that clarity allows planting to shine.
- **Think about sightlines:** What do you see from your windows? From your seats? From the street? Framing some views, blocking others and creating glimpses are all part of the experience of being in and around a garden. If you have a small space, then permeable solutions such as timber-and-wire fencing or lifted tree canopies will help to make it feel expansive.
- **Anchor the garden with focal points:** This might be a large pot, a clipped shrub, a chair, a tree or even a sculptural log (like the cypress block in my western verge garden). Focal points make you pause, creating rhythm as you move through a space.
- **Work with the seasons:** I often leave perennials standing through winter for their seed heads and structure. I choose evergreen shrubs or pruned trees to hold the form when everything else is sleeping. I plan for bulbs to come up just as I'm ready to cut back the rest of the plants. A garden with a quiet season still holds shape.

Your garden doesn't need to be complicated. But it should offer something to the senses through structure, simplicity and rhythm.

***Opposite page*_**From the street, a permeable fence and repeated structure draw the eye from the verge to the main garden.

DESIGN TAKEAWAYS

Design is a layered process of observation, adjustment and gentle evolution. Here are some takeaways to guide your own design journey:

- **Begin with a brief:** Start with what you want. What do you value? What kind of life do you want to experience in this space? Create a garden vision that's grounded in feeling and purpose.
- **Create a base plan:** Use an aerial photo or a hand sketch. Mark fixed elements – house, sheds, trees, driveways – before designing anything new.
- **Observe your site:** For a full year (if you can manage it) or at least midsummer to midwinter (so you experience the seasonal extremes), track sun angles, wind direction, frost pockets, water movement, shade and sound. What are the constraints and the opportunities? Map these on layers of tracing paper, or digitally.
- **Try fast sketching:** Use fat markers to sketch three-minute design options on tracing paper. Try ten variations. Push your thinking. The best ideas often come once you stop trying to get it 'right', so don't get stuck in perfectionism. Work through multiple versions and trust your instincts.
- **Start with structure:** Use paths, beds, trees and verticals to create your framework. Then layer in rhythm and planting.
- **Think adjacency:** Where are your kitchen windows? Where do you want to sit in the winter sun? What connects easily with what? Design to support your real-life rhythms.
- **Plan for multifunction:** Don't assume that every space has a single job. A gravel courtyard might be a driveway, a fire-pit zone or a dining space at different times of the year.

Western verge at Little Cottage on a Hill. The visually permeable fence line reimagines the boundary between private home and public land, so the verge reads as part of the garden. Adjacency, material echo and layered planting work together to make the interface usable and generous.

A morning in early summer on the verge. A clear structure holds the planting, while the street edge stays open, workable and generous.

- **Design for all seasons:** Choose a few structural plants that hold through winter. Include bulbs for spring lift, perennials for summer joy, and grasses or seed heads for autumn texture.
- **Make space for memory and rhythm:** Good design is functional, but great design remembers. It holds emotion, experience, movement and time. Think about what you want the space to offer you daily, seasonally and over the years.
- **Review and refine:** Place your concept sketches over your base plan and site analysis. What works? What surprises you? What needs adjusting? Let the design evolve as you test ideas.

You don't need to follow this exactly. But having a rhythm helps. It gives you structure, permission and a starting point.

Things to remember

Design gives us a way to translate what we observe into something lasting. It's how we take the cues from our place – its light, slope, texture, boundaries – and shape them into a space that nourishes us. Whether you're working within constraints or beginning with a clean slate, the invitation is the same: to consider and create with intention.

There's no one right way to design. But when you listen closely to the land, and to yourself, your garden will begin to reflect not just what you grow, but how you live.

VALUABLE VOICES OF DESIGN

The following voices offer international insight into what it means to design a productive garden where structure meets beauty, and function lives alongside care. These are not one-size-fits-all designers. They are people who respond to place, just as I do. Their work sharpens and extends the conversations in this chapter, showing that no matter the garden's climate or scale, good design begins with listening to land and designing with generosity.

SIMONE BLISS

Designing with care

What if design was less about control and more about invitation? What if the garden could become a kind of soft threshold between worlds, between memory and possibility, between hardship and healing? For landscape architect Simone Bliss, a dear friend of mine, these questions sit serenely behind her work. As founder of SBLA Studio in Tasmania, and former senior designer at Taylor Cullity Lethlean, Simone has spent two decades crafting spaces that offer safety and emotional presence. Her gardens don't shout. They hold.

Simone's design practice is inseparable from her own lived experience. She designs for people who've experienced trauma, for systems that need rebalancing, for ecosystems trying to regenerate. And she does it by holding space for others to

Central Park All Abilities Playground, Malvern East, Victoria, by SBLA Studio. Simone Bliss's work is a reminder that good design can hold people by leaving space for life to unfold.

fully participate. 'There's no wizardry,' she says. 'It's about leaving space for cracks: spaces for others to bring their own story into the garden.'

Her studio began not as a business plan, but as a mutual support structure, a means to gather other women navigating motherhood and work, and to design in ways that acknowledged both. That same spirit of reciprocity and care infuses the way she approaches a site. Whether designing for a healing refuge, a riverside art centre or a fermentation hub in Tasmania, her work listens first. She starts by sitting on the land alone, gathering clues, asking what wants to be revealed rather than imposed. 'A lot of the time,' she says, 'we're undoing more than we're adding.'

This layered responsiveness extends to her understanding of productivity. It's never just about yield. For Simone, a productive garden might grow food, but it might also cultivate cultural story, community care or a sense of belonging. 'It's about seeing change and beauty in the microscopic,' she reflects. 'When you witness those moments, they hold you.'

In her designs, healing and function are inseparable. There's a clear rigour to her use of materials, her structure, her planting palette, but there's also space for intuition and softness. A pause point might be shaped to hold the crook of your back. A horizon line might be revealed just enough to re-anchor your nervous system.

Simone's design theories provoke interesting questions. What if we designed gardens that invited people to be fully themselves? What if restraint was not the absence of abundance, but the ground from which it could emerge?

'It's about leaving space for cracks: spaces for others to bring their own story into the garden.'

Scan to hear my full conversation with Simone Bliss, where we talk about the intersection of productive and healing gardens, and the importance of reading the site to choose forms and materials that help people to feel held.

MARK McDOWALL

Designing as revelation

When Mark McDowall speaks about gardens, it's not to describe a finished product. It's to describe something always there, waiting. His work is about unearthing. Not just in the physical sense, though there's plenty of that. But in the layered act of seeing what's already present, and letting design become the way he uncovers and honours it.

Mark began his landscape architecture career in Australia, spending many years alongside me and supporting me as a young graduate at Taylor Cullity Lethlean, and he now works across Ireland and the United Kingdom as co-founder of CMD Studio. His projects range from large-scale civic parks to private gardens that wrap around Georgian homes. But scale is not the point. The throughline is clarity. 'We're not just shaping space,' he tells me. 'We're revealing it.'

In his own garden, that clarity becomes an ethic. There are no grand gestures. Instead, rhythm and restraint do the work. Repeated elements create structure. Boundaries dissolve through visual rhythm. Planting is edited to support form, not overwhelm it. Even his material palette is tightly held. The result isn't minimalist; it's distilled. 'I don't want people to be awed by a garden,' he says. 'I want them to be stilled by it.'

Kinnitty Garden in County Offaly is one of Mark's projects that exemplifies this thinking. Rather than erase what was there, Mark worked with the site's existing

Scan to hear my full conversation with Mark McDowall, where we talk about revealing the unseen in garden design, using local materials and site immersion, and gardens as evolving retreats that give beyond harvest.

River Oaks Garden, Ireland, by Mark McDowall of CMD Studio. This garden was shaped through restraint and careful editing; the existing elements were clarified, not overwritten.

structure: a walnut (*Juglans regia*) tree at the turning circle, a forgotten copper beech (*Fagus sylvatica*), a neglected barbecue nook. He didn't remove these things. He recalibrated them. The barbecue area became a circular portal to the garden beyond. The walnut tree became an axis. When it came to the lawn, it was transformed into a conversation between formality and freedom. 'The garden already had good bones,' he says. 'We just needed to edit.'

This approach is deeply aligned with the premise of a productive oasis. In Mark's world, productivity isn't maximised. It's revealed, held and framed. Not everything has to be designed. In fact, he's wary of overdesigning. 'The most successful gardens,' he says, 'are the ones where the designer has stepped back just enough.'

'The most successful gardens are the ones where the designer has stepped back just enough.'

PAUL THOMPSON

Planting with structure

If there's anyone who can translate the poetry of plants into a system of design, then it's Paul Thompson. Having just retired after more than 50 years of working across Australia, Paul is widely known for his Australian Garden planting design at the Royal Botanic Gardens Cranbourne, created alongside collaborators Taylor Cullity Lethlean. Paul's work has shaped how a generation of designers think about landscape, resilience and beauty as structure. But he's quick to remind us that the best gardens aren't exhibitions. They're places of constant adjustment, humble learning and generosity.

When we speak, Paul offers one of the most useful lenses for planting design: structure, supporting layer and display. Paul sometimes calls the middle tier the 'supporting structure'. It is not a formula. It is a framework. 'The structure is the reliable form of your design,' he says. 'They might be trees, they might be low plants, but they're the bones. If you get that right, the garden can hold itself together even if other things shift.'

The supporting layer embellishes those bones. These plants might not be essential, but they bring depth, rhythm and texture. 'They might be experimental. Some might come and go,' Paul notes. 'But they shouldn't destabilise the structure.' And then there's the dressing, what others might call the display. 'This is your ephemeral layer. It can be high-diversity, even unreliable. But it's joy. If it disappears, the garden still stands.'

This isn't just a philosophical idea. It's a working model, developed over years on projects such as Victoria Square, where Paul used it to help quantify the labour required across categories. 'You can structure a planting design based on the amount of care needed,' he explains. 'So if a council wants high display, they also need high budget and maintenance. If not, you scale accordingly. It's simple, but it works.'

Paul doesn't purely offer techniques, he expands our idea of what a garden can be. He's not interested in perfection or fads. He's interested in resonance. In planting that belongs to its place. In gardens that evolve and hold form over time. 'A good garden is part of the system,' he says. 'It contributes. It doesn't just sit there to be admired.'

'The structure is the reliable form of your design . . . If you get that right, the garden can hold itself together even if other things shift.'

Melaleuca Spits, part of the Australian Garden (Stage 2) at the Royal Botanic Gardens Cranbourne. The planting was designed by Paul Thompson with Taylor Cullity Lethlean. A painterly vision of the Australian landscape, Melaleuca Spits was built in layers of tone, texture and rhythm, with structure holding it all together.

PART -II- Shaping the garden

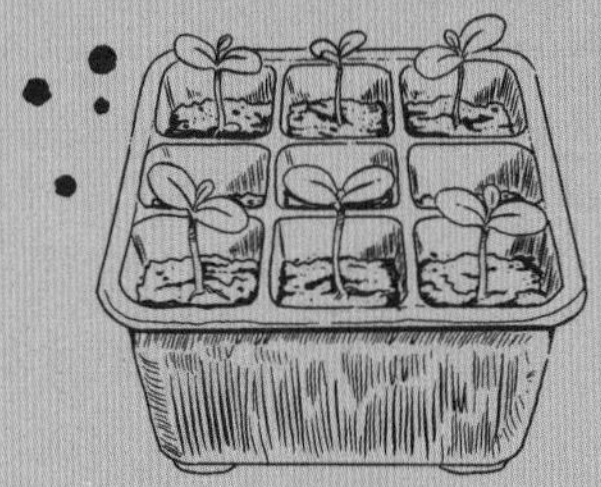

5 PLANNING FOR ABUNDANCE

Before a single seed is planted,
the garden begins to take shape in your mind.
This chapter is about planning as possibility.
Planning as a form of care.

LOOKING AND LEARNING

There's a phrase I often return to when I'm teaching or mentoring: there are no mistakes in garden design, only insights. These are invitations to look again. The rest will follow.

'There are no mistakes in garden design, only insights.'

I often meet people who feel overwhelmed at this point in the process. They've got grand visions and dozens of seed packets and maybe a few raised beds already in place, but they don't know where to go from there. It's easy to feel like you need to get everything right from the outset, but I don't believe in perfect plans. I believe in learning by doing. In my experience, every iteration, every scrappy sketch or season that doesn't quite work brings you closer to clarity.

Even now, I'm surprised by some things I could never have anticipated that happen in my garden. On the sloped verge at Little Cottage on a Hill, I planted globe thistle (*Echinops ritro*) and *Calamagrostis* 'Karl Foerster' alongside each other because I liked the contrast between their forms. What I didn't expect was that the globe thistle would become a structural support, holding the grass upright through high winds and heavy rain. This is a combination I now use as a planning device. I've seen how it works over time, and I've learned from it. I'll plant more globe thistle next year for exactly that reason.

Planning is full of small revelations, such as lucky pairings, visual continuities and patterns you don't always notice until you sit with the space. There's a moment in winter when I look out of the window and see how the plants in my front verge and in the garden beds inside the fence seem to flow together. From a certain angle, the lawn disappears. The *Miscanthus* cultivars (such as 'Eileen Quinn', 'Kleine Fontaine' and 'Yakushima Dwarf') and the panicle hydrangea (*Hydrangea paniculata*) inside the fence merge visually with the plantings on the verge. And all it takes is one addition – maybe a few *Hylotelephium* cultivars (such as *H. spectabile* 'Autumn Joy' and *H.* 'Gooseberry Fool') behind the fence line – to bring that continuity into focus.

Two different methods

At Oak & Monkey Puzzle, I planned with precision. It was a 5-acre property, and I came to it from a background of large-scale public design. I'd just finished working on the Australian Garden (Stage 2) at the Royal Botanic Gardens Cranbourne, with every millimetre documented and every detail calibrated. So I brought that accuracy with me, drawing up everything on the computer. The size of the garden beds was based on the length of wood available at the timber yard, so there would be no offcuts, no waste. Each bed had to be wide enough for a wheelbarrow and accessible from both sides. There was no room for error. We had spent every cent buying the place, and everything else had to be scraped together.

'The size of the garden beds was based on the length of wood available at the timber yard, so there would be no offcuts, no waste.'

Little Cottage on a Hill was a different story entirely. It's a small block, just over 500 square metres (5400 square feet) inside the fence, and I planned it on the ground. I used builder's string, spray paint and a lot of standing around. I moved things with my feet. I kept the plants in their pots, grouped them by height, and then played with form and texture until the combinations felt right; only then did I put them into the ground. It was intuitive and physical and joyful. There was no drawing. There didn't need to be.

Lists and questions

I believe that planning works best when it honours the way you already think. For me, that's lists. My kids joke that I have lists for my lists. One time, when my car had been broken into, the only clue was that all of my notes had been pulled out of the centre console and scattered across the seat. My kids just laughed. 'They didn't steal anything,' they said. 'Except maybe one of your lists.'

I make notes in my phone. I write them on scraps of paper. I pin them to the fridge and stick them onto walls. I keep photos in my phone as well as on Instagram (this started as a personal visual diary long before I realised that other people could see it!). And I walk. I wander through the garden every day, often with a cup of tea or a glass of wine, and I notice things. The way the light hits a fence. The way the soil sticks to my boots or doesn't. The way the lorikeets have eaten all the *Echinacea* 'Magnus Superior' seed heads and left the stalks waving.

Planning begins with noticing and then asking questions. What do I want from this space? How will I move through it? What do I want to eat, cut, admire, give away? What do I want to remember each year, and what do I want to change?

Planning is deeply hopeful. It's not just about logistics, it's about seeing what might be possible. When I plan, I'm building the scaffold for what's to come. I'm not chasing perfection. I'm imagining joy. I'm investing in beauty. I'm making space for surprise.

So, if you're feeling unsure about where to start, or worried about getting it right, then let go of those feelings. This chapter isn't about rigid diagrams or perfect formulas. It's about learning to listen to your garden. To yourself. To the forces and relationships that shape the space you tend.

CORE FRAMING FOR ABUNDANCE PLANNING

Planning isn't just about plotting beds and crop rotations. It's not a masterplan in the architectural sense, or a spreadsheet showing what to sow each week. For me, planning is a conversation between light and form, between what you love to eat and what your soil can offer, between what you imagine and what your site can hold. I call this approach 'relational design'.

When I was a university student, one of my lecturers often spoke about forces and relationships in design (thanks, SueAnne!). I didn't fully understand this idea in the very early days because it felt so abstract; at least, I often struggled with giving it form. But now I see it everywhere. The strong wind that shapes how a plant grows. The deep shadow cast by a fence. The way a path carves its own rhythm through repeated use. The way parsley (*Petroselinum crispum*), Caucasian cornflower (*Psephellus bellus*) and spring onion (*Allium fistulosum*) – one of my favourite combinations – can sit together in a garden bed, each holding its own form, each offering something different.

Planning for abundance means tuning in to these relationships. It means understanding that productivity isn't about perfection; it's about resonance: that

Opposite page,
Top_The northern verge in late winter at Little Cottage on a Hill. Grasses, stakes and frames hold structure while I watch light, wind and movement, and begin making the next set of decisions.
Bottom_Winter seed heads on the western verge. Repetition, texture and layering are left standing as a record of what worked and as a quiet scaffolding for what comes next.

sense of coherence you feel when the garden begins to hum with alignment. When the paths lead where your feet naturally want to go. When the plantings support each other structurally and visually. When the garden is meeting your needs, and vice versa. It's not about imposing control. It's about noticing what works together and designing with that in mind. Resonance is what happens when the garden starts to feel *whole*.

There's a reason I don't teach using design templates. Every garden is different. The forces are different. The hands that tend the plants are different. But there are questions I always come back to, ones that I use in my own planning, and that I encourage others to ask:

— What experience do you want this space to offer?
— How do you want to move through it, daily, seasonally and emotionally?
— Where does the light fall in midwinter? Where does it pool in summer?
— How does the wind move across your site?
— Where does water collect or run away?
— What are the existing plants telling you?
— What do you want to eat, to share, to cut, to admire?

These questions aren't meant to overwhelm. They're meant to reveal. Because every garden already holds clues, and the way you want to live in your garden does, too. You just have to know how to read them.

Sometimes that means sketching. Or walking with a cup of tea and noticing what your body is drawn to. Occasionally it means moving pots around until something clicks. And sometimes you just have to plant something to see what happens.

You don't need to name every force or understand every dynamic. But when you start to observe and notice, you're already planning. You're already relating to your space.

Practical and personal

For me, this relationship begins long before a layout is fixed. It starts in winter, when the garden rests and I return to my lists. It starts with a flick through photos from the previous year, the smell of the soil after rain, a memory of the sun hitting a fence line at a certain angle. I don't follow a calendar. I follow the cues.

Planning, in this sense, is a steady accumulation of understanding. It's not just a strategy, it's also a rhythm. It's the compost bay unobtrusively filling in one corner, the garlic going in before the solstice, the first asparagus spears nosing up through the mulch.

Planning for abundance is also highly practical. Just because a garden feels intuitive doesn't mean it lacks logic. There's intention beneath the texture, structure beneath the softness. I plan by thinking through both function and rhythm. I consider how I move through the garden, what I want to harvest each season, and where the high-use zones are. For plants I'm harvesting regularly, I lay out beds so that I can reach the centre from either side. I group things based on their needs, such as light, moisture and fertility. I start with hungry crops in the best-prepared soil and follow them with something more forgiving. But I hold all of this lightly. Because each year, the conditions change. And so does the plan.

That's why I believe that planning should be personal. It should respond to how you live as well as how you want your garden to look. At Little Cottage on a Hill, everything was planned on the ground. But at Oak & Monkey Puzzle, I planned on computer. Designing 5 acres on the ground wouldn't have worked for me at that stage. The space was too big, the resources too tight, and the urgency too real. I had two small children, a house in mid-renovation, and not a dollar to spare. I required a plan that would let us build the garden ourselves, methodically and efficiently. I needed to have absolute faith in my dimensions and costings, and to have drawings that we could measure against on the land. It was a practical decision born from constraint and a set of skills I could put to hand. And like all good planning, it matched the life I was living at the time.

My two gardens had two completely different design approaches. But both were valid because they were shaped by scale, resources and time. There's no right way to plan. Only a way that helps you to feel connected to your space, your season, your intention.

So, in this chapter, I'll walk you through the ways I plan, not to offer a rulebook but to share what works for me and why. I'll show you how I think about zones, layout, crop rotation and succession. I'll share how I plan differently across scales. And I'll bring in the voices of others, describing a garden that was imagined on the first sketch, and one that emerged season by season.

But before we go there, I want you to know that planning isn't just a stage of the garden. It's a mindset and a way of listening. When you approach it with care, curiosity and attention, it becomes one of the most generous acts you can offer your garden.

PLANNING AS REAL GARDEN LOGIC

My approach to planning has always grown out of the space I'm in physically, emotionally and seasonally. I've never followed a set system. I don't draw planting charts for the year ahead or work to a fixed schedule. Instead, I plan by noticing. By responding to what's happening now, what the garden did last season, and what it's asking for next. I build things from rhythm and need, not from templates. This is where planning becomes a lived experience.

'I build things from rhythm and need, not from templates. This is where planning becomes a lived experience.'

The garden at Oak & Monkey Puzzle had to be pragmatic. Everything was designed precisely to avoid wastage. There was no money for fancy landscaping, and we had to construct the garden ourselves (we even bought up pallets of gabion cages on clearance when Masters Home Improvement shut down). I placed enormous pressure on myself to create my dream garden and to get everything right, from the beds and the cuts to the cost. I planned the kitchen garden down to the centimetre, laying out the beds so we could reach the centre from either side for tending and harvesting. The paths were wide enough to move freely, to make maintenance feel like a pleasure, not a chore.

We built the garden in stages, making choices about what could be done at the time and what had to wait. And even though the garden was designed digitally, the logic came from lived experience. From knowing how it feels to walk a muddy

Planning as real garden logic.
***Above left*_**Abundant produce in the wicking beds during summer.
***Above middle*_**A thornless blackberry, *Rubus ulmifolius* 'Waldo'.
***Above right*_**Propagating seeds and tomatoes so planting can be timed and staged.

path with tools in hand; from being time-poor and weatherworn; from building with a toddler who wanted to help, and another child who would happily wander aimlessly far beyond the non-existent fence lines. There was an 80-kilometre-per-hour (50-mile-per-hour) speed zone on one side, and the entire Wombat State Forest on the other.

Later at Oak & Monkey Puzzle, I tried to shortcut the process. I wanted to turn the teardrop-shaped garden that formed the entry into a layered perennial bed. But instead of preparing the ground properly, I dug holes into root-choked soil and hoped for the best (yes, even I have made my fair share of mistakes!). I mulched over the top and planted. It didn't work. The roots of nearby Monterey cypresses (*Hesperocyparis macrocarpa*) were everywhere, stealing water and air. The new plants struggled.

A couple of years later, I returned to it, sweaty, tired and determined. I spent two weeks digging through that soil, turning it over, building it up, trying to give those plants the conditions they deserved, as well as somewhere for their roots to go. It taught me an important lesson: preparation matters. Foundation is everything.

Designing 5 acres on the ground would have been impossible for me. The sheer scale and my need to resolve all of the details before they hit the ground meant that I needed drawings. I needed certainty around materials, costs and layout because there was no room for error. That kind of planning gave me confidence when time, money and capacity were stretched. But in a small garden, especially one I can see almost in its entirety from a kitchen window, I plan by feel. By standing in the space. By responding directly to what's in front of me.

Planning across different scales

No two gardens are the same, and how you plan your garden will shift depending on the scale, the layout and the way you're existing within it. But the core principles still hold: observe, respond and plan for how you want to live.

In larger gardens:

- Drawing helps to clarify layout, access, materials and staging.
- Compost bays, nursery zones, animal systems and circulation paths all need more spatial logic.
- Weather, water and workflow matter, so plan around what's practical to reach and tend.
- Design decisions often need to be costed and sequenced, especially when you're building the garden yourself on a budget.

In smaller gardens:

- You can plan by feel, walking through the space and adjusting as you go.
- Proximity becomes everything, so plant what you use most where you can see and access it easily.
- Beds need to work harder. Layering, companion planting and rhythm really matter.
- Spaces for seating, harvesting, tending and observing all have to be intentional.

What stays the same, regardless of scale:

- Ask yourself how you want to live in the space.
- Plan around the movement of sun, water and wind, as well as the shade of trees.
- Think in seasons, not just in squares.
- Leave room to adjust, because your garden will teach you what it needs.

A new approach

When I moved to Little Cottage on a Hill, my approach altered entirely. This is a much smaller space – just over 500 square metres (5400 square feet) inside the fence line – and that scale changed how I worked. Here, everything is always planned on the ground.

I love seeing the garden in real time, such as watching the way the shadows fall and how certain plants catch the morning light. In the verge garden along the northern boundary, a 27-metre (89-foot) sloped stretch of public planting, I stood and watched for weeks before I committed to a layout. When I finally planted, I used what I had: stakes, builder's string, a tape measure, surveyor's paint and my eye. That garden came together by walking it, watching it and working it out on the ground.

I'm constantly making decisions based on how things feel, how they function and how I want to experience the space. Sometimes it's aesthetic. Sometimes it's structural. A step-over Huonville crabapple (*Malus* sp.) has become a low wall. Red-barked dogwood (*Cornus alba*) offers beauty, but also gives me cane material for weaving and supports. Sunflowers (*Helianthus* spp.) underplanted with sweet alyssum (*Lobularia maritima*) as a living mulch and threaded with scarlet runner beans (*Phaseolus coccineus*) makes a pocket that is beautiful and productive; the sweet alyssum knits the soil and nourishes beneficial insects, the scarlet runner beans climb the sturdy stems, and the ripened sunflower heads feed birds. These are combinations that I've learned to love, not just for what they do, but for how they sit together.

I pay attention to scale and depth. I've learned from experience that narrow garden beds are hard to work with because they lack spatial richness. You can't have layering and texture in a thin ribbon of soil; narrow beds tend to become decorative rather than multifunctional. At Oak & Monkey Puzzle, I found that beds measuring 3 × 3 metres (10 × 10 feet) or 3 × 5 metres (10 × 16 feet) offered something different because they were immersive. Each one felt like its own garden. A place to step into, not just a border to walk past.

At Little Cottage on a Hill, I've had to think differently about rhythm and movement. The garden still has structure, but it's just more tightly held. The verge layout had to meet council planting guidelines, but within those I still worked intuitively. I planned for access, for visibility, for beauty across the seasons. I layered in time and in texture.

Seasonal cues

'I don't sit down with a blank calendar and fill in the dates . . . I work with cues. I watch the garden.'

I don't sit down with a blank calendar and fill in the dates. That's never worked for me. Instead, I work with cues. I watch the garden. I scroll back through old photos to see when the roses flowered last year. I pay attention to when the soil has dried out enough so it's no longer boggy. I walk across the lawn and see when the postie's tyres are still leaving marks. I notice how much further thc sun stretches into the kitchen on a winter's day. I plan from what I see, not from what the calendar says.

Sometimes the birds tell me, especially when superb fairy-wrens flit through with fine grasses in their beaks for making nests. At other times it's the spiders, their webs laced through the garden like jewellery. Sometimes it's the wind direction, the colour of the clouds or the way the air changes before a storm.

In winter, my planning is inward. I rest. I imagine. I let the garden pause. I sit at my table, surrounded by seed packets and scraps of paper. I make lists, and I sort my seeds into boxes, containers and piles. I jot down notes in my phone, scrawl on butcher's paper, tape things to the fridge. My studio space is part commercial kitchen, part workshop and part writing room, and it's tucked up against my hybrid potting shed and greenhouse. I sit there, watching the light shift across the day, and begin planning again.

That's why I always return to rhythm before detail, and seasonal energy not just seasonal tasks. The arc reminds me what kind of season I'm in, before I try to decide what to do.

Planning, for me, is both fluid and detailed. It happens through walking and sketching, dreaming and trialling. I rarely draw formal plans these days, but I still think quite deeply about access, orientation, material use, plant combinations, and movement. It's embedded in the way I live with the space. Some people journal about their gardens on paper. For me, that record has become digital, captured through my

Opposite page_From the kitchen window, the wicking beds and verge open the view, and I read the light and seasonal cues before I act.

Alice Vincent

Northern verge garden in early summer. Repeated beds and grass paths keep the layout clear and workable, while simple frames extend the growing plane vertically as crops rotate and change through the season.

phone, my posts, my photo library. It's not always organised, but it's there. And some years, I change the plan entirely. A bed that was meant for beans becomes a cutting garden. Or I skip a crop altogether because the weather's shifted and I missed the window. That's part of it, too.

And I return to it all the time. Because this garden, like every garden, is constantly teaching me. I plan from what I remember, from what I observe, from what I feel. I plan based on what we love to eat. I don't follow strict crop-rotation diagrams, but I do pay attention to the soil (see the box opposite for an easy crop-rotation plan). In the verge beds, I think in layers across time: the clipped English box (*Buxus sempervirens*) balls and perennials hold structure while the seasonal crops move through. Sugar snap peas (*Pisum sativum*) for my son, cucumbers (*Cucumis sativus*) and garlic (*Allium sativum*) and roses for me. I plan for scent, for cutting, for giving away. I plan for joy and all the ways I can make my life feel abundant and rich.

I also plan for preserving. It's not always written down, but it's in the back of my mind as I decide what to grow. I think about the garlic I'll dehydrate and blitz with rosemary (*Salvia rosmarinus*) for salt blends. I grow extra cucumbers so I can pickle them for the months to come. I plant herbs that I'll dry for tea or bundle for kitchen use once the frosts have hit, such as lemon verbena (*Aloysia citriodora*), spearmint

(*Mentha spicata*) and sage (*Salvia officinalis*). When I choose a variety, I'm thinking not just about what we'll eat fresh, but what we'll want to bring into the quieter months, planning for the future flavour, the favourite things that I definitely don't want to run out of because they carry me through the seasons.

There's no one way to do it. But over time, what I've come to trust is this: a plan is not a fixed thing. It's a way of listening. It's a way of thinking through what the garden might offer and how I can meet it there.

A crop-rotation plan that you can actually use

This simple four-step rotation keeps soil lively, reduces disease carryover and makes planning feel easy. Think in plant families, and move each family to a new bed each year. Hold this plan lightly, and adjust it to what your household eats.

1. Start with legumes, such as sugar snap pea (*Pisum sativum*) and common bean (*Phaseolus vulgaris*). These help to fix nitrogen in the soil and set up the bed for the next crop.
2. Follow with leafy greens, such as lettuce (*Lactuca sativa*), spinach (*Spinacia oleracea*), Asian greens and celery (*Apium graveolens*). They benefit from the available nitrogen.
3. Move to fruiting crops, such as tomato (*Solanum lycopersicum*), capsicum (*Capsicum annuum*), eggplant (*Solanum melongena*), zucchini (*Cucurbita pepo*), cucumber (*Cucumis sativus*) and butternut pumpkin/squash (*Cucurbita moschata*). These draw more energy from the soil.
4. Finish with root vegies, such as carrot (*Daucus carota* subsp. *sativus*), beetroot (*Beta vulgaris*), parsnip (*Pastinaca sativa*) and radish (*Raphanus sativus*). They are lighter feeders.

When planting, keep families together. Brassicas go with brassicas, such as broccoli (*Brassica oleracea* Italica Group), cabbage (*B. o.* Capitata Group), kale (*B. o.* Acephala Group) and cauliflower (*B. o.* Botrytis Group). Alliums go with alliums, such as garlic (*Allium sativum*), onion (*A. cepa*), leek (*A. ampeloprasum* Porrum Group) and chives (*A. schoenoprasum*). Solanums go with solanums, such as tomato, capsicum, eggplant and potato (*Solanum tuberosum*). When planting subsequent crops, aim to keep members of the same family out of the same bed for three to four years. This helps to break pest and disease cycles and balances nutrients over time.

Use green-manure (cover) crops during resting windows. Oat (*Avena sativa*) and common vetch (*Vicia sativa*) add organic matter and protect soil structure. Cut before flowering and return to the soil.

If space is tight, rotate in three or even two beds. Pair legumes with leafy crops in one year, then fruiting crops, then root vegies. The principle is movement and balance, not a perfect diagram.

And don't forget to record what was where. A quick note or photo each season is enough to guide next year's layout.

***Above left*_**Raking the last of the autumn leaves. This is a simple seasonal task that closes one cycle and reveals what needs attention next.
***Above right*_**Willow and Ivy in the golden autumn sun. In this season, I watch the light shift and let the garden exhale into its slower rhythm.

Planning across different seasons

I don't plan by calendar; I plan by noticing. These are some of the cues and seasonal rhythms I return to each year, not fixed rules, just the kinds of things that guide what happens next.

In autumn:

— I watch how the light shifts – the golden hours stretch out sideways, and shadows start to elongate.
— I plant garlic (*Allium sativum*) somewhere between March and the winter solstice.
— I let the garden start to relax – less sowing, more gathering, more cutting back.
— I observe what held through summer and what didn't – this helps to shape what I'll plant again.
— The energy in the garden softens – it's a season of harvest and reflection.

In winter:

- — This is my planning season – I gather seed catalogues, sort my boxes, make lists, think about what I'll propagate.
- — I let the soil rest, and I rest, too – it's a calmer rhythm, with more space for imagining and dreaming what's next.
- — I leave all of the seed heads standing – for beauty, for wildlife.
- — I notice where the sun reaches inside and outside – it comes deep into my living room, and the dogs stretch out to find it.
- — I take time to sit in the garden and look – where does frost settle? What's protected? What's exposed?
- — I start to mark things in my mind – where paths could be widened, where light is lacking, where structure is needed.
- — This is when I start to prepare the beds – composting, mulching, building the foundations for what's to come.

Above left_Winter woollens and a hot mug in hand. I still walk the garden, noticing frost pockets, sun angles and the cues that shape the next plan.
Above right_Brassicas cloaked in frost. Winter makes structure visible, and reminds me to plan by observation, not dates.

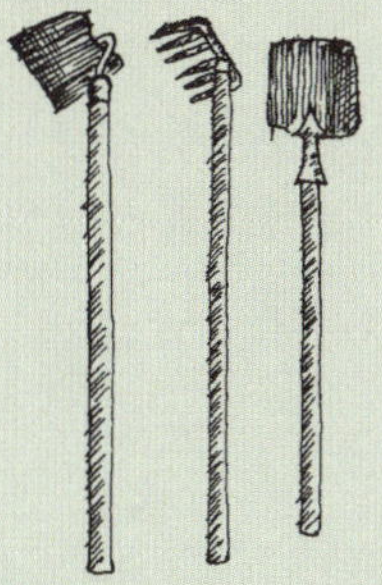

***Above left*_**A spring posy of double black Lenten roses (*Helleborus × hybridus*) and barrenworts (*Epimedium* spp.), the season's first quietly cut flowers.
***Above right*_**Iceland poppy (*Oreomecon nudicaulis*) in early bloom. This small, bright spring marker reminds me to start my garden tasks and to continue steadily, week by week.

In spring:

— If I stop, I can notice the sap rising – in the plants, in me.
— I start planting in earnest – not everything at once, but steadily, week by week.
— I pay attention to wind patterns – which beds need shelter, which plants need staking early.
— In my garden, spring doesn't really begin until late October. In early spring, I cut back the perennial garden – this helps me to see what's thriving and what's not; what needs to be replaced and which plants have overstayed their welcome.
— I look at what survived winter and what struggled – and I make adjustments.
— I often walk in the garden with a cup of tea and a list – observing where gaps have opened up or where things are crowding.
— This is a season of doing, but also adapting – no plan is fixed once the garden starts growing.

In summer:

- — This season is full of tending, watering, harvesting, preserving.
- — I plan successions, especially for quick growers such as lettuces (*Lactuca sativa*) and radishes (*Raphanus sativus*).
- — I give the perennials some room to breathe, and I'm more forgiving of things going a bit wild.
- — I let some plants go to seed for beauty, for pollinators, for the birds and for next year.
- — I notice where I've overplanted or where the path is too tight.
- — I tuck away seeds, make preserving lists and start thinking about what I'll want more of next year.
- — I take stock of what's working and what isn't while it's all still in front of me.

Above left_Summer harvest: zucchinis (courgettes), onions, cucumbers, tomatoes and a melon. This is the season of tending, gathering and taking stock of what the garden is offering while it is all in front of you.
Above right_A basket of overgrown zucchinis (courgettes), already edging into marrow territory. In summer, timing is everything. Blink and you'll miss the harvesting window, which is why I keep picking and adjusting as I go.

How I plan

When it comes to tools, habits and seasonal rhythm, I don't plan everything at once. I plan in layers: some of them intuitive, some written down, some remembered in the body. The rhythm of the garden guides me more than a calendar does, but there are tools I return to every season to keep things manageable and clear.

I observe:

— where the sun falls in midwinter and midsummer
— where frost lingers or water runs off
— what's thriving where (without effort)
— what I naturally walk past or reach for every day.

I use:

— a basic site map (hand-drawn, messy, edited over time)
— a garden notebook (not every day, just when it matters)
— my seasonal arc (to tune in to the energy of the moment; see pages 63–5)
— zone overlays or transparent tracing paper to shift ideas around.

I ask:

— What needs to be close? What can be further away?
— What's giving back? What's struggling?
— Where can I plant once and harvest often?
— What season are we in, not just the month, but the feeling?

Then I turn to the regular activities that help me to plan well for this season and the next:

— I keep my seeds in seasonal groups, sorted into boxes or containers with dividers for spring, summer, autumn and winter.
— I make lists in my phone, on butcher's paper, in notebooks and occasionally on paper stuck to the fridge or walls. They're not always to-do lists; often they're just prompts or reminders.
— I walk through the garden and take photos of what's working and what's not, especially when something surprises me or comes into flower.
— I look back through old images and Instagram posts to track what was happening this time last year, or several years before.
— I plan on the ground using wooden stakes hammered into the soil, builder's string, surveyor's paint and a tape measure. I group plants in their pots and move them around until the layout feels right.
— I keep track of things I want to preserve, such as garlic (*Allium sativum*) for salt blends, cucumbers (*Cucumis sativus*) for pickles, herbs for tea, fragrant roses for vases and bath soaks, and tomatoes (*Solanum lycopersicum*) for sauce and passata, and I plan extra space for those.
— I pay attention to the shape of paths, how I'll carry a basket and whether I can get a wheelbarrow through without pushing against the plants.
— I make decisions based on what I'll want to eat, share, cut or bring inside.
— I sit in different parts of the garden throughout the seasons, with a cup of tea, a notebook or just time, and notice what comes to mind.

Scan to download a printable zone-planning worksheet and a blank seasonal-arc template that you can adapt for your own garden. They're simple, flexible and designed to help you plan with rhythm, not rules.

This isn't about control. It's about clarity. I plan to reduce friction, not to fill every bed. Planning well means I can do more with less effort, stay responsive and keep the garden from becoming a burden. The tools help, but it's the rhythm that leads.

Northern verge garden in winter. The lawn provides clear space for working and strolling, while repeated beds, vertical structures and an espaliered edge give the narrow space its form through the cold months.

SEASONAL ARC AND CUES

Every productive garden has its own rhythm. Before diving into calendars and checklists, it helps to step back and observe how the year moves through light, scent, temperature and tempo.

This seasonal arc isn't prescriptive. It's an invitation to tune in. To notice what shifts in your own garden and in your energy. Where some seasons are about planning and pruning, others are about rest or generosity. Use this arc as a way to orientate your own pace and planting, and to remember that rhythm, not perfection, is what makes a garden thrive.

Seasonal planning cues help you to see what's needed or shifting in your garden, and guide your actions. They're seasonal signals: things to look for, consider or respond to as the year unfolds in your green space. See the table on page 64 for common cues.

Season	Focus	Cues + considerations
Late autumn to midwinter	Resting and planning	Observe frost and water flow. Let some beds rest. Prune deciduous trees. Check structure. Sketch layout changes. Sow green manure. Pay attention to precious seasonal scent.
Late winter to early spring	Waking and warming	Sow early seeds. Watch day length. Cut back perennials. Layer compost. Look for first blossoms. Shift mulch. Mark scent, colour or wildlife returns.
Mid-spring to early summer	Building and adjusting	Succession is key. Plant, observe, adjust. Check flowering sequences. Stake where needed. Prepare for preserving. Take note of pollinator activity and gaps.
Midsummer to late summer	Harvesting and preserving	Gather what the garden offers. Preserve gluts. Braid garlic. Collect seeds. Monitor wildlife. Remove spent blooms. Make space for late sowings or resting beds.
Early autumn to mid-autumn	Resetting and reflecting	Clean up edges. Cut back if needed. Sow overwinter crops. Plant spring bulbs. Reflect on timing, gaps, scent, structure. Let some mess remain.

Productivity can mean food, flowers, seeds, scents or structure. These cues are prompts, not prescriptions. Build your own seasonal rhythm around what matters most in your garden.

This rhythm works as a soft overlay to whatever tool you use, whether it's a notebook, a planting calendar or a map of your zones. Pair it with the seasonal arc to guide the energy of your planning. There's no right pace, just the one that works for your life, your climate and your garden.

Flora and fauna

Whether you're growing flowers for scent, colour, cuttings or the pleasure of the blooms, consider how your flowering rhythm weaves into the seasons. Think about:

- what blooms when (and for how long)
- where you want scent to gather or move
- which flowers support pollinators early or late in the season
- how structure, seed heads or spent blooms can remain beautiful long after flowering.

This is a small sample of what I gathered from six 1 × 1 metre (3 × 3 foot) wicking beds. I harvested over 160 kilograms (350 pounds) of produce in just eight weeks.

Seasonal cues aren't just about plants. Birds, insects, frogs and worms can all help you read your garden. Watch for:

- — the first ladybirds or bees
- — migrating or nesting birds
- — lizard movements or frog calls
- — which plants draw in life, and which are left alone.

This kind of observation deepens your connection with the living system around you. It also builds long-term rhythm and trust in seasonal patterns.

THINGS TO REMEMBER

Whatever your starting point – an idea, a layout or simply a space you're ready to reclaim – planning helps to give shape to your intentions, and makes room for both structure and surprise.

You don't need to have it all mapped out in the beginning. Good planning holds space for rhythm, for change, for life. It asks you to notice more than you control, and to return more than you take. It can be layered. Imperfect. Built over time.

Some seasons you'll plan by notebook. Some seasons you'll plan by feel. But when planning begins with observation – with walking mindfully around your garden, with witnessing the winter light, with acknowledging the signals of soil and scent – what grows from it will last.

You already know more than you think. And the rhythm of the garden will meet you where you are.

A productive space where growing is built into the architecture, Daylesford Longhouse blurs the line between garden and shelter. It is a place to propagate, gather, teach and preserve, with greenery threaded through the structure, and daily life shaped by seasonal patterns.

DAYLESFORD LONGHOUSE

A new kind of productive space

At Daylesford Longhouse in Victoria's Central Highlands, landscape and architecture are not separate gestures. They are one continuous act of planning, a choreography of growing, gathering, preserving, teaching and inhabiting.

Imagined by Ronnen Goren and Trace Streeter, and designed by Timothy Hill (Partners Hill) as a place to live, to learn and to host, Daylesford Longhouse defies classification. It's a building, a garden, a working farm and a school, but it's also a system. One where animals, compost, crops and people move in rhythm. One where beauty is functional, structure is generous, and every decision is rooted in care. 'There was no model for this,' says Ronnen. 'We had to imagine it from first principles.'

That act of imagining has yielded something extraordinary. A long, translucent structure – low-slung, steel-framed and open to the land – stretches across the ridgeline. It looks at once like a woolshed and a glasshouse, but step inside and the lines blur completely. Garden beds extend through the building. Cooking anchors one side. The other is open for pruning, preserving and preparing. There are no hard thresholds. The transition from garden to kitchen to guestroom happens in subdued stages, but everything is connected. 'We wanted to collapse those distances,' says Ronnen. 'The one between where food is grown and where it's eaten. The one between work and life. The one between learning and doing.'

A structure that grows with the land

Daylesford Longhouse is not ornamental, despite being exquisitely architecturally detailed. Every part of the building serves a function, often more than one. The roofline harvests rain into large tanks along the building's edge (around 340,000 litres or 90,000 gallons in total), and the water is used for both domestic purposes and the productive systems. The internal beds grow crops for the kitchen and teaching areas. The building's large volume traps warmth during the day, making it a true hybrid: part shelter, part growing house, part seasonal clock.

The steel frame is wrapped in translucent cladding made from Ampelite glass reinforced polyester, so the light inside is diffuse and soft; from outside, the building glows. Never dominating, it's always responsive to the landscape within which it sits. On foggy mornings, it disappears into cloud. On clear evenings, it hums with warmth. 'We knew we didn't want this to be a "feature" in the landscape,' says Ronnen. 'We wanted it to be of the place, to hold the line of the ridge, to make sense spatially, seasonally and socially.'

The building's axis is aligned with the fall of the land. One long edge looks over the orchard. The other catches the morning light through vegetables and herbs that run in and out of the central bays.

A living plan, not a retrofit

Where most productive landscapes are fitted around architecture, Daylesford Longhouse was always imagined as an integrated loop. Planning here did not begin with the garden beds, or even the building footprint. It began with rhythm: the daily, seasonal and ecological cycles that would shape how the place would be lived in. 'There are patterns to what happens here,' Trace reflects. 'It's not a plan on paper. It's a pattern that repeats and refines, and we've learned it by living here.'

'There are patterns to what happens here. It's not a plan on paper.'

That pattern includes animal movements across rotational grazing zones, composting in active and resting bays, teaching spaces that shift with the seasons, and a food-growing system that links seamlessly with the kitchen and the preserving room.

Beds extend outwards from the building. Pathways for people, animals and wheelbarrows are legible and layered. The orchard feeds the kitchen. The garden feeds the classes. The classes produce compost. The compost goes back to the soil. It's not just proximity; it's a feedback loop designed from day one.

Living systems and spatial logic

Planning at Daylesford Longhouse is not a set-and-forget diagram. It's an ecology of decisions, each one shaped by season, scale, use and care.

Beds are aligned to sun and access. The compost system is flanked by both garden and paddock, bridging animal input with plant need. Orchard trees are spaced for airflow, beauty and picking lines. Chickens are moved between zones, depending on what the soil, pasture and predators are doing each week.

There is no aspect of the design that stands alone. Each function – growing, cooking, tending, teaching, preserving – is linked to another. The firewood storage supports heating and seasonal cooking. The propagation bench doubles as a workspace and teaching surface. Even the livestock paddocks are integrated, positioned

Scan to watch my full conversation with Ronnen Goren and Trace Streeter, where we talk about compost systems, site logic, planning decisions and the long view of living with a landscape.

to support pasture health, guest access and a sense of presence. 'Everything has to serve more than one role,' says Trace. 'It's not about efficiency for its own sake, it's about making every system hold its own weight, and then some.'

One of the planning elements is the composting system. Built for scale and cycle, the compost bays are sited where they're visible to guests and accessible to the working paddocks – in line with the rhythm of activity – not hidden away. They are designed not only to function, but also to teach. Guests can see the process, contribute to it, and understand how waste becomes resource. 'We didn't want the productive systems to be invisible,' says Ronnen. 'They're part of the welcome.'

'We didn't want the productive systems to be invisible. They're part of the welcome.'

Inside Daylesford Longhouse, that same ethos holds. The indoor garden beds are not ornamental. They grow food for the kitchen, which is not a performative space, it's where the real work of preservation, education and daily nourishment happens. Guests learn to bake bread using grains from local regenerative farms, or join preserving sessions using stone fruits from the orchard outside. The experience is seamless because the planning was deep.

Planning as choreography

This is not static design; it's responsive, seasonally intelligent planning. Daylesford Longhouse embodies what it means to choreograph abundance: not to control it, but to set the stage for it to arise.

'We walk the length of Daylesford Longhouse several times before lunch,' Ronnen says. 'It's not a rule, it's just how the day unfolds. There's always something to check, adjust, respond to.'

Seasonal animal cycles shape how and where animals move. Weather and temperature shifts determine whether beds are sown inside or outside. A preserving class in late summer is held within metres of where the ingredients have been picked that morning, and the cooking occurs while stories are told around the table.

'The goats tell us a lot,' Trace says. 'We feed them by watching them. We know the compost is ready not because of a date, but because it's steaming or the texture shifts or it smells right.'

These are rhythms that can't be captured by diagrams alone. They're learned through attention and enabled through planning that allows space for those observations to become decisions.

Planning as hospitality

Daylesford Longhouse is not just productive; it's generous. Guestrooms face the landscape, not as a vista to be observed, but as a system in which to exist. Paths from the rooms lead directly to the orchard, the garden, the animal pens. Visitors don't peer into the productive systems. They are part of them.

Hospitality here is not an overlay; it's an outcome of planning. 'We wanted people to feel held by the place,' says Ronnen. 'To feel close to the work, to the food, to the rhythm, but also to be comfortable, to have space.'

The flow is deliberate. There are no jarring transitions. The distance from compost to kitchen to table to rest has been designed for ease. The experience of visiting Daylesford Longhouse mirrors the experience of tending it: unhurried, layered, satisfying.

Trace and Ronnen describe it as 'designing for interaction'. A kitchen bench that invites conversation. An orchard that's close enough to harvest, but set back enough to keep the sense of calm.

Everything is deliberate. Everything flows.

Planning as a productive loop

Built on observation, feedback and care, the planning style at Daylesford Longhouse is responsive, iterative and ecological. It ensures that the property's systems work together seamlessly:

- **Animal movement:** Rotational grazing is based on pasture health and weather patterns.
- **Compost system:** Located between the paddock and the garden, it's fed by animals, guests and kitchen waste.
- **Growing beds:** Extending inside and outside the building, they are structured for accessibility and rhythm.
- **Kitchen system:** It's tied directly to season and harvest, focusing on moment, not menu.
- **Guest experience:** This is integrated into the cycle through picking, eating, walking and learning.

What Daylesford Longhouse teaches us

Daylesford Longhouse is not a template. It's not a structure to replicate, or a scale to which we should aspire. It's an invitation to think differently about how we plan and how we live, as well as how those two things can move closer together.

It shows us what's possible when planning is generous. When structure exists to support rhythm. When systems are built not just to function, but to teach, to hold and to evolve. 'This place teaches us,' Trace says. 'Every season. Every year. You can't ever think you've got it all figured out. You have to be open.'

That mindset of listening, observing and responding is what makes Daylesford Longhouse such a powerful example of abundance planning. It's a place where nothing is wasted, but also where nothing is rushed. Where design holds space for change. Where compost is as important as light. Where pruning, baking, teaching and tending all belong to the same garden.

Daylesford Longhouse reminds us that productivity is not a task list. It's a conversation between land, season and structure, and the people who move through them. And it challenges us to learn from its choreography. To ask ourselves:

- What do I want my garden to support?
- How can I design for ease, not effort?
- Where does the energy flow? Where does it get stuck?
- What could I let go of, or do differently, to allow abundance to emerge?

Although the questions are the same for every gardener, the answers will look different. And Daylesford Longhouse offers one beautifully built response.

BANK HOUSE

Seasonal rhythm and intuitive rooms

Bank House isn't a masterplan; it's a rhythm. A process. A garden that has unfolded leisurely yet deliberately across more than a decade of shared living. Designed by Andrew Lowth and Nigel Smith, the property sits at the edge of Newlyn, a small town in the Central Highlands of Victoria, Australia. When Andrew and Nigel purchased it in 2005, it was a near-vacant paddock. Just a weatherboard former Bank of Australasia building (*c.* 1880), a few outbuildings and a treeless field that held potential. 'We bought it the same day we saw it,' Andrew recalls. 'There was no fence, there was no house to live in. There were the outbuildings, and a garden that had once been there, but had long gone.'

This wasn't a site that was mapped and divided from day one. 'We didn't draw anything up,' Nigel explains. 'We just lived it.' Instead of laying out zones or calculating yield, they began with the land itself: walking it, watching it, and gradually shaping spaces that responded to what they noticed over time.

The result is not a single garden, but a sequence of named rooms and connective walks, each with its own function, character and planting logic. These aren't decorative gestures. They hold vegetables, flowers, herbs and fruit trees. They shape space, guide movement and anchor seasonal structure. And every part of the garden, every clipped edge, every untamed border, is maintained by hand. 'We've never had help in the garden,' says Andrew. 'This is all us, every part of it. We built it slowly, and we still do everything ourselves.'

That slowness isn't incidental. It's central to how the garden works. Each room was created as capacity allowed. There were no rushed weekends or pre-booked trades. Instead, the garden was shaped by habit, by returning again and again to prune, to plant, to observe, to try. 'We did it all incrementally,' Nigel explains. 'Each room has been added in sequence, not in a way that was designed to be connected from the beginning, but in a way that's become cohesive over time.'

In the early days, they planted in areas that turned out to be frost-prone, windblown and challenging. 'I thought nothing was going to survive,' Andrew recalls. 'But if you go up there now, it's like its own microclimate.' Over fifteen years, the space transformed not through plans, but through presence. As Andrew puts it, 'We'd add a bed or build a wall when we had the time. Or the energy. Or when we couldn't live without it anymore.' That kind of responsiveness is what gives the garden its coherence. Over time, a structure has emerged not imposed from the outset, but built through habit, use and care.

Scan to watch my full conversation with Andrew Lowth and Nigel Smith, where we talk about seasonal rhythms, generous garden rooms and planning for joy.

Unique garden rooms

At Bank House, the garden is divided into a number of rooms and walks, each boasting its own role and personality. These functional spaces have evolved over time. Some are framed by shaped hedges, while others are revealed through arches. Each one adds to the layered rhythm of the garden as a whole.

- **Parterre beds:** Four formal quadrants sit just behind the house, and are planted seasonally with tulips (*Tulipa* hybrids), heritage roses with the classic 'old rose' scent, and annuals.
- **Scots rose garden:** Enclosed by European hornbeam (*Carpinus betulus*) hedges, this 'anteroom' is planted with beautiful old burnet roses (*Rosa spinosissima*) and seasonal layers.
- **Pear walk:** This central axis, flanked by espaliered *Pyrus calleryana* 'Chanticleer' trees underplanted with dwarf periwinkle (*Vinca minor*), draws the eye uphill to a pair of antique iron gates; the walk is enclosed by privet (*Ligustrum vulgare*) hedging.
- **Vegetable garden:** A productive and pragmatic growing space, it has been refined over time through rhythm and restraint, held by architecturally sculptural hedges.
- **Grass garden:** A smaller pocket space, it has been planted with ornamental grasses for softness and seasonal movement.
- **Hornbeam walk:** A linear passageway shaped by hornbeam hedging, it connects garden rooms across the middle slopes.
- **Beech and oak woodland:** This is a looser, more natural precinct near the garden's edge, with mown paths through understorey planting.

These rooms have grown from observation and care, not from complex planning. As Nigel notes, 'Each space has its own personality. It tells you what it wants to do next.'

A garden that teaches over time

For all its beauty, Bank House isn't a precious garden. It's lived in. Worked. Weathered. And built entirely for use. Every decision comes from experience: from being in the space day after day, month after month, year after year. 'We've grown into the rhythm of it,' Andrew says. 'We didn't know the soil, the sun, the seasons, not really. But we learned it all by doing. You just start. You try.'

'Each space has its own personality. It tells you what it wants to do next.'

One of the early lessons was scale. They planted more vegetables than they could use. More tomatoes (*Solanum lycopersicum*), more zucchinis (*Cucurbita pepo*), more of everything . . . until it became unmanageable. They don't do that now. What they grow, they use. And what they can't use fresh, they preserve. 'We bottle, we pickle, we make passata,' Andrew says. 'And then we give it away.'

Preserving isn't a separate activity, it's a seasonal rhythm. It's part of how they plan. Quinces are turned into paste. Crabapples become jelly. Tomatoes become sauce, and garlic becomes braids. Every season has its own cadence. Every fruit and vegetable gets its moment. And they've learned not to chase variety for its own sake. 'We don't need twenty different types of everything,' Andrew explains. 'We've worked out what suits us, what suits the garden, what we actually use.'

This, too, is a form of planning. Not the kind that happens on paper, but the kind that emerges through return. Over time, they've shifted from planting to see what would grow, to planting what they know will thrive and nourish. They still experiment, still try new things, but the core rhythm is now known. Beds are rotated gently. Crops move across the garden. There's no rigid diagram. Just attention. Observation. A memory of what was where and when. Sometimes that's recorded in a notebook. Sometimes it's just known by the feel of the soil.

The Scots rose garden, enclosed by European hornbeam (*Carpinus betulus*) hedging, follows a different rhythm, one that's as visual as it is practical, and there's a layering to bloom and structure. 'When I walk in there and it's in the height of its flowering, it's intoxicating,' Andrew says. This small anteroom holds seasonal shifts: the bulbs give way to burnet roses (*Rosa spinosissima*), and the roses to annuals. The space is a favourite not just for its beauty, but for its generosity.

The long axis at Bank House is held by clipped hedging, a lifted canopy and a simple lawn walk. Thresholds and gateways draw you forwards, room by room, giving the garden its quiet structure.

Planting for joy, planning through trust

At Bank House, planning doesn't always begin with a need. Sometimes it starts with a joy. Nigel remembers how poppies (*Papaver* spp.) kept returning each year. 'They're just beautiful,' he says. What thrives is allowed to stay. What doesn't is let go.

'Everything has a season,' Andrew says. 'And everything teaches you something.' This speaks to the spirit of the garden. This isn't a space built to a prescription. It's one that listens, adapts and holds.

The vegetable garden provides a different kind of rhythm, one shaped by daily habit. Meals are guided by what's ready to pick. Breakfasts in autumn come with poached fruits. Summer lunches feature zucchini and herbs. Winter focuses on stored goods. Spring is for greens and waiting. There's a pragmatism in what's grown here: fewer varieties, more intention.

While it's an extraordinarily beautiful garden, there are no showy gestures at Bank House. Nothing is designed to impress. But wander through the garden and you soon feel the quiet choreography: a bench tucked beside the roses, a path that turns towards the view at the top of the pear walk, the seasonal shifts in the parterre beds, the buzz of bees in the hedges. The spaces feed more than the table, they nourish a way of living. 'We grow things because we love them,' Nigel says, 'and because they love growing here.'

At Bank House, hedged rooms contain generous planting and colour, with gravel underfoot and clear edges that guide movement. Structure is considered first, then the softness of perennials is allowed to unfold within it.

6 DESIGNING WITH BEAUTY AND FUNCTION

There's a common misconception in gardening that beauty is optional. But in my world, beauty is a foundational part of how the garden works. In fact, it's what makes the work sustainable.

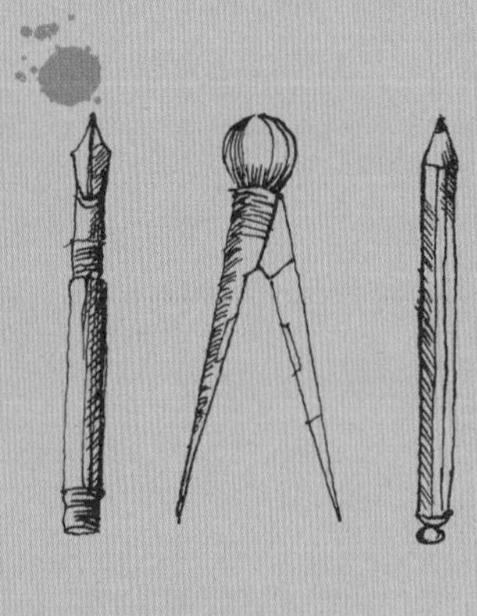

A BALANCING ACT

At Little Cottage on a Hill, there isn't room for waste, whether that's space, time or effort. Every part of the garden has to serve more than one role. The black-painted wicking beds are functional: they retain heat, reduce water use and are easy to tend. But they also provide strong visual anchors, breaking up the space with height and rhythm. The trellises carry sugar snap peas (*Pisum sativum*) in spring and *Cucurbita maxima* 'Coventry' pumpkins in summer, but they also create shade and softness, three-dimensionality, and a layered edge between the house and the street. The planting does its job, but it also makes me pause. That's the balance I look for. That's where beauty meets purpose.

This is not about perfection. It's not about maintaining a pristine show garden (although I'm inclined to be that way because my gardens are often outward-facing demonstrations to the world of all that I do, love and am!). There are days when the weeds creep in, when the roses need deadheading, when the mulch has thinned and the weather is too hot for me to care. But even on those days, the structure holds. The rhythm remains. The garden still gives back. And that offering, whether it's a dinner-plate-sized bloom, a soft and inviting shadow, or the way fennel (*Foeniculum vulgare*) catches the morning sun, is enough to call me outside.

In this chapter, I want to invite you into the craft of that balance. The design thinking that underpins what might look effortless. The systems of care that keep things growing. The tools I use to plan, prune, propagate and plant. But most of all, the way that beauty can become a kind of infrastructure and a framework for function. A very real and human need.

Because when we treat beauty as integral, the garden becomes something different. It stops being a task list. It becomes a place in which you want to be. And that desire, however quiet and simple, is what transforms maintenance into ritual, ritual into rhythm; and rhythm into living by the seasons.

We begin not with diagrams, but with intent. We design not to impress, but to support. And we tend not because we must, but because we're drawn to it. I certainly don't ever want the care for the spaces that bring me the greatest joy to feel like a chore! That's the power of a beautiful, functional garden. It gives and keeps giving.

'I certainly don't ever want the care for the spaces that bring me the greatest joy to feel like a chore!'

THE ART OF BLENDING ORNAMENTALS AND EDIBLES

In my garden, there is no clear divide between what is productive and what is beautiful. Garlic (*Allium sativum*) bulbs fill the gaps between English lavender (*Lavandula angustifolia*) bushes and cheery Iceland poppies (*Oreomecon nudicaulis*). Pot marigolds (*Calendula officinalis*) brighten the base of a bare growing frame that held last summer's cucumbers (*Cucumis sativus*). Rhubarb (*Rheum rhabarbarum*) mingles with thickets of vibrant red-barked dogwood (*Cornus alba*). Silverbeet (*Beta vulgaris* Cicla Group) holds the line beside sweet peas (*Lathyrus odoratus*). These aren't quirks or aesthetic accidents, they're considered placements. Small, everyday design decisions. I don't see ornamental and edible as separate categories; they're layers of the same system. One feeds the eye, the other the body, but both feed the soul.

Blending these elements isn't about tucking a vegetable into a flowerbed, or sneaking a few herbs in for fragrance. It's about understanding the physical, visual and seasonal roles played by a plant, and then placing that plant accordingly. But you don't need to overthink it. I consider form first. Is it upright or sprawling? Rounded or soft? Will it catch light or cast shadow? Will it allow me to reach into the bed or block the way? Then I look at rhythm and contrast. Is there enough repetition to ground the planting? Enough variety to keep it alive? Then I mull over the timing. Will this plant peak when another is waning? Will it leave a gap, or a moment of rest?

At Little Cottage on a Hill, the constraint of space sharpened this thinking. The front verge facing west, for example, comprises two big beds intersected by a gravel circle that makes sense of our slightly off-centre silver birch (*Betula pendula*) tree and the monolithic cypress seat that I hold so dear. While the two garden beds are predominantly planted with perennials and, between the colder seasons, bulbs, they're actually a beautiful riot of flowers, foliage, medicinal plants and herbs. The clipped English box (*Buxus sempervirens*) balls anchor them. Beneath the balls, thyme (*Thymus vulgaris*) varieties and ornamental oregano (*Origanum libanoticum*) knit the ground plane, while grasses, *Hylotelephium* cultivars (such as *H. spectabile* 'Autumn Joy' and *H.* 'Gooseberry Fool'), *Echinacea* cultivars (such as 'Magnus Yellow' and 'Primadonna Pink') and a tapestry of texture and form weave through. Self-sown field pansies (*Viola arvensis*) dance with sprouting garlic (*Allium sativum*). It's layered, but not messy. Even the green-manure crop that replenishes the soil is a textural feast: vertical oats (*Avena sativa*), twisted and tangled sugar snap peas (*Pisum sativum*), and broad beans (*Vicia faba*) as sentinels. The repetition of textures and tones keeps the beds legible. And the beauty is immersive. You can smell it, touch it, gather from it. The scent of a rosemary (*Salvia rosmarinus*) hedge clings to your fingers. You brush past the tomatoes (*Solanum lycopersicum*), and the unmistakable aroma of their foliage lingers on your sleeve.

This isn't a new idea, of course. Cottage gardens did this intuitively. Monastic gardens did it with reverence. And many of the plants we now call 'ornamental' began as medicine or food. But somewhere along the line, we separated the useful from the beautiful. As garden designer Christian Douglas reminds us, we isolated food to the back corner. We celebrated aesthetic gardens for being purely visual. And in doing so, we lost something vital: the deep satisfaction of a space that gives in every way.

Plants for all purposes

What I love about designing in this way is how responsive it becomes. You're no longer choosing plants just for yield or performance, you're selecting them for structure, tactility, scent, habitat, seasonal rhythm. You're inviting diversity, and letting function and delight exist in the same breath. And you're planting not only for yourself, but also for the pollinators, the soil life, and the visitors drawn in by colour and form.

This is where the thinking of Jac Semmler (of Super Bloom fame) has been so influential for me (see pages 109–11). Her framing of productivity as generosity,

Opposite page_ Western verge in spring at Little Cottage on a Hill. Daffodils (*Narcissus* spp.) and jonquils (*N. jonquilla*) thread through *Geum* 'Totally Tangerine' and oriental poppies (*Papaver orientale*). The cypress slab seat carries a piece of Oak & Monkey Puzzle into the present, while the planting shifts and rewrites itself each season.

*Above*_Northern verge from the street at Little Cottage on a Hill. Edibles and ornamentals are planted as one language, held by clear structure, verticals and repeated forms, so the garden can keep changing without losing its rhythm. ***Opposite page***_Rhubarb (*Rheum rhabarbarum*) weaves through grasses and globe thistle (*Echinops ritro*), with pale purple coneflower (*Echinacea pallida*) lifting through and red-barked dogwood (*Cornus alba*) behind. This palette decision uses stem colour and texture to stitch edibles and ornamentals together.

seasonality and presence has helped me to articulate something I've long felt. That high-performance planting isn't just about resilience or yield, it's about what a garden offers across time. It's about plants doing multiple things at once: holding the structure, feeding the soil, delighting the senses, offering moments of respite. It's not about labelling plants as either edible or ornamental, it's about understanding their role, their rhythm and their ability to hold experience.

My dear friend Lily Langham's garden, Three Chimneys, embodies this principle at a landscape scale (see pages 113–15). Her garden isn't compartmentalised; it flows. You move through a sequence of spaces that feel abundant, intentional and expressive, where texture, colour and function are choreographed with generosity. Lily's planting works hard, but it never feels like it's doing the heavy lifting. The lines are soft, and the forms are grounded. There's structure, but also the most soul-touching spirit. It's one of the most immersive planting experiences I know, and it reinforces that this approach of interweaving of purpose and beauty isn't about scale. It's about sensibility.

A beautiful blend

For those starting out, blending edibles and ornamentals can feel like a risk. There's a fear that it will look haphazard, or be hard to maintain. But my experience has been the opposite. When designed well, these mixed plantings are easier to tend. The diversity supports pollinators and soil health. The structure gives you visual rhythm and practical flow. And the joy these plants bring, such as walking out to harvest herbs from a bed that's also humming with bees, is incomparable. And can't we just value plants for their uniqueness, rather than place the emphasis on whether they're edible or ornamental?

There's no one way to do it. Sometimes it's as easy as pairing upright *Allium* species such as spring onion (*A. fistulosum*) with low-growing herbs such as French sorrel (*Rumex scutatus*). Sometimes it's a textural contrast: the softness of lamb's ear (*Stachys byzantina*) beside the crinkled form of Tuscan kale (*Brassica oleracea* Acephala Group). Sometimes it's planting by scent: rosemary (*Salvia rosmarinus*) holding the line; thyme (*Thymus vulgaris*) spilling over a stone edge. Sometimes it's a palette decision: deep maroon radicchio (*Cichorium intybus*) against silvery English lavender (*Lavandula angustifolia*), framed by Flanders poppies (*Papaver rhoeas*) and soft-toned pansies (*Viola × wittrockiana*). These are the combinations I return to, not because they're fixed, but because they hold. They feel good. They just work.

This section of the garden with an edible–ornamental blend is where design and daily life most clearly meet. It's the space from which I cut flowers and harvest herbs as well as aromatic and medicinal plants. A space that I inhabit, pass through as I leave home for the day, and find myself noticing most closely. It teaches me, season by season, how form, function and care can coexist.

Once you begin seeing your garden this way, there's no going back. The categories dissolve. The labels blur. What's left is a planting language that is expressive, alive and generous. And you realise that what your garden offers is more than just food. It's connection. Rhythm. A beauty that feeds you.

What is an edimental?

The term 'edimental' is a portmanteau of 'edible' and 'ornamental', and it's used to describe a plant that is both beautiful and useful. It might offer colour, structure or seasonal drama in a design, while also being harvestable for food, medicine or tea. Think artichoke (*Cynara cardunculus*), pot marigold (*Calendula officinalis*), fennel (*Foeniculum vulgare*), nasturtium (*Tropaeolum majus*), the flowers of chives (*Allium schoenoprasum*) and the purple form of basil (*Ocimum basilicum*). The term is popular in the United Kingdom and Europe, especially in design circles and publications such as *Gardens Illustrated*. While it's less commonly used here in Australia, the philosophy aligns beautifully with the way that many of us already grow plants, integrating beauty and yield in one expressive palette.

DESIGN TOOLS FOR LAYERED AND SENSORY GARDENS

When people ask me what makes a planting scheme feel resolved, I often say that it's not about the plants themselves, but how they've been composed. A garden isn't a collection of plants, it's a composition of forms, lines, textures, moments and experiences. The best gardens don't overwhelm or try to impress. They feel balanced, grounded and spacious. They allow your eyes to settle, your body to wind down, and your senses to switch on. You breathe differently in them. Your shoulders relax a little without you noticing.

But that sense of resolution usually doesn't happen by accident (although I do love an unexpected surprise because it's where some of my favourite and fortuitous plant pairings have come from). It's shaped through rhythm, contrast, repetition and space. Through an understanding of how light and shadow move across an area. Through the balance of structure and softness. Through restraint as much as variety.

In my own gardens, especially at Little Cottage on a Hill, space has been my most exacting teacher. A smaller footprint means that you notice when a bed is too busy or under-scaled. A poorly placed plant becomes a barrier or visual impediment. A bed without rhythm or soft logic becomes noisy. I'm certainly not immune to getting it 'wrong', or struggling with a patch that just doesn't sing. There are spaces I've had to refine, replant or recalibrate. This has taught me to see more clearly: to recognise how shape, texture and light work together. And how design, when done well, is a form of generosity.

Effective techniques

'One of the most powerful tools I use is layering, both vertically and horizontally.'

One of the most powerful tools I use is layering, both vertically and horizontally. Vertically, I think of the canopy, the understorey and the ground plane. The Lebanese crabapple (*Malus trilobata*) in my hybrid driveway/courtyard space has had the lower branches removed in order to lift the canopy, and this lets the eye travel further in a seemingly small but equally expansive space. Upright perennials create interludes. Cascading forms soften edges. Horizontally, I think in swathes and sequences. A path edged with ornamental oregano (*Origanum libanoticum*) and English lavender (*Lavandula angustifolia*) gives way to a broader plane of purple coneflowers (*Echinacea purpurea*) and *Rudbeckia hirta* 'Green-Eyed Lady', anchored by clipped forms or trellises beyond. The planting pulls you in, but it also provides room to breathe.

Zoning also plays a key role. This doesn't mean rigid boundaries, it means thinking in experiential moments. I group by microclimate, yes, but also by mood. A loose, textural edge to draw you in. A tighter, more upright structure to lead the eye along. A change in gravel texture to create subtle division between path and pause. These transitions help the garden to feel intuitive, like it's unfolding as you move through it.

Contrast and cohesion are other essentials. If there are too many similar forms, then the garden loses definition. Too much contrast, and it loses flow. To create rhythm, I repeat plant forms, colours or textures across a space. Silver stems.

Seed heads. Clipped English box (*Buxus sempervirens*) balls. These echoes allow the eye to travel comfortably. But then I gently disrupt the repetition with a wild card, such as a band of vertical Russian sage (*Salvia yangii*) or a bobble of dancing *Geum* 'Totally Tangerine' plants. Something a little unruly that stops you in your tracks.

Negative space matters, too. It's tempting to fill every pocket in a garden, especially when you adore plants, but I've learned to love the value of restraint. A simple gravel circle. An area of mulch left clean. These quiet zones allow the planting to shine. They give contrast. And they grant the inhabitant room to rest and move.

The power of sensory observation

Sound, scent, texture and light are all part of the design, even if they're not visible on a plan. I listen for how the breeze moves through different plants; grasses are brilliant for this. I note which blooms attract bees, and find it's *Hylotelephium spectabile* 'Autumn Joy' and borage (*Borago officinalis*) almost every single time! I plant for scent near doorways, windows and pathways, so the garden speaks to you when you enter, and stays with you after you've gone. And I always watch how the light lands. In my eyes, a tree with foliage that catches the morning sun is just as valuable as a tree that offers fruits.

To refine this thinking, I often use photography. Not staged garden shots, but honest image captures of what the garden actually looks like from a kitchen window, or how a path reads when you're walking with a basket in hand. Sometimes I sketch over these pictures. Or I wander through the garden at different times of day, noticing where I like to return. This helps me to see what's working and what's not. To find the magic in a busy and noisy world.

Autumn on the western boundary path. The canopy, the clear line of movement and the layered edge planting create texture, rhythm and pause.

The seating nook within the gravel circle. A visually permeable fence and a tight material palette blur the line between street verge and garden room.

This is also where I connect deeply with Tim Pilgrim's planting ethos (see pages 111–12). His gardens are immersive, not curated. They feel alive and rhythmic, like they've grown into their own momentum, but you can tell how much observation sits underneath. Tim's language is texture, timing and succession. He works with nature, not against it. His blocks of planting are confident but not loud. And he's not afraid of decay, imperfection or a plant going to seed. His gardens remind me that structure doesn't have to mean stiffness. That rhythm doesn't have to be formal.

That ethos of observation and working with what the garden offers sits at the heart of Lily Langham's planting, too. Her curved beds hug the contours of her land and flow in drifts, with moments of density and delay. She plays with height, space and bloom time, always attentive to how it feels to inhabit each space. Her gardens aren't overdesigned; they're felt. You can sense the human scale in them, and the seasonal care that shapes them. They are tapestries woven together with a rich and diverse palette of plants, but the threads that bind them together still remain visible.

All of these tools, from layering and rhythm to contrast and observation, help a garden to become more than the sum of its parts. They help it to move. To sing. To settle. And, most importantly, they help it to feel generous to live with. A well-designed planting scheme doesn't just look good; it's enjoyable to be in, and it gives so much. And that feeling of ease, coherence and delight is the most powerful design principle I know.

SMALL-SPACE DESIGN STRATEGIES

A small garden asks more of the design and rewards deliberation. The constraints are tighter, so the thinking has to be smarter. There's no room to hide poor planning or wishful plant choices. Every metre matters. Every decision is felt. Because of this, small gardens are some of the most generous teachers of landscape design.

When I moved from 5 acres at Oak & Monkey Puzzle to 515 square metres (5545 square feet) at Little Cottage on a Hill, the scale of everything changed. I was no longer designing long sightlines or layered field transitions. I was designing a courtyard. A verge. A space between a chicken run and a compost heap. And instead of resisting that shift, I leaned into it. Because when space is limited, your intention sharpens. The garden becomes more personal, more responsive and more precise.

'Because when space is limited, your intention sharpens.'

At Little Cottage on a Hill, one of the most important tools I've used is layering with legibility. A garden can be rich and complex, but still feel calm and ordered. The key is in how you structure the space, how you use rhythm, negative space and materiality to guide the eye and body. A structural palette of ornamental grasses planted in groups of five or more, a vertical trellis and a soft silver layer at the edge of a bed are small cues that create orientation. They allow your brain to make sense of the space, and your body to feel centred, which means that you can relax in the garden.

Multifunctionality is also critical. I don't ask a plant or structure to do just one thing. A cladding screen hides the bins but also forms a backdrop for a climbing hydrangea (*Hydrangea petiolaris*) or espaliered fruit trees. A gravel path stalls water and invites visitors. A raised wicking bed near the house serves as a heat trap, a growing zone and a convenient spot to rest a basket. The logic is layered. Everything does more than one job.

One of my favourite areas to design has been the verge, the garden beyond the formal boundary of our front fence. Being on a corner block, it comprises a more squat western section and a long, north-facing strip that performs hard. They both provide street presence and pollinator habitat. They act as a teaching tool during workshops. They feed our household with herbs, greens and seasonal colour. But they also frame the whole house and invite people to visit. And because the verge area is public-facing, it required careful attention to rhythm, repetition and transitions so it felt generous rather than chaotic, expressive rather than overfull. It also had to align with the nature-strip planting guidelines drawn up by Hepburn Shire Council.

Permeability, containment and calm

In small spaces, visual permeability becomes a design asset. You want to be able to see through and beyond. A light gravel path edged with wispy foliage. An open-structured plant that offers movement without blocking views. A timber-batten fence that holds the boundary without feeling heavy. These simple moves expand space perceptually rather than literally. They help the garden to feel more spacious than it is.

Containment is just as important. In a small garden, you need anchors such as forms or edges that hold the space and keep it from feeling busy. That might be a clipped hedge, a defined courtyard or a bed framed in stone. These elements offer visual rest and allow looser planting to breathe. In addition, they ground the garden emotionally, especially for those of us who feel the world keenly.

There's a phrase I come back to often: designing for calm. In my own life, especially as a solo parent of neurodivergent children, my garden needs to do more than grow food or look good. It needs to regulate. To hold space. To offer peace, rhythm or constraint, depending on the season and the state of things. And while I speak from lived experience rather than in clinical terms, I've found that small gardens can offer profound support and delight when they've been designed with sensitivity. They become sensory sanctuaries, places where scent and softness and structure work together to restore clarity. Where the edges are legible, and the transitions are smooth. Where there's enough order to feel safe, and enough wildness to feel alive. At Little Cottage on a Hill, that often means:

— planting by feel, not just by textbook
— tempering thresholds with scent or sound
— choosing forms that move gently with the wind
— making sure that each corner has a purpose, but also a softness.

Western verge at Little Cottage on a Hill, in autumn. The gravel axis and circle make sense of the off-centre birch, with the cypress slab seat and fire pit forming a small room within the public verge. Visually permeable fencing and layered planting give structure, containment and an invitation to pause.

It also means creating spaces so the eye knows where to land. So the foot knows where to step. So the feel of a soft-mulched path or the aroma of thyme (*Thymus vulgaris*) against a warm wall can shift the mood of a whole day.

These garden spaces don't need to be large. In fact, it often works best when they're close at hand: just outside the kitchen, or lining the path to the front gate. These are the places we pass through every day, and engage with through incidental movements. And when they're designed with care, they become more than circulation. They become spaces for noticing. Spaces for settling.

In many ways, Little Cottage on a Hill has taught me more than any property I've ever had or visited. Because in a small space, nothing is wasted. Every patch of soil holds potential. Every design choice echoes. Every season is felt in full. It's not about doing more with less, it's about doing purposeful things in meaningful places. And that's design at its most powerful.

DESIGNING WITH STRUCTURE AND SUPPORT

Structure gives a garden its bones. It's what allows a space to hold form through the quiet seasons, to feel intentional even in moments of pause or dormancy. Without it, a garden can feel like it's drifting or untethered. But with structure, even the loosest planting can shine. It becomes legible. Grounded. Able to breathe.

In my gardens, structure is where I begin. Not with what I want to plant, but with how I want to shape space. How I want to move through it. What I want to feel held by, orientated or framed by, or drawn towards.

At Little Cottage on a Hill, the bones are few but they're hardworking. A central path with a soft and generous axis. A gravel circle that forms the heart of the front garden. Low, clipped elements that hold edges and rhythm. Upright supports for seasonal verticals. Espaliered fruit trees against a fence line, where they add beauty, structure and yield in a bed that measures less than 30 centimetres (12 inches) from front to back.

One of the most powerful tools in a small garden is the vertical frame, not just as a means of growing, but as a spatial design device. A basic wire-mesh arch or arbour over a path gives a sense of threshold and arrival. A metal tripod lets common beans (*Phaseolus vulgaris*) or cucumbers (*Cucumis sativus*) reach for light, while providing seasonal punctuation. A trellis clad with climbing pumpkins (such as *Cucurbita maxima* 'Coventry') becomes a green wall. These structures carry more than just plants. They convey rhythm, containment and three-dimensional form. They guide the eye, emphasise space and provide repetition. In addition, they provide sculptural elements and help the garden to move.

My double-layered, espaliered orchard, comprising step-over Huonville crab-apples (*Malus* sp.) at hip height, with pears (*Pyrus communis* 'Bonne de Maline' and *P. c.* 'Doyenné du Comice') and quinces (*Cydonia oblonga* 'Smyrna') above, is one of the key intentional design elements. When we moved to Little Cottage on a Hill, space was tight but the urge to grow fruits was strong. I'd had a 16 × 16-metre (52 × 52-foot) orchard for nearly ten years at Oak & Monkey Puzzle, and I absolutely didn't want to let go of the seasonal abundance idea. But rather than filling the small garden area with fruit trees, I trained them against the 27-metre (89-foot), full-sun-facing fence line. The spacing was deliberate. The underplanting – initially foxgloves (*Digitalis purpurea*), then later English lavender (*Lavandula angustifolia*) and soft drifts of bulbs and annuals – was all part of the logic. It wasn't just about squeezing things in. It was about hiding an ugly fence that I couldn't justify replacing. It was about reading the space from multiple angles: from the garden, from the street and from beyond. And letting the structure do the work of cohesion.

Go with the flow

Good structure also holds movement. It guides flow and circulation. It tells you where to step and where to stop. In larger gardens, that might be a long axis or a hedged path. In smaller spaces, it might be as simple as a change in surface texture, a planted curve or a framed view. These are the design moves that turn a garden from a space you walk through into a space you inhabit.

This is where The Stones, created by Jeremy Valentine and Grant Francis, offers such clarity (see pages 107–9). Their work, forged in the extremes of Central Victoria, is a masterclass in restraint, re-use and rhythm. Faced with heat, wind and exposure, they didn't fight the elements, they designed with them. Using old fencing wire, bush timber and industrial scrap, they created vertical forms that are both poetic and practical. Screens and trellises frame long views and hold vegetables. Arbours support vines and invite you into their cocoon-like embrace. Sculptural elements are as beautiful bare in winter as they are cloaked in greenery in spring. Nothing is wasted. Everything serves. And yet the garden feels anything but utilitarian.

As Jeremy puts it, 'We didn't want to mimic what we'd seen in books. We just built what made sense for this place. And, over time, it's become a space that holds us. Holds the heat, the cold, the wind, but also holds beauty.'

What I find so resonant in their approach is their willingness to use structure not as a backdrop, but as a participant in the garden. Their frames don't disappear: they hold the space and anchor the experience. And like the clipped forms or gravel paths in my own two gardens, they help to shape the rhythm of the day: the way light strikes, the way bodies move, the way tasks unfold.

Because when structure is well placed, it frees the garden to be more expressive elsewhere. It gives you something to lean against, visually and physically. It carries weight so that other parts of the garden can stay light. And it allows for the kind of seasonal generosity I value most, where sugar snap peas (*Pisum sativum*) and pumpkins (such as *Cucurbita maxima* 'Coventry') share the same verticals, and form and function become inseparable.

In any garden, structure is a kind of long-view thinking. It's what stays when the annuals fade. What steadies the eye in spring abundance, and what holds the line in high summer. It's the thing you return to when everything else is shifting. And it doesn't need to be elaborate. It just needs to be intentional.

1

2

3

4

5

6

1_Reinforcing-mesh uprights between wicking beds have been bent into sculptural frames to pull the growing surface up into the vertical plane.
2_Training tomatoes (*Solanum lycopersicum*) to grow up sheets of reinforcing mesh on the northern verge. Strong structure comes first, then the plants do the rest.
3_Reinforcing mesh is used along the boundary fence as a strong trellis for step-over and espaliered fruit trees, creating a compact, vertical orchard.
4_A young fig (*Ficus carica*) has been trained low with a single bamboo cane. The horizontal ribbon becomes both edible structure and a green line in the garden.
5_A simple A-frame made from timber-and-wire fencing, tied together with cables, holds plants upright and lets softness sit within a clear geometry.
6_Steel bars, reinforcing mesh and wire are a tough, repeatable kit of parts. This restricted material palette can be used to make robust frames for almost anything that needs height.

LIVING SYSTEMS OF CARE AND CULTIVATION

There are rhythms that underpin every thriving garden. You won't find them in a how-to book or a seasonal planner. They're the rhythms that comes from showing up regularly, from watching closely, from letting the work of care become part of how you live. Over time, the garden teaches you when to sow and when to rest. When to cut back hard and when to leave things be. When to step in and when to observe from the edges.

These rhythms aren't fixed. They shift with the seasons, the weather, the microclimates of your particular patch, the changing world. But once you start listening to them and noticing what the garden is asking for, they become a guiding compass. A pleasant, practical logic that anchors your growing life.

Seed starting

For me, seed starting is one of the most grounding parts of the growing rhythm, but I don't always cultivate plants from seed. Some seasons I sow seeds; other times I buy punnets from the nursery. There's no judgement here! You don't have to grow everything from scratch, but you do need to know when to start. That timing is everything. I don't follow a rigid calendar, but I do work by local rhythms: by forecast, by habit and by seasonal ritual.

Below left_Foraging dried seed heads from wild teasel (*Dipsacus fullonum*) for wreaths and winter arrangements.
Below right_Harvesting seed heads from purple coneflowers (*Echinacea purpurea*) for next season's sowing.

*Above left*_Visiting the local nursery to choose seedlings, working with what the season offers.

*Above right*_Propagating tomatoes and other summer crops in the hybrid potting shed and greenhouse.

Every place has its markers. I've learned from Lily Langham to plant brassica family crops when the hawkmoths arrive. I don't expect everyone to spot hawkmoths – I certainly wouldn't have recognised them if Lily hadn't shown me what they looked like – but I do know to move early, before the ground cools too much in late autumn. Here in Central Victoria, the seedlings of frost-tender crops such as tomatoes (*Solanum lycopersicum*), capsicums (*Capsicum annuum*), zucchinis (*Cucurbita pepo*) and various pumpkins (*Cucurbita* spp.) should be planted out after Melbourne Cup Day, the first Tuesday in November, although that's starting to shift as the climate becomes more erratic.

My propagation bench is small but hardworking, and one of my favourite tools is my heat mat because it has transformed how and when I grow. It extends the season and lets me start earlier. Sometimes I use the greenhouse. At other times I make do with a plank across the bathtub, angled to catch the nearby window's strongest light. In fact, in the early days of Covid, at Oak & Monkey Puzzle, the bath itself became a propagation zone for an entire tomato-seedling system before the garden warmed enough to take them. It's not high-tech, but it's resourceful. And that's what matters.

Pruning

Pruning also follows a rhythm, but it's important to be clear about why a plant is being cut back. For deciduous fruit trees and certain woody perennials, a harder prune often happens in winter, once the leaves have dropped and the structure is visible. This kind of pruning is about regeneration. It encourages new growth, but it can also trigger water shoots and vigorous upright laterals. This is why I follow it

Above left _Cutting down green-manure crops and leaving them on the surface, in order to keep the soil covered in a no-dig system. ***Above right*** _Winter pruning an espaliered Huonville crab-apple (*Malus* sp.) to maintain form and let light in.

with a more measured, formative prune in summer, especially on espaliered and clipped forms. That summer shaping softens the plant's outline, directs its energy and refines its place in the space.

I don't prune just for yield or health, I prune for clarity. For how the plant holds itself in the composition. How it catches the light. How it supports what's planted nearby. A clipped rosemary (*Salvia rosmarinus*) becomes a living bench edge. A pruned fig (*Ficus carica*) lets sunlight reach the core of the bed. These aren't chores. They're gestures that are part of the garden's sculptural language.

Fertilising

Feeding the garden is less about product and more about process. I don't have a fertilising schedule taped to a shed wall. I have a rhythm. And even that rhythm has shifted as I've moved deeper into no-dig principles (see pages 205–10). These days, I rely more on compost than I ever used to because I've learned that when you grow the soil, the plants follow. This doesn't mean that fertilising isn't needed, just that the focus changes.

I feed in spring and autumn, but lightly. Observationally. I watch the plants and the soil. Sometimes I top up with diluted worm tea (used in low concentrations), or add aged chicken manure if a bed feels depleted. If brassica family plants are coming in, I might add a dusting of wood ash from the fire, but sparingly, and only if the soil isn't already too alkaline (soil pH test kits are available from garden centres). Sometimes I sow a green mulch such as rye (*Secale cereale*) or oat (*Avena sativa*), and even add spent seedlings. Sometimes I sprinkle a watering-can's worth of well-diluted

seaweed solution over the garden bed. It's never rigid. It's always guided by what the garden's asking for, and how the soil is holding.

Too much feed, especially the wrong kind, can push soft, leggy growth. I learned that the hard way with *Hylotelephium* cultivars (such as *H. spectabile* 'Autumn Joy' and *H.* 'Gooseberry Fool') that grew so fast they couldn't bear the weight of their own blooms (it's like the heartbreaking scenario found in some commercial poultry businesses, where poor chooks are encouraged to grow so fast that they can't hold themselves up). What I want is strength and resilience, enough for the garden to support itself, with the soil as the foundation.

Above left_Top-dressing with worm castings helps to feed the soil rather than the plant. ***Above right***_Composting worms are ideal for turning scraps into castings that support the whole garden system.

Composting

My relationship with compost has shifted over time. In my twenties, I built a hot compost that would make any permaculturist proud: manure, straw and green waste, turned with zeal. At Oak & Monkey Puzzle, I had three bays on the go: one filling, one resting and one ready to use. It was an efficient system, both practical and predictable, but none of the bays ever got hot.

Composting at Little Cottage on a Hill is deliberately cold. I could hot compost if I wanted to, with a tumbler or a dedicated bay and bulk inputs, but I prefer a slower, steadier method that suits the scale and rhythm of this garden. The layered heaps are tucked into towers made from wire and leftover fencing, and they allow me to add small amounts at a time. Weeds and kitchen scraps go to the chooks and the worm systems first, which keeps the towers free of weed seeds, odours and rodent interest. The result is sweet, crumbly humus that feeds the beds reliably with very little fuss.

I don't always turn the compost; I often let it sit and transform gradually. It's less of a system and more of a living archive of seasons past. Corn husks, pea vines, coffee grounds and autumn leaves break down together and teach me patience. They remind me that the garden is always in motion. That what fed me in summer will feed the soil in winter. That transformation doesn't have to be loud to be complete.

I also like to double-up tasks and uses, so my composting towers often get layered with seed potatoes. As the garden material breaks down, it nourishes the emerging potato plants. When the plants grow up through the composting material, I add more just like you would with a potato bed and layers of straw. The result has been almost 1 cubic metre (35 cubic feet) of compost and a basket bigger than I can carry of incredible Dutch cream potatoes (a cultivar of *Solanum tuberosum*). (For more detailed information on how to compost, turn to pages 211–17.)

And so, these days I compost with purpose. But I also compost with curiosity. What will happen if I leave this? What will it become? What will the worms find in here in six weeks' time? What if I pop potatoes between the layers? That curiosity has become part of the rhythm, too. Because in the end, tending a garden is just a series of responses. You notice. You feed. You prune. You sow. You get curious. And in doing so, you build a life alongside the garden, not just in it.

Managing pests, diseases and waste

Dealing with pests and diseases in the garden starts with one simple principle: observation first. When the cabbage moths arrive, I don't reach for sprays. I protect plants with insect netting to keep the moths at bay. When the aphids cluster, I wait for the ladybirds. When a plant is struggling, I ask questions. Is it in the wrong place or under stress? Is the soil too rich or too wet? Is there not enough sunshine? I may intervene with a soft solution, such as a diluted oil spray, a soap wash, a good cutback or compost feed. But mostly I do nothing at all. I trust that a diverse garden with healthy soil and thoughtful design will return to balance more often than not.

Far left_Ladybird on a double black Lenten rose (*Helleborus × hybridus*). An early spring ally, it arrives with the aphids and is a clear sign that the garden is balancing itself.
Left_Cabbage moth caterpillar on a brassica leaf. I do not spray pests. I net plants, and I pick off unwanted insects. If a plant is badly infested, then I hand it to the chickens – turning a problem into protein in the form of eggs.

Otherwise, my chickens are very happy with a fancy homegrown protein meal of pests. They love nothing more than a head of aphid-infested broccoli! Nothing goes to waste, and even what might be perceived as failure, I can usually reframe into an opportunity to make more eggs. I like to think of myself as a glass-half-full kind of girl.

That balance extends into how I manage garden waste. Pruning doesn't create rubbish; it makes useful material. Woody offcuts become stakes or mulch. Spent crops are chopped and dropped into the wicking beds, feeding the soil in place. Autumn leaves are piled into my composting towers or pushed under shrubs. The garden feeds itself, in silent cycles.

A retrofitted garbage bin worm farm hums along, and worm tunnels are tucked into wicking beds, fed with scraps and covered with a cap. The worms are part of the garden team. They remind me that decomposition is just as important as growth. That every stem, every leaf, every so-called failure becomes food for what's next.

There are seasons where all this care is energising. And there are seasons where it's effortful. But the rhythms hold. And the more I return to them, the more I see that this is the real work of gardening: not the Instagram moments, but the layering of systems that support life.

Notes from the garden

These notes gather the touchstones I return to when I'm shaping a planting to be both beautiful and useful. They're a summary of practice, not a checklist. Read them as a way to keep your eye on rhythm, to welcome imperfection, to trust the quiet work of soil, and to notice the seasonal cues that guide good decisions. Let these notes sit beside your own so the garden can keep teaching you.

Design and rhythm:

- The garden tells me when something's not working, usually with silence, or a sense that the space has lost its rhythm.
- Sometimes a clipped form says more than a bloom.
- Good design doesn't shout. It lets the plants do the talking.
- I plant by rhythm, not by variety.

Imperfection and process:

- I've never once followed the textbook exactly, and the garden still grows.
- Not everything needs to be tidied (note to self!). Some things are better left to seed and soften.
- It doesn't have to be perfect to be generous.

Compost and care:

- Compost doesn't need to be perfect. It just needs to be consistent.
- There's so much happening underground while we go about our day.
- Most of the good work in a garden happens slowly. Silently. Out of view.

Seasonal and sensory:

- I plant scent near a threshold as a soft welcome and a beautiful hello.
- I know that it's time to sow when the light starts landing differently on the garden.

'Compost doesn't need to be perfect. It just needs to be consistent.'

1

2

A potato-growing composting tower is a simple, beautiful way to turn soft green and brown garden material into compost while growing a crop in the same footprint. Each tower produces around 10 kilograms (22 pounds) of potatoes and about 1 cubic metre (35 cubic feet) of finished compost. To create your own potato-growing composting tower, follow these step-by-step instructions:

*1*_Build the cylindrical tower using wire mesh, then start adding the initial layers: dry leaves and soft green material, topped with a thin layer of soil.
*2*_Add seed potatoes (my favourite type is Dutch cream).
*3*_Cover with more dry leaves and soft green material.
*4*_Top up with soil to settle the layer.
*5*_Add the next layer of seed potatoes.
*6*_Cover again with dry leaves and soft green material as the tower builds.
*7*_Close and secure the tower with wire, cable ties or non-perishable twine.
*8*_I clad my finished potato composting tower in repurposed fence posts to match my garden's material palette. Choose something that suits your garden style.

5

6

3

4

7

8

PLANTING PALETTES AND SEASONAL COMBINATIONS

I don't design planting combinations around aesthetics alone. What looks good is rarely the only consideration. I ask what the plants do, and what they do together. Do they feed us, heal us, shelter us, catch the light? Do they hold the space in summer, or offer shade, scent, softness? Do they invite the bees, capture a memory or stop me mid-task with their beauty? With the space constraints here at Little Cottage on a Hill, these questions are vital for the way I want to live within this small footprint.

When I talk about palettes, I'm not just referring to which colours go together. I'm interested in the living relationships, the patterns of support, contrast and rhythm that help the garden to work not just in a visual sense, but in deeply human, seasonal and ecological ways.

This kind of thinking is hard to teach as a set of rules. But it can be felt, and it can be practised. It starts by noticing what a plant offers across more than one dimension. And then seeing what happens when you place that plant in various relationships: with other plants, with the soil, with time.

One of the most enduring examples of this is known as the Three Sisters, a traditional Indigenous North American planting system that places corn/maize (*Zea mays*), common beans (*Phaseolus vulgaris*) and various pumpkins/squashes (*Cucurbita* spp.) together. Corn grows tall, offering support. Beans climb the corn, fixing nitrogen in the soil. Pumpkin sprawls below, suppressing weeds and holding moisture. It's not just a productive trio, it's a philosophy of mutual support. Each plant benefits the others. The system is successful because the relationships work.

I don't grow corn in my current garden, because the large space required and the plant's thirsty nature both make this tricky, and I just can't be bothered going out there every day to tend to the watering. But I think in that same pattern: what supports what? What anchors? What follows? What fills the gaps or feeds the pollinators or soothes the eye when the rest of the bed is in transition?

Where do I begin?

Often, I start with structure: a clipped form, a trained espalier, a spire of rosemary (*Salvia rosmarinus*) or the bold silhouette of an artichoke (*Cynara cardunculus*). But equally, I also consider sensation and experience. A shift in light. A fragrance that is released as I brush past while carrying compost. A plant that has self-seeded in the perfect spot and changed how the whole space feels. The best combinations in my garden aren't always built, they emerge. From curiosity. From need. From those happy accidents I love so much. From memory and season and small, recurring gestures of daily life.

'The best combinations in my garden aren't always built, they emerge. From curiosity. From need. From those happy accidents I love so much.'

That's why there's lemon-scented geranium (*Pelargonium crispum*) in the wicking-bed garden located just outside the living-room window. The foliage is deeply fragrant, incredible in little posies, and keeps the mosquitoes at bay. It's not ornamental (although I do love having the lime green leaves as a foil to the black wicking beds). It's relational. The pot marigold (*Calendula officinalis*) that lines a garden bed does more than brighten the space: it heals, it self-seeds, it holds the line when other plants are in transition. The wormwood (*Artemisia absinthium*) by the chicken yard isn't a feature. It's a protector, cut when it gets too big and cast into the chicken coop as a natural pest deterrent. The comfrey (*Symphytum officinale*) tucked near the compost tower catches nutrients and tells me when the soil is warming. Harvested when the leaves threaten to take over, it's added to the compost heaps or brewed into a batch of compost tea. These are not placements. They are patterns of support.

While I was living at Oak & Monkey Puzzle, I separated the formal garden into kitchen, berry and cut-flower terraces; these days, with the small space I have, I don't divide my garden into categories. There's no bed for cut flowers, no zone for tea plants, no section marked medicinal. Instead, plants are chosen for what they offer across time and experience. Yarrow (*Achillea millefolium*) softens the edge of a path, draws in pollinators and finds its way into bundles for drying or infusions; it's also used during wonderful workshops with my beautiful friend Caroline Parker, a herbalist. Oregano (*Origanum vulgare*) sits beside the yuzu (*Citrus × junos*) I'm trying to espalier, and I brush past its healing, familiar, generous form a dozen times a day. Rosemary (*Salvia rosmarinus*) is both a clipped structure and a fragrant addition to a bath. It's also what I run my hands over when I need to reset between wicking-bed garden and composting towers.

Some plants stay because they surprise me. Rhubarb (*Rheum rhabarbarum*), planted alongside red-barked dogwood (*Cornus alba*) and ornamental grasses, doesn't just offer its stalks; it echoes structure and shifts colour across the season. Kale (*Brassica oleracea* Acephala Group), left to grow into its full scale (if the possums

From the street in late summer, the northern and western verge gardens read as one palette. Seed heads, grasses and clipped structure carry the planting as colour begins to soften.

ever leave it alone!), becomes a living hedge. Strawberries (*Fragaria × ananassa*) underplant the fragrant climbing roses, softening the ground plane and offering unexpected sweetness at ankle height. And English lavender (*Lavandula angustifolia*), even when not blooming, holds its late clipped form through winter, which allows looser forms to breathe around it.

I've learned to think in systems, not combinations. One plant might feed the soil, repel pests, scent a corner and bring joy in a vase. And when those qualities meet in a place that also embraces the light, responds to wind or marks a threshold, this is when I know that the plant belongs. These groupings are not designed. They're responses to space, to climate, to what I return to again and again with my hands, my scissors, my senses.

Roles, rituals and resilience

When I'm planning or reworking a space, I don't think in terms of 'companions'. I think of garden roles. What holds the structure? What entices the bees and hoverflies? What self-seeds and fills the gaps? What brings scent in high summer when the rest of the garden is starting to tire?

Sometimes it's pale purple coneflower (*Echinacea pallida*), standing tall through late summer, its seed heads catching low sun as the garden relaxes. Sometimes it's nasturtium (*Tropaeolum majus*), cascading down wicking beds and protecting the black cladding from the sting of the sun's heat; every part is edible, and it also holds moisture and provides a pop of colour. And sometimes it's a trio I hadn't planned, such as comfrey (*Symphytum officinale*), wormwood (*Artemisia absinthium*) and pot marigold (*Calendula officinalis*), all growing near the compost towers and chicken yard. One draws nutrients from deep in the soil. One repels pests. One soothes both skin and space.

None of it is fixed. What works one year might shift the next. The strawberries (*Fragaria × ananassa*) may migrate. The yarrow (*Achillea millefolium*) may claim a new edge (and probably will; it can be tricky like that). But the things that I watch for are the ways that plants support each other or make moments in the garden more livable. That's what I trust.

I also plant for ritual. Rosemary (*Salvia rosmarinus*) grows near where I plan to build a wood-fired pizza oven. So does soft, generous and forgiving lemon balm (*Melissa officinalis*). These are plants I've learned to reach for without thinking. Put into the bath. Into tea. Into bundles hung in the laundry or tucked into drawers. They're part of how I live, not just how I grow.

And I plant for resilience, not just in terms of drought tolerance or pest resistance, but emotional resilience. Plants that hold space for when life gets difficult. Plants that ask little of me but offer much: roses, German chamomile (*Matricaria chamomilla*), giant hyssop (*Agastache aurantiaca*), English lavender (*Lavandula angustifolia*). These are a few of my constants.

The older I get, the less interested I am in planting plans that prescribe. What I care about is showing what's possible when you notice what works, not just for the garden, but for you. What returns. What surprises. What nourishes more than one part of your life. I want you to embrace curiosity and create plant combinations that resonate with and enrich you.

Here are eight combinations I return to, not as rules, but as rhythms:

1 **Jerusalem sage (*Phlomis fruticosa*), *Hylotelephium spectabile* 'Autumn Joy', anise hyssop (*Agastache foeniculum*)**

Why it works: it combines evergreen mounds, late seed heads that hold, and aromatic verticals for pollinators and tea.

2 ***Geum* 'Totally Tangerine', purple coneflower (*Echinacea purpurea*), *Calamagrostis* 'Karl Foerster'**

Why it works: it provides early amber lift, a long season of structure and seeds for birds, and a steady vertical grass to bind the bed.

3 **Rhubarb (*Rheum rhabarbarum*), *Cornus alba* 'Sibirica', *Panicum virgatum* 'Rubrum'**

Why it works: it offers edible drama with a colour echo, winter stems as a backbone, and fine plumes for movement.

4 **Parsley (*Petroselinum crispum*), spring onion (*Allium fistulosum*), cornflower (*Centaurea cyanus*)**

Why it works: a trio of edible companions, alongside upright lines that age into seed heads, plus blue nectar for beneficial creatures.

5 **Purpletop (*Verbena bonariensis*), artichoke (*Cynara cardunculus*), Queen Anne's lace (*Daucus carota*)**

Why it works: it features light vertical mesh as well as architectural, edible, airy umbels to stitch layers and feed insects.

6 **Pale purple coneflower (*Echinacea pallida*), *Calamagrostis* 'Karl Foerster', globe thistle (*Echinops ritro*)**

Why it works: it blends elegant spires and winter seeds, a reliable vertical curtain, and blue orbs for contrast and drying. The coneflower also provides a valuable support for 'Karl Foerster' in strong wind.

7 **Panicle hydrangea (*Hydrangea paniculata*), *Panicum virgatum* 'Rubrum', *Rosa* 'Just Joey'**

Why it works: matches colour-shifting flamboyant flowers and winter heads with copper tone through the season plus apricot saucer-sized fragrance.

8 **Lemon-scented geranium (*Pelargonium crispum*), borage (*Borago officinalis*), purple cabbage (*Brassica oleracea* Capitata Group)**

Why it works: it gives brush-released scent and insect deterrence, edible blue stars for pollinators, plus edible structure and winter colour.

Combo notes

These eight combinations are not formulas; they are signals. What to watch for, what to notice, what might work together, not just in form or colour, but in use, rhythm and experience. Let these combinations be prompts, not prescriptions. Let them open a door to your own logic of scent, space, memory and need.

Once you begin to plant not for category, but for feeling, function and flow, you'll never walk through your garden in the same way again. You'll move through it not as a set of tasks, but as a series of relationships. And those relationships, season by season, are what hold you and the garden together.

SEASONAL TASKS AND TAKEAWAYS

By this point in the book, you don't need a checklist. You already know that the garden isn't a job to get through, it's a rhythm to live by. But rhythm doesn't mean sameness.

Some years I start everything early and still feel behind. Other years I barely touch the garden in alignment with the seasonal cues, and it carries me anyway. Sometimes I don't need to feel useful. Other times I just have to be out there, doing something with my hands. Some seasons you'll feel tired and just want to keep things ticking over. Some years it'll be the vegetables that teach you. Other years, it'll be the weeds.

There isn't just one right way to do things. But there are elements and actions that I come back to. Markers. Moves. Little habits that hold the season in place, even when the rest of life feels like it's going too fast. These aren't tasks. They're ways of staying in relationship with the garden, with the body, with time.

Opposite page_At the end of the day in the garden, I pause to take it all in as the light drops. ***Below left***_Potting up self-sown anise hyssop (*Agastache foeniculum*) from the garden. ***Below right***_Strawberries (*Fragaria × ananassa*) under cover in the hybrid potting shed and greenhouse, a small experiment in extending the season.

***Above left*_**Spears of asparagus (*Asparagus officinalis*) pushing through in spring. This is the first clear sign that enough warmth has arrived to begin planting.
***Above right*_**Delicate blossoms of an apple (*Malus* sp.). Nature is signalling that the season has turned and that pollination is beginning. The promise of fruits starts here.

In spring:

- **Notice where warmth takes hold:** Watch the garden. Where does the sun remain the longest? That's where you start.
- **Plant for scent first:** You'll forget what you planted, but you won't forget what you brushed past. Lemon verbena (*Aloysia citriodora*). Winter daphne (*Daphne odora*) first thing in the morning. A heritage rose with the classic 'old rose' scent that begs to be cut for a blowsy posy.
- **Try a trio that works together:** Maybe a plant to draw pollinators. One to feed you. One to hold the shape of the garden. The combo doesn't need to be clever. It just has to make sense when you look at it.
- **Cut the path before you plant:** Don't fight the way your body wants to move through the space. Use it as your cue. Design for it.

In summer:

- **Watch what copes:** When the heat hits, you'll know which plants are show and which ones are spine. Keep the spine. Bravely turn off the water, and see what still thrives!
- **Let something spill:** Trailing herbs. Unruly grasses. Mock orange (*Philadelphus coronarius*) that sends its arching, fragrant stems into the walkway. Not everything needs to be clipped into line.
- **Ignore a corner:** Let it go for a few weeks. You'll learn more from what self-seeds than from anything you planned.
- **Bring it in:** A single stem. A tangle of spearmint (*Mentha spicata*). An armful of 'this and that' blooms. Harvest because it steadies you, not just because it's ripe.

***Above left*_**Foraging for ripe elderberries from European elder (*Sambucus nigra*). Summer is the seasonal window for syrup making and preserving what the home garden and country lanes offer. ***Above right*_**A freshly gathered red capsicum (*Capsicum annuum*). It is summer's bright proof of what thrives when the heat arrives.

Above left_Autumn on the western verge. Seed heads, texture and low light come to the fore, and I walk slowly, noticing what held and what wants to change.
Above right_Fallen autumn leaves are gathered and kept in motion. They will feed the garden as compost and mulch, helping to build the next season's fertility.

In autumn:

- **Walk with a notebook:** Not for a list. Just to mark what held. What bloomed longer than expected. What needed more air. What you could definitely live without.
- **Feed with what's falling:** Don't tidy it. Use it. Chop it. Mulch it. Pile it by hand. What's spent at season's end feeds the next flush of growth. That's how the garden earns from every one of its cycles.
- **Watch what fades well:** Some plants collapse with grace. Some don't. You'll start to see the difference. You'll see which plants are worth fighting for.
- **Photograph the garden:** Shoot pics through the kitchen window. Past the compost heap. On your way to the bin. With an armful of groceries from the car. These are the views that matter.

In winter:

- — **Don't clean it all up:** The garden is still telling you something. Wait. Observe. There's form in decay.
- — **Stop and look:** Does the structure still hold? Walk along the paths. Sit in the cold corners. Do they still make sense? If not, adjust before spring wakes up.
- — **Look for hardworking plants:** Sound, shelter, tension, the way they hold the frost. These are structural companions that offer you something this season.
- — **Design in fragments:** Don't write a plant list. Write what you need more of: quiet, shade, colour in July. That's where you begin.

You don't need to do any of this on time. Sometimes I don't do these things at all. But I still return to these ideas. Not because I have to, but because the garden keeps a version of me I don't want to lose and supports a way of life that brings me closer, season after season, to what it feels like to live well.

***Above left*_**Frost on a sun rose (*Helianthemum* sp.) ground cover. It is a winter morning cue to stop and look, and to see structure and form with fresh eyes.
***Above right*_**Sitting in the winter sun, with a cup of tea in my hands. I'm not doing, just witnessing.

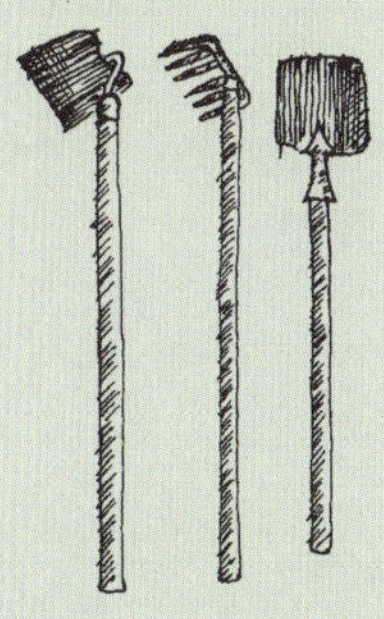

WHEN BEAUTY MEETS PURPOSE

Beauty is often dismissed as optional. A finish. A flourish. A thing to reach for once the rest of the work is done. But in this chapter, we've seen the opposite. We've seen that beauty, when rooted in function and purpose, becomes the thing that holds the garden together. It's what draws us in and keeps us there. What gives the work its shape.

The gardens in the following pages don't follow the same rules. But they have something in common. Each one shows what's possible when we let beauty do more than decorate, when we let it guide. When we design with feeling, repeat with intention, layer with memory, plant with generosity.

Jeremy Valentine and Grant Francis find their beauty in restraint. In the decisions they didn't make. Their design begins with climate, wind and context, and holds through editing. Texture meets structure. Creativity meets constraint. Every material is asked to justify itself. Every bed is shaped to hold meaning, not excess.

Jac Semmler redefines productivity through beauty. She asks plants to work hard, to give texture, tone, structure and succession. It's high-performance planting, but without aggression. With softness. With seasonal generosity. Her garden isn't just functional, it's emotionally intelligent.

Tim Pilgrim looks at a garden like a body needing rest, rhythm and contrast. He builds in texture, looks for what survives without his help, and designs in succession. Not for performance. For persistence. His beauty comes from the resilience, time and confidence that emerge through stepping back.

Lily Langham speaks through rhythm. Through drifts, grasses, edited mistakes. Her garden is a place of return. A place of moths and memory. Not designed, but felt. Grown from movement, from childhood, from the desire to belong. A system made not from drawing but from repetition, built in layers across wind and slope. She doesn't say it's beautiful. But it holds.

And then there's you. The reader. The grower. The person sitting with your own garden, or the hope of one. Your version of beauty might not look like any of these. It doesn't have to. What matters is that it feels like yours. That it means something. That it keeps you in the garden a little longer, adjusting something, walking the edges, cutting a stem for the table, stopping to notice what's changed. Because beauty, when it meets purpose, becomes a way of staying.

It's not an extra. It's the architecture of care. It's what turns maintenance into noticing. Tending into rhythm. Labour into something to which you want to return. You don't need a finished design to start planting. You don't need everything to be in place before you begin. What matters is that you start. That you trust your eye. That you trust the garden to teach you.

Let beauty do more than decorate. Let it help you stay.

THE STONES

Designing with rhythm and constraint

The Stones, Central Victoria. Grant Francis (left) and Jeremy Valentine walk the garden they have shaped through restraint. It is a landscape designed to listen to its site, hold rhythm and structure, and let what survives belong.

The first thing you notice about The Stones isn't what's been planted, it's what hasn't. There's no rush to fill space, no scramble for variety, no apology for the rawness of the site. What holds you is the restraint. The composition. The clarity of the plant palette. A garden designed not in defiance of climate, but in collaboration with it.

Set in the exposed, shifting landscape of Central Victoria, The Stones is a lesson in what can emerge when creativity is grounded in limits. Jeremy Valentine and Grant Francis came to the site with a background in textiles, vintage design and interior aesthetics, a design language shaped by cohesion, repetition and disciplined curiosity. And that same language now flows through the garden. As Jeremy says, 'In textiles, I only ever worked with six colours. That's it. So it makes perfect sense that I've ended up with a planting palette that's equally tight. Foliage, shape, tone, scale – it's all about control.'

'In textiles, I only ever worked with six colours . . . So it makes perfect sense that I've ended up with a planting palette that's equally tight.'

But control here doesn't mean sterility. It's not a clipped or over-curated space. It's a study in atmosphere: soft movement held by strong bones. Swathes of different agaves and grasses. Gridded stone paths. Walls that feel like they've been there forever. The garden literally rises from the bones of the site. Much of it was built by hand from local materials. Jeremy describes 'hauling stone, digging paths, putting the structure in place ourselves', a process that embedded them deeply in the land's rhythm. That rhythm shaped not just the paths, but the plants, too.

The climate offered no softness. Frost. Heat. Wind. Long dry stretches. 'It's tough here,' Jeremy says. 'If it doesn't work, it's out. We tried plants that just couldn't cope, and it was clear quickly. So now, everything that's still here . . . it's earned its place.' What survives is not just tough, it's tonal. Textural. Plants that thrive on neglect, yes, but that also hold structure and presence across the seasons.

This is a garden of boundaries and balance. Light and shadow. Texture and scale. Strength and stillness. It's deeply influenced by Jeremy and Grant's shared creative background, but never indulgent. 'Our aesthetic history absolutely shapes it,' Jeremy notes. But it's not about ego. They've learned to listen to what the garden wants to be.

That philosophy of listening and of designing with restraint runs through every aspect of The Stones. Early versions of the garden were much more crowded, and much more eager. 'We planted too much. It didn't feel right. And eventually we realised: we needed to take things away,' says Jeremy. Over time, the garden became subdued. More intentional. They're more interested in letting a plant hold space than filling every pocket.

And then there's the history. The Stones sits on land once shaped by miners, with old ruins, stone remnants and a landscape marked by extraction. That history isn't hidden; it's honoured. Jeremy and Grant's garden doesn't erase the past. It works with it: the buildings, the wind, the shadows. Everything is a layer. Everything is memory.

If Edna Walling were to walk through the site, Jeremy suspects that she'd appreciate the sense of containment. The curve of the paths. The absence of trend. 'She might tell us to let it spill a bit more,' he says with a smile. 'But I think she'd recognise that we're trying to create something lasting.'

And there is a lastingness here, not in permanence but in presence. The Stones isn't finished. It's evolving. But its principles are steady: work with what you have. Use what's on hand. Resist the temptation to overdesign. Let the climate shape you, not the other way around.

When asked what advice he'd give to others designing under constraint, Jeremy doesn't hesitate: 'Stop fighting the site. Let it speak. Strip back. Edit. Start with fewer plants, not more. Trust that the limits are the design. The garden is already there; you just have to get out of the way.'

'Stop fighting the site. Let it speak. Strip back. Edit. Start with fewer plants, not more. Trust that the limits are the design.'

What The Stones teaches us

Amid the challenges of The Stones' site conditions, limits are not a hurdle. They are the design. Jeremy and Grant show how restraint, local stone, a tight plant palette and clear structure can hold softness through the seasons. When I walk this garden, I am reminded to use what I have, edit until the spaces can breathe, and let rhythm and repetition do more work than variety ever could.

— **Constraint sharpens design:** Working with a brutal climate, a limited plant tolerance and local materials led to a pared-back aesthetic that feels deliberate, resolved and deeply grounded in place.
— **Restraint is a form of respect:** Jeremy and Grant learned to edit their garden over time, removing more than they added and allowing the plants to breathe.
— **Texture and repetition do more than variety:** Their background in textiles shows through in their disciplined use of form, foliage and tonal cohesion, proving that richness doesn't require abundance.

Scan to hear my full conversation with Jeremy and Grant, where we talk about constraint, composition and the beauty that emerges when you stop fighting the land.

— **Materials are memory:** Hand-built paths, stonework and re-use of what the land offers give the garden emotional depth and physical honesty.
— **A garden should settle into its site:** The Stones doesn't announce itself, or impose a vision on the land. It listens, pares back and responds.

JAC SEMMLER

Supercharged planting and emotional resonance

Jac Semmler of Super Bloom doesn't just grow gardens. She builds whole worlds with plants. A maximalist, an experimenter, a teacher and an advocate for rethinking what gardens can offer, Jac takes an approach that is both radical and grounded, rooted in a belief that beauty, resilience and performance can and should coexist.

At the centre of her practice is the idea of high-performance planting, a concept she defines as plants doing more than one thing. 'It's not about single-purpose planting,' she explains. 'It's about layers. Edible and ornamental. Structure and softness. Pollination and shade. Something that can surprise you at different times of the year.' In Jac's work, performance isn't just about function, it's about generosity. Plants are chosen for what they offer to people, place, ecosystem and memory. A garden becomes more than simply yield. It transforms into a system of relationships.

Her own home garden, Heartland, is both a test site and a living canvas; it's part laboratory, part love letter to what's possible. 'I always say it's a plant lab. It's

Jac Semmler of Super Bloom. A plant practitioner known for high-performance planting with emotional resonance, she layers edible and ornamental plants to support biodiversity and hold people through the seasons.

where we test everything: ideas, combinations, responses to climate, soil, conditions.'
There's no separation between ornamentals and edibles in her work. She doesn't talk about categories, she talks about community. 'Everything is in conversation. That's what makes it feel alive.'

Jac's planting is often bold, abundant, layered and textural. But what underpins it is a deep respect for time, rhythm and seasonal responsiveness. She designs for longevity. For beauty across decline. For gardens that move with people through grief, change and joy. 'Plants offer us more than we ask of them. They hold memory. They shape our days. They support our nervous systems. They make us feel held.'

'Plants offer us more than we ask of them. They hold memory. They shape our days. They support our nervous systems. They make us feel held.'

This emotional dimension isn't an afterthought in her work, it's central. 'Gardens are not just for growing things. They're for healing. They're for experiencing. That is a form of productivity. That's something that should be designed for.'

Her challenge to gardeners is a generous one: raise your expectations. Demand more of your plants and garden. Not in a way that needs perfection, but in a way that asks what's possible if we start looking beyond yield. 'I make productive gardens,' she says. 'Yes, there might be edibles, but that's not the point. It's not about produce. It's about experience. It's about what the garden gives back across time.'

Her voice is also one of permission: to love plants for the way they make you feel. To garden with emotion. To choose colour because it lights up something inside you. To start messy, and stay curious. To try again. 'Grow what you love,' she says. 'Grow what calls to you. That's enough.'

When asked what advice she'd give to someone starting out, she doesn't hesitate: 'The sooner you start gardening like yourself, the better.' That's not an aesthetic position. It's a way of being in relationship with place.

In a world that often reduces gardening to yield, output or ornamental display, Jac Semmler's voice is one of generous resistance. Her gardens are beautiful, yes, but they're also brave. Unapologetic. Functional in ways that expand the word's meaning. They offer space for biodiversity, but also for pause, for emotion, for aliveness.

'We need to remember what gardens have always done. They hold us. They remind us. They teach us to pay attention.' And through that act of attention, something changes in the gardener, the garden and the world.

What Jac's gardening method teaches us

Jac invites us to expect more from planting. Not more plants, but more layers of purpose and care. She shows how beauty, function and emotion can sit together, how generosity in planting can support biodiversity and people, and how curiosity turns a garden into a conversation with place. Use the notes that follow to tune your garden for season, structure and feeling so it gives back over time.

- **High-performance planting is layered:** Plants can and should be chosen for what they offer across seasons: structure, pollination, resilience, edibility.
- **Productivity is not just food:** A garden that offers joy, healing, ecological connection and place-making is productive. Jac reframes productivity as experiential and ecological, not agricultural.
- **Emotional design is real design:** Planting can (and should) be tuned in to emotional tone. Joyful. Grounding. Bold. Soft. These aren't embellishments, they're part of how a space holds us.

Scan to hear my full conversation with Jac Semmler, where we talk emotional resonance and gardening as an act of creative resistance.

- — **The garden is a co-creator:** Planting isn't about imposing order. It's about entering into a conversation with plants, with place, with climate. Curiosity leads.
- — **Generosity is a design principle:** Jac's gardens don't strive for minimalism, they aim for giving. Generously planted. Generously shared. Generously alive.

TIM PILGRIM

Learning by letting go

Tim Pilgrim is a landscape designer known for immersive, naturalistic planting that's guided by instinct, succession and ecological resilience. His work prioritises structure, texture and time, and he designs gardens that evolve, adapt and often outgrow their original plans. Based in Victoria, he's just released his first book, *Wild by Design*, which explores plant-led practice and garden-making that holds both emotional and ecological space.

In this chapter, Tim speaks about what it means to design with restraint, to trust what the land is already doing, and to let the garden breathe beyond the page. What follows is a conversation about natural succession, modest confidence, and designing with observation rather than control.

When you speak with Tim, there's a lull before each answer: not hesitation, but thoughtfulness. The same quality runs through his gardens. They're immersive. Rhythmic. Designed not to impose, but to respond.

*Below left*_Tim Pilgrim is a skilled designer of naturalistic gardens shaped by observation, succession and restraint. *Below right*_Rhonda's Garden in Central Victoria, created by Tim Pilgrim. This garden is true choreography in planting: pause, contrast and movement, held by structure and allowed to evolve.

Tim doesn't build gardens around trends or visual impact, he constructs them based on what will last. He talks about designing for succession, for texture over time, for structure that holds when everything else has faded. 'If it doesn't survive with just rainfall, it doesn't stay. That's where I'm at now.' That's not a metaphor; it's a test. In his own garden, he literally turned off the tap to see what could endure unaided.

He speaks often about resilience, not just in an ecological sense, but in terms of design. The ability of a garden to hold its own shape. To carry itself across seasons. To give something even in absence. He doesn't expect a design to stay static; in fact, if it does, that's a problem. 'If I go back a year later and it looks exactly like my renders, something's wrong.'

Tim doesn't start a design with a planting list. He begins by walking through the site and getting a feel for what the wind is doing, where the shadows sit, what the soil wants. He listens for tension. For pressure points. For where the site already knows more than he does. Sometimes, he notices a plant already doing the job: thriving, self-seeding, signalling. In that case, he follows its lead. 'You're trying to feel what the land wants.'

'There's a choreography to how a space should move. You need contrast. You need rest.'

His designs are grounded in the way a garden flows across time. 'There's a choreography to how a space should move. You need contrast. You need rest.' For him, structure is not just vertical, it's emotional. Gardens must include places to land. To recover. Not everything should perform at once.

He talks about plants as collaborators rather than just materials. He doesn't force outcomes. He lets the garden suggest the next move. The plants that survive are the ones that belong. And underlying all of it is humility. Tim doesn't claim certainty. He knows that he gets things wrong. But he's interested in what happens when you stop trying to be perfect. 'There's a difference between a designed space and a held space. I'm interested in the ones that feel held.'

What Tim's gardening method teaches us

Tim's naturalistic planting begins with observation and builds towards a living plant community. He reads the site first, sets a clear structure, then lets plants settle and self-select. Irrigation helps them start, then it is removed so resilience can show. Succession, self-sown drifts and light editing do the shaping, which is why his gardens feel made by their place rather than imposed on it.

- **Succession is design**: Tim designs for how a garden holds over time. Planting is never static, it's about layers, longevity and allowing space for change.
- **Resilience must be tested**: Turning off irrigation reveals which plants truly belong in the system. What survives shapes what stays.
- **Observation comes before action:** Each garden begins with a walk, not a plan. Tension, shade and movement reveal what's needed before a single plant is chosen.
- **A garden is choreography, not spectacle**: Tim plants for rhythm, contrast and rest. He designs for presence, not performance.
- **Let the garden breathe beyond the plan**: A garden should evolve. If it looks exactly like the drawings a year later, then something's off. The best spaces shift and teach as they do.

Scan to hear my full conversation with Tim Pilgrim, where we talk about natural succession, letting go of perfection, and designing spaces that are felt as much as they are seen.

Walking the paths of Three Chimneys with Lily Langham, whose gardens are made by staying close. She plants, edits and returns, again and again, until the whole place begins to hold you.

LILY LANGHAM

Movement and closeness at Three Chimneys

There was no grand plan at Three Chimneys. When Lily Langham first arrived, there were no garden beds. No vision. Just three old chimneys, an overgrown 2-hectare (5-acre) block, and a single gesture that changed everything: she mowed a path. 'That was the first thing I did. Just mowed a line of invitation from the bush.'

That small act, not decorative, not strategic, was the beginning. It was how she marked her presence. How she said to the landscape, 'I'm here now. I'm listening.'

Everything that's followed – the plants, the layering, the rhythm, the gathering spaces, the movement – has grown out of that initial instinct. Lily builds her garden the way she lives in it: by doing. There is no drawing. No plan. No site analysis. She plants, then shifts, then edits, then watches. Then begins again. 'I'm constantly editing. Things often get moved a few times.'

She uses bamboo stakes to physically lay out things, often in colour-coded clusters, to test groupings, rhythms and gaps. Not because it's a system, but because it works.

The garden is shaped by conditions: wind, slope, time. There's no shielding. No formal edge. The bush presses right in, and Lily likes it that way. She doesn't try to hold it back. Her planting isn't an intervention, it's a conversation. 'There's no real boundary. I want the bush to press in. The planting should be in conversation with it.'

'There's no real boundary. I want the bush to press in. The planting should be in conversation with it.'

The ground is uneven. The plant palette is a mixture of perennials, herbs, shrubs, self-seeders and grasses – reed grasses (*Calamagrostis* spp.), silvergrasses (*Miscanthus* spp.) and feather grasses (*Stipa* spp.) – chosen for their ability to move,

Three Chimneys is a garden built through movement and repetition. Perennials, grasses and self-seeders are guided rather than controlled, and the planting is allowed to press in, soften edges and evolve with the season.

to hold the slope and to soften the shifts. She uses the grasses to ensure that the garden makes sense. 'They bring movement. They do so much. I couldn't do this garden without them.'

Drifts anchor the space. She plants in repetition not to impress, but to calm. Too much contrast agitates her. Bigger blocks settle the space. She'll often plant four or five of the same species, then step back and adjust the group.

There's no use of pesticides. No decorative pruning. She lets things blow out. Lets them lean. Lets them rot back and then sees what returns. Her logic is always seasonal not stylised.

The hawkmoth is her signal for late summer. The scarlet robin tells her when the seasons are turning. She plants for pollinators but not performatively: anise hyssop (*Agastache foeniculum*) and Cleveland sage (*Salvia clevelandii*). If it draws in insects, if it holds its space, if it survives, then it stays. 'Once I waited two years for the hawkmoth to come back. When it did, it was the best day.'

She walks through her garden at night. Not to check on anything, but to witness. That's when she sees and hears what wouldn't be apparent during the day. The way the insects behave. The things that shimmer. The sounds that don't exist at other times. 'That's when it feels most alive. That's when I'm not trying to do anything.'

The old yellow plum tree (*Prunus* sp.) is one of her earliest anchors; it helped her understand the site. After that came the English oaks (*Quercus robur*). The windbreak. The loose hedges. The grass paths that are not laid, but mown through both shape and use.

Beds emerge as the garden tells her what it needs. Some are built on compost drops. Some are unplanned. 'I'll think I'm doing something else, and suddenly I'm making a bed.' Some she's called her last, then changed her mind again. Nothing is fixed. Nothing is finished. 'I can never call it done. It's too alive for that.'

There's a line she uses that holds everything she's made: 'It's not a project. It's just part of life.'

She works quickly. On weekends. In stolen time. She's a mother. A jeweller. A sculptor. Her studio holds flax, dried seed heads, copper, moths, grass. She's working now on a body of pieces about vanishing grasslands, trying to freeze a moment. Capture something that might not be here much longer. 'Jewellery is small and slow. Gardening is big and slow. But they both let me listen.'

What Lily is building is not a garden in the conventional sense. It's a place for return. For seasonal noticing. For slowness. There's sculpture welded into it. Benches tucked under trees. No fixed perspective. No big reveal. Just things to come across. Things to share. Things to rest in. 'I want people to feel like the garden is embracing them. That they don't have to be on their best behaviour.'

There are failures. Whole sections that didn't work. Things she's taken out. Plantings that never made sense until a third species was added. She doesn't hide that. She learns through it. Learns through doing. What remains is not perfect. Not styled. But it holds. 'It's how I stay in place.'

'I want people to feel like the garden is embracing them. That they don't have to be on their best behaviour.'

What Lily's gardening method teaches us

Three Chimneys began with a single mown line and the habit of returning. Lily works on the ground first, watching how wind and slope affect things, then testing where to place plants with coloured stakes as proxies, then adjusting by feel. She lets grasses hold the edges, invites the bush to press in, and edits in real time so the garden stays alive. The notes that follow set out the habits behind this way of working so you can read place with your body and let pattern emerge over time.

— **Gardening is a language:** For Lily, gardening isn't a skill, it's a body-memory. A landscape-memory. It's not something she learned to do, it's something she already spoke.

— **Site analysis doesn't have to be recorded to be real:** Lily reads the slope, the wind, the light and the sound of insects, not with a notebook, but with her body. Her design choices come from watching, mending, returning.

— **Grasses offer memory and rhythm:** She uses grasses to hold space, soften transitions and shape the garden's tempo across seasons.

— **Repetition is how you calm a space:** She plants in drifts not because of design theory, but because it settles her. Because big groupings soothe. Because contrast disturbs her. That feeling drives her form.

— **Gardens are not performance, they are return:** Lily gardens for presence, not for audience. She doesn't document much. She shares quietly. But when people come, they feel the invitation.

— **Something that's still alive is never finished:** Beds shift. Plants move. Some disappear. Some return. There's always another chance. Always something still listening.

Scan to hear my full conversation with Lily Langham, where we talk about learning by doing, hawkmoths, sculpture, repetition and building a garden you can live inside.

7

THE MAKING OF OAK & MONKEY PUZZLE

I moved on from Oak & Monkey Puzzle in 2022, but that place represents my biggest awakening and my biggest returning to myself. Everything I believed about design, about productivity, about what a garden could be and do was all tested there.

MAGICAL MOMENTS

The landscape at Oak & Monkey Puzzle was a canvas on which everything I loved could finally be painted. If I close my eyes and think about it, there's still one moment that comes to me over and over again. Standing in the garden in the golden light of early evening, the glow coming from the west, pouring through the forest behind the arc of the hill that held the back of the formal garden. The way the light would cut through the trees and land on something specific and fleeting: glistening jostaberries (*Ribes × nidigrolaria*) or blackcurrants (*R. nigrum*), backlit bees on the borage (*Borago officinalis*), a single *Alcea rosea* 'Nigra' gleaming dark and rich like silk. Maybe it was the European hornbeams (*Carpinus betulus*) catching the low sun, or a tendril on the sugar snap peas (*Pisum sativum*) reaching skywards. Sometimes it was the scent of wintersweet (*Chimonanthus praecox*) on a cold day, calling me over to it. Other times it was lily of the valley (*Convallaria majalis*), catching a sliver of evening light.

These moments were so small, so quick, sometimes only a minute long. But they were profound. They stopped me in my tracks every single time. They brought me into the present so fully that it was like I was made of the same cells as the plants around me. And even now, thinking about them, I get teary. Because in those moments, I felt so utterly myself. So completely alive. So totally on the right path. And I didn't know who to thank. The sun? The soil? Myself, maybe? For having the presence to stop. For letting myself be called outside, away from interior chores, to catch each precious moment.

The formal garden in its infancy: the new terraces and kitchen garden set on the lawn spine, rising to the forest edge.

***Opposite page*_**Oak & Monkey Puzzle is a beacon in the forest clearing. A mown line through the meadow crosses the old cricket pitch from its recreation reserve days and leads to the house and the life built there.

Instagram became my gratitude journal at that time. No matter how hard life was, those moments of light and season and scent and presence were everything. They were my reminders. My anchors.

There were so many turning points during those years. But one of the biggest came during Covid. That was the season when everything was stripped back. There were no workshops, no people, no events, no income, no collaborations. No guests sitting under the English oaks (*Quercus robur*) at long tables. No money raised for young people in the community. No open garden. No way to share what I'd created. No validation. All I had was soil, sky, air and water. My children and myself.

What I really felt in my bones during that season was that if I had those things, I had everything I needed. It was the most grounding time of my life. Everything else had been taken away from me. Stripped back to nothing. But the garden was still there. The stars were still above me. The air still smelled of damp earth. And I was still here.

Held by greenery

The landscape at Oak & Monkey Puzzle was a canvas on which everything I loved could finally be painted. This period of time marked the beginning of the end. Not in a sad way, but in a manner that spoke of transformation. The garden had done something extraordinary. It had taken everything I couldn't carry and converted it into something rich. Something that could grow. I found myself flourishing again, in the smallest and most essential ways. I stopped looking outwards for recognition. I started finding it in the compost warming through winter. In the trees holding snow. In the garden as it kept rhythm even when the rest of my life felt like chaos.

There's a photo of me and the kids, the first one after we became a family of three. Although it was awkward to take, I love that it captures a precious moment with two sleeping children in my arms, all in one bed. That's how we slept for years. It was the only way I could manage it. The garden embraced me like no person did. It gave me somewhere to put my energy, somewhere to care, to make, to witness life happening. And in return, it held me as I grieved and as I rebuilt.

I'd feed the kids, settle them, and then I'd go out on the verandah and just look at the sky. It's different out there in the forest. Black and thick and full of stars, satellites, the Milky Way. I'd talk to the sky. I'd stand there and whisper, 'I'm trusting you. I'm trusting that this is going to work. That I'm being held.'

I used to stand on that same verandah after late nights of drafting legal documents. Mum and I working through weekends together, desperately trying to save a place that was more than a home. I'd step outside and look at that same night sky, exhaling everything. That air felt like it remembered me. That garden, that view, it didn't ask anything of me. It just allowed me to be.

It was never just a garden. Oak & Monkey Puzzle was a teacher and a confidant. It was my mirror. It showed me my strength, how exhausted I was, how capable I was. It reflected my edges, and then it held me through them. It reminded me that rhythm is real. That nothing blooms all year. That rest is part of the cycle.

Scan to watch a video of a walk through Oak & Monkey Puzzle, captured during one of the quietest seasons of my life.

It was a place that held every season of my life. The high points, including the workshops and long lunches, the full flower beds, the excitement of new plantings. But also the quiet days. The days when I'd weed with tears streaming down my face, or sit on the ground and stare into the middle distance, grasping a trowel but not planting anything. It held that, too.

A new chapter

I can't count the number of barrowloads of leaves I raked each year. Probably hundreds. The English oaks (*Quercus robur*) would start dropping their foliage, and I'd think, *here we go*. Every second day for weeks. Some seasons it brought me joy. At other times I dreaded it. Occasionally, even the change of season felt like a weight. The first falling oak leaf would land like a warning: here comes the upkeep, the exhaustion. And that's when I knew the scale had started to tip. That something was shifting. That maybe it was time for a new chapter.

People said, 'How could you sell it? That place was you.' And in a way, they were right. But they were also wrong. Because it had been me. And the garden had done its job. It had held me long enough to let me go. It had brought me back to myself. And once I returned to myself, I required less. I wasn't craving anything. I didn't need to achieve or to prove or to perform. I just wanted to live. I wanted to be.

So I did let go. And I moved to a tiny place on a hill. Although the new plot was just 515 square metres (5545 square feet), I felt free. I felt more expansive. Because the garden had moved from being outside me to being within me. It was carried. Still is.

An oblique aerial view of the weatherboard homestead and wraparound verandah at Oak & Monkey Puzzle in Spargo Creek, Victoria. The layout of the formal garden took its cues from the dimensions of the house and the surrounding forest.

Even now, when I tend the wicking bed or walk along the small western verge at Little Cottage on a Hill, Oak & Monkey Puzzle is there. In the way I observe. In the way I pause. In the way I notice the light catching a pot marigold (*Calendula officinalis*) petal or hear the rustle of straw or the stillness of a winter bed. Oak & Monkey Puzzle made me. It broke me open so I could live differently. And what a gift that was.

It gave me a new definition of beauty. Not just lush growth and peak bloom, but endurance. Adaptation. Silence. A flower head left to seed. A plant learning to survive with less water. A compost pile doing its unassuming work under a hessian cover. It gave me a new language for grief and joy. It gave me myself back, without ever asking for anything in return.

And in all of the resilience, the rhythm and the remembering, I discovered that a garden doesn't just mirror the seasons. It gives you back to yourself . . . one harvest, one heartbreak, one healing moment at a time.

The formal garden at Oak & Monkey Puzzle, looking back towards the house. A strong lawn spine aligns with the library window and front door, drawing you through layered beds and down the terraces, with western red cedars (*Thuja plicata*) and Douglas firs (*Pseudotsuga menziesii*) rising beyond.

OAK & MONKEY PUZZLE IN PRACTICE

If the first half of this chapter is about what Oak & Monkey Puzzle meant to me, then this second half is about what it taught me. How it challenged me. And how I shaped it, one considered decision at a time.

This was never a textbook garden. It was a layered, living system that evolved through observation, experimentation and seasonal refinement. The scale of it meant that every decision had to be pragmatic, but this never came at the cost of beauty or intention. It was an anchor, a testing ground and a canvas for ideas that had long lived only in the margins of notebooks and on the chalkboard walls at our former scout-hall home. These floating words soon found a place in the work, becoming actions and elements that held the garden together. Fragmented ideas were made three-dimensional and lived with season by season.

Reading the site

Spargo Creek has a very particular climate. Weather rolls in from the south and hits the Great Dividing Range just near Leonards Hill, about 7 kilometres (4 miles) away, which drops heavy rain over the area. It's cooler and wetter than nearby regions within a cool temperate zone. You can read it in the trees, in their girth, height and history. In winter, the temperature regularly falls to –8 degrees Celsius (17 degrees Fahrenheit).

I learned quickly. Someone gave me an entire ute-load of yellow clivias (*Clivia miniata* var. *citrina*) in the early years; I planted them under the English oaks (*Quercus robur*), thinking they'd thrive. But they liquefied in the frost. It was a wake-up call. This place wasn't going to let me impose a vision. I had to work with what was already there.

The site was defined by clay soil, significant grade change, weedy blackberries (*Rubus fruticosus*), tree stumps and remnants of colonial plantings: oaks, Douglas firs (*Pseudotsuga menziesii*), spruces (*Picea* spp.) and an old monkey puzzle tree (*Araucaria araucana*). The forest formed one edge, and the house stood elevated, sitting between sunrise and sunset; forest to the west, entry to the east.

From the very beginning, we observed. Not just in the first few months, but every day, across many years. We watched where frost landed. How the water flowed. Where icicles formed. How the topography told us what it needed. The pond in the berry terrace froze solid in winter. Shade shifted with the seasons. We built gradually. Responsively.

We started with the infrastructure: water first. The dam didn't hold water, so we sank a bore and extended large-capacity pipes throughout the property. We fenced the dam as a safety measure, as we had toddlers who liked to wander. That fencing was one of the first gestures of care and containment.

Opposite page,
Top left_Oak & Monkey Puzzle in the early renovation phase, 2014. In a pause before planting, the cleared ground was used to read the landscape and begin shaping what would become the orchard.
Top right_Oak & Monkey Puzzle as we found it, 2013. The half-finished house on five acres awaited repair, care and a new life.
Bottom_The first working bee, 2015. Garden beds were set out with string lines and marker paint before timber edges were built. This is the earliest structure of the formal garden as it took shape in front of the renovated house.

'Water is one of the most revealing forces in the garden. It doesn't just nourish, it teaches. It shows you where the land yields, where it resists, where it stores, where it sheds.'

Reading your site through water

Water is one of the most revealing forces in the garden. It doesn't just nourish, it teaches. It shows you where the land yields, where it resists, where it stores, where it sheds. And if you pay attention, then it tells you exactly how to design.

At Oak & Monkey Puzzle, water was both a gift and a challenge. The climate was cool, the rainfall generous. But excellent rainfall doesn't always mean easy gardening, especially when you're working with compacted clay, undulating ground, and the memory of livestock underfoot.

Design begins with observation

Before we planted a single thing, we watched. We observed after every downpour. Where did the water sit? Where did it flow? What areas stayed boggy days after the rain had passed? Where did frost settle hardest? We learned that the dam, while picturesque, didn't hold water reliably. We discovered that overflow moved southwards, towards the orchard. And we found out that clay soil held water in the wrong places and repelled it in others.

Only through watching could we respond. Only through repetition could we understand.

Water: the first infrastructure

Before garden beds, before trees, before anything else, we drilled the bore. We knew that we couldn't rely on rainfall alone, even in this high-rainfall zone. The dam was no help. Rainwater tanks would never be enough. We needed reliable water access across the property.

We also needed ways to move water around. Crushed rock paths helped with permeability. In the kitchen garden, we built terraces graded just enough to let water shed gently rather than stagnate. And retaining walls made from gabions allowed water to percolate down through levels.

Gabions: a design response to flow

Our terracing wasn't just about shape, it was about hydrology. Gabions became both retaining walls and water channels. Made from cages filled with rocks, they were beautiful, textural and permeable. Rainwater could move between garden levels without pooling. We paired them with geotextile membranes to hold soil in place, and planted near their edges to stabilise them.

Gabions offered a resilience that matched the land. They flexed where concrete might crack. They filtered where brick might block. They became part of the site's logic.

What water taught us

Water informed a way of designing that was grounded in evidence and observation. By tracing its paths and pauses, I read the site with precision, then shaped structure, grading and planting to work with those patterns. The procedure was clear: observe first, act second, and let the garden follow the logic of water.

- **To plant high in wet areas:** Trees in the orchard had to be mounded to survive.
- **To stall and spread, not just drain:** Gravel surfaces and mulch helped to absorb water and soften its impact.
- **To watch for microclimates:** In winter, dam overflow made one side boggy, while another stayed dry.
- **To read frost lines as water behaviour:** Moisture pooled where air was stillest, and those pockets became frost traps.
- **To accept the site as it was, not as we hoped it might be:** That meant letting some areas be boggy. Letting others remain tough. Working with, not over, the site.

Practical tips for reading your own site

Start with what you can witness. Keep simple records, test small changes, then repeat through the seasons. The aim is not to fix everything at once, but to let patterns reveal the next right move.

- After rain, walk around the garden. Look for puddles, rivulets and dry zones.
- Use a spade to check how water moves through your soil. Dig a small hole, fill it once, and let it drain to wet the sides. Refill, then measure how far the water level drops in one hour. Around 25 to 75 millimetres (1 to 3 inches) is a healthy amount for most gardens. Less than 25 millimetres (1 inch) suggests heavy clay or compacted soil. More than 75 millimetres (3 inches) indicates very free-draining, often sandy soil.
- If you have heavy clay soil, then plant higher. Build beds up, not down. Allow space for root aeration, keep traffic off wet soil, and build in organic matter.
- For free-draining sandy soil, add compost, mulch more thickly, and water more deeply but less often.
- Watch throughout the seasons. Winter frost can show you where cold air pools. Those same low points can also be places where moisture lingers after rain.
- Map where moisture-loving plants thrive naturally. This will tell you something that no textbook can.

Water doesn't just feed a garden. It reveals its memory. Where the animals walked. Where the trees once were. Where the land still breathes deeply. Let it teach you.

Gabions as edges, walls and water tools

Gabions are wire-mesh cages filled with rocks. In gardens, they can act as retaining walls, terrace edges, steps, seats and low boundary elements. Because they are permeable, they allow water to move through rather than push hard against a solid wall. That single quality makes them useful in wet soils, on sloping sites, and anywhere you're trying to slow, spread and guide water so it doesn't pool.

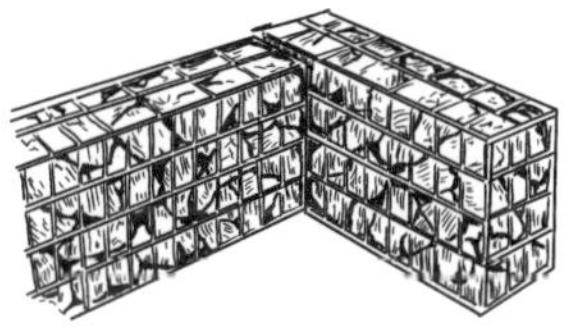

Design logic and terracing

The grade change from the house up towards the forest had to be mediated, so we created three terraces. The walls were built with gabions: permeable cages of rock that allowed water to move between levels, preventing pooling during heavy rain. We used a crushed rock base, compacted by hand, and placed geotextile membrane behind the gabions to stop soil clogging the rocks.

The soil itself was precious. We had deep, black, fertile topsoil beneath the colonial trees, built up over 150-plus years, so we carefully stockpiled that during earthworks. A local contractor came in with a mini excavator to help with ripping. Every bed was mapped out with builder's string and surveyor's paint, then ripped with narrow tines. Then into the beds we worked gypsum (to break up the clay), organic rock dust (to re-mineralise the depleted subsoil), mushroom compost (to add stable organic matter and improve water-holding ability) and organic-certified Perma-Fert (a piggery by-product that provides slow, balanced nutrients and beneficial biology).

We built the garden beds with non-arsenic-treated pine, which is safe for growing food plants, and filled them with a blend of stockpiled soil and rich organic matter, such as aged chicken manure and mulch. We planted, bed by bed, knowing full well that the weather would teach us what would stay and what would go.

Garden zones and spatial rhythm

The property moved from east to west, from Ballan-Daylesford Road and the entry driveway, through the house and out towards the forest. The formal garden sat directly west of the house across three terraced levels: kitchen garden, berry terrace, and cut-flower garden. To the north, under the oak trees, was the woodland garden: thousands of naturalised bulbs revealed themselves that first spring. To the south, a long, mown lawn formed a spine from the house towards the far southern paddocks. Other key zones included:

- **the hornbeam meadow:** Pleached fastigiate European hornbeams (*Carpinus betulus*) planted on the south side of the entry trees
- **the birch forest:** Silver birches (*Betula pendula*) and swamp birches (*B. alleghaniensis*) located between the hornbeams and the dam, thriving in the dam's overflow
- **the gravel circle:** a reimagined former round yard turned fire-pit and gathering space
- **the orchard:** a four by four grid of heirloom fruit trees, established with green manure and deep ripping
- **the chicken folly:** a tall, architectural coop that became a centrepiece
- **the studio and shed:** for making, storing and teaching.

We used mowing as a design device. Alleys were created by mowing paths. Grasses grew long in transition zones to create verticality and softness. Thresholds were framed, not fenced. The garden was always in motion, but never chaotic.

This masterplan for Oak & Monkey Puzzle shows the full design layout, with the top of the plan pointing west. The house sits central to the site. The three formal terraces step up westwards towards the forest from the back of the home. The terraces house the kitchen, berry and cut-flower gardens. The studio sits on the north-western corner of the cut-flower garden, against the forest edge. To the north sits the woodland. To the south, there is the hornbeam meadow, birch forest, orchard, paddocks, gravel circle, chicken folly and bushland beyond. To the south-west lies the shed, with the dam beyond.

*Top, middle and bottom*_Mowing as a design tool at Oak & Monkey Puzzle. A simple change in height creates paths, edges and outdoor rooms, with mown lines holding space against billowing grasses and seed heads. It is low-cost, human-scaled structure, shaped by movement, season and rhythm.

Mowing as a design tool

Mowing might not be the first technique that comes to mind when you think of landscape design. But at Oak & Monkey Puzzle, it became one of the most powerful and adaptable techniques we used.

With just a mower, I could carve movement into the land. A simple line through grass, cut at a different height, could define a path, establish an axis or create an outdoor room. There was no hardscaping, no infrastructure. Just a gesture. An invitation. A way of drawing with absence.

Structure in the meadow

Long grass becomes your walls. Mown grass becomes your paths. It's a contrast not only in texture and height but also in experience. Mowing introduces spatial rhythm to a loose landscape. Paths lead. Clearings invite pause. Alleys frame. A mown axis can ground an entire garden. And all of it is dynamic. Changeable. Responsive to mood, season, growth. At Oak & Monkey Puzzle, mowing was used to:

- trace out straight alleys through the birch forest
- shape winding paths through emerging meadows
- create circular clearings for rest and gathering
- direct the eye towards focal points: trees, the gravel circle, the horizon.

In many ways, mowing became my sketchbook. A test site. It allowed me to trial a geometry or rhythm before committing to structure.

Form follows function (and wildlife)

Mown paths weren't just design, they were also practical. In a landscape shared with snakes and other wildlife, they offered safe passage. I taught my children never to walk through tall grass. Not because they weren't allowed, but because it demanded awareness. Mown paths became a way of moving with respect. Of seeing the ground clearly, and inhabiting the land with care.

Cost-effective, dynamic, human-scaled

There's an accessibility to mowing as a design tool. It doesn't require a team or materials. Just time, presence, a willingness to observe and a mower. At Oak & Monkey Puzzle, it was one of the few gestures that could be made instantly, shaping space in a single morning. As the garden matured, those gestures matured, too. Pathways changed. Clearings grew. Grass seeded and softened. And the design evolved with it.

Try it in your own garden

Begin with one gesture. Cut a single line through long grass to test a path, an axis or a small clearing, then live with it for a week and adjust. Treat the mower as a sketching tool that lets you trial movement and rooms at full scale before you commit to structure.

- **Start small:** A single path cut through long grass can reorientate how you move through the space.
- **Draw the eye:** Use mowing to create sightlines or to frame key trees or features.
- **Introduce three-dimensionality:** Allow surrounding grass or wildflowers to grow tall.
- **Vary the rhythm:** A mix of tight winding paths and wide straight alleys changes the feel dramatically.
- **Let mowing be fluid:** Treat it as a seasonal, responsive task. You can always mow again. Or not.

At its best, mowing is a dialogue with the land. One that says: I see you. I move with you. I mark the way, not as a dominator, but as a participant.

Planting palette and combinations

The plantings at Oak & Monkey Puzzle were never just about aesthetics. They were about response to clay soil, to sharp frosts, to shade, wind and forest edge. But they were also about rhythm and emotion. I chose plants for what they offered across the year. Not just in peak bloom, but in their buds, in their structures, in their fading.

I've always loved the way that fastigiate European hornbeams (*Carpinus betulus*) sit upright, refined and serenely commanding in a space, so they were the first things we planted. Part of the structure, the architecture, they framed the edge of the cut-flower garden and gave it something to push against. They also held the view to the forest and provided a sense of enclosure in an otherwise open clearing. We used them as hedging, too, particularly around the shed, where they acted as a green veil for the back-of-house areas.

I planted for structure. For contrast. For fragrance and for gathering. For sensory interest and seasonal punctuation. Panicle hydrangeas (*Hydrangea paniculata*) became a hallmark of the garden, not just in bloom, but as the months wore on. Their skeletal seed heads caught the low light of winter. Their presence gave shape to the space long after their colour had faded.

Always fragrant and repeat flowering, roses anchored many of the garden beds. Some were climbers trained along the edges. Others were shrub forms bordered by low, clipped English box (*Buxus sempervirens*) hedging. I wasn't precious about varieties, but they had to earn their place. They had to be resilient, generous and scented.

The cut-flower garden was designed as individual beds within a larger space. Some focused on drama, such as the beds with foxgloves (*Digitalis purpurea*), mollis azaleas (*Rhododendron* Mollis Hybrids), Siberian larkspurs (*Delphinium grandiflorum*),

The lawn spine of the formal garden visually cuts through the terraces, as seen from the kitchen garden through the berry terrace and cut-flower beds to the forest edge beyond.

tree peonies (*Paeonia × suffruticosa*) and *Alcea rosea* 'Nigra'. Others were about structure and texture, with artichokes (*Cynara cardunculus*), *Eryngium planum* 'Blue Sea Holly', *Echinacea* 'Sombrero Baja', garden angelicas (*Angelica archangelica*), *Echinops ritro* 'Veitch's Blue' and *Sanguisorba officinalis* 'St Philibert'. I loved watching their silhouettes shift as the seasons changed. *Hylotelephium spectabile* 'Autumn Joy' was planted not just for its flowers, but for the green buds that are useful in floral arrangements and beautiful in their own right.

The berry terrace, nestled between the kitchen garden and the cut-flower beds, was planted for rhythm and form. The blueberry cultivar *Vaccinium corymbosum* 'Brigitta', jostaberries (*Ribes × nidigrolaria*) and blackcurrants (*R. nigrum*) created dense, fruiting hedges. Strawberries (*Fragaria × ananassa*) formed a generous ground cover beneath. I loved seeing the contrast of foliage types and the way that the garden changed when the berries ripened. In some beds I added in *Echinacea* cultivars (such as 'Double Scoop Lemon Cream' and 'Double Scoop Raspberry') and *Hydrangea arborescens* 'Annabelle'.

The woodland area, under the established English oaks (*Quercus robur*), revealed itself over time. That first spring, thousands of bluebells (*Hyacynthoides* spp.) and daffodils (*Narcissus* spp.) emerged. We planted jonquils (*Narcissus jonquilla*), Lenten roses (*Helleborus × hybridus*), oakleaf hydrangeas (*Hydrangea quercifolia*) and *Hydrangea arborescens* 'Annabelle' into the understorey, choosing varieties that could handle the filtered light and clay soil. It became one of the most restful parts of the garden.

The hornbeam meadow was seeded with a mix of bulbs, some planted in the rain, others by crowbar on cold days. *Miscanthus* 'Eileen Quinn' was a favourite grass throughout the garden, especially in the teardrop-shaped entry space, where it was planted alongside purpletops (*Verbena bonariensis*), Queen Anne's lace (*Daucus carota*), purple coneflowers (*Echinacea purpurea*), *Hylotelephium spectabile* 'Autumn Joy', artichokes (*Cynara cardunculus*), *Calamagrostis* 'Karl Foerster', *Sanguisorba officinalis* 'St Philibert', snowdrop windflowers (*Anemonoides sylvestris*) and a diamond-pattern grid of English box (*Buxus sempervirens*) balls that I jokingly called the Chesterfield garden (billowing perennials held by gridded buttons of clipped box balls like the form of a Chesterfield settee). Even in winter, the green bones of that space held.

In the more functional spaces, such as the kitchen garden, we let things move in and out depending on the season. Lovage (*Levisticum officinale*), horseradish (*Armoracia rusticana*), rhubarb (*Rheum rhabarbarum*), edible flowers such as pot marigolds (*Calendula officinalis*) and sweet alyssum (*Lobularia maritima*), and herbs such as parsley (*Petroselinum crispum*) and thyme (*Thymus vulgaris*) were planted alongside more ephemeral crops. Sometimes I planted foxgloves (*Digitalis purpurea*) or sweet peas (*Lathyrus odoratus*) among the edibles, just because they belonged.

What unified everything wasn't a strict planting plan. It was rhythm. The garden was always about layering texture, scent and movement. I'd find myself planting by feel. If something worked, then it stayed. If it didn't, then it moved. That's the freedom of a garden like this: it wasn't formal, but it had bones. It could hold the looseness.

Over time, the planting became less static. I stopped trying to keep things in their place and started watching to see how they wanted to move. The beds softened. Combinations self-seeded. The garden started speaking back.

It wasn't about having a list, it was about knowing the conditions and trusting the process. Some plants occasionally failed. Some thrived. Some became signatures. The point was never perfection; it was presence. Beauty that could withstand rain and frost, and the repetition of seasonal work. Beauty that evolved.

Snipping some Siberian larkspur (*Delphinium grandiflorum*) in the cut-flower beds. The tall spires are grown in well-prepared clay, and are gathered for the house, special events and florists.

Begin with the structural planting

You can change perennials, move annuals, shift colour palettes. But in any garden, big or small, structure is what holds the space together. It establishes the bones of the garden, the rhythm of movement, the sense of scale. It's what gives a garden presence when everything else has died back, when the seasons turn, when colour and softness are fleeting. Without structure, a garden is just a collection of plants. With it, a garden transforms into an integrated place.

Structural plants often take years to reach maturity. That's exactly why they go in first. While they grow, the rest of the garden can unfold around them. Perennials can be tested and tweaked, ground covers can knit together, self-seeders can show you what they want. But those bones? They're what give you confidence and clarity as the garden evolves.

At Oak & Monkey Puzzle, structural planting was the foundation upon which everything else could evolve. We knew that if we wanted structure in five years, then we had to plant for it in year one. Consequently, we planted structure early:

- a row of fastigiate European hornbeams (*Carpinus betulus*) along the western edge of the cut-flower terrace, standing like sentinels and creating a threshold before the forest beyond
- hedging to mask sheds and back-of-house zones, this time using clipped European hornbeam for its resilience and beauty
- a cross-shaped axis of pleached fastigiate European hornbeams to define four quadrants of hornbeam meadow
- English box (*Buxus sempervirens*) hedging, clipped into low, sculptural forms, defining certain edges of the cut-flower beds; not everywhere, but enough to establish a visual rhythm
- silver birch (*Betula pendula*) and swamp birch (*B. alleghaniensis*) trees planted en masse to create a forested threshold that would thrive in the outflow of the dam between the 'designed landscape' and a gradient back to bushland.

Plants that shape a garden

Structural planting doesn't have to involve hedges and symmetry. It can simply mean choosing species that:

- anchor the view (visually or emotionally)
- hold their form through the seasons
- create contrast with softer or looser companions
- respond to the site conditions by being resilient, reliable or regenerative.

My go-to structural plants at Oak & Monkey Puzzle included:

- European hornbeam (*Carpinus betulus*), for hedging, meadow framing and vertical rhythm
- English box (*Buxus sempervirens*), used sculpturally, in grids and balls, to counterbalance loose perennial combinations

Late afternoon in the cut-flower garden, where Siberian larkspurs (*Delphinium grandiflorum*) and foxgloves (*Digitalis purpurea*) echo the vertical forest beyond. They are held by a dry-stone wall and a line of European hornbeams (*Carpinus betulus*) that mark the threshold between the designed garden and the inherited landscape.

- silver birch (*Betula pendula*), as a foresting gesture, creating immersive shade and winter beauty
- Huonville crabapple (*Malus* sp.), espaliered to define the edge of the kitchen garden in front of gabion walls
- English oak (*Quercus robur*), longleaf pine (*Pinus palustris*) and existing conifers, inherited and enhanced to shape backdrop and rhythm.

Even under the old colonial oak trees in the woodland garden, we let structure emerge through form, not just plant choice. The verticality of mature trunks and the shadows cast by height became part of the structural language.

Start your garden like a designer

When designing your own productive or ornamental garden, ask yourself:

- What will this space look like in winter?
- Where does your eye need to be led or to be held?
- What plants will still maintain their form after the frost flattens everything else?
- Where do you want enclosure, rhythm or hierarchy?

Put in your structural plants first. Don't rush the rest. Let the structure guide the layers that follow. Design is not about perfection, it's about intention. And structure allows you to return to intention, again and again, no matter what changes.

***Above left*_**The three-step threshold located between the berry terrace and the cut-flower garden, with a reclaimed cypress branch arbour marking the shift in level and use.
***Above right*_**The small, spired chicken housing, a functional folly set among the heirloom fruit trees in the orchard.

Design challenges and adaptation

No garden unfolds without challenges. For us, the biggest constraint was water. The clay soil held moisture, and the ground in the orchard would often become boggy, especially after heavy rains and dam overflow. We lost trees early on, so we learned to plant higher. We decided to work with the site's gradients, not against them. Sometimes the overflow couldn't be redirected, so it had to be understood and absorbed.

The climate was harsh in its own way. Winters could plummet to well below freezing. And while wind wasn't a regular problem, thanks to our thickly forested protection, shade from the growing trees became a challenge over time. Some beds eventually lost access to the sun. Others became more protected than expected. We had to keep shifting, adapting.

'The storm' – what I've come to think of as the cold-climate cyclone – was one of the most confronting moments. A once-in-a-lifetime weather event that tore through the landscape in 2021, turning trees into matchsticks. We lost trees. Big ones. An old Monterey cypress (*Hesperocyparis macrocarpa*) was so damaged that we had to chop it down. We mourned a gold-rush era Douglas fir (*Pseudotsuga menziesii*). Blackwoods (*Acacia melanoxylon*) shattered in the back bushland. Before removing any tree, I left offerings at the base. Flowers from the garden. Words of thanks. It mattered to me; it still does.

Even in the planting, we had to unlearn. Initially, we worked in grids: bed layouts, planting intervals. But nature doesn't grow in grids. Over time, I softened.

Allowed drifts to take shape. Gave permission for plants to go where they wanted. The structure didn't vanish, it matured.

We slowly transitioned to no-dig gardening (see pages 205–10), despite initial disagreements. My former partner preferred to follow a more traditional horticultural approach favouring rotary hoeing. But as I learned, watched and trialled, I began to trust different methods. Green-manure crops, arborist mulch left to break down over time, pine bark in some areas, mushroom compost in others. Towards the end, the influence of English no-dig pioneer Charles Dowding started to take hold. From him I took a clear discipline: protect soil structure, feed with surface compost, keep beds covered and active, and let observation guide the next move. But it was at Little Cottage on a Hill that those practices became fully embedded.

Seasonal rhythms and lived experience

Every season brought its rituals. Armfuls of roses, gathered in early summer. Wild blackberries (*Rubus fruticosus*) foraged from the bushland fire track. Pine mushrooms gathered from hiding spots at the forest's edge (always making sure that we'd correctly identified them first).

We moved through it all as a family. I remember the feel of frost underfoot on an early morning. The silence of snow. The golden rustle of silver birch (*Betula pendula*) leaves in autumn. These weren't just sensory markers. They were cues. Anchors. Invitations to presence.

We planted bulbs by the boxful, most gifted to us by friends. I never knew what would bloom where. But that was part of the magic. Surprise becomes its own rhythm.

Workshops, long lunches and gatherings certainly happened. But the real experience was in the daily tending. The unnoticed work. The barrows of mulch. The repetition of care. Oak & Monkey Puzzle taught me that looking after a garden is not just about shaping a landscape, it's about shaping time. Shaping relationship. Shaping self.

What I carry forwards

Oak & Monkey Puzzle was more than a garden. It was my crucible. My classroom. My companion. It taught me:

- — that no system is fixed; everything must evolve
- — that observation is more powerful than any design tool
- — that beauty can be resilient, and resilience can be beautiful
- — that gardens are not escapes; they are returns to body, to breath, to belonging.

So much of what I practise now began there in the compost bays, in the frost pockets, in the softened geometry of a once rigidly planted bed. I carry those lessons forwards. Into every design. Every workshop. Every morning in the verges of Little Cottage on a Hill.

And when people ask me if I miss it, I say this: I don't need to. It's still with me. In my hands. In my eyes. In the way I move through the garden. Oak & Monkey Puzzle gave me back to myself. And I carry that gift every day.

Avoid weedy berries

While some berries are beautiful and useful, brambleberries such as raspberry (*Rubus idaeus*) and blackberry (*R. fruticosus*) should be avoided where you don't have the space or means to manage them, because they can be invasive. Their roots resist containment, travelling under soil and gravel, and the plant can reappear metres away. Note that European blackberry (*R. fruticosus* aggregate) is a Weed of National Significance in Australia and has been declared a noxious weed in most Australian states. Check your local guidelines for control requirements.

In the United Kingdom and much of Europe, brambleberries are often native; however, in parts of North America, blackberries are invasive. Obtain local guidance before planting.

What to plant when you're starting from scratch

Designing a garden from a blank slate can be thrilling and completely overwhelming. What to plant? What performs? I trialled many plants at Oak & Monkey Puzzle, and some were discarded. But the plants listed below earned their place.

Begin with structure

First put in plants that will hold the garden through every season:

- English box (*Buxus sempervirens*), used sparingly but powerfully as a low, clipped, sculptural anchor
- European hornbeam (*Carpinus betulus*), as fastigiate (narrow, upright) form, hedging or structural rhythm
- reed grasses (*Calamagrostis* spp.) and silvergrasses (*Miscanthus* spp.), for interest and movement, plus structure from early summer onwards.

For spring drama

These plants arrive like a sigh of relief after winter:

- Lenten rose (*Helleborus × hybridus*) – late-winter to early-spring beauty, often the first sign of renewal
- mollis azalea (*Rhododendron* Mollis Hybrid) – luminous and underrated, delivering extraordinary colour at the turn of spring
- Siberian larkspur (*Delphinium grandiflorum*) – statuesque and fleeting, but worth every second of its early-summer reign.

For summer succession

These plants carry the show once the spring display fades:

- foxglove (*Digitalis purpurea*) – tall, romantic, and irresistible to pollinators
- globe thistle (*Echinops ritro*) and flat sea holly (*Eryngium planum*) – textural, sculptural and superb dried or fresh in floral work
- panicle hydrangea (*Hydrangea paniculata*) – structural, changing through the seasons and spectacular year-round.

For grounded abundance

These plants fill the ground plane or in-between spaces, feed the family and soften the edges:

- redcurrant (*Ribes rubrum*) and gooseberry (*R. uva crispa*) – productive and well-behaved in structured beds that need a bit of substance
- rhubarb (*Rheum rhabarbarum*) – textural and generous.
- strawberry (*Fragaria × ananassa*) – a reliable, spreading ground cover with returns for both garden and kitchen.

A RUMINATION ON THE GARDEN

Oak & Monkey Puzzle in the late afternoon light. The view from the berry terrace up through the cut-flower garden reveals a spine of lawn that draws you towards the forest edge. Structure, glow and threshold are held in the same moment.

When I look back now, it's not the scale of Oak & Monkey Puzzle that I remember. It's the feeling. The way the land seemed to lean in. The way the garden held shape, even when I couldn't. The way it asked everything of me, and somehow still gave more.

This wasn't just a garden I built. It was the place I became. The place I learned to hold grief and joy in the same breath. To plant without guarantees. To stay in the middle, not rushing towards the bloom or the harvest, but discovering how to live inside the growing.

I found a different kind of strength there. Not the kind you boast about. The kind that builds slowly, season by season, through muddy boots, wheelbarrows and winter bones. Through doing the work even when no one is watching. Especially then.

It taught me to see structure as something generous. To let rhythm be a kind of care. To notice the things that didn't need fixing. To trust that beauty can be unruly and resilient, and that nothing worth growing arrives fully formed.

And all of that lives in me now, not just as memory, but as method. I still mark out beds with string. Still listen to the soil before I speak into it. Still pause at the edge of a space and wait for the right entry point. I carry the shape of that garden in the way I move, the way I decide, the way I stay present with a place. The scale is smaller now, but the depth is not. Because this wasn't just a garden I shaped. It was the garden that shaped everything that came next.

A REFLECTION ON THE MACLENNANS

Joanna Maclennan came to Oak & Monkey Puzzle in late 2019.

She moved gently, without imposition, hosting photography workshops, walking around the garden with a soft gaze yet documentary sense of perception, sharing meals, noticing light. She watched the way we lived with the place. Not just how I planted or designed, but how the days unfolded. The ordinary rituals. The way the garden held us.

Her lens was unhurried and calm. And through it, I saw something that I hadn't been able to name. The garden had become something larger than its form. It wasn't just a project, or a design; it was a life. Her photographs offered it back to me with tenderness and precision. And then her brother Oliver wrote the words.

What they captured together – the stillness, the shape of the days, the kind of domestic wildness that lived in that space – reflected a life lived through simple seasonal moments. This excerpt from their book, shared here with their permission, isn't just a snapshot of the garden. It's a portrait of a life, in a moment of clarity. A rare window through which someone else, someone deeply perceptive, saw the place for what it truly was.

EXCERPT FROM *LIVING WILD:*

New beginnings in the great outdoors

– written by Oliver Maclennan, photographs by Joanna Maclennan

The house and garden had been several different things over the years, not only a post office, dating to the 1860s, but also a farm shop, a pub and a recreational reserve with a cricket pitch. 'The horses had grazed everything,' Natasha says. 'Bits of the wall were missing, glass was missing, bats flew in the house at night. A sorry state.' But within this 'sorry state' lay the house's essence. 'It was covered in so many different layers of materials,' she adds.

'First thing, before the renovation, was to start on the garden,' she says, 'planting some trees, such as hornbeams, to give it some form, and a fruit orchard. I wanted the garden to have a productive focus, and to sustain me and my family. I grow as much as I possibly can, using heirloom varieties.'

Owing to her experience at the florist's, Natasha knows just where to look for unusual things. 'We have a particular micro-climate, with a long and cold winter (for Australia), drizzly and misty. I was interested in plants like peonies and lily of the valley: scented, fragrant, a bit architectural. I was creating a garden for me, but also a place to be lived in.'

The terrace provides space for groups, big or small, and can expand or contract accordingly. 'Spaces not just to be viewed, not just compositional, but that also provide an experience. It brings together my skills in landscape architecture, floristry and urban design. I have a passion for place-making.'

A converted shipping container overlooks the garden, and provides the scene for a lunch of local and homegrown produce. There are also workshops on garden design, fermenting, dry-stone walling, cheese-making, marketing for small businesses, shibori, creative writing and more. 'It's an evolving programme, generated by local connections and talented people,' Natasha adds. 'They need to be inspiring and full of passion.'

The same, of course, can be said for her garden, and no one knows this more than her children. Initially, after moving to the country from Melbourne, Natasha was worried that she was somehow depriving them, limiting their access to resources and education. But she has found completely the opposite.

'They spend lots of time outdoors, learning from what's around them. We walk in the forest, forage for mushrooms, pick raspberries.

'They eat carrots without washing them . . . They are present to changes in the seasons . . . It's everything you would imagine a country upbringing to be.'

Quite unexpectedly, Natasha has become a country person. 'I don't miss the city,' she muses. 'I've had to make sacrifices, but my life is so much richer than it was.'

Less is sometimes more. What is vital is that strong sense of place, with guaranteed surprises all year round.

In the garden

The region's micro-climate, with a long, cold winter and lots of rain and mist, led Natasha to search for plants that would thrive in cooler climates, such as peonies and lily of the valley, and were also fragrant and would provide structure.

'It's cold, it's wet, it's dirty,' she says, 'but it's also an incredibly sincere way of life, and abundant.' There's always something to enjoy in the garden, from eating homegrown vegetables to observing changes in the light and experiencing the passage of the seasons. There is also time to slow down and appreciate what is around you. For children, the added benefit is that they are connected to the land, the seasons and the people around them.

Cutting flowers at Oak & Monkey Puzzle, photographed by Joanna Maclennan during her week with us. Joanna's lens holds the rhythms and rituals of garden life: slow, attentive and full of quiet detail.

PART -III-

The seasonal garden

8
LITTLE COTTAGE ON A HILL IN ACTION

My move to Little Cottage on a Hill began with a question: could I start again? How do you distil the lessons of a garden and let them take root in a different landscape? This chapter is my answer.

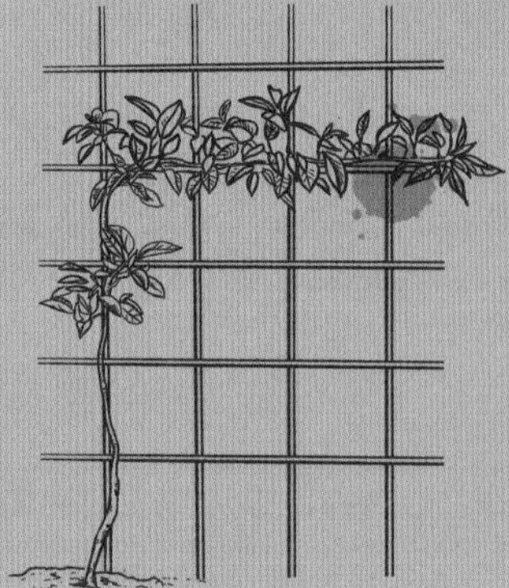

NEW BEGINNINGS

When we landed at Little Cottage on a Hill in April 2022, everything was still very raw. Oak & Monkey Puzzle wasn't just a place I built. It was the place that built me.

But moving to Little Cottage on a Hill was about choosing to be closer to town, to put my kids first: two autistic children at a pivotal age who needed community around them, not just forest. I chose to make their school days easier, to support the friendships that were growing and to give them roots. I chose a smaller garden so I could create more and maintain less. Because I love creating. It's who I am and what I do.

There were practicalities, too. I was a solo parent. I'd found an incredible school for the kids, but how was I going to fund it from 5 acres, twenty minutes out of town, and no buffer if something went wrong? I wanted to live well, but also wisely. I also wanted to design something that reflected who I am now, not who I used to be.

And I was ready to be close to Daylesford. Really close. No more 100-kilometre (60-mile) days just doing school drop-offs and pick-ups and workshops and errands. No more driving home through kangaroo country in the dark. I wanted to walk to the bakery. I wanted to bump into people at the market. I wanted to belong more fully to this community that had been part of my orbit for years.

Then there was the epiphany, the one that landed in the middle of a pandemic when shelves were empty and everything felt precarious: if I have soil, sun, water and fresh air, what more do I actually need?

'Then there was the epiphany . . . if I have soil, sun, water and fresh air, what more do I actually need?'

That thought changed me. It made the decision not just logical, but joyful, exciting, inspiring. It was like a creative door opened. What if I recontextualised everything I'd learned at Oak & Monkey Puzzle? What if I translated the whole thing through the lens of constraint? What if the very act of shrinking the footprint made the ideas grow stronger?

View south from Wombat Hill Botanic Gardens across Daylesford's rolling hills and out to the Wombat State Forest beyond. This fertile volcanic landscape, shaped by deep soils and mineral springs, has long supported gardens, farming and community life. For me, it remains one of the clearest expressions of why beginning again here felt so right.

FINDING MY FEET

I actually bought Little Cottage on a Hill before I sold Oak & Monkey Puzzle. The property market was in a frenzy. Daylesford had almost no rentals. I was desperate. I needed to know that we had somewhere to go. Somewhere safe. I took out bridging finance, something I'd never imagined doing, because I couldn't take the risk of being left without a roof over our heads.

I'd been looking everywhere. I'd (thankfully) just missed out on securing an acreage on the edge of town in a blind auction. And then this cottage came up. I rang the agent immediately. I told him: 'You cannot sell this without me seeing it.' I was emphatic.

He was surprised. 'That place?' he said. 'Won't it be too small?'

I said, 'Let me decide that.'

I organised the kids, my dad and a builder for the inspection the next morning. That night, the sale documents came through. My heart skipped a beat. The vendor was one of the agents selling Oak & Monkey Puzzle.

The next day, we walked through. And the moment we stepped into the hallway, Oliver looked around and said, 'This feels safe, Mum.'

It wasn't big. It wasn't grand. It didn't have high ceilings or architectural bravado. But it had my signature palette. White walls. Dark floors. A calmness. And I knew I could imagine myself here.

I could see the garden instantly. What I wanted to create, how it would work. But the house? That was the unknown. Until I was in it. And then it wasn't.

'I wrote the owner a real letter, pouring out my heart. It wasn't just a pitch; it was a moment of full surrender.'

I wrote the owner a letter, pouring out my heart. It wasn't just a pitch; it was a moment of full surrender: please don't sell this to someone else. Please let me begin again here. I'd like to think that this was the clincher, but it was probably the serendipity of economics. I just happened to be the person with the most compelling offer.

We moved in before we even had furniture. *The Block*, Australia's biggest reality TV show, was filming at Oak & Monkey Puzzle, and I couldn't move a thing. Everything had to stay as it was. So we sat on a couch kindly left behind by the previous owner. Used a bar fridge. Slept on borrowed mattresses. We camped in our future.

And then came the accident.

I was on my way to hand over Oak & Monkey Puzzle to its new owners. Hit black ice. Lost control. Both cars totalled. The kids, thankfully uninjured, were collected by their dad from the roadside. Paramedics looked me over. One of the agents picked me up from the accident site, and I went to the handover. That's how I am. I knew something was wrong, but my adrenaline was pumping. When I saw my osteo later that day, she took one look and sent me to hospital. Neuropathy. Trauma MRI. I spent nine hours on my back, ramped in a Ballarat hospital corridor, crying. I couldn't move, not even to wipe away my tears.

And the thought hit me hard: if I were still living at Oak & Monkey Puzzle, there's no way I would have managed.

The house was too remote. Too hard. Too far. But here, I was enveloped by community. People dropped off food. Checked in. Took the kids to and from school. Held space. I wasn't alone.

Doing more with less

Little Cottage on a Hill was never meant to be the next big project. I didn't want to replicate 5 acres in miniature. I wanted something else. Something more distilled. More intentional. Synthesised. Evolved. Humble. Could I carry the essence of everything I'd learned in a tree change with a purpose, and still live well on less . . . far less?

This chapter is where that question lives.

It's not just about design. It's about freedom. Clarity. Letting go of what no longer fits and starting again with what still does. It's about choosing beauty, but making it work hard. About layering yield with rhythm. About designing a garden that lives almost in full view of the street, and deciding not to hide.

The early days here weren't easy. I was in a neck brace, recovering from the car accident. Unable to lift anything heavy. The garden had to wait, which, in hindsight, was exactly what I needed. Time to watch the light. To trace the lines. To test what it felt like to live in this new rhythm.

And then I held the first workshops. Too early maybe, as the garden wasn't close to being finished. But people came. They stood in this partially formed place with its marked-out beds and grassed paths and baby plantings, and they said, 'This. This I can do.'

That was the moment, the turning point. This garden isn't aspirational; it's translatable. It's not a fantasy; it's a prototype. And it's the first time I've had enough clarity under my feet, enough chapters under my belt, to write a book about my experience.

There is no back-of-house here. Every corner is visible. Every element earns its place. Every gesture carries the whole. It's not about hiding function behind beauty. It's about letting function be beautiful: the compost towers, the wicking beds, the espaliered boundary, the worm tunnels tucked into beds. Even the path that splits around the silver birch (*Betula pendula*) in a circle of gravel and light.

This is a garden that doesn't apologise for what it is.

***Above left*_**First gestures at Little Cottage on a Hill, marked directly onto the lawn with survey paint. A mini excavator begins cutting the lines, with the position of the silver birch (*Betula pendula*) guiding what would become the gravel circle. ***Above right*_**Northern verge beds, measured and set out on the ground. Survey paint, pegs and cloche arcs were used to test curves and widths; the garden was designed at full scale before a single edge was built.

Little Cottage on a Hill, as we found it. There were two wide verges, a few silver birches (*Betula pendula*) and a lot of lawn. This blank canvas was the beginning of doing more with less.

REDEFINING SCALE, RECLAIMING SELF

From my bedroom window, when I lie down in bed, I can see the canopy line of the Wombat Hill Botanic Gardens. It's not a grand view, not one that stretches forever. But it's layered. It's familiar. It's full of texture and memory. The same exotic species I lived among at Oak & Monkey Puzzle – English oak (*Quercus robur*), Himalayan cedar (*Cedrus deodara*), Douglas fir (*Pseudotsuga menziesii*) – now make up the skyline that frames the end of my day. There's a beautiful echo in that. A comforting continuity. I haven't left everything behind. I've just shifted orientation. What once wrapped around me as forest now meets me at eye level in the morning light. It's a view that feels like home without being the same place. And that, in itself, is profound.

I thought that I'd miss the size of Oak & Monkey Puzzle. The terraces. The orchard. The sound of wind approaching through tall trees before you saw the foliage move. But that space wasn't vast openness, it was a clearing in the forest. A garden encircled and held by trees. It was private. Secluded. Protected.

Little Cottage on a Hill is the opposite. Here, I live in full view. In relationship with the street. With the community. With the botanic gardens just across the way. There are days I can hear the school bell from my front door. And there's something about this visibility that has brought a surprising sense of ease and presence.

Everything here feels manageable. Knowable. Every big task is a one-day job. Pruning. Mulching. Shaping. Hosting. It's all possible in a way that doesn't cost me more than I have to give. And that feeling of being in rhythm with the work changes everything. It allows me space. It feels expansive. Liberating. Light.

This is the first garden that is wholly mine. No shared decision-making. No old griefs held in the soil. No past love etched into the planting lines. Just me. And the work. And the ideas I'm still growing into.

It's a continuum, yes. But it's also a clean slate. A fresh start with roots, hope and promise.

A cottage within a community

I haven't given up anything. I've gained spaciousness. Clarity. Confidence. The ideas have become bigger even as the footprint got smaller. And I feel more connected to my landscape than ever before because now I'm designing from within my community.

It's the first time in years that I haven't had to explain where I live. I can just say 'the one with the garden'. Everyone knows it. This is a kind of belonging that feels like home.

The garden and I are both visible now. It's a special kind of intimacy. A sense of shared generosity.

And it brought things I didn't expect. Every day for the first year, people would stop. On the verge. In their cars. While walking their dogs. Some would stand in silence, watching. Others were overwhelmed with joy. One neighbour left a handful of limes and a bunch of garlic. Another deposited a box of homegrown cherries at the front door with a note (thank you 'Jxx', whoever you are).

And then there was the phone call to council. Someone thought that I must be doing something illegal. That no one was allowed to make a verge like this: growing a garden on public land. The compliance officer came by, took one look and said, 'Keep going. It's wonderful.'

The garden kept speaking. And the community listened. Not just politely. Actively. Generously. It was the opposite of what I'd feared. I didn't have to retreat. I didn't have to explain. I just had to keep planting, making, sharing, doing what made me feel alive.

The silver birch trees (*Betula pendula*) of Little Cottage On A Hill became an unexpected anchor in this shift, a botanical thread tying one life to another. At Oak & Monkey Puzzle, we planted a birch forest. Rows of silver trunks, soft movement, dappled shade. It was a space inspired by the work I witnessed during my time at Taylor Cullity Lethlean and their design of the National Arboretum Canberra. A place of a hundred forests and a hundred gardens. Trees planted close together to create a rhythm of tall, slender trunks, a constellation of greenery to stand within.

And here, at Little Cottage on a Hill, the birch trees were already waiting for me. Not just one. Almost all of the trees on the property are birch. In the western verge and also along the house, tucked behind the front fence, flanking the driveway courtyard. They line the entry, mark the rhythm of the space, give shape to the sky. They shimmer and shift and drop golden leaves in autumn like scattered coins.

When I realised this, I felt something settle in me. Like a seed of continuity. Not forced, not planned, just . . . meant. I shaped the new entry path around one slightly off-centre birch. I didn't want to centre it; I couldn't have, even if I'd tried. I wanted to honour its position but also anchor it as the feature of this space. To orientate the gravel circle off-centre in a dance between elements, and to make the circle wide enough so that the tree could breathe. So that I could sit beside the tree, under it. So that the tree could still move and become part of a new story. A different scale. But the same kind of quiet magic.

The birches here don't just offer beauty. They hold memory. They remind me of what I planted before, and why. And they let me begin again, without starting from nothing. For the first time, I don't feel the need to prove anything. The garden speaks. The garden holds. The garden teaches.

Living with destructive birds

Many gardeners in Australia have to deal with cockatoos. These noisy birds will rip off seedling tops and snap off flower heads just because they can. And they will come in numbers. You can spend your days feeling rage and resentment, or you can design your garden for coexistence.

I have a cockatoo deterrent that isn't high-tech. It's a bottle or jar, loosely wrapped in white fabric or plastic, laid gently on the soil. From above, it resembles a dead cockatoo. And cockatoos – being intelligent, deeply social creatures – avoid it. I've tested this not only at Little Cottage on a Hill but also at Oak & Monkey Puzzle, and it's worked for me just about every time. There may be the odd occasion when there's so little for cockatoos to eat that they'll risk visiting the garden, but in eleven years of living in the country, it's been my go-to solution. The design principle for this deterrent is universal, but the decoy itself is cockatoo-specific; if you live outside Australia, then adapt the idea using a locally relevant bird deterrent.

I don't plant my most fragile or prized edibles in the verge anymore. Out there, it's tougher things: herbs, hardy greens, polyculture mixes, garlic (*Allium sativum*), flowers, climbing annuals and perennials. If these plants get trimmed by a beak, they are resilient enough to bounce back. Even if someone picks a sprig, I'm still perfectly happy.

Tanya Loos reminded me that this isn't just a garden; it's a habitat. In our conversation (see pages 16–17), Tanya spoke about the need to garden with fauna, not against it. Her book *Living with Wildlife* helped me to reframe the cockatoos as participants rather than pests. The garden isn't mine alone: it's part of a broader system. And my role isn't to dominate it, but to listen. To adjust. To belong.

Designing for cohabitation is a practice. Not everything is protected. But everything is chosen with consideration and with the knowledge that I'm not the only one moving through this space.

DISTILLING A DECADE OF KNOWLEDGE

Oak & Monkey Puzzle taught me everything. And yet, it wasn't the beginning. I had an entire career behind me by the time I broke ground there. I'd worked on award-winning public landscapes, taught design and mentored students. I knew the principles and understood the mechanics. But none of that compares to what happens when you do it for yourself.

When it's your land and livelihood, your grief and joy and resilience are all rooted in the soil. Every compost bay, every cut flower, every path you rake at dusk is both functional and emotional. That's what Oak & Monkey Puzzle was for me. A place that embraced me when I needed to rebuild, and taught me what it meant to create with full presence and deep intention. Taught me scale and rhythm and layering. How to plant for beauty and yield. How to host with warmth and purpose. How to hold space for other people while still holding my own.

But gardens, like people, have seasons. And the season in which I found myself was changing. I wanted to create again. To reimagine. To begin a new conversation with the land, not just maintain what was already built. And so I brought the best of that decade at Oak & Monkey Puzzle with me to Little Cottage on a Hill.

Northern verge at Little Cottage on a Hill. I distilled a decade of gardening at Oak & Monkey Puzzle and adapted it for the smaller footprint here, using the verge to extend space, hold structure and keep the garden offering what mattered most.

***Above left*_**Ripe cucumbers gathered from the wicking beds, proof of what good soil can offer.
***Above right*_**A working corner. Sieves, tools and pots are kept close because small gardens run on rhythm and readiness.

What came with me:

- — The rhythm of repetition. Beds shaped by season, not trend.
- — The line of sight that pulls you through. From kitchen to espalier. From gravel circle to soft western hills.
- — Compost systems that close loops. Chickens that feed the soil and the spirit.
- — Raised beds and well-prepared soil that turn sunlight into garden offerings.
- — Vertical growing. Working with structure. Restraint that makes room for abundance.
- — The principle that every square metre earns its place.

What I reimagined:

- — Orchard zones became espaliered boundaries. Repetition along the fence line.
- — A converted shipping container workshop space became a driveway courtyard studio.
- — Line-of-sight thinking, reinterpreted through a smaller garden. From the gravel circle to the soft western hills beyond.
- — Compost bays became sculptural composting towers.
- — Privacy became permeability.
- — Scale became system.

What surprised me:

- — How generous a small space can be.
- — How quickly a garden can grow if you prepare the ground properly.
- — How deeply people respond to something that feels possible.

It's not just about constraint. It's about recalibration. Reconnection. Realising that I didn't have to scale back my thinking, just the footprint.

Little Cottage on a Hill doesn't try to be Oak & Monkey Puzzle. It doesn't need to. It carries the lessons and lets them breathe. Everything is sharper. There's no fluff. No filler. Just a deeply designed, deeply lived space that gives more than it asks.

It's not a downscale; it's a distillation. And it's changed the way I see everything.

Below _Secateurs in hand. What I prune or cut from the garden is returned as mulch or compost, creating a closed-loop system. ***Bottom*** _Purple coneflower (*Echinacea purpurea*) seed heads are gathered for their seeds. Today's cutback becomes tomorrow's plants.

Closing the loop

A closed-loop garden system ensures that waste is reduced and no resources are lost. At Little Cottage on a Hill, everything that leaves my hand – offcuts, peels, faded foliage – goes back into the system; it's just how I like to work, and it feels right. I feel responsible for the waste I create. Yes, sometimes it goes into the green-waste bin, but mostly I try to deal with my waste on-site and close the loop whenever I can.

Every wicking bed has a worm tunnel buried in it. I drop in scraps and walk away. The worms do the rest: breaking down organic matter, building fertility from within. There's no hauling compost across the garden. No extra bins. The beds feed themselves. The soil stays alive. The loop is closed. Wicking-bed water overflow also contains plant-nourishing worm wee, so that gets collected and shared around.

The paths compost, too. I use bark mulch between the beds, but not just for cohesion. It's a chop-and-drop system. The mulch breaks down gradually underfoot, adding structure and life to the soil. It softens the garden. Grounds the raised beds. And once the mulch has decomposed, it gets scooped up as compost to top up the beds. Then new bark mulch starts the cycle all over again.

No-dig gardening isn't a method; it's a mindset (see pages 205–10). English no-dig educator Charles Dowding's voice is in my head every time I top up a bed. Feed the soil, and the soil feeds the garden. Grow good soil, and the soil will grow the plants! It's that simple. At Little Cottage on a Hill, every input is as local as I can source. Composted goat manure (thanks, Rosie!). Kitchen scraps. Mushroom compost. All layered in no-dig beds.

The systems aren't hidden; they're celebrated. The worm tunnels. The compost towers. The mulch. They're not tucked away behind a screen. They're part of the garden's rhythm. Part of the visual language. Part of the invitation to think differently about what a garden can be.

It's not a closed loop just for the sake of sustainability. It's a closed loop because it works. Because it's alive. Because it belongs here.

THE WAY I APPROACHED THE GARDEN

In the first weeks at Little Cottage on a Hill, I did almost nothing. Not by choice. The car accident had left me injured, and I had strict instructions not to lift anything heavier than a kettle. That was a hard adjustment. I'm not someone who sits still easily, but it turned out to be a gift in disguise. Because, instead of action, I had time to walk the site, again and again. To watch how the light moved. To track the shadows of trees across the gravel. To sit on the front step and see where my eye was drawn. I watched people pass, imagined the seasons, noted the slope, the drainage, the views. I noticed.

That forced stillness shaped everything that came after. I didn't rush to build the garden. I learned it first. And when I did begin, I started with what was most visible: the verge.

It was the easiest place to begin logistically, but it was also the most exposed. That tension pushed me to think carefully about how I'd use it. I wasn't just planting the verge. I was planting a message. Not as a statement. Just in that calm, confident way that a garden speaks.

I started at the boundaries. With 27 metres (89 feet) of unsightly fence to reckon with, I knew that I wanted to obscure it, soften it, use it. But I also needed to respect the local council's nature-strip planting guidelines and maintain space for a possible future footpath. (I dearly hope it never eventuates!) So, I started thinking vertically. The first things planted were the espaliered fruit trees along the northern fence. It became a way to house an entire orchard on a flat plane. Two layers: quinces (*Cydonia oblonga* 'Smyrna') and pears (*Pyrus communis* 'Bonne de Maline' and *P. c.* 'Doyenné du Comice') along the top half, step-over Huonville crabapples (*Malus* sp.) underneath. Sometimes, that's how design happens. You look at a fence and see layered rows of fruit trees instead.

On the western verge, I dug out a ring of *Agapanthus* plants from around the silver birch (*Betula pendula*), lifted its canopy by removing the low branches, and designed the gravel circle and wide path that now hold the entire axis of that space. It was one of the first real design decisions at Little Cottage on a Hill: to let the tree stay off-centre, and instead shape the space and path to embrace it.

I marked out beds with builder's string and spray paint, and measured clearances for wheelbarrow access. I made sure that every line I drew was human-scaled, manageable, readable. Nothing gratuitous. Nothing oversized for the sake of drama. This would come in drifts of purple coneflowers (*Echinacea purpurea*) and plume poppies (*Macleaya cordata*), not in overbuilt paths or hard structures.

Vertical thinking in small gardens

I didn't have space to spread out. So I went up. Not in a flashy way. Just in a quiet, structural, necessary way, where every vertical surface became an invitation.

- A new idea of double-layered espaliered fruit trees got me curious. Could I stack them one above the other and get more real estate bang for my buck? Yes! This softened the fence, gave rhythm to the garden, and put the whole harvest on a vertical plane.
- Mesh is more than a support; it's a design device. I use rusted steel mesh in the wicking beds, not just for climbing plants to use, but to extend the growing surface, to lift the visual line, and to add texture and height. It makes the space feel taller than it is. Fuller. But not heavy.
- Sun capture isn't just about orientation, it's about elevation. The raised wicking beds are composed of full-height intermediate bulk containers (IBCs) with their tops cut off. This brings the growing surface closer to the sun. The black cladding holds warmth. And the climbing crops reach for the light. The wicking beds have become a useful microclimate.
- Planting height is a layering strategy. Not everything is flat or low. There are the English box (*Buxus sempervirens*) balls, the erect Lebanese crabapples (*Malus trilobata*), the tall grasses. They all play a role: marking space, catching light, holding rhythm. It's how you get a garden that feels generous, even when the footprint is narrow.

In a small garden, verticality isn't a feature. It's a necessity. And it's part of the choreography.

Above left_Common beans (*Phaseolus vulgaris*) climbing a reclaimed steel reinforcing-mesh arbour on the northern verge, using height instead of ground space.
Above middle_A *Cucurbita maxima* 'Coventry' pumpkin, grown on the same structure in the narrow zone between beds over the grass.
Above right_A young pumpkin (*Cucurbita* sp.) setting fruit while the beans keep climbing, one structure supporting a double-layered crop in a small footprint.

A slow unfolding

The northern and western verges came first. Then the entry garden – the zone between the western verge and the house – tucked inside the fence line. Then the gravel courtyard. Then the wicking-bed garden, between the northern verge and the house. Each zone unfolded based on a mix of necessity and rhythm. What needed water first? What needed structural planting for orientation? What areas could be held off while the weather did its thing? What made sense to do with help, and what could I manage once I could lift more than a kettle?

The wicking beds came after a shock: my first $900 water bill. At Oak & Monkey Puzzle, I'd been on tank and bore water for ten years, and I'd never seen a water bill. Suddenly I was paying for every drop. And I asked myself: is this sustainable? What am I doing here that could be done differently?

In addition, I'd started to grow food plants on the verges. This made sense, as they were open, generous, beautiful. But as the gardens grew and the interactions with people increased, I realised that someone might pinch a tomato or snip a herb, and I never wanted to feel resentful or annoyed if that happened. The verges had to remain open-hearted, so that meant I had to move anything precious behind the fence.

The wicking beds became a way to pull the kitchen garden closer. Not to hide it. Just to honour the relationship I wanted to have with it. These were the plants I interacted with daily. The herbs, the greens, the ingredients for dinner. I wanted them nearby. Easy to reach. Waterwise. Contained. And joyful to look at.

And so the IBC wicking beds were installed along the house side of the northern fence. They were raised high for sunlight and ease, and worm tunnels were integrated into the beds. A bark-mulched ground plane ran in between, and vertical mesh was installed for climbing crops. Every bed was positioned with precision, but not fussiness. I didn't draw plans. I laid it out so it felt right.

The hybrid potting shed and greenhouse came with the studio renovation. A basic extrusion of the existing roofline, it kept the morphology clean. Underneath that roofline sit the propagation zone, the nursery benches, the tool hooks, the chickens. All in one run. Like a little 'Longhouse'. One end for food, one end for life, and the in-between for making and tending.

There was never a masterplan. Only intention, and trust in the process. And something else, too: rhythm. When everything is visible, you think carefully about what happens when. You don't pile compost in a corner to get to later; you build a system that composts as you go. You don't hide the worm farm; you find ways to make it part of the structure and story.

'I approached every zone of this garden not as a stand-alone vignette, but as part of a larger choreography.'

I approached every zone of this garden not as a stand-alone vignette, but as part of a larger choreography. Each element moving in step with the next. Every line leading somewhere. Each material echoing something else. Gravel underfoot. Timber-and-wire fencing. Folded steel mesh for climbing crops. Dark fences to visually recede and to hold the heat.

Each part of the garden was conceived with spatial logic: the northern verge along the roadside; the wicking-bed garden just inside the fence; the entry garden linking the western verge to the house; the gravel courtyard wrapping into the rear garden; the rear edge housing the potting shed, chickens, berries and workspace. Each zone taught me something new about sequencing, rhythm, exposure and constraint.

Creating the garden wasn't fast or flashy. But it was faithful to the site, to the seasons, to my energy. And slowly, the garden began to unfold.

Designing for all seasons

In a small garden, every plant has to do more than one thing. There's no room for one-hit wonders. This garden is built on rhythm. On return. On plants that hold space not just for a moment, but across time. Here are my essentials:

- ***Agastache* 'Liquorice Blue' and *A.* 'Tango'**: Perennial backbones. Long flowering seasons. Offer scent and colour, as well as being magnets for pollinators. A joy to walk past, and gentle punctuations in the rhythm of the verge.
- **great burnet (*Sanguisorba officinalis*)**: Feathery spring growth. Summer spires like wine-red commas hovering in the breeze. Autumn seed heads that stay sculptural through winter's frost. Textural. Resilient. Always doing something.
- ***Penstemon* 'Electric Blue'**: Extended flowering window. Holds its shape without staking. Good colour contrast against grasses and perennials. Returns year after year with minimal intervention.
- **plume poppy (*Macleaya cordata*)**: Tall, architectural foliage. Light, foamy, upright flowers that work at scale. Silvery leaves and russet flowers weave their way through plantings for vertical punctuations. Chosen for height, presence and the way it moves air through the planting.
- **purple coneflower (*Echinacea purpurea*):** Strong through summer. Holds vertical structure in the middle of the growing season. Seed heads stay intact into winter, keeping form and feeding birds. Reliable. Purposeful. Structural.

When I choose a plant, I'm looking for interest across the year. What it offers in spring. How it holds in summer. How it works in winter. It's not about a single moment. It's about staying useful to the space in every season.

A small garden doesn't limit your palette. It just asks much more of every decision.

Top_Red-barked dogwood (*Cornus alba*) against feathery *Calamagrostis* 'Karl Foerster', held for winter colour, structure and cut stems for weaving.
Above_Plume poppy (*Macleaya cordata*) and purple coneflower (*Echinacea purpurea*) are a reliable summer to autumn partnership.

ZONES AND SYSTEMS: LIVING SMALL, LIVING LAYERED

This garden may be small, but it operates like a full ecosystem. Every part has a role. Every metre does something. Nothing is wasted. No zone is idle.

In addition, there's no room to hide the compost or stash the bins or let things get scrappy. So every system had to be designed not only to work, but also to be seen. To be understood as part of the beauty, not separate from it.

Above left_Picking from the western verge, where the planting is as much for cut flowers and seasonal pleasure as it is for productivity.
Above right_The western verge, anchored by an off-centre silver birch (*Betula pendula*) and a gravel circle that give the space its logic. The fire pit is set within a garden that stays visually permeable at the public edge.
Opposite page_The corner where the northern and western verges meet is kept open to comply with council guidelines. Clipped English box (*Buxus sempervirens*) balls hold structure and rhythm through the seasons.

The western verge

This is where the relationship with the street begins. It's public, yes, but not in a showy sense. There's a silver birch (*Betula pendula*) that anchors the space, a gravel circle that holds it, and two large garden beds flanking the wide path that runs to the front gate and entry stairs beyond. These beds are layered with perennials and grasses, such as:

— *Agastache* 'Liquorice Blue'
— *Aster* 'Orpheus'
— Caucasian cornflower (*Psephellus bellus*)
— *Echinacea* 'Magnus Superior'
— *Geum* 'Totally Tangerine'
— *Hylotelephium spectabile* 'Autumn Joy'
— oriental poppy (*Papaver orientale*)
— *Penstemon* 'Electric Blue'
— plume poppy (*Macleaya cordata*)
— Russian sage (*Salvia yangii*)
— *Sanguisorba officinalis* 'St Philibert'
— thyme (*Thymus vulgaris*).

These plants have been chosen for structure, rhythm, movement and multi-seasonal interest. Nearly a thousand bulbs are tucked underneath. The drama is seasonal. The repetition is intentional.

Throughout this zone, clusters of clipped English box (*Buxus sempervirens*) balls are placed into the planting as a juxtaposition to the soft and billowing mix of form, colour and perennial texture. They're evergreen anchors used sparingly but deliberately to create rhythm, hold space and offer visual cohesion during winter.

The entire verge planting was shaped in response to Hepburn Shire Council's nature-strip planting guidelines, which included no hard edges to garden beds, and no raised beds. Instead, the wide, spade-cut beds have open edges, respectful offsets from road infrastructure, and lower-growing plants that won't impact corner visibility or driver sightlines. The guidelines were a constraint but also a creative brief.

On the fence line, I planted step-over espaliered apples: *Malus* 'Cox's Orange Pippin' and *M.* 'Pomme de Neige'. They create a low, edible threshold. Behind them, the visually permeable fence brings a useful transparency that's structural without being severe. It holds climbers, frames the view and gives visual continuity to the planting behind.

Within the gravel circle of the western verge, there's a fire pit because public space should be lived in, not just looked at. And on certain evenings, when the light is soft and the western hills catch fire with the sunset, I sit out there on the large cypress slab. Sometimes with a cup of tea. Sometimes just to watch the sky.

The northern verge

This 27-metre (89-foot), north-facing strip with a slope runs the full length of the property. It began as my kitchen garden. The beds are edged with spade cuts and filled with polyculture plantings: various brassicas and beans, cornflowers (*Centaurea cyanus*), asparagus (*Asparagus officinalis*), sage (*Salvia officinalis*), spring onions (*Allium fistulosum*). No hard edges. No raised beds. Just careful soil prep, mushroom compost, no-dig principles (see pages 205–10) and seasonal rotation.

Plant spotlight: English box (*Buxus sempervirens*) balls

I use these clipped forms sparingly. That's what makes them work. They're not fillers; they're anchors.

In the western verge, they're tucked into the beds in clusters of two or three, marking corners, repeating at just the right intervals so the rhythm carries through all of the seasons. In the entry garden, they sit in the bark mulch, picking up that same repetition and carrying it right through to the wicking-bed garden. And in the driveway courtyard, they're planted directly into the gravel in clusters rather than in lines, set so they read as sculptural weights rather than as hedging.

They hold a space without dominating it. Evergreen, unchanging, but never static. In winter, when the perennials have died back and the grasses have thinned, they hold the shape of the garden. In summer, they're part of the composition, not competing with it. It's a small-scale garden, so every constant counts.

This area, too, was shaped by the council's nature-strip planting guidelines: spatially restrained and height aware; always leaving space for foot traffic, services and the possibility of a future footpath installation. The slope was addressed through careful bed shaping and layering. Nothing here was arbitrary.

Over time, I shifted the crops with higher care needs or value back inside the fence. The verge still grows food. But it's the kind that can tick along reliably. The kind that doesn't ask too much of me or of others.

Along the northern fence, I built a double-layered espaliered orchard: Huonville crabapples (*Malus* sp.) below, pears (*Pyrus communis* 'Bonne de Maline' and *P. c.* 'Doyenné du Comice') and quinces (*Cydonia oblonga* 'Smyrna') above. I'd never seen a double-layered espalier, but I knew that doubling the plane would allow for a tight lower tier and an equally productive upper tier. It has become one of the strongest features in the garden: productive, ordered and deeply satisfying. Every year it fills out a little more. It's an investment in the future and a way to create my own living sculptural wall.

Above left_A quiet moment on the front verandah in the late light, with furry companions Willow and Ivy.
Above right_The entry garden, where mulch forms a continuous ground plane. You move through planting rather than along a path.
Opposite page_The wicking-bed garden: full-height intermediate bulk container (IBC) beds with reinforcing mesh to extend the growing surface upwards.

The entry garden

Just behind the western fence, the entry garden is where planting and movement become blurred. It uses the same species palette as the western verge, but the materiality shifts: the entire ground plane is bark mulch. There are no hard paths here, just mulch and movement. The idea is that, when viewed from the verandah, the planting reads as one continuous composition.

There's no dominant axis in this space. Access moves around and between the plants, loosely following the soft forms. English box (*Buxus sempervirens*) balls are again used here within the mulch to echo the verge and provide architectural rhythm.

The bark mulch that covers the ground becomes a unifying canvas. It runs through the entry garden and continues into the wicking-bed garden, creating one seamless ground plane and softening the transition between zones. It was a deliberate decision, one that lets each element (beds, containers, structures) sit within, rather than compete with, the space.

The wicking-bed garden

Located between the house and the northern verge, the wicking-bed garden is where form meets function. I used full-height intermediate bulk containers (IBCs), clad for thermal mass and visual consistency. The extra height allows me to work in and around the beds while standing upright, a crucial consideration after years of heavy physical labour and the impact of my car accident.

It also lifts the plants into more direct sunlight and creates a microclimate that I hadn't anticipated. The bark mulch, the black cladding and the orientation combine to create a pocket of warmth and shelter. Even after hard frosts, the nasturtiums (*Tropaeolum majus*) still flower here. Vertical mesh for climbing plants adds to the three-dimensionality of the space, making it feel sculptural and seasonal all at once.

Between the beds, the mulch acts as a chop-and-drop composting path. The whole space is rhythmic, productive and easy to tend. These are the plants I interact with daily. The ingredients for dinner. The greens I reach for without even thinking.

Entry garden as visual extension

From the elevated verandah, the lawn between the fence line and western verge planting disappears. That's deliberate.

The entry garden is all about the view from the house. Bark mulch runs across the entire ground plane here, the same as in the wicking-bed garden beyond, and the planting palette mirrors that of the western verge. From the house, this continuity means that the two spaces read as one with no visual break, no disconnection.

There are no obvious paths. Movement happens where planting allows it. You wander through, following the planting rather than being funnelled by an axis. This space fills the gap between the house and the fence without feeling like a separate garden room. From above, from the vantage of the verandah, the entry garden seems to be part of the same sweep as the verge outside. That's the point: visual expansion without adding square metres.

Driveway courtyard: Where gravel meets structure

This is the arrival zone and the working zone, all in one. The surface is gravel right to the edges; there's no mitigation with lawn. It connects to the studio, so the materiality runs right through. Clusters of English box (*Buxus sempervirens*) balls are planted directly into the gravel here, echoing their use elsewhere in the garden and holding the space without blocking movement.

The Lebanese crabapple (*Malus trilobata*) stands just before the fence line on the southern edge, canopy lifted high enough so car doors can open underneath. It gives upright structure and seasonal change – autumn colour, winter tracery, spring blossoms – without creating shade that would rob light from the nearby planting. Behind it, the fence is layered with silver vein creeper (*Parthenocissus henryana*) and *Clematis* 'Huldine', softening the line and adding seasonal movement.

The driveway courtyard has to work hard. But it must still sit within the garden's rhythm. The gravel, the plant repetition and the lifted tree canopy work together to make the space part of the whole garden, so it doesn't look like an afterthought.

The inner garden

This also includes the driveway courtyard and the rear garden. The driveway courtyard wraps around the studio and softens the transition between driveway and garden. The edges of the courtyard feature English box (*Buxus sempervirens*) balls planted directly into the gravel, a subtle gesture that brings structure without heaviness. Repetition and placement make the difference. The box balls mark the corners, hold the rhythm and feel deliberate without shouting.

Alongside these is a perimeter planting of fastigiate (narrow, upright) Lebanese crabapples (*Malus trilobata*) that punctuate the garden, providing productive verticality without dominating the area. They stand like sentinels, allowing cars to park, doors to be opened and depth to be achieved even in the smallest of spaces. They gift me unique cut leaves and autumn glory that sings a symphony alongside the autumn colours of *Clematis* 'Huldine' and the silver vein creeper (*Parthenocissus henryana*) cloaking the rusty mesh frame attached to the black-painted fence line.

The rear garden

This is still evolving. It's currently home to the last patch of lawn (a non-functional compromise for my kids); a sprawling cherry laurel (*Prunus laurocerasus*), which provides too much shade and drops toxic berries; and a zone I'm still learning how to resolve. There's potential here. But for now, it holds tension. And that's part of the story, too.

The fence lines

Along the perimeter fence lines, every surface is growing. The southern boundary of the driveway courtyard holds silver vein creeper (*Parthenocissus henryana*) and *Clematis* 'Huldine'. The eastern fence is home to thornless blackberry (*Rubus ulmifolius*), an old apple (*Malus* sp.), yuzu (*Citrus × junos*) and persimmon (*Diospyros kaki*).

The back of the northern fence – where the espaliered orchard lives – also hosts *Philadelphus* 'Silver Showers', lots of climbing roses (such as *Rosa* 'Abraham Darby', *R.* 'Bathsheba' and *R.* 'Crepuscule') and *Clematis* 'Rooguchi'. Every boundary is softened. Every line is layered.

The potting shed

Tucked beneath the extended roofline of the studio, the potting shed is used as a nursery, workspace and greenhouse, as well as for storage. It's where propagation happens, where seed trays sit in the filtered light and warmth, where tools are kept within easy reach. The chickens live adjacent to the far end, under the same roof. It's a simple, elegant structure that evolved as the garden did.

THINGS TO REMEMBER

Nothing here is accidental. But nothing is overdesigned. It's a system. A flow. A garden that offers beauty, yes, but also practicality, resilience and abundance.

Plants weren't chosen for beauty alone. They were selected for rhythm, performance and utility. Jac Semmler might call them 'high-performance plants'. Lily Langham would call them 'triple whammies'. I just call them honest. They earn their place; they offer more than they take. And the garden continues to change. Because I do. This is what the Cottage on a Hill garden teaches us:

- Constraint is a design tool, not a compromise. The trick is to work with it, not against it.
- Every element should serve more than one role: beauty, yield, rhythm, structure.
- Observation before action creates better long-term outcomes.
- Public-facing gardens can be generous without losing personal value.

Fence lines that expand space

Solid fences enclose a garden. Timber-and-wire fencing opens it up.

Along the western boundary, the timber-and-wire fencing holds climbers and frames the planting behind. It doesn't block the view; it extends it. From inside, your eye runs through the planting and past the fence, catching layers of green beyond. From the street, the transparency draws you in rather than shutting you out.

It's a small garden, so visual permeability matters. A solid wall would make the space feel tight. Timber-and-wire fencing, layered with perennials, gives depth. The fence isn't just a boundary, it's part of the planting composition. It's a structural element that disappears into the garden's rhythm.

Opposite page_The driveway as a courtyard, widened into a working forecourt for the studio, where cars, gatherings and workshops share the same gravel ground plane.
Above left_The driveway courtyard in front of the studio is designed to be multipurpose and expansive. Gravelled right to the edges, it has English box (*Buxus sempervirens*) balls planted straight into the stone, and boundary planting layered against the black-painted fence.

Designing with constraints

I didn't start with a blank canvas. I started with rules. With injuries. With tired arms. With time pressure, council guidelines, slope, shade, street frontage and kids needing space to belong. But here's the thing: constraint doesn't limit or close down design. It clarifies and opens up possibilities.

- **Nature-strip rules aren't a hurdle:** They're a brief. The Hepburn Shire Council planting guidelines told me: no raised beds, no solid garden edges, no permanent structures, no sightline interruptions, no blocking of services or impeding possible future footpaths. So I created offsets, planted wide spade-cut beds, kept the edges open, layered low plants at the corners. And that made the design stronger, considered, cohesive.
- **I sequenced the garden to my ability:** After my car accident, I couldn't lift heavy objects. So the first zones I created were the ones I could reach without much effort. The verge. Then the entry. Then the wicking beds. Recovery shaped rhythm. And that rhythm gave the garden its spine.
- **Shade, slope and setbacks were part of the choreography:** The driveway had to stay open. Car doors needed clearance. Trees couldn't impede circulation or access. So I lifted the canopy on the Lebanese crabapple (*Malus trilobata*), chose the eastern fence for additional espaliered fruit trees, and found the microclimates by living with the site.
- **Every metre had to do something:** There's no filler here. No feature beds for their own sake. Everything has a purpose: yield, shade, structure, softness, privacy, rhythm. It's not about cramming more in. It's about doing more with what you've got.

Western verge at Little Cottage on a Hill. The grass path and the gravel edge are held open for a possible future footpath, with the garden shaped around the negative space. Nature-strip rules are a brief, not a hurdle.

A workshop moment on the western verge, where the garden is both public-facing planting and a demonstration space, shaped by constraint and lived in every day.

A RUMINATION ON THE GARDEN

Every time I drive up Wombat Hill, there's a point where the corner block slips into view. First the open grassed corner, then the colour, texture and form against a mown ground plane, then the silhouette of a climbing structure, the backdrop of silver birch shimmer, the fence. Finally, the whole garden reveals itself. And each time, a wave of contentment washes over me. This is home, yes. A town block doing more than it should by any sensible measure, and yet here we are.

When the workshops first started, I was nervous. Anxious, in fact. I wondered whether this space was enough for people to feel it was worth their while, worth their hard-earned money. It was a clever rural suburban block, but it certainly wasn't grand or expansive like Oak & Monkey Puzzle. The garden was so new, with smaller bones, closer held; every decision and every corner was visible. Oak & Monkey Puzzle caught your breath, like walking into the realm of Narnia; it felt otherworldly, extraordinary. This was just a little cottage on a hill.

I wasn't sure if 515 square metres (5545 square feet) could support everything that 5 acres could. But gosh, I was willing to give it a good try.

Design for the life you live

Country living hasn't gone anywhere; it's just more embedded, integrated. Condensed into small moments. Held by the seasons and the soil. The light tells me what to do. The wind does, too. I know when the sap's rising; I feel it in my bones before I see it. I notice when the Japanese apricot (*Prunus mume*) starts to blossom in August because it's too early. It's a note I file away in the body first, the diary second. Will winter actually be too short? It's not time to wish the cold away. Twelve country-life years in and I'm not ready for winter to end. I imagined a lot but never that!

People stop. They take photos, ask the name of this or that. Some share the contribution this garden now makes to their lives, their daily rituals, always slowing down right here to see what's happening, what's changed. Someone leaves cherries on Christmas Eve with a note. A compliance officer says to keep going. A kid on a scooter with his black hoodie shrouding his face points at the espalier and asks what kind of tree makes lines like that. These are the exchanges a small, visible garden sets in motion. This is the work as much as the planting.

My dear friend Pip (Phyllida) saw it the way I hope strangers will: not as a neat trick, but as generosity under constraint. The edges pushed out without stealing anything that isn't ours.

So, what does this place prove? That scale is a frame. That rhythm can do more than square metres. That a fence can be an orchard. That a mulched path can work as a slow-acting compost bin. That beauty can be put to work, and utility can be beautiful. Not as a slogan, just as the way things are built when you refuse to hide the doing.

I said at the start: if I have soil, sun, water and fresh air, what more do I need? Not much as it turns out. Enough is plenty when you design for the life you actually live.

From here, we travel from making to inhabiting. Rhythm, light, season and movement are not ideas on a plan, but the daily reality of how a garden feels and what it makes possible. That's Chapter 9. For now, I'm at the gate, looking out, watching a small place hold a big life, and thinking that beginning again wasn't starting over. It was carrying what mattered and letting it take root where I stand.

Opposite page_A candid moment with my son, Oliver, in the wicking-bed garden, the day's harvest piled high on the bench, all from a small space designed for the life we live.

PHYLLIDA STEELE-WAREHAM COMES TO VISIT

When someone visits your garden and sees it for the first time, they often discern things that you've stopped noticing, and sometimes they spot things that you didn't realise were there at all. When writer and gardener Phyllida Steele-Wareham came to Little Cottage on a Hill, she captured it in ways that surprised me. Her words hold the threads of this place – its scale, its rhythm, its generosity – and they remind me of what it means to begin again. I'm honoured to share her thoughts here.

PHYLLIDA STEELE-WAREHAM

Reflection

I have butterflies on my way to visit Natasha's new home and garden, Little Cottage on a Hill, because I know that I am going to step out of my car and into something special. It's what Natasha does, and from all I have seen online of the new haven Natasha is creating on a small corner block around a quaint white cottage, on the edges of picturesque Daylesford, I know that the true magic will lie in the detail, and that there will be a lot of it.

I visit twice in early autumn to try to capture Natasha's new creation. The air has begun to pinch at my cheeks with a clue to the cold that will arrive in Daylesford in the coming months, sitting just over 300 metres (1000 feet) higher than where we are at Moorfield, yet only a 45-minute drive away. The light is crystalline and catches the feathery tips of a dense wall of *Miscanthus* 'Yakushima Dwarf', glinting madly in the sun. It makes you smile as it greets you, the living division that it is between the verge and the road, your first hint that there is magic to this place, your first hint that this garden has been created by someone who understands plants and how to use them to their maximum potential.

What you might miss within the dense floriferousness of *Miscanthus* at peak high summer/autumn growth is that interspersed between it is red-barked dogwood (*Cornus alba*). A plant that holds the crown for looking the most impressive, in my book, in winter when it has lost all its leaves, and so has mostly everything else, if your garden is largely deciduous or perennial. Left to stay, against the bitter cold, are unmissable clusters of upright, vibrant red stems that burn hot on an otherwise muted landscape, a relief to a winter-weary eye. And therein lies your first inkling of the level of thoughtfulness and expertise lying in this once unremarkable suburban block. When the *Miscanthus* is cut back, you're not left with the coarse stumps of its wintry slumber and the impatience for it to fill back out, but rather a show that is equally impressive and unexpected.

'Little Cottage on a Hill is so beautiful from the street that I imagine it might send most drivers, not expecting to see it, careening off the bitumen.'

Little Cottage on a Hill is so beautiful from the street that I imagine it might send most drivers, not expecting to see it, careening off the bitumen. As one ascends the hill and drops over the top of it on the road that runs off the Daylesford main drag and skirts the Wombat Hill Botanic Gardens, it is impossible not to notice Natasha's new home, place of work and where her many gardening and lifestyle workshops are held, a practice brought with her from Oak & Monkey Puzzle. It is stunning, as you might expect from such a highly trained and practised landscape architect. A small white cottage sits within walls of garden, both ornamental and productive, but it's something else that makes this place extra special in the world of regional urban gardens – nay all urban gardens – that first strikes you as it comes into view: how sagaciously and resourcefully it pushes its own boundaries, quite literally.

It is genius how Natasha uses the deep corner verge she could have easily ignored, or seen as an obvious end to her garden, like most people would have and do, but then Natasha's gardens reflect her own tenacity. Like their maker, they are clever, layered and well considered. Little Cottage on a Hill almost screams at the passer-by that this is a place to be enjoyed, be you human or insect or bird, or any other living thing. One cannot help but be enveloped in its generosity, and I imagine that it exudes this energy out into the streets and homes around it.

It beckons us all to explore not just a garden, but the idea of what is possible. I suspect that for many folks who live on smaller municipal blocks, who happen by or mean to arrive at this epicentre of biodiversity and beauty in country suburbia, it is a light-bulb moment. For when space is not your privilege, this need not be seen as an impediment to creativity or to the variation and abundance in what you can grow.

***Below left*_**Phyllida Steele-Wareham visiting Little Cottage on a Hill.
***Below right*_**A glimpse through to the wicking-bed garden, photographed by Phyllida.

9

CREATING A GARDEN EXPERIENCE

I stop gardening and stand still, struck by the beauty of it all. These are the moments I live for, design for, the ones that can only be experienced by being in the garden, not passing through it on the way to somewhere else.

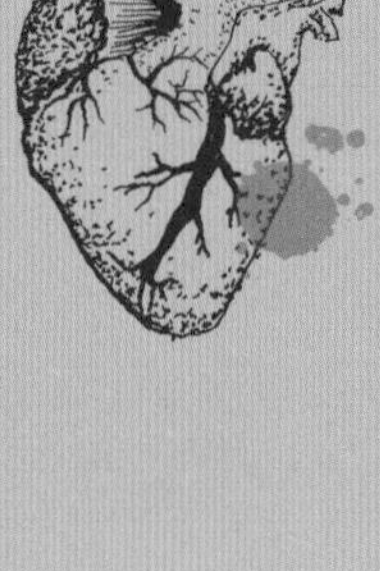

MOVEMENT WITH MEANING

In earlier chapters, we've looked at the mechanics of design, how to think spatially and how to plan for seasonal abundance. Here, we move into the layer that holds all of that together: inhabitation. How a garden is lived in, not just how it is made. Because no matter how beautiful or well considered and executed a design is, its true worth lies in the quality of life it supports once the tools are down.

This is not the same as 'styling' a space. Styling can be applied after the fact, like a garnish or a decoration. Experience is designed from the beginning. It's in the position of a bench so that the winter sun finds your chest. It's in the choice to widen a path just before a view opens, so the body feels the change in pace and can't help but slow down. It's in planting a drift of English lavender (*Lavandula angustifolia*) by the front gate because you want to smell it every time you brush past it when it's in bloom.

When I dreamed up my Melbourne Food and Wine Festival Regional Longest Lunches at Oak & Monkey Puzzle, the 154 guests didn't arrive through the front gate. They were ushered from their cars at the forest's edge towards the far end of the property, and they walked along the old fire track, taking in the sounds and scents of the Wombat State Forest. They arrived at and were held by the gravel circle (the previous owner's round yard, I presume, used for breaking horses), where they were greeted with cocktails and canapés, away from the sight of the day's hero: the formal garden. A sense of anticipation built up before the guests were finally escorted towards the long tables set out within the central garden, where they were treated to dishes by chefs from five different restaurants, the best local produce and the finest wines.

Melbourne Food and Wine Festival Regional Longest Lunch at Oak & Monkey Puzzle. The lawn spine became a procession to the long table, in a garden designed to expand, host and add meaning to movement.

Above left to right_Melbourne Food and Wine Festival Regional Longest Lunch at Oak & Monkey Puzzle. The gravel circle hosted cocktails and canapés as the first pause before the long lunch. Foraged hawthorn branches and rosehips decorated the table and filled wheelbarrows, shaping the whole experience.

Orchestrating a transformative arrival

You don't need an event, a forest or a country estate to shape arrival. Begin by imagining how you want people to feel in those very first impressionable moments. Do you want them to be led on a journey, to exhale, become curious, feel held, look up, smile? Let that intention steer what comes next. Consider these three steps that work at any scale:

1. **Threshold:** Think about the act of entering. Does it involve a gate latch to open, a corner to turn, a small change in materiality underfoot that signals you are arriving?
2. **Hold:** Offer a brief pause before the reveal. An overlap in a hedge that only gives way to the entry once you're close enough to discern it. A widened landing, a shift in the rhythm of elements, a place where air slows and scent lingers long enough to be noticed.
3. **Reveal:** Open the view so the eye lands cleanly. One anchor is enough: a framed garden bed, a long sightline, a single tree catching the light.

Reflect on the experience of the garden as you move through and inhabit it. Crunch slows the step, while mulch softens it. Place fragrance where people pause, not where they rush. Backlight one element at the reveal so the eye knows where to land. Give the hand a place to land: a touch point such as a smooth timber handrail.

Design that first half-minute of arrival with intention, and then let the path, the pause and the reveal do the quiet work.

Transforming a garden entrance

The design of the garden at Oak & Monkey Puzzle employed the same sort of thinking about arrival and movement at its core. The converted shipping container that hosted workshops wasn't just located at the garden's edge because that was the easiest place for a crane to lower it. This spot also overlooked the main formal garden, offering a vantage point across the terraces, and was a 'bridge' to the Wombat State Forest backdrop; the glassed end behind the freestanding fireplace transported visitors deep into the forest's heart. The orchard wasn't just situated between the formal garden and paddocks for ease of access, or to take in the light. It provided a visual gradient between the most highly designed spaces and the more naturalistic qualities of the landscape beyond.

At Little Cottage on a Hill, with its smaller footprint, the principle is the same but the cues are finer: the apertures of the fence line define the threshold between public and private, but they also allow the lived experience of the garden to spread far beyond the 515 square metres (5545 square feet) of the cottage's own extent. Here, inside and outside merge. A little cottage on a hill feels expansive and invites you not just onto the verge, but along the sightline of the rolling hills and evening sunset beyond. A monolithic slab of cypress wood takes on the role of a seat, the respite between time and place, between garden and the last light of a glowing golden sunset. With their conical form and lifted canopy, Lebanese crabapples (*Malus trilobata*) act like sentinels along the driveway courtyard, giving even the shortest walk a sense of arrival.

Morning light along the northern verge, a long planted edge that turns the road into an arrival sequence rather than a boundary.

DESIGNING FOR EXPERIENCE, NOT JUST OUTCOME

When I talk about a garden's 'experience', I mean the sum of what it gives you when you're in it: how it engages your body, your senses and your emotions over time. It's the difference between looking at a space and fully feeling the visceral impact of the space on you; between admiring the composition from a distance and noticing the warmth of a wall on your back, the smell of lemon verbena (*Aloysia citriodora*) as you brush past, the way your pace changes instinctively. This chapter is about shaping those lived encounters that root you to a place in ways that photographs never can.

Designing for experience means shaping spaces that reveal themselves over the years, not just in the first weeks after planting. It's not about a single, frozen image, it's about creating a rhythm in which you can live.

Rhythm comes from more than planting repetition. It's in the alternation of open and enclosed spaces, the predictability of certain scents or colours in particular months, and the places you always seem to stop, whether to take in a view, greet a neighbour or watch a bee work its way through a smorgasbord of perennial blooms. Repetition anchors the body in a place; it creates familiarity rather than routine.

At Little Cottage on a Hill, the verge garden was designed with this in mind. It isn't a boundary to keep people out, it's an invitation to step closer. The planting leans towards the street, safely spilling scent and texture into the public space. In spring, passers by brush against billowing grasses and hear the constant hum of bees. In summer, various beans (*Phaseolus* spp.) and pumpkins (*Cucurbita* spp.) clamber across steel-mesh structures and wire A-frames, their rhythm echoing down the length of the space and pulling visitors visually into the verge. The garden asks for interaction; in return, it gives a sensory and seductive moment to anyone who walks past.

At Oak & Monkey Puzzle, the principle showed up differently. There, scale allowed for long approaches and wide sightlines, so I used seating as a cue to linger. Benches were placed where the light was filtered in late afternoon, or where the lawn spine terminated at the garden's end, creating a quiet place to look back on the house rather than from within it. These weren't afterthoughts; they were part of the garden's bones, spaces imagined, considered and set during design so they would feel almost inevitable when you found them.

***Opposite page*_**A vertical pumpkin (*Cucurbita* sp.) arbour on the northern verge. Edible and ornamental plants share the same frame, growing upwards and overhead so the garden feels deeper than its footprint.

'At Little Cottage on a Hill, the verge is my most public room . . . The line between street and garden has softened so neighbours slow, look, ask and sometimes linger.'

Turning a boundary into an invitation

At Little Cottage on a Hill, the verge is my most public room. I built a visually permeable fence that frames the inner edge of the property but doesn't shut it out. Billowing grasses lean out to brush passing sleeves. Climbing vegies clamber up light A-frames. In spring, the hum of bees meets people before I do. The line between street and garden has softened so neighbours slow, look, ask and sometimes linger.

Begin by picturing how you want your street edge to feel in the first half minute: quiet welcome, seasonal theatre, edible commons, simple calm. Let that intention guide the moves. These three prompts will work at any scale:

1. **Signal:** Mark a clear yet permeable edge. A low fence, a clipped line, a simple gate within a generously spaced picket fence that you need to open to enter. Show that intention and a sense of deep care live here while providing a gentle yet considered invitation to the 'outside' world.
2. **Share:** Offer a small gesture at the threshold between public and private. Herbs where a hand can reach. A single beautiful flowering climber on a light frame that smiles outward. A modest sign that says, 'Feel free to pick one'.
3. **Safeguard:** Keep your most precious crops inside the fence, where you can tend, water and net them. Think about where you place seating, both inside and outside the fence line, either for communal chats or for private reflective time. Protect your calm as much as you share. Find the balance that feels right for you.

You don't need an expansive frontage. You need a coherent and considered edge that invites a sense of exchange and generosity, physically or visually, while respecting what you want and can offer publicly or privately. Shape the verge to convey your invitation, then let the materials, plants and small gestures facilitate the everyday conversations.

Clipping as choreography. This small seasonal task keeps the verge structure legible.

Benefits of design for experience

It matters just as much in small domestic gardens as it does in public landscapes or therapeutic settings. In hospitals, aged-care facilities and community spaces, design for experience has been shown to lower stress, improve recovery times and foster social connection. At home, the same principles apply; they simply take on a more personal scale. A garden designed for experience will meet you where you are, on the days you're full of energy as well as during those times when you can do no more than stand and breathe deeply for ten minutes.

Ultimately, designing for experience is an act of generosity. It acknowledges that a garden's life is not just in its productivity or visual appeal, but in how it shapes the days of the people who inhabit it. This is what makes a garden somewhere you want to return to, again and again. Not because it needs you, but because it offers you something new and nourishing each time you step into it.

Design for experience is as much about what happens inside you as it is about what happens in the space. A widened path before a view doesn't just look generous, it physically feels expansive and slows your breath. Sitting on a bench in the winter sun doesn't only offer delicate warmth to the skin, it also lifts the mood and mutes racing thoughts.

Where in your garden do you always halt without thinking? How could you design more of those moments on purpose?

DYNAMIC AND SPATIAL CHOREOGRAPHY

Gardens teach the body before the mind catches up. A narrow path gathers you in; a widening path opens your chest. A clipped threshold curbs your stride; an expansion across gravel asks you to look up. When done well, movement is designed less like a corridor and more like a piece of music: tempo, rest, crescendo, release.

At Little Cottage on a Hill, I lean on that sequence. The western verge begins at its heart with the generous gravel circle. A path cuts through it from the front door to the verge, but the silver birch (*Betula pendula*) we inherited with the property sits slightly off-centre in the gravel so the path effectively splits around it. That gentle deflection is enough to make you notice the tree, to register the sound of your steps shifting on the gravel screenings, to glance at the shadows thrown by the canopy. The cypress slab seat is anchored there, too, a deliberate pause point in one of the most public parts of the property, set within a space that belongs to the garden but also to the street. Even in a small footprint, you can choreograph pace: narrow enough to draw you in, expansive enough to hold you for a while.

Texture does some of the work. Your choice of ground-plane material makes you aware of your steps. A brush of thyme (*Thymus vulgaris*) on your ankle is a soft signal to reduce speed. Sound shifts, too: birds are louder in enclosure, the wind is more present as you tread into open light. This is circulation as lived rhythm, not just access.

Bank House balance

When I consider containment and reveal at the scale of a country garden, I think of Bank House in Newlyn (see pages 70–3). Andrew Lowth and Nigel Smith say it plainly: 'We didn't draw anything up . . . we just lived it.' The garden was made incrementally, room by room, over many years, which is why the movement feels learned rather than imposed. 'We thought it would take two years. It took twenty,' Andrew says, and the generosity of that timeline shows in how the body is guided through the garden without being pushed. 'It gives me a reason to keep going outside.'

From the road there is no fanfare. The garden hides behind the house. You enter through an arch in a box leaf privet (*Ligustrum undulatum*) hedge, and the sequence begins: the stone terrace with its four formal parterre beds; the threshold in a European hornbeam (*Carpinus betulus*) hedge that tightens the frame; the anteroom of Scots roses; the pear walk that pulls you up the slope to antique iron gates on the skyline. To the sides, other rooms open on cue: the vegetable garden; the autumn garden, with its swaying grasses; the hornbeam walk; and the woodland, where bluebells (*Hyacinthoides non-scripta*) have naturalised in swathes. The structure edits your attention; the sequence calibrates your pace.

What I admire in Andrew and Nigel's work is how they use hedging as architecture to make thresholds you feel before you see the reveal. It's a language that sits comfortably in an Australian rural setting but carries the resonance of English gardens they have visited, interpreted entirely through their own site and experience. The design lesson translates anywhere:

— **Define the narrow:** Create a deliberate constriction in the space (a hedge corridor, an arch, a path pinch point) so that the body registers intimacy, focus or anticipation.

— **Protect the quiet:** Hold that enclosed or contained space long enough so that the visitor settles into it; this becomes a place of hiatus, safety or calm before the next change.

— **Let the view go:** Open the space out to an expansive view, light or wider volume. The release is felt physically and emotionally because of the preceding containment.

This pattern has become a shorthand within their composition, a rhythm of funnelling, holding and revealing that repeats through the garden.

Scale, sound and structure

Scan to hear my full conversation with Andrew Lowth and Nigel Smith, where we talk about hedging and garden rooms as architecture for thresholds, containment and reveal; following desire lines; and letting the garden teach the route.

Scale changes how you write the same sentence. In a large rural setting, you can stretch the phrase: a long, lightly crowned walk; a clipped passage that opens to an orchard; a bench placed exactly where the slope slackens, so the body registers 'arrival'. In a small urban garden, a change in path material, a half-height hedge or a single held view can do the work that a long axis does in an expansive country setting. Either way, you're composing movement with containment, expansion and reveal. And when you get it right, people don't talk about the path at all. They talk about how the place makes them feel.

Sound is part of this choreography. In narrow rooms, you notice close sounds: insect hums braided with the brush of grass against corduroy pants. In open volumes,

ambient sound expands: wind tracking across a hedge face, birdsong carrying from a neighbouring tree canopy. Your ear takes the cue, and your body follows.

At Oak & Monkey Puzzle, transitions were long enough to register as journeys. The enclosed forest precinct held you in filtered shade, then the mown pathway released you into open meadow, with a change in light and sky that you felt as much as saw. In that shift, there was a physiological response: a small lift in the breath, an easing in the step. It's the same release you get at Bank House when moving from the tight hornbeam walk into the pear walk's long, clean view.

Bank House shows how structure sets tempo while planting sets phrasing. The hedges keep time; the herbaceous and grass layers add syncopation. The parterre promises patterned stillness in one season and buoyant colour in another; the autumn garden adds softness and sway. The hornbeam walk is a measured interlude between more declarative spaces; the woodland loosens the score. It's 'controlled romanticism' that is layered and generous without tipping into chaos.

Designing movement in this way is a commitment to be taught by the site, by the weather and by the return. It's why the walk never gets old. It's why a small space can feel generous, and a large one can feel intimate. And it's why, when you arrive at a seat with your back protected and your view set, the body understands without being told that this is where it can rest and enjoy the vista.

Whether it's a clipped hedge walk on a country estate or a single espaliered fruit tree leading you down a narrow terrace path, the principle is the same: define, protect, release. The scale may change, but the body's small shift in pace, that readiness for what comes next, remains universal.

Walk your garden as if for the first time. Where does your body speed up or slow down? Where could you heighten or inject impact?

Bank House in Newlyn, Victoria. Hedges are used as architecture, shaping a sequence of garden rooms along a clear axis. Each threshold compresses the space, edits the view, then releases you into light and depth, so your body registers arrival before your eyes take in the next reveal.

SEASONAL CHOREOGRAPHY AND TEMPORALITY

Tim Pilgrim works in a naturalistic style (see pages 111–12). His planting looks effortless, but it's underpinned by deliberate planning and an eye for seasonal rhythm. He thinks in successions: not just spring colour or summer height, but how each combination moves through emergence, fullness and decline. 'It's not all about the flowers, it's the whole picture, and it changes through the seasons,' Tim says. 'You've got to think about what's coming next, not just the moment you're in.'

In his borders, one plant hands over to the next with no abrupt cut. The rhythm is seasonal but also day-to-day: in the morning light, grasses read as soft haze; in the low sun of evening, the same planting flares into gold. Imperfection isn't an accident, it's an ingredient: seed heads left for frost, stems left to catch dew, gaps left for self-sown seedlings to test their luck.

At Little Cottage on a Hill, I see the same arcs on a smaller stage. In late autumn, the silver birch (*Betula pendula*) leaves fall like coins across the gravel circle: bright gold for a day or two, then curling into copper that crunches underfoot. After the first frost, purple coneflower (*Echinacea purpurea*) seed heads go from orange-umber to black almost overnight. On a warm morning in late February, the smell of the soil after rain (petrichor) is so deep and visceral that it makes me want to kneel and press my hands into the ground. These are moments you can't order from a nursery catalogue; you have to be there, at the right time, to experience them.

Rhonda's Garden in Central Victoria, designed by Tim Pilgrim. His naturalistic planting offers seasonal choreography, with each combination moving through emergence, fullness and decline rather than being held at a single peak. Grasses, seed heads and stems are left to speak, so the garden carries structure and atmosphere from morning to evening, and from late summer to winter.

At Oak & Monkey Puzzle, I learned the discipline of waiting through a full cycle before changing anything. The first year, I left the Chinese wisteria (*Wisteria sinensis*) to flower without interference. Its one-week window in spring was well worth the patience; buds fattened over months, then suddenly strings of blooms draped the verandah like poured silk. In the European hornbeam (*Carpinus betulus*) meadow, the trees forming the central axis held their leaves long into winter, their russet crowns a warm counterpoint to the pale trunks of the silver birches (*Betula pendula*) behind them. You could feel the garden drawing inwards, holding its energy until spring.

The value of transience

Daily temporality is another layer. The same path can be a completely different experience depending on the hour. In morning softness, the birch canopy at Little Cottage on a Hill filters the sun into silver-green pools; in the evening, the same leaves become translucent discs, each one jewel-like with golden light. A winter sun trap – a bench set against a north-facing wall – draws you in for ten minutes of stillness when the air is too cold to linger elsewhere. In summer, you gravitate to shade, and the route you take through the garden changes to match.

Tim designs for those shifts deliberately. Watching him work, it feels like he's scoring a piece of music: knowing which notes will carry early in the season, which will hold the middle, and which will close the piece. In his naturalistic gardens, seed heads and standing stems aren't just tolerated; they're essential to the late-season structure. He values plants past their perceived prime, seeing them as part of the whole picture and the next chapter of the season.

Working with temporality also means resisting the urge to edit too quickly. One winter of observation can transform a gardener's understanding. You see where frost lingers longest, which beds warm first, where low light falls in the late afternoon. These patterns tell you where to plant early bulbs, where to place late blooming *Salvia* species, where a deciduous tree could provide shade in summer and allow light through in winter.

Designing well for seasonal arcs is also about transition. A path edged with *Hylotelephium* 'Gooseberry Fool' in late summer becomes a path edged with seed heads in autumn, with low light catching on every dried flower. Clumps of silvergrass (*Miscanthus* spp.) aren't just appealing for their midsummer plumes, but for the way those plumes bleach and fray through winter, catching frost and backlight. A single specimen tree might be chosen for four different reasons across the seasons: bud, bloom, leaf and bare silhouette.

The ultimate reward for designing with time in mind is that the garden is never 'finished' in the static sense; it's always mid-conversation, constantly in a state of becoming. And whether you are there in the warm gold of evening or the washed light of morning, in the flush of spring or the pared-back bones of winter, the garden meets you with something true for that moment, and something you'll only see if you're paying close attention. This keeps curiosity alive and anchors you to the seasonal flow.

Which seasonal change in your garden do you look forward to most? How could you frame it so it becomes a focal experience?

Scan to hear my full conversation with Tim Pilgrim, where we talk about designing in successions and reading the whole picture across seasons, building structure-first plantings that create movement and rhythm, and the discipline of watching for one full winter before you edit.

LAYERING THE SENSES

Jac Semmler's philosophy (see pages 109–11) encompasses immersive planting, high-performance plants and sensory density without chaos, and it begins with the body in the space. She builds compositions that you can't stand back from; they invite you to move, touch and linger. 'These aren't gardens to view; they're gardens to be within,' Jac says. 'For me, it's about an immersive quality, about not being able to be a bystander.' That same intention shapes how I work with the senses.

Form is the first read. It frames the experience before colour or scent arrive. In my western approach at Little Cottage on a Hill, a dark steel edge holds a line while planting softens and lifts against it: Russian sage (*Salvia yangii*), *Eryngium* 'Oxford Blue', *Geum* 'Totally Tangerine' and the vertical threads of purple moor grass (*Molinia arundinacea*). The edge gives the planting something to play off; the planting stops the edge from becoming static. Form here is both anchor and foil.

Ironically, sound is often the quietest design tool, but it changes the pace. Gravel underfoot makes each step deliberate; a shift to bark mulch softens the tread. In the open, wind threads through tall grasses, lifting the rhythm of walking. In enclosed garden rooms, birdsong collects and holds you for a moment before you move on.

Scent works best where the air slows. I use it to signal arrival or rest: winter daphne (*Daphne odora*) at a shaded turn, *Agastache* 'Liquorice Blue' catching late summer warmth beside a seat. These placements are deliberate. Fragrance holds memory; it fixes the experience of a place in a way that nothing else can.

Texture is how the hand remembers. I keep contrasts legible year-round: upright against billowing; fine filigree against opacity. Along the verge, the crisp cut garden edge meets the froth of summer planting; in winter, seed heads and grass stems carry the structure forwards without losing softness.

A sensory team

These layers are most powerful when they work together. The cypress bench seat has enveloping plants rising up behind it; they gently move in the breeze, carrying a light fragrance, but that's not a backdrop. That's a designed moment of inhabitation.

High-performance plants make this possible. A grass that moves, flowers, seeds and stands through frost offers four seasons of work. A perennial with good leaves, blooms, seed heads and a clean fall holds its place in every month. With these, density stays legible, abundance stays navigable.

In my own gardens, edible and ornamental plants share the same frame. Rosemary (*Salvia rosmarinus*) is structure and scent. Bolting parsley (*Petroselinum crispum*) proffers seeds and architecture. Any pumpkin (*Cucurbita* sp.) growing up mesh becomes both food and a seasonal curtain that moves with the wind. The garden produces presence as much as it produces harvest.

Designing for the senses isn't an afterthought. It's set in the intentions from the first sketch: where the back will rest, where a scent will meet you, where texture will curtail your step. Layer by layer, sense by sense, the garden shifts from idea and image to experience.

What's the first scent you notice when you step into your garden? Could you make it the first thing you encounter every time you walk outside?

Scan to hear my full conversation with Jac Semmler, where we talk about layering the senses and refusing the bystander position, high-performance 'plants for the people' practice, and dissolving the ornamental–edible divide in dry-dynamic plantings.

LIGHT AND SHADOW AS DESIGN MATERIALS

Jac Semmler believes that designing for an immersive garden experience begins with the body, then builds outwards through layered planting, texture and scent. High-performance, sensory-rich plants create density, movement and seasonal continuity, inviting you to slow down, step in close and experience the garden from within rather than as a bystander.

At Three Chimneys, Lily Langham's magic spaces, 'where the garden feels like it's embracing you,' she notes, are not static. They're alive with wildlife: birds crossing a shaft of sunlight, bees lifting through a cloud of seed heads, the quick movement of an insect's wing. She intuitively designs with plant textures, light angles and shade points in mind so that each season reveals something different: the translucent lift of grasses in autumn, frost along the edges of winter foliage, the filtered green of the spring canopy. Her planting becomes a moving canvas for light, shifting in colour, texture and sound as the day and year turn.

Light is not decoration; it is structure. It shapes mood and pace as surely as a path or wall. Morning light softens the garden, dissolving edges; sharp evening light rakes across surfaces so every line and texture stands out. I work with both deliberately, keeping in mind where the low sun will hit; I set taller stems where they will catch the first or last light and throw shade across a path.

Shadow is the counterweight. It frames, edits and cools. The shadow of a steel-mesh climbing frame becomes a pattern on freshly cut lawn, shifting through the day until it disappears into the evening. A softly clipped pineapple guava (*Feijoa*

Lily Langham's Three Chimneys is a garden read as a journey, not as a snapshot. The path curves through layered planting, where texture and light steer pace and attention, with each bend offering a new microclimate, a new edge and a new moment of pause.

sellowiana) hedge throws a solid block of shade that holds the eye before the next reveal. On high summer days, a narrow shaded corner can be as much a destination as an open view.

At Little Cottage on a Hill, light and shadow are part of the daily choreography. In the morning, dew in the beds catches the sun in glints, each droplet a small flare before it burns away. By late afternoon, the western verge is illuminated on the diagonal, and the *Echinops bannaticus* 'Blue Glow' heads are backlit so they seem to hover. In winter, the sun sits low enough to stream through the bare silver birch (*Betula pendula*) canopy, drawing long lines across the gravel. At Oak & Monkey Puzzle, the long east–west axis meant mornings were all about lateral light through the entry garden, while evenings turned the upper terraces gold.

Scan to hear my full conversation with Lily Langham, where we talk about choreographing light and shade across the day and seasons; planting for wildlife so the garden becomes a moving canvas; and designing for night and moonlight.

Patterns and planning

Working with light means thinking in journeys, not snapshots. Where does the first light fall in winter? Which spaces are in shade at midday in summer? I map these patterns (often just briefly in my mind) before I plant. A deciduous tree might be placed to filter the high sun in summer and to allow light in during winter. A water surface might be sited to catch a low reflection in autumn, so the whole space shimmers for one glorious hour. In fact, when we were living in our scout hall in inner-city Melbourne, we designed a 7-metre-long (23-foot) water rill so that it perfectly aligned with the glass panes of the front door. In the morning, the reflection glowed like a runway beckoning you out into the light, the garden and the new day.

Shadow design is just as active. A dense planting can cast a dapple that cools the ground and hinders evaporation. An arbour or pergola can throw patterned shade that becomes part of the garden's texture. At Three Chimneys, Lily uses both, creating places where people and wildlife can pause, where the air stills and the eye can adjust before gliding back into light.

Light and shadow are not static conditions. They are moving materials, shaping the experience as you walk, work or rest. Designing with them is about anticipation – knowing what the sun and shade will do tomorrow, next month, next season – and setting the stage so those changes are felt. When it works, the garden is different every time you step into it, even if nothing else has been altered.

Some of the most intimate garden experiences happen under moonlight: leaves silvered, scent carrying further in the cool air, shadows turning familiar paths into something new. In fact, my children's father wooed me right at the very beginning in exactly this way. After asking me if I'd ever smelled the scent of wintersweet (*Chimonanthus praecox*), he spontaneously took me to Burnley Gardens in the dark of night so I could experience it firsthand.

Designing for night is part of planning for the whole diurnal cycle: a bench where the moon rises over a hedge, a spot to catch the frenzy of insect activity on a hot summer night, a pale planting that glows after dusk, or a tree that throws dramatic shadows while bright stars shine above.

Where does moonlight fall in your garden? Could you make it a place to linger?

An arbour at Three Chimneys is a threshold that shapes the shade, frames the sky and draws the eye outwards to the horizon line of Lalgambuk (Mount Franklin). Structure and planting work together to create a place to linger before you are released back into the wider landscape.

PLANTS AS STRUCTURE, RHYTHM AND CONVERSATION

*1*_Northern verge planting on the 27-metre (89-foot) slope. *Miscanthus* and *Calamagrostis* cultivars hold the road edge in soft, repeating swathes, with red-barked dogwood (*Cornus alba*) rising through for winter structure.
*2*_Globe thistle (*Echinops ritro*) threaded into the grasses, a happy accident that holds *Calamagrostis* 'Karl Foerster' upright and keeps the rhythm clean at the lawn edge.
*3*_An informal pineapple guava (*Feijoa sellowiana*) hedge, fruiting and evergreen, marks the space without a hard boundary.
*4*_*Geum* 'Totally Tangerine' bobs at the garden edge, a soft line that keeps the conversation going through the season.
*5*_Winter structure in close up: Turkish sage (*Phlomis russeliana*) in the foreground, with Russian sage (*Salvia yangii*) just behind. Texture and vertical form do the work when flowers have faded.

Plants hold space as surely as any wall or fence. They set the frame, carry the rhythm, and keep the conversation going through the seasons. Garden architecture isn't just built form. It's in the trees that anchor a view, the hedges that define a threshold, the clipped forms that own their ground in winter, the drifts of grasses that catch the light and shift the pace.

I often tell my workshop guests that my planting is never 'salt and peppered' – one of this, one of that – but built in drifts. I want to feel the immersion that comes from repetition, the way a mass of a single plant can hold you in its colour or movement. At Oak & Monkey Puzzle, whole swathes of *Calamagrostis* 'Karl Foerster' and *Miscanthus* 'Eileen Quinn' ran through the entry garden, the same restricted palette of plants cultivated in wave after wave so the eye could rest. At Little Cottage on a Hill, the repetition is smaller in scale: espaliered fruit trees repeating along the fence, Lebanese crabapple (*Malus trilobata*) at intervals along the driveway courtyard. But the effect is the same. The body finds the rhythm and relaxes into it.

Tim Pilgrim puts it plainly: 'Structure first – tree, shrub, clipped forms – then you bring in your verticals, then movement with grasses. Bulbs, perennials, seasonal layers come after that.' His planting plans start with anchors, the long-term framework, before he adds the mid-height plants that move, flower and shift with the year. In his naturalistic designs, he'll often use eleven, twelve, thirteen, even 25 plants in

1

2

3

a group to make a swathe that you feel with your whole body. I tend to use smaller numbers such as four, five, six or seven, but the principle is the same: immersion through mass, not distraction through variety.

Structure gives you the bones; rhythm is how you move through them. Tim uses repetition like a metronome: the same grass appearing at intervals to pull your eye along a border, the same perennial catching light in different parts of the garden so that each space is linked to the others. Grasses and perennials are his rhythm-makers, working hard even when they're not in flower. 'A plant's got to do more than one thing,' he says. 'It has to earn its place across the year.' That might mean holding a clean seed head through winter, colouring well in autumn or offering movement in the slightest breeze.

Jac Semmler takes the idea of performance and layers it into abundance. For her, immersive planting means using high-performance plants – those that offer structure, movement, colour and texture across multiple seasons – and placing them close enough to dissolve the boundaries between you and the planting. In her hands, edible and ornamental aren't separate categories. A bed might carry pomegranate (*Punica granatum*) for its clusters of ruby-red sculptural fruits, Tuscan kale (*Brassica oleracea* Acephala Group) for its velvety grey vertical stems and structure, perennial basil (*Ocimum gratissimum*) for its scent and flower, and mid-east sage (*Salvia viscosa*) for pollinators, with all plants working together to hold the space and feed both body and eye.

4

5

The power of planting in drifts

At Oak & Monkey Puzzle, the entry garden carried whole swathes of ornamental grasses, including *Calamagrostis* 'Karl Foerster' and *Miscanthus* 'Eileen Quinn', alongside supporting plantings of English box (*Buxus sempervirens*), artichoke (*Cynara cardunculus*), *Sanguisorba officinalis* 'St Philibert' and purple coneflower (*Echinacea purpurea*), to name a few. Wind activated the planting like a series of billowing sails; low sun turned the grasses into ribbons of golden light.

Along Little Cottage on a Hill's northern verge, repeated red-barked dogwoods (*Cornus alba*) make a winter thicket of luminous scarlet stems alongside the summer and autumn heroes of *Calamagrostis* 'Karl Foerster' and *Miscanthus* 'Yakushima Dwarf'. When you repeat a plant, the eye rests and the space settles. Plants become the material rather than the decoration. Consider the following that work at any scale:

- **Lead plant:** Pick one plant that you want to read as the 'field' or 'base fabric'. It must carry across the seasons that you care about most, and provide interest and cohesion from any distance. If you hesitate before choosing the plant, then it's not quite right for your garden. The lead plant should hold the composition like a painter's canvas.
- **Run and repeat:** Plant in generous runs (or drifts, as I call them), and repeat the same run so it resolves as a rhythm, not a salt-and-pepper shaker of 'spots'. Aim for depth as well as width. Do the 'squint' test from a distance. If it still looks speckled, the groups of plants are too small or the palette is too busy.
- **Lift the field:** Add one quiet lift so the drift doesn't feel flat. Thread a finer texture through, or underplant bulbs for the handover between seasons. One move is enough.

Plant for movement you can read from the street or kitchen on a windy day. Backlight stems that hold winter structure. Keep colour families close so the bed appears as one field, not a scatter. Plant in blocks, not pinches. If you feel the planting as a whole, then the space reads in one glance and the work is easier.

***Top*_**Planting in drifts. A lead grass establishes the field, then repetition builds immersion, movement and a sense of the garden as a single composition rather than scattered moments. ***Above*_**Red-barked dogwood (*Cornus alba*) threaded through silvergrass (*Miscanthus* sp.). A strong base 'fabric' carries the planting, while seasonal stems and seed heads add lift, light and structure as the garden shifts through the colder months.

Mood, movement and plant dialogue

At Little Cottage on a Hill, my western verge of precision spade-cut edges between garden and mown lawn carries exactly the same logic. Against that stark dividing line, I've planted Russian sage (*Salvia yangii*), *Sanguisorba officinalis* 'St Philibert', *Agastache* 'Liquorice Blue', *Stachys byzantina* 'Silky Fleece', plus soft and billowy ornamental oregano (*Origanum libanoticum*). It's structure and movement in the same frame: the crisp edge keeps its line while the planting leans, sways and lifts in the wind or catches the sunlight in the early evening. That unique tension in the juxtaposition between the hard edge and the loose planting keeps the space vibrant and alive.

Plants can also be the hinge between one mood and another. At Oak & Monkey Puzzle, a long run of low, clipped hedging would give way to a drift of mollis azaleas (*Rhododendron* Mollis Hybrids), the stillness opening into movement just as the view widened. At the National Arboretum Canberra, the 'hundred forests, hundred gardens' approach delivers this immersion at a monumental scale. Standing inside a grove of a single species is like being held inside a note, with every leaf, trunk and shadow in tune.

This is the heart of planting as conversation: the push and pull between stability and change. Whether it's a mown lawn spine, a line of espaliered fruit trees or a clipped evergreen shrub, structure holds the space steady. Seasonal layers bring the lightness, the improvisation, the unexpected line in the music. Without one, the other loses its meaning.

When plants are used as structure, rhythm and conversation, the garden reads in complete and robust sentences, not fragments. You move from one space to the next with a sense of continuity, your body unconsciously registering the repetitions and the shifts. And, like any good conversation, it's not about a single voice dominating, it's about the interplay, even the tension. The long-term anchors give the short-term players a stage; the seasonal changes stop the permanent plantings from feeling static.

Whether you're planting with thirteen in a group or with five, the intent is the same: to let plants hold the space, set the tempo and carry the dialogue from season to season. It's an approach that works at any scale, from the hundred forests of the arboretum to the 27 red barked dogwoods (*Cornus alba*) along my northern verge, because it's built on the same truth: plants are the architecture you live inside.

Choose one plant in your garden that already 'earns its place' across multiple seasons. How could you repeat it to create rhythm?

Plume poppy (*Macleaya cordata*) and *Miscanthus* 'Yakushima Dwarf' in a drift. The conversation comprises bold, sage-toned leaves and a coppery flower haze, with an upright grass rhythm threading through.

Early morning on the verge in autumn light, walking the garden slowly and reading the shift from late-season flower into seed-head structure that will hold through winter.

RITUAL, REPETITION AND DAILY INHABITATION

Gardens are not only shaped by the seasons, they are shaped by the ways we move through them every day. The morning check before breakfast. The evening loop to see what's changed. The hushed reset after the last harvest. These small acts repeated over weeks, months or years are what bind you to a place. They are not just maintenance. They are the ongoing conversation between gardener and garden.

At Little Cottage on a Hill, my day often starts with a slow circuit before the kettle boils. I walk past the espaliered fruit trees on the northern verge, noting which buds have broken and which tips need tying down. I check the wicking beds for signs of overnight visitors: a scratch of soil, a nibble in a leaf (I've been super happy, but the possums did steal the cauliflowers once!). In autumn, I clear and prep the beds for spring planting, tucking cloves of garlic (*Allium sativum*) into cooler soil and covering them with composted goat manure. The actions themselves are simple, but the repetition anchors me. I know these beds in all their stages – sown, sprouting, thriving, fading – and that familiarity is its own form of belonging.

I know how those small repetitions can take root in a life; I've watched it happen. Meg Travis's journey into creating, gardening and growing began with one of those moments, and it's stayed with both of us ever since.

The first day of forever

Meg Travis arrived serendipitously at Oak & Monkey Puzzle in February 2016. A Facebook post, a single photo exchanged in a leap of faith by way of a brief email, and a dash to the airport with the kids in tow, right when I was launching my business and embarking on the very first workshops. Meg and I found each other practically by accident as she embarked on a long season of journey and intention, setting herself the task of travelling the world for a year in 'trades' under the persona of 'Girl Friday', a self-described generalist, working alongside makers, doers, growers and food producers in different landscapes and seasons, swapping labour for experience as a way of finding her footing. The travel wasn't aimless; it was a deliberate education in real time. She wanted to learn by doing, to see how people inhabited the world through their skills and passions. To work inside the pulse of places where artisanship, food, soil and season shaped the day. Oak & Monkey Puzzle was only the second stop on that search.

Before Meg came through my front gate, she had never really gardened. She'd grown up doing bits and pieces with her mum, but this was different; it was the kind of immersion that can set the course of a life. She folded herself into the rhythm of the place, offering a hand when needed, documenting those early days with tenderness. She became part of the landscape of my own becoming. In her words: 'What is clear is the day I walked up the front steps of your verandah was 100 per cent the first day of forever for me.'

That time became in part a foundation for everything she has grown since. It also marked the beginning of a friendship rooted in shared work, a shared table and a shared belief that a garden can anchor an entire way of living.

We worked side by side in the beds, in the kitchen, in the quiet intervals between jobs. Looking back, I think both of us can see it for what it was: the first hinge in a door that hasn't stopped swinging open.

One Field Farm: Rhythm as anchor

One Field Farm in Crantock, Cornwall, is where Meg's work has found a steady rhythm. She doesn't live there, but she goes every day. Farmer Chris has loaned the field to her, an arrangement that began in exchange for helping him pick his crop and has grown into a rhythm of trust and reciprocity. Chris also lets her borrow his tractor for the heavy work. The beds feed her household and a circle of local cafés and restaurants, where relationships have grown to the point that a few select chefs are trusted to pick direct. What began as a private sanctuary now has a community radius, its seasons and repetitions reaching beyond the fence line and into kitchens and plates across the region.

She describes One Field Farm as the place where she feels most at home in her work, where the flow of the day and the tasks in the garden are inseparable, each shaping the other. It's her sanctuary, but also a space that sometimes opens outwards: a long lunch among the beds, a dinner with friends, an occasional public event. Most days, though, it's hers alone: the everyday space she inhabits season after season.

The rhythms here are shared. In the polytunnel, a mud kitchen has transformed the way the space is used. Her young daughters will happily spend hours there, playing in their own corner while she works nearby. These parallel rhythms of adult and child, tending and play, are part of the texture of her days.

One Field Farm is not a garden in the traditional sense. It's a small, windswept field with the polytunnel at its heart. There's no formal design here, no clipped edges or coordinated palettes, but it holds all of the qualities of a true garden: rhythm, care, seasonality and nourishment. Inside the tunnel's filtered light and damp soil, Meg grows food for her family, seedlings for neighbours, and time for herself.

This life wasn't a grand plan, but a choice to live more simply and seasonally, letting the work of growing shape the rest. Field meals are shared with muddy boots still on, seed swaps are acts of community, and notes to her children are tucked into seed packets. Early spring light on the polytunnel plastic is a memory she carries alongside each new season. In her world, a garden is not a place but an experience: full, generous and deeply felt.

Designing for ritual

Rituals don't just happen; they can be designed for. Crops you need daily, such as herbs and salad leaves, belong close to the kitchen door. A path you love to walk can be planted for scent in the evening. At One Field Farm, Meg's working areas are set so she can move easily from one anchor point to another: polytunnel to outdoor beds, picking to washing, seedling bench to planting rows.

Some of her planting is shaped by the relationships that have grown alongside the garden itself. From those early days of the farm, when veg boxes containing her surplus produce were sent out into the world, through the occasional gatherings and shared meals, the field's rituals now extend beyond Meg's own day and into the kitchens and plates of the community, with the same respect for season and quality that she brings to her own table.

My own gardens have always been shaped with similar intent, where the tasks I return to often are the ones that give me the most back.

Some rituals are inherited: a grandmother's habit of planting bulbs after the first frost, or a neighbour's solstice gathering under a particular tree. These cultural threads can be woven into your garden's own rhythm, layering your story over the place's longer memory.

Scan to hear my full conversation with Meg Travis, where we talk about the serendipity of her 'Girl Friday' year of trades and how it led to Oak & Monkey Puzzle; the immersion of those first months together; and how friendship, making and garden rituals have shaped the life she's built since.

Seasonal markers

Meg marks her year by the natural turning points in the garden: the moments when a crop is ready to plant, harvest or cut back. They're not dates on a calendar, but cues from the land: what's flowering, what's coming to an end, what's beginning again. They tell her where she is in the season and guide the work ahead.

For me, the same markers have shaped every garden I've lived in: the first bed prepared in autumn for spring planting, the last harvest before frost, the cutting back that signals winter's pause. These repetitions give structure to the year, not as deadlines, but as invitations to notice, respond and tend.

Oak & Monkey Puzzle, 2016, photographed by Meg Travis. This is a snapshot of the garden as the anchor of Meg's time here, holding the daily rhythms and the life being lived around it.

At One Field Farm, Meg's harvests often become both a practical and a personal ritual. Seasons offer narrow windows – often just a few weeks between flushes – and she moves through them with purpose, gathering berries and currants for cordials and the spiced elderberry syrup we dreamed up over the kitchen bench at Oak & Monkey Puzzle many moons ago (see page 312). The process is physical and sensory: the scent heavy in the still air, the stain of juice on her hands, the sound of fruits softly landing in the basket. It's work, but it's also a way of marking time, one of the recurring beats in the score of her year.

Why ritual matters

When we return to the same tasks over years, they become more than maintenance. They are a way of knowing a place, of reading its changes. They deepen our skill and strengthen our connection. Not in a rush of achievement, but in the slow accrual of understanding.

For Meg, that connection began the day she stepped onto the verandah at Oak & Monkey Puzzle. For me, it's in every garden I've walked through at first light, watching for the tiny signs that the season has changed: the first frost turning leaves to glass, the smell of damp earth after summer rain, the sound of seeds rattling in their pods. These are the moments that remind me the garden is not just something I keep, but something that keeps me.

What daily or seasonal act in your garden could you turn into a ritual that grounds you?

WELLBEING THROUGH PRESENCE, NOT PERFORMANCE

Sometimes I go into the garden like a bull at a gate. Usually, it's in the days immediately before a workshop, or when the season is shifting and seasonal markers are letting me know that things need to be done. Maybe it's the winter pruning of the roses, or the celery (*Apium graveolens*) is threatening to swallow an entire wicking bed. Occasionally it's the first green shoots of late winter to early spring ('sprinter' we call it here in Daylesford; it's practically a season of its own!). I've got the list running in my head before I've even stepped outside: shift the hose, deadhead the roses, check for eggs with one eye on the chickens, thinking that it's probably time to dig out their deep litter before they compact it after the rain.

I'm moving fast, almost always wearing the wrong clothes, shoes wet from the grass, thinking about the next job before I've finished the one I'm on. Then something interrupts me. It could be the sudden heady scent of *Philadelphus* 'Silver Showers' filling the air. Maybe it's the way the light has caught on a plant that I wasn't even looking at. By now, you should know that I'm a sucker for the afternoon's 'pretty light' and the way it turns every plant it touches into its own mesmerising jewel!

That's when it happens, that little interlude when the whole pace of the day alters. My shoulders drop. My breathing changes. I notice where I am. I'm not rushing anymore. And that shift is why I keep coming back. Not for the 'got it all done' feeling because mostly I never do, but for that flick of a switch from doing to being.

Care goes both ways

While I'm a stickler for a tidy space, the garden is here to keep me steady, not to keep up appearances. I look for the smallest shifts, the kind most people would miss, and those become the anchors. Grow with these anchors, bend with them, and the landscape becomes somewhere you go to steady yourself, not just somewhere you work.

I'll be tying in stems or hauling mulch, and suddenly the 'doing' falls away. I'm just there. The sun's warm on the back of my neck. I can smell compost on my hands. I think that's why my favourite thing to do is to 'potter', to amble between doing and being. The work and the presence blur together until they're the same thing. It's hard to describe in words because it's actually not really an action; it's truly a way of being, connecting and grounding. I feel so intimately entwined with time and space, life and land. It's in the garden that I can face my most torturous battles (and I have), and I feel most held and alive.

It's a rhythm I recognise when I speak to Mark McDowall, who lives in Ireland. We discuss the making and remaking of his own garden, and how spaces change by being inhabited. Part of his place is a sand garden, a quiet ground where raking draws and redraws the day. In the Japanese dry-garden tradition, raked gravel stands for water, and rocks hold like mountains; the emptiness between them – what is left white – carries as much weight as any object. That is *yohaku no bi* and *ma* at work, the field where attention lives. The patterns he creates with the rake last only until the next breeze or the next pass, yet the doing is the point. You tend the surface, and it tends you. I feel it in my own work, that shift when maintenance becomes incidental care, when I stop chasing a list and start being in the season that is embracing me.

I think we lose something when we strip gardens back to the point where there's hardly anything to do. People call it low-maintenance, but all the texture and invitation to connect disappear with it. The gardens that matter most to me are the ones I actually live in, the ones I can walk into wound up and walk out of with a different kind of breath.

'I think we lose something when we strip gardens back to the point where there's hardly anything to do. People call it low-maintenance, but all the texture and invitation to connect disappear with it.'

And it's nearly always the small, unplanned moments that make the difference. Leaning on the gate for a few minutes before you go inside. Sitting in the polytunnel while the kids play in the mud kitchen. Watching a bee work one flower until it's done. Those are the moments that stitch you back together. They're the reason I keep walking back out the door.

AN INVITATION TO INHABIT

It's late afternoon once again. The sun slips under the silver birch (*Betula pendula*) canopy, catching the *Miscanthus* hybrids on the verge so each blade is edged in that glorious gold to which I always return. Bees hum in the pollen-filled crowns of *Hylotelephium spectabile* 'Autumn Joy', working the last of the light, and the air holds that gentle breathing space before evening. It's the same glorious time of day that I described at the beginning of this chapter, only the season has shifted, and so has the garden's offering.

A garden's greatest gift is not its neatness or even its productivity, but how it holds you in the pauses, the repetitions, the sensory moments that make you feel at home in your own skin. Design for the experiences that you want to have again and again, and the garden will keep them for you.

This is your invitation to slow down, to notice, to let the seasons teach you. Because in the end, the most powerful gardens are not those you visit once, but those you live inside day after day, season after season; always returning, always noticing, always being met by something new.

10 SUSTAINABLE PRACTICES FOR LASTING ABUNDANCE

Sustainability isn't a style or a checklist. It's a way of shaping your garden and your life so that every decision works with nature, instead of against it.

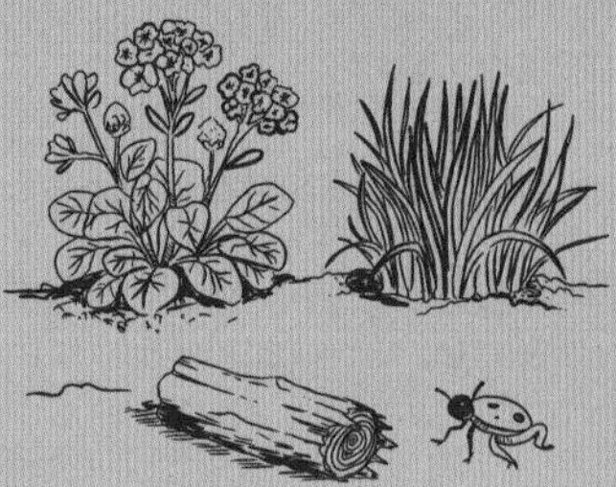

A SUSTAINABLE CHAIN

This chapter is about incorporating sustainability as a natural flow in your garden. It's also about trial and error, curiosity and the understanding that there are no failures, only lessons taught by your garden. You don't need to do everything at once. Start with one change – a worm farm, a single wicking bed, planting flowers for pollinators – and let it lead to the next. Over time, the systems link together, each one feeding the others, building resilience and beauty across the whole garden.

And beauty matters here. Sustainable solutions can be as appealing as they are practical. It isn't only about what works; it's also about what you'll love enough to keep. When a system is thoughtfully placed, well-made and visually integrated with its surroundings, you'll want to use it because it has become part of the pleasure of gardening: a growing panel and plant-clad rainwater tank that also frames a view, a sculptural collection of compost towers that doubles as a backdrop for seasonal planting, an architecturally designed collection of wicking beds that catches the day's warmth and creates a season-extending microclimate.

We'll begin, quite deliberately, with the most important system of all: the soil. Healthy, living soil is the foundation of everything you grow. Build the soil, and you build the garden. From there, we'll explore how to protect and feed the soil, grow organically, regenerate your space, propagate plants and save seeds, work with water wisely, integrate animals and biodiversity, build climate resilience, and connect everything in a circular design.

By the end of this chapter, you'll have a toolkit of systems and ideas to design and sustain abundance in a space of any size, anywhere in the world. Systems that don't just keep a garden alive, but make it thrive in a way that's uniquely yours.

Raking autumn leaves at Little Cottage on a Hill, with Willow and Ivy. I return this carbon-rich garden litter to the soil through a composting tower. It is one small loop in the sustainable chain.

Cover beats bare

Here are three tips for protecting soil:

1 Aim to have living cover or mulch year-round to buffer temperature extremes, soften rain impact and shield soil life from sun and temperature extremes.

2 In cool, wet climates, try a thin compost mulch if straw or sugarcane mulches harbour slugs.

3 During the germination of fine seeds, such as those for carrot (*Daucus carota* subsp. *sativus*), protect the surface with boards or cloth until seedlings emerge, then remove the boards/cloth and maintain soft cover.

DESIGNING SUSTAINABILITY FROM A LANDSCAPE PERSPECTIVE

As a landscape architect, I don't separate sustainability from design; I see it as a material, a rhythm and a structuring device. Good design, at any scale, integrates systems from the outset. It's not about retrofitting compost bays or tacking on a rainwater tank. It's about reading the site, shaping spatial logic and making each component feel inevitable, like it belongs, both visually and functionally.

Edges, rhythm and repetition matter here. Compost towers aren't tucked away as afterthoughts, they're sited like vertical punctuation marks in the garden, part of the visual cadence. Wicking beds aren't just containers, they're laid in a deliberate grid, their height and alignment offering a rhythm that structures the space. Even my worm tunnels align with bed geometry, so the eye reads the system as both productive and resolved.

I pay close attention to thresholds, transitions and material continuity. The timber used to wrap the composting towers echoes the visually permeable timber-and-wire fence lines and the slatted frame of the chicken run. The aim is to create cohesion, not through uniformity, but through resonance. It's not about hiding the function; it's about making it sing in tune with the rest of the space. This is what excites me: when a space works well, or, better yet, when beauty supports the systems of abundance.

Every sustainable system in the garden has to earn its place spatially, visually and practically. If it doesn't support the way you move, live and feel in the space, then it will become visual and/or physical clutter. When it's integrated from the beginning in form, function and rhythm, it becomes a joy to use. It becomes part of the architecture of the garden, not separate from it.

Many of these choices align with the principles of permaculture: stacking functions, closing loops, designing with observation and care. While I don't practise permaculture in a formal sense, it's one of many traditions I draw from. I've always been a bit of a magpie, gleaning ideas that hold up in the real world and refining them through use. My own path has been shaped just as much by spatial rhythm, material resonance and how systems feel in a designed space. What matters most to me is that sustainability becomes part of how we live, not something we add on. Later in this chapter, you'll hear from growers, educators and systems thinkers whose work continues to deepen and challenge my own, and each of them brings a different kind of rigour to what it means to live and design sustainably.

SOIL: THE LIVING FOUNDATION

Beneath every thriving landscape lies a living architecture that breathes, breaks down and builds the garden we see: soil. Think of it as a community rather than a material. When the soil is alive and well structured, plants grow with less fuss and more resilience, water sinks in instead of running off, and your garden copes better with heat, wind and sudden rain.

You don't need a laboratory to understand your soil. You can use your hands, your nose and a few simple tests to find out what you need to know. Try this: after the next rainfall, smell your soil. That earthy scent (geosmin) is a little burst of joy and a sure sign your soil is alive.

In the pages ahead, you'll learn how to read your soil, how to build it (preferably without unnecessary disturbance), and how to keep it covered and fed. The result is more life under your feet, which means stronger plant roots, fewer problems and a garden that gives back, season after season.

What is living soil?

Healthy soil is alive. Bacteria, fungi, protozoa, nematodes, arthropods and earthworms all recycle organic matter into things that plants can use. As they move and feed, these tiny creatures bind mineral particles and humus into crumbs that contain minute spaces for air and water. This is the physical structure that plant roots need to breathe, drink and anchor. Here are five ideas to hold in mind:

1. Structure is the arrangement of soil crumbs and pores. It is as vital as fertility.
2. Texture is the mix of sand, silt and clay (as a guide, a balanced loam is roughly 40 per cent sand, 40 per cent silt and 20 per cent clay). You cannot completely change the texture, but you can improve its structure.
3. Organic matter is the fuel for life in the soil. Add it gently and regularly.
4. The pH of the soil influences nutrient availability. Most productive crops prefer slightly acidic to neutral soil, roughly pH 6–7.
5. Cover is care. Bare soil loses life, moisture and structure very quickly.

I spoke with chef-turned-farmer Matthew Evans, whose book *Soil* explores the living complexity beneath our feet with clarity and care. Both his work and our conversation reminded me that when we treat soil as alive, everything changes: flavour, resilience, the way we tend and what the garden gives back.

Taste what biology does

Try this simple comparison to understand how living soil changes what the garden offers.

1. Grow the same crop in two different beds. Plant one in an established bed that has been fed with compost and kept covered over time, and the other in a newer or recently rebuilt bed with less organic matter and soil life.
2. At harvest, pay attention to sweetness, texture and aroma. Note how the plants grew, and what you see in the soil: crumb structure, moisture, worms and surface cover.
3. Use what you observe and taste to guide your practice: steady compost inputs, living cover, and diverse rotations that build soil life year by year.

'A single teaspoon of soil can have up to ten billion living things in it.'

MATTHEW EVANS

Soil as the skin of the earth

Matthew Evans came to soil through taste. A chef and restaurant critic who became a farmer in southern Tasmania, he discovered that the best food he ate came from people who looked after their soil. His move to Fat Pig Farm turned curiosity into practice. He writes and speaks about soil as a living ecosystem rather than a substance, and he urges ordinary gardeners to become stewards of that life.

Evans' core principles are empoweringly simple. Feed the soil with compost. Keep it covered with living plants or mulch. Avoid unnecessary disturbance. Grow diverse crops through the seasons. In his own beds, he top-dresses rather than digs, keeps living roots in the ground, and lets structure and biology do the heavy lifting. Over the years, he has tasted the difference. A plant grown in well-fed, biologically rich beds has sweeter and more complex produce than the same species grown in nearby beds that have a low amount of organic matter and less active biology.

He reminds us that soil is a climate buffer and biodiversity hotspot, home to extraordinary numbers of organisms in every teaspoon, and that this underground life underpins flavour, nutrition, resilience and our wellbeing. The human microbiome benefits when we eat widely from plants grown in healthy soil and when we spend time on living ground. For gardeners at any scale, his message lands cleanly. These are the key takeaways from our conversation:

— Soil is a living, breathing superorganism that needs air, water and food.
— Flavour follows biology. Produce grown in soil with a high level of organic matter and active biology tastes markedly better.
— Roots growing in protected soil provide a steady food source for soil life.
— Use no-dig principles as a default, not a dogma (see pages 205–10).
— Eating a range of plants nourishes the human microbiome, while growing a range of plants is good for the diversity of farmers' crop rotations.

Matthew Evans' book *Soil* brings the hidden life beneath our feet into sharper focus. It makes a compelling case that healthy soil underpins flavour, resilience, biodiversity and human wellbeing. This is one of the books that has helped to strengthen and affirm my own commitment to building living soil as the basis of any productive garden.

Scan to watch my full conversation with Matthew Evans, where we discuss soil as 'living skin' as well as the garden microbiome.

Ways to read your soil

There are a number of sensory techniques that you can use to check your soil quality before you pay for soil-sample tests:

- **Squeeze test:** Moisten a handful of soil from the root zone, and try to squeeze it into a ball. Clay-rich soil will hold together in a tight clump. Sandy soil will fall apart. A crumbly ball that just holds together is ideal.
- **Jar test:** Fill a clear jar about one-third full with dried, crumbled soil, and top up with water. Add a drop of plain dishwashing liquid. Place the lid on tightly, shake the jar hard for one minute, and allow the contents to settle for 24–48 hours. Sand will quickly fall to the bottom, followed later by silt and then clay. This shows the relative proportions of sand, silt and clay in your soil, which largely determine the soil's texture.
- **Infiltration test:** Sink a bottomless tin or plastic bottle 'collar' into a garden bed, pour in enough water to reach 25 millimetres (1 inch) up the side, and then time how long it takes for the water to disappear. If it's absorbed in less than five minutes, then the soil is loose or sandy. If the water is still there after two hours, then the soil is compacted or heavy clay.
- **Smell and colour:** Grab a handful of soil. Healthy soil smells earthy rather than sour, and it tends to be brown rather than grey.
- **Worm count:** Lift a spade of soil, and count how many worms you see. Ten or more is a good sign in a temperate-climate bed; in tropical, arid or alpine regions, expect fewer worms overall, and place more emphasis on soil structure, moisture content and organic matter.

However, if you're gardening near old industry, busy roads or very old houses where toxic lead paint may have been used in the past, then consider a lab test for heavy metals. Where I am in Victoria, Australia, we have the GardenSafe program, a science-based soil-testing initiative run by EPA Victoria. You can register, send in three garden-soil samples and have them analysed for free (except for postage), to assess contamination risks, including trace metals such as lead, arsenic and chromium. Participants receive a report that helps to guide vegetable gardening and raises awareness about urban soil quality. Many places around the world have these sorts of programs, so it's well worth checking for one in your region.

Where contamination is possible, choose raised beds, wicking beds or large containers. Bring in the best-quality growing medium you can afford, and keep root crops in clean areas only.

Disturb less, and build more

Many plants partner with fungal threads (mycellium) to explore soil beyond their roots. That partnership improves both nutrition and resilience. Consequently, you should disturb your soil as little as possible. Every time you turn it, fungal networks and soil crumbs break apart, and life then needs to rebuild.

However, disturbance may be useful if you have a compacted pan or rubble just below the soil's surface, and plants are failing. In this instance, a one-off fork to crack the layer can be justified. Avoid inverting the soil. Lift and wiggle to open channels, then return to no-dig gardening (see pages 205–10) with compost and mulch. A broadfork is a great tool for this. I don't actually have one, so I use a regular garden fork; it takes longer and a bit more effort to achieve the same result.

The least disruptive way to add organic matter to and protect the structure of established beds is to top them up with 2–5 centimetres (3/4–2 inches) of mature compost once or twice a year. Keep living plants, compost and mulch cycling rather than emptying and reworking beds.

Feeding and protecting soil

You have three main choices here, and they are useful for gardens of all sizes:

1. **Compost:** This comprises concentrated organic matter plus a diverse inoculum of life. For productive beds, a typical annual total of 2–5 kilograms (4–11 pounds) per square metre is plenty. Spread it thinly and often rather than in rare heavy doses.
2. **Mulch:** As well as protecting the soil's surface, mulch moderates temperature and reduces evaporation. In addition, it's part of the visual language of a garden. It can be warm and textural or quiet and recessive, so choose a material that suits your planting palette and garden conditions as well as your purpose and climate, but always keep the mulch clear of plant stems. For hot and dry conditions, use 7–10 centimetres (2 3/4–4 inches) of paler, reflective mulch (woodchips or straw) to shade the surface. For cold and wet conditions, use a lighter layer in spring to allow soil to warm, and a thicker layer in autumn once the soil has stored heat. For easy-walk pathways, woodchips break down slowly and feel comfortable to tread on.
3. **Green manures and living covers:** Where there is space, sow quick-cover crops and green manures between seasons to protect soil, feed life and maintain structure. In small gardens, underplanting with living ground covers can offer similar benefits while adding beauty.

'Pot-cap' mulching hack

When I'm mulching a lot of plants, I don't tiptoe around stems. I use protective 'caps' over the plants, then mulch quickly and confidently.

This method protects soft stems and crowns from breakage and rot (especially in cold and wet areas), while speeding up the mulching job. You can shovel and rake without fiddling around each plant.

Of course, you'll need to choose a pot size that's a little wider than the plant. In slug/snail-prone areas, lift the pots promptly so you don't create temporary hide-outs. For woody roses or plants that form spiky rosettes, utilise a ring cut from old irrigation pipe or a corflute as a re-usable collar.

This is how to 'pot-cap' mulch:
*1*_Cover each plant with an upturned nursery pot.
*2*_Check that all of the foliage is inside the pots.
*3*_Spread mulch evenly around the pots.
*4*_Carefully lift off the pots.
*5*_The mulch is in place, with a clean edge.
*6*_The end result is a mulch-free ring around the stems and efficient mulching in the rest of the garden bed.

Why green manure is great

The greatest success I've had in improving soil structure within the hardest environments, such as ground that has been waterlogged then baked hard into concrete, has come from sowing green-manure crops.

Years ago, at a previous home of mine, a spring in the front yard destroyed any structure the soil had once had. The ground was either mud you'd lose a boot in, or like solid concrete in summer. Over just two seasons of green-manure crops, the transformation was extraordinary. The compacted, lifeless ground became friable (crumbly), patterned with roots and air channels, teeming with worms, and able to hold water without drowning plants.

Green manures do far more than add surface cover. Their roots drive deep into the soil, breaking up compaction and creating pathways for air, water and microbial life. Leguminous plants, such as broad bean (*Vicia faba*) and sugar snap pea (*Pisum sativum*), fix nitrogen from the air into the soil, delivering it right down into the profile where future crops can access it. Grasses and cereals, such as oat (*Avena sativa*), add bulk organic matter through both their roots and their top growth, feeding soil organisms as they decompose. Brown mustard (*Brassica juncea*), white mustard (*Sinapis alba*), radish (*Raphanus sativus*) and rocket (*Eruca vesicaria* subsp. *sativa*) in a mix can help to biofumigate and loosen heavy soil.

My own mix often includes broad beans, oats and peas, but there are countless other choices, such as clover (*Trifolium repens*), common vetch (*Vicia sativa*), rye (*Secale cereale*) and narrow-leaved lupin (*Lupinus angustifolius*), all with their own strengths. Regardless of which ones you choose, a well-grown green manure can restore structure, build fertility and leave the ground ready to support a productive garden again.

Far left_Florian's green-manure mix from Mount Franklin Organics is a locally grown organic blend that I keep on hand to build soil structure and fertility between growing seasons.
Left_A green-manure crop before flowering. Chop and drop the plant onto the soil while it is still green (and before it sets seed) to protect soil structure, feed soil life and add organic matter.

Soil inputs and amendments

Consider amending your soil if the structure is compacted, the organic matter is low, the pH is extreme, or crops show persistent deficiency or poor growth despite adequate water. Lead with observation and test results rather than habit. I always take a less-is-more approach and rarely intervene unless absolutely necessary!

- Lime raises pH and can release nutrients in acidic soils. Use only if a pH test indicates a need.
- Elemental sulphur lowers pH in alkaline soils. Apply in small amounts and retest.
- Compost and surface mulch help with heavy clay soils. Over time, roots and soil life will open channels and improve infiltration.
- Gypsum can disperse tight clays where sodicity (salt imbalance) is an issue. It will not fix drainage in non-sodic/stable clays.
- For sandy soils, incorporate 3–5 centimetres (1¼–2 inches) of mature compost each growing season to improve organic matter and moisture retention. Add 2–5 kilograms (4–11 pounds) per square metre of fine clay (such as kaolin or clay-rich loam) or 1–2 litres (35–70 fluid ounces) per square metre of quality biochar that has been charged with compost tea to enhance nutrient and water-holding capacity. Finally, apply a 5–7-centimetre (2–2¾-inch) layer of organic mulch to slow soil-moisture evaporation and moderate soil temperature.
- Rock minerals, trace elements and sea-mineral products can be useful where tests show deficiencies. Use modestly and retest.
- Avoid quick-fix salt-based fertilisers in living soil systems. They can upset the biology you are trying to foster.

Climate and scale adaptations

These quick notes will help you no matter where you live and what kind of soil you have in your garden.

Hot and dry climates:

- Keep soil covered at all times. Bare soil is dying soil.
- Prioritise wind protection and afternoon shade for tender crops.
- Use deeper mulch and consider wicking beds or sub-surface irrigation to deliver water slowly to the root zone. I like to use drip irrigation laid between the soil and mulch.

Cold and wet climates:

- Improve drainage first. Raised beds or wicking beds can lift roots into warmer, better-aerated soil.
- Go easy on spring mulch until the soil warms, or it can lock in the cold.
- Where frost lingers, protect early plantings with cloches or low tunnels.

Heavy clay soil:

- Avoid digging when wet because this will destroy structure.
- Regularly add compost and surface mulch.
- Use gypsum only where sodicity (salt imbalance) is confirmed.

Sandy soil:

- — Add compost often, and keep beds mulched.
- — Use windbreaks and living edges to reduce the effect of drying breezes.
- — Water more frequently but in smaller doses to reduce leaching.

Garden scale:

- — **Balcony and courtyard:** Containers, troughs and wicking beds become your soil. Use a living potting mix, top-dress with compost, and keep the surface mulched.
- — **Suburban gardens:** Use a bed width of 75–150 centimetres (30–60 inches), with paths 40–60 centimetres (16–24 inches) wide. These proportions allow you to reach the middle of the bed without stepping on the soil, and provide wheelbarrow access. Make the paths wider if you require wheelchair access.
- — **Larger plots:** Repeat simple bed and path modules so maintenance stays human-scaled.

Design integration and beauty

I keep soil care visible and elegant. Bed edges in timber, steel or stone serve to frame planting and give crisp lines without becoming hard barriers to water. Even a spade-cut edge, such as the one on my verge gardens, creates a beautiful, clean line (although it does require more maintenance).

Path materials should be permeable and comfortable underfoot. Mulch can read as a warm ground plane that sets off foliage and bloom. Compost bays and worm farms can borrow the same material palette as fences, arbours or screens so the whole garden feels resolved and visually cohesive.

At Oak & Monkey Puzzle, the three-bay compost system was part of a timber and steel language that repeated throughout paths and edges. At Little Cottage on a Hill, compost towers are dotted across the garden like sculptures, where they read as vertical rhythms rather than mess or clutter.

A seasonal rhythm for living soil

Here's a guide to what you can do for your soil in the coming months:

- — **Autumn**: Feed beds with a thin dressing of mature compost, and remulch. Plant living covers where possible. Gather leaves for future mulch and leaf mould.
- — **Winter**: Protect bare ground, avoid working saturated soil, and plan rotations. Repair edges and paths so spring traffic does not damage beds.
- — **Spring**: Assess moisture, keep mulch light where soil needs to warm, and top up compost in thin layers. Plant intensively so living roots occupy the soil.
- — **Summer**: Maintain mulch depth, add compost as a light side dressing around hungry crops, and water slowly so it penetrates rather than runs off.

To get you started, try these two things this week:

1. Read your soil with a squeeze test, a smell and a quick worm count.
2. Top-dress one bed with 2 centimetres (3/4 inch) of mature compost, and cover any bare patches with mulch. Observe how moisture and crumb change over the next month.

NO-DIG GARDENING

Healthy soil is a living structure. The less you disturb it, the better it performs. No-dig gardening is the practice of building and protecting that structure by adding organic matter on the surface, then letting soil life do the mixing for you. The result is better drainage, steadier moisture, fewer weeds, stronger roots and an easier garden to live with and to love. No-dig visionary Charles Dowding has even put it to the test with ten years of data proving that no-dig gardening is the best style. But you don't need to be obsessive about it. Some crops, such as potatoes (*Solanum tuberosum*), have to be dug from the soil . That's the reality of growing them.

For decades, Charles has shown that the lightest touch can produce the most abundance. No-dig gardening isn't a trend; it's a commitment to soil structure, fungal networks and time saved on weeding. Here's how no-dig gardening works:

- It protects soil crumbs and fungal networks so water and air move freely.
- It feeds the soil community steadily with compost and mulch.
- It keeps weed seeds buried where they are less likely to germinate.
- It turns routine care into a light seasonal rhythm rather than heavy reworking.
- Compost is thc cnginc: thin, regular top dressings maintain a steady 'diet'.
- You can start anywhere, even on lawn or rough ground. Lay down cardboard, add a layer of compost and a layer of mulch, then plant into the bed.

My no-dig beds read as finished elements: consistent edges (timber and steel), permeable paths for quiet movement, and a mulch plane tying productivity to beauty.

Charles Dowding's no-dig work has long shaped the way I think about soil and structure, not just in theory, but in how I live with my garden. In speaking with him, what struck me was the clarity and humility he brings to decades of careful observation. What follows is drawn from that exchange: grounded, practical and permission-giving.

Working on one of my potato-growing composting towers at Little Cottage on a Hill (see pages 94–5). For me, compost is central to no-dig gardening, and each tower produces both a potato harvest and around 1 cubic metre (35 cubic feet) of compost to feed my verge beds and no-dig wicking beds.

> *'You will gain time . . . and you will gain harvests. So it's just win–win.'*

CHARLES DOWDING

No-dig gardening as layered care

Charles Dowding has spent more than 40 years refining and teaching no-dig gardening principles, pairing a grower's intuition with careful trials at his Somerset garden, Homeacres. Side-by-side beds there have shown a consistent yield advantage for no-dig gardening of roughly 12–13 per cent over dug beds, results he shares to demonstrate that surface feeding and minimal disturbance build living soil and productivity.

At the heart of his method are two simple ideas. First, disturb the soil as little as possible. Second, feed soil life from the top with compost and mulch. You can still lift potatoes (*Solanum tuberosum*), make a planting hole for a tomato (*S. lycopersicum*) or set a tree correctly, but you avoid needless excavation and subsequently keep biology intact.

Charles is equally clear about common misunderstandings. Cardboard is a tool for smothering weeds at the start, not an annual requirement. An initial 10–15 centimetres (4–6 inches) of compost is an investment to establish a clean, fertile surface, not a yearly prescription. Layering undecomposed materials in wet climates invites slugs, so ensure that the surface comprises a finished compost mulch rather than a lasagne of raw organics.

His trials also test widely repeated rules. A ten-year comparison found that forking to aerate soil produced about 8 per cent less food than undisturbed no-dig strips, likely from breaking fungal and bacterial networks. Separate measures at Homeacres recorded higher soil carbon in no-dig beds than in dug ones, reinforcing the long-term fertility gains of leaving soil structure to grow.

What we learn from Charles is as much about practice as perspective. Curiosity beats routine. Observe first, intervene last. In design terms, a composted surface reads as one material across beds, while paths and edges carry the structure. Layered soil care then becomes visible rhythm as well as function. These are the key takeaways from our conversation:

- No-dig gardening involves minimal soil disturbance plus feeding soil life from the surface, applied with common sense rather than rigid rules.
- Use cardboard only to smother weeds when establishing beds, not every year.
- Start with a generous compost top dressing, then maintain with lighter annual additions (2–3 centimetres; ¾–1¼ inches) rather than repeating the initial depth.
- Homeacres trials show no-dig beds yield 12–13 per cent more than dug beds, with higher soil carbon in no-dig beds.
- Forking to aerate reduced yields in Charles's ten-year strip trial, pointing to the value of leaving soil networks intact.
- Adapt the method to the climate. In wetter regions, avoid thick raw-material layers (such as straw or hay) that can harbour slugs; favour a 5–7-centimetre (2–2¾-inch) layer of finished compost as mulch.
- Question inherited rules, such as fixed four-year rotations. Observe your site and respond accordingly.

Scan to watch my full conversation with Charles Dowding, where we talk about no-dig fundamentals and why 'less' yields more.

Soil
Matthew Evans
Charles Dowding
No Dig
Charles Dowding No Dig

Setting up and maintaining a no-dig bed

To create a new bed on lawn or rough ground:

1. Mow or slash the grass down to the base. Leave the roots in place to feed the soil as they decay.
2. Lay out a well-soaked layer of plain cardboard (no tape or glossy print), with overlaps of 10–15 centimetres (4–6 inches). This will smother any remaining grass and weeds.
3. Add 10–15 centimetres (4–6 inches) of mature compost as the initial surface.
4. Top with 5–8 centimetres (2–3¼ inches) of mulch that suits your climate and crop-rotation plan (see page 57).

To plant into a no-dig bed:

— **Seedlings:** Part the mulch, tuck the seedling roots into the compost layer, then return the mulch loosely.

— **Small seeds:** Pull back the mulch to create a narrow strip of exposed compost. Scatter the seeds, and water them in. Once the seeds have grown into seedlings, mulch them very lightly with fine mulch.

— **Large seeds:** Use your finger or dibber to create holes through the mulch and into the compost below. Place one seed into each hole, cover it with soil or compost and water it in, then return the mulch.

To renew an established no-dig bed:

— Once or twice a year, top-dress with 2–5 centimetres (¾–2 inches) of mature compost.

— Keep the surface covered with living plants or mulch.

— Avoid empty beds. If a bed needs to rest, then sow a quick green manure or lay a light protective mulch over it.

Materials you can use in your no-dig bed, and why:

— Mature compost is the primary feed; apply it before planting or as a 2–3-centimetre (¾–1¼-inch) top dressing. Aim for a material that smells earthy (like mushrooms) rather than sour, ammonia-like or rotten.

— Use a 5–10-centimetre (2–4-inch) layer of leaf mould as a gentle conditioner to improve moisture-holding.

— Place a 5–10-centimetre (2–4-inch) layer of straw or shredded prunings as a protective blanket. Choose clean straw that is free of seed heads; soaking straw in water for a week can start breaking it down and encourage any seeds to sprout, so you can remove them. (Avoid straw in wet climates because it can harbour slugs and snails.)

— Well-rotted manure is ideal for hungry crops; use it sparingly and always cover it with compost or mulch.

— Avoid fresh lawn clippings in thick layers because they can mat and become anaerobic. Use thin layers, mixed into other mulches.

Opposite page,
Top left_Green manure is cut back and left on the surface to break down, feeding soil life without any need to turn the bed.
Top right_A light top dressing of mature compost, with mineral inputs and worm castings, builds fertility from the top down.
Bottom left_A protective layer of sugarcane mulch keeps the moisture in and the soil surface covered as the bed settles.
Bottom right_I'm planting seedlings that have been raised in toilet-roll tubes. The roots stay undisturbed, and the cardboard tube breaks down in situ.

Troubleshooting for no-dig beds

Here are the most common problems associated with no-dig beds, and what you can do about them:

- **Slugs and snails in thick mulch:** Use simple barriers around seedlings, create dry zones around slug-prone crops, and encourage predators by adding habitat. Eggshells or coffee grounds make great slug and snail deterrents. Beer traps attract slugs, which then drown. I also use iron-based snail pellets sparingly; they are an eco-friendly and animal-friendly alternative for controlling infestations.
- **Nitrogen drawdown after heavy straw mulching:** Nitrogen drawdown occurs when microbes use up nitrogen in the soil while breaking down carbon-rich materials such as straw or sawdust, leaving less available for plants. To remedy this, add a thin layer of compost under the straw, or water the bed with diluted worm liquid.
- **Persistent perennial weeds under the cardboard:** Double the size of the overlaps, leave the cardboard in place for a longer period before adding soil or mulch, and hand-pull any shoots that appear.
- **Waterlogging on heavy clay:** Increase the amount of organic matter, raise the bed height by a few centimetres, add surface drains in winter, and keep off the soil when it is wet (use paths or boards to spread the weight).
- **Slow soil warming in spring:** In cold or persistently wet climates, thick mulch can delay soil warming. Pull back mulch temporarily in early spring to let the soil absorb warmth, then replace it once growth is underway.

Climate and scale adaptations

These quick notes will help you no matter where you live:

- **Hot and dry climates:** Use deeper mulch. Ensure that there is afternoon shade for tender crops. Deliver water slowly to the root zone.
- **Cold and wet climates:** Build no-dig beds higher, and improve drainage. Hold back on spring mulch until the soil warms.
- **Balcony or courtyard:** Your containers become your no-dig beds. Top-dress with compost, keep the surface mulched with fine materials, and refresh little and often.
- **Larger plots:** Repeat basic modules of bed and path so maintenance stays human-scaled.

Design integration and beauty

No-dig gardens can be elegant and visible. Use a consistent material palette for edges if needed, and incorporate compost bays and worm tunnels to blend with the garden's language. Let mulch become a ground plane that visually sets off foliage and bloom.

In highly visible zones, choose a finer textured mulch for a considered finish, and repeat it so the space feels unified. Paths should be permeable and generous so that moving through the garden is effortless.

The studio, the hybrid potting shed and greenhouse, and the chicken housing form the working spine of the garden, with composting towers closing the nutrient loop. Repeated materials keep the hardworking structures cohesive, so function and beauty can sit comfortably together.

COMPOSTING SYSTEMS AND NUTRIENT CYCLING

Compost is concentrated life for your soil. It turns what the garden casts off and the kitchen discards into stable organic matter that feeds the soil community, improves structure and holds moisture. When composting is designed into daily life, it becomes effortless. You empty a caddy, you add browns, you turn or top up, and the garden keeps closing its own loop.

At Oak & Monkey Puzzle, there was enough space to have an entire back-of-house area that included a generous three-bay compost system. At Little Cottage on a Hill, in a much smaller space, compost towers and neat worm tunnels become vertical rhythms in the garden and in wicking beds; they're structural, discreet and beautiful. Compost sits at the heart of a productive garden because it:

- returns nutrients to the soil in a steady, safe form
- improves soil structure so roots can breathe and water can move
- reduces the amount of waste leaving your property, which saves money and builds resilience
- is adaptable to any scale, from a balcony tub to a 1-cubic-metre (35-cubic-foot) bay.

Compost can also be beautiful. Bins and bays can share materials with fences and edges so they read as part of the same garden language. Towers can become eye-catching vertical accents in a garden. When the composting system looks considered, you will use it more often. It will become a point of pride rather than something to hide.

The basics, in plain language

Think in pairs of 'browns' and 'greens'. Browns are dry, carbon-rich materials, while greens are fresh, nitrogen-rich materials. You can include things such as:

- straw and hay (browns)
- dry leaves and twigs (browns)
- shredded newspaper and cardboard (browns)
- cut-up pieces of cotton fabric (browns)
- vegetable and fruit scraps (greens)
- coffee grounds and tea leaves (greens)
- fresh lawn clippings (greens)
- new garden prunings (greens).

You can also add eggshells as a mineral input. Crushing them first helps them to break down more quickly, though they can remain visible as flecks for a while, which is fine. However, there are some things you should avoid or handle with care:

- meat, fish or dairy in open heaps where animals visit; these are safe only in sealed hot-composting systems (see below)
- weed roots and seed heads, if you don't plan to hot compost
- glossy paper, plastic stickers and produce ties
- thermal receipts and PFAS-coated takeaway papers; test paper with a drop of olive oil (if it beads, then avoid it)
- paper featuring home-printer inks, as they're unsafe (newspaper ink is fine)
- dog and cat droppings in compost for food crops; keep these in a separate composting system for ornamental plants (if used at all).

To create your compost heap, follow this simple rule: add the browns and greens in layers, with a ratio of two or three buckets of browns for every bucket of greens. Chop up pieces so they're 3–5 centimetres (1¼–2 inches) long. Keep the heap as moist as a wrung-out sponge. Give it air by turning it regularly (hot heaps: turn every two or three days for one or two weeks, then weekly; cold heaps: turn monthly), or by building in many small voids.

Hot composting happens when the pile is large enough (about 1 cubic metre; 35 cubic feet) and has the right mix of greens and browns, plus good moisture and airflow. It's faster than cold composting and can kill many weed seeds and pathogens if the centre spends time at 55–65 degrees Celsius (130–150 degrees Fahrenheit). Cold composting happens in smaller or less actively managed piles that don't heat up much, and it breaks down materials over months or years. It's slower than hot composting and easier to manage. However, both methods make good compost if you give them time and balance. To know if your compost is ready to use, look out for these signs:

- It smells earthy, never sour or ammonia-like.
- You're unable to recognise the original ingredients.

— For hot composts, the temperature has cooled to match the atmospheric conditions and has stayed there for a week.
— Seeds germinated in a portion of the compost show healthy, even growth.

Choose the system that suits your life and space

The three-bay system is reliable and scalable. It's best where you have steady inputs and room to work. Place the bays where you have water and wheelbarrow access, with morning sun to warm the heaps and some shade later in the day.

— An ideal bay size is 1 cubic metre (35 cubic feet).
— Line pallet compost bays with cardboard to retain warmth and moisture for better decomposition.
— Regularly add layers of browns and greens to the first bay. When it's full, move the compost into the second bay. When the heap temperature drops in the second bay and the material is dark, crumbly and earthy, move the compost to the third bay to mature.
— Actively turn the compost in the first bay; weekly turns bring faster results, but monthly turns still work well. Occasionally turn the compost in the second bay, but don't turn the compost in the third bay.

Tumblers are clean and contained. They're best where rodents are a concern or space is tight.

— Load with a balanced mix of browns and greens, then spin every few days to aerate.
— Keep moisture at the right level; most failed tumblers are too dry. Add a watering-can's worth if the materials look pale and dusty. They should feel as moist as a wrung-out sponge.
— If space permits, use two tumblers in rotation for a smoother supply.

Compost towers and compact cylinders are best for small gardens. They can also become sculptural features. I've used leftover bits of timber-and-wire fencing to clad my composting towers and turn these utilitarian objects into things of architectural beauty!

— For each tower, use a wire-mesh cylinder that is 60–100 centimetres (24–39½ inches) in diameter and 90–120 centimetres (35½–47 inches) tall.
— Tuck a loose inner 'skirt' of straw around the mesh (if you are after a neater finish), then add alternating layers of chopped browns and greens. The compost layers pin the straw in place as you build.
— For a potato (*Solanum tuberosum*) tower, the holes in the wire mesh need to be big enough so the plants can grow through, but small enough so most of the compost does not fall out as it decomposes. Nestle seed potatoes around the edge as you build your compost layers, so they will be able to access the light when they grow.
— Keep the tower moist. Place it in a part of the garden that would benefit from subtle nutrient leaching.

***Above left*_**Inside my retrofitted wheelie bin worm farm, kitchen scraps and browns (such as dry leaves) break down into castings and worm liquid for the garden. ***Above right*_**Built around aged compost and leaf mould, my homemade potting mix is gentle enough to be used as a top dressing or a seed-raising mix.

Sheet composting and trench composting are best for quiet soil building and for beds that will rest.

- For sheet composting, start with a 1–2-centimetre (½–¾-inch) layer of browns, then add a 1–2-centimetre (½–¾-inch) layer of greens. Repeat, alternating browns and greens, until the heap is around 10 centimetres (4 inches) in height. End with a brown layer before covering with mulch. Plant large seedlings through it, or let it rest for a few weeks.
- For trench composting, bury food scraps 20–30 centimetres (8–12 inches) deep, between crop rows, so the scraps are well covered. Soil life will process them in place.

Leaf mould is a gentle conditioner.

- Pile dry leaves in an upright cage. Wet well, and leave for six to eighteen months, ensuring that they never fully dry out.
- The result is a fine, dark, spongy material that improves the moisture-holding ability and structure of soil.
- Use leaf mould as a top dressing under fruit trees and ornamentals, and as a component in homemade seed-raising mixes (see page 231).

Easy fixes for food scraps

Bokashi bins are ideal for busy gardeners and apartment dwellers. They ferment all food scraps, including meat and dairy, without smells when the lid is closed. Add food waste to the bucket, sprinkling a handful of Bokashi mix over every new layer. To check if it's working, open the lid: you should notice a sour, pickled aroma and a white bloom, especially during warm weather. When the bin is full, set it aside for ten to fourteen days to finish fermenting. After this, bury the fermented scraps in a garden bed or compost bay, add them to a soil factory (a container where fermented scraps are mixed with soil and left for a few weeks to finish decomposing before planting), or feed them to a worm farm for a nitrogen and microbe boost. You can even siphon off the Bokashi liquid regularly and pour it down household drains to keep them clear and fresh.

Terracotta in-ground worm farms work well in small gardens where a traditional worm farm would be too bulky. Soak discarded terracotta pots overnight, drill a few extra holes in the bottom with a masonry bit, then bury the pots in garden beds or large containers so the rim is just above the soil's surface. Add chopped food scraps, and let worms move nutrients in and out through the holes. After two to six months, harvest the worm castings ('vermicompost') or move the pot to another area, as most of the contents should be broken down. There are many benefits: no microplastics, beautiful materiality and easy access within arm's reach.

Compost placement and design integration

Place your compost heap within easy reach of both the kitchen and the garden. If you can see it, then you're more likely to use it. Mirror the same timber, steel or stone that you've utilised elsewhere so bays and screening read as part of the garden.

Allow space to keep browns until needed. Store leaves, aged woodchips, cardboard and toilet paper rolls to cover every caddy of scraps.

Give the system room to turn, air and some sun, and ensure that water is nearby. A hose point within a few steps is ideal so you can keep the heap moist.

A word of caution: keep compost heaps out of the reach of pets and livestock. Certain moulds that grow during decomposition can produce toxins that cause serious issues in animals, including tremors and seizures. My friend's dog had to be rushed to emergency veterinary care after getting into the compost.

Staying safe with compost

Wash your hands after handling fresh compost heaps, and keep raw compost away from edible leaves. If you need to be extra cautious – for example, for pregnancy or immune-health reasons – then favour sealed systems and apply compost to the soil, then place mulch on top. Remember that time is your ally. Mature compost and leaf mould are gentle, stable and safe when handled with care.

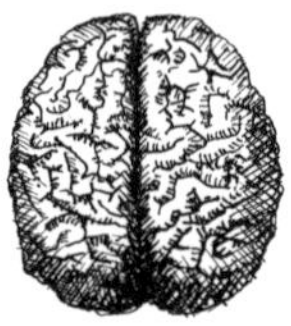

Using compost well

Productive beds often thrive with a total of 2–5 kilograms (4–11 pounds) of mature compost per square metre each year. Spread it thinly and often rather than in rare heavy doses.

Place it on the soil's surface under a light mulch, rather than dug through. Soil life will do the mixing. You can also use it as a planting pocket for hungry crops, and as a side dressing around plants during the fruiting season, followed by a soft mulch.

Note that evidence is mixed about compost teas and extracts, so it's best to treat them as gentle complements rather than cure-alls. If you choose to use teas/extracts, then make them from mature compost, aerate them well, and apply them to the soil rather than edible leaves. When using compost, try to link it to the wider garden cycle:

- Feed a little mature compost into worm farms to seed them with diverse life.
- Use spent chicken bedding as a brown layer in bays, then allow a full maturation period before returning it to beds.
- Save excess dry leaves each autumn to restore balance in spring when greens are plentiful.

To get you started, try these two things this week:

1. Start a browns store. Fill three breathable sacks with dry leaves or shredded cardboard. Label and stack them neatly beside your compost area.
2. Build one compact compost tower. Use a cylinder, add alternating thin layers of chopped browns and greens, and water as you build. Place it where a nearby bed will enjoy the slow release of goodness.

Troubleshooting for compost

Here are the most common problems associated with compost, and what you can do about them:

- **Bad stink:** If the compost smells sour or like ammonia, then add browns, mix to incorporate air, check the moisture, and cover the top with a dry cap of autumn leaves, shredded cardboard or straw.
- **Too dry:** If the compost is parched and not breaking down, then add water through the pile, layer in fresh greens, and consider a light cover to slow evaporation.
- **Rodents are visiting:** If mice and rats are an issue, then use a tumbler or a rodent-resistant bin with a secure base. Avoid cooked food and meat in open systems.
- **Weeds are sprouting:** If finished hot compost has weed seedlings, then the heap did not reach a high enough temperature or was not hot for long enough. Use this batch under trees and ornamentals. Next time, check that the volume of your heap is at least 1 cubic metre (35 cubic feet) when you construct it. If you have a weed problem with cold compost, then be more selective about what you add. (Some of the best pumpkins I have ever grown have come out of accidentally seeded compost!)

*Above left*_An earthworm from the compost pile, one of the simplest indicators that the system is active and cycling.
*Above right*_Finished compost and worm castings, crumbly and sweet-smelling, can be added as a top dressing to feed a garden bed before planting.

Climate and scale adaptations

These quick notes will help you no matter where you live.

- **Hot and dry climates:** Shade the sides of bays, increase brown layers to keep structure airy, and water compost heaps while building them and during hot spells.
- **Cold and wet climates:** Site on free-draining ground, give compost heaps a roof, and use lighter layers until the weather warms. Turning is best done when materials are not sodden.
- **Small gardens, balcony or courtyard:** Choose a sealed tumbler or a compact aerated bin. Use leaf-mould cages that double as vertical features. A single worm tunnel within a large pot can be both practical and discreet.
- **Larger plots:** Build a three-bay system, and keep a dedicated leaf-mould cage. Repeat the material palette of your edges and screens so the whole area feels resolved and visually cohesive.

KATE FLOOD

Compost as culture, care and everyday joy

Kate Flood – known as Compostable Kate – is an educator and author who has turned compost into an approachable, joyful practice for every kind of gardener. She grew up in the inner suburbs of Sydney, where a backyard compost heap was part of normal life, a habit she has now passed on to her own children. Her work makes the case for compost as a practical climate action and a design choice that belongs in plain sight.

'Decay is not an end; it is the beginning of transformation.'

Kate's philosophy is disarmingly simple. Decay is not an end; it is the beginning of transformation. When composted food scraps are returned to the soil, we reduce landfill methane and build living structure where roots can thrive. She asks us to put on compost-coloured glasses and see waste as resource, then keep as much organic matter on-site as possible. The result is a garden that is more resilient, less reliant on purchased inputs, and richer in microbial life.

Design matters. Kate encourages visible and beautiful composting systems that you will actually use, placed near the kitchen door or a daily pathway. She is moving away from plastic enclosures and towards natural materials, including terracotta vessels repurposed as in-ground worm farms, which avoid microplastics and integrate quietly with planting.

Her core principles are practical. Great compost is made from four universal ingredients – carbon, nitrogen, oxygen and water – so set up a carbon-collection corner with leaves, aged woodchips and safe papers to balance kitchen nitrogen. For busy households, a Bokashi bin pre-ferments everything, including meat and dairy, without odour, and the fermented mix can feed a worm farm, a soil factory or a hot heap. She cautions against contaminated commercial inputs and shares easy ways to avoid PFAS-coated papers and other hidden hazards. Compost begins at home, yet it scales through community in all sorts of ways, such as sharing caddies with neighbours and closing the loop at street level. Kate's beliefs include:

- **Visibility beats perfection:** Put compost where you'll use it, with no shame and no hiding.
- **Rhythm over rules:** All you need is scraps, browns, air and cover; adjust them by smell/feel.
- **Scale fluidly:** Work up from a sealed benchtop caddy to a worm farm/tower to a three-bay system.
- **Share it:** Noticing excess heat, discovering steam coming from the heap, and sifting worm castings ('black gold') are teaching moments.
- **Celebrate the loop:** Compost makes your garden more yours with every bucket.

In Kate's hands, compost is transformation, participation and everyday design, all in service of soil that gives back. Compost is technique, yes, but Kate frames it as culture. When scraps become soil, you're not just making fertiliser, you're building a daily ritual that connects kitchen, season and community.

Scan to watch my full conversation with Kate Flood, where we talk about compost as culture.

WORM FARMS AND WORM TUNNELS

Worms turn kitchen scraps into a fine, stable material that plants love. A worm system is clean, compact and easy to live with. It fits balconies and backyards, and it brings the biology right to the roots. When placed well and fed little and often, it becomes a subtle engine for your garden. Here is a quick overview of a worm system:

- Use composting worms (often sold as 'red wigglers') rather than earthworms. They live in rich surface layers, not in deep soil.
- A comfortable temperature for composting worms is 15–25 degrees Celsius (59–77 degrees Fahrenheit). Brief peaks outside that range are fine if the bedding stays moist and shaded.
- The bedding should be springy and absorbent. Use a mix of shredded cardboard, coir, leaf mould and a little finished compost. Moisten to the level of a wrung-out sponge.
- Feed your composting worms small amounts often rather than big loads rarely. Chop scraps to 2–3 centimetres (¾–1¼ inches) in length.

Choose a system that suits your space

Stand-alone worm farms are best for balconies, courtyards and small gardens. They can comprise stacked bins or a single ventilated box. Both work equally well. Place your chosen worm farm in bright shade, never in full sun. In the southern hemisphere, a southern or eastern aspect is ideal.

Add a 5–10-centimetre (2–4-inch) layer of bedding (such as shredded cardboard or coconut coir, aged compost, moist newspaper or straw) to the bottom of the worm farm. Bedding should feel like a wrung-out sponge: damp but not soggy. Favour a bedding to food scraps ratio of at least 3:1 by volume, and replenish bedding as it breaks down or compacts. Add a light cover of damp hessian, cardboard or newspaper to minimise vinegar flies and to retain moisture.

Ensure your worm farm has drainage holes in the base so excess moisture can escape. Collect any leachate ('worm juice') from the outlet, and store it in a separate container. For suggestions on how to use the leachate in the garden, see page 222.

Worm tunnels are the best choice for bringing biology straight into garden beds and wicking systems. Drill ten to fifteen holes (10–25 millimetres; ½–1 inch diameter) into a 150–300-millimetre (6–12-inch) section of pipe, spaced every 5–10 centimetres (2–4 inches) around the pipe. Sink the pipe so the holes are below the soil's surface, and place a handful of food scraps into the pipe. Cap the top of the pipe between feeds to keep out pests and to maintain moisture. Seed the tunnel with a small handful of composting worms and a scoop of castings from a worm farm or local supplier.

If you're placing your worm tunnel into a wicking bed, ensure that it stays in the upper soil layer above the water reservoir. Never feed directly into the water reservoir. Favour small, frequent feeds because excessive scraps can turn sour in the cool lower soil.

What to feed, what to avoid

Feed your worms like you would season a dish – just a small handful – then cover with bedding material. If the worms chomp through the material quickly, then you can always add more next time.

Include fruit and vegetable scraps, coffee grounds, tea leaves, crushed eggshells, soaked shredded cardboard and soft prunings. Limit or avoid:

— large quantities of citrus and onions (if you must add them, then do it in small amounts and bury them well)
— very salty, oily or spicy foods
— meat, fish and dairy in open inlets that animals can reach
— large amounts of grass clippings (mix thinly with bedding to prevent compaction).

Harvesting and using worm castings and leachate

Worm castings (also called vermicompost) are rich in stable organic matter and microbial life. In stacked farms, harvest from the lower tray, which will contain no fresh food but might have a few tiny white cocoons. In worm tunnels, lift the cap, scoop out a small amount of castings, and replace with fresh bedding. If you have a single box, scoop out finished castings from one side. Sift the material and return any worms or large bits to the box with fresh bedding and food; this keeps your worm population healthy and the process continuous.

Use castings as a light top dressing, about 0.5–1 kilograms (1–2 pounds) per square metre. You can mix a handful into planting holes for seedlings. Apply castings 'little and often'. For example, every two to three months for pots, or two to three times a year for garden beds. They add life and organic matter without excessive nutrients.

*Right*_Feeding a worm tunnel in a wicking bed with spent leaves and garden debris. This returns scraps straight back to the soil rather than carrying them out of the bed.
*Far right*_Replacing the cap to keep the worm tunnel moist and free of pests. This simple closed-loop system is built into each of my wicking beds.

'Leachate is the liquid that drains from a worm farm. Use it only if it smells clean and earthy; discard it if it's sour.'

Leachate is the liquid that drains from a worm farm. Use it only if it smells clean and earthy; discard it if it's sour. Dilute the leachate with water in a ratio of 1:10 before using it on the soil around ornamental plants or trees; don't apply it directly to edible leafy greens or herbs. Leachate provides soluble nutrients and beneficial microbes, giving the soil a mild nutrient and microbial boost, so use it thoughtfully.

To make an aerated extract, soak 2–4 cups of finished castings in water, stir briskly, and let the mixture sit for up to 24 hours before using it promptly. Like leachate, apply diluted extract to the soil. Liquids are a supplement; the real value is in the worm castings themselves.

Troubleshooting for worm farms

Here are simple tips and solutions to help keep your worm farm thriving, with guidance for common situations you might encounter:

- **Sour smell:** Add dry bedding, improve airflow, stop feeding for a week, and check drainage.
- **Vinegar flies:** Bury food, use a damp cover, and freeze or microwave scraps before placing them in worm farms if necessary.
- **Ants:** Raise the moisture level slightly, and sit the worm-farm legs in small bowls of water for a few days.
- **Worms trying to escape:** Check the heat and moisture levels, as well as the recent feed, because the conditions are off. Correct gradually, not all at once.
- **Mites or springtails:** These are normal fellow travellers. If numbers boom, then reduce feeding and add bedding.

Climate and scale adaptations

*Opposite page*_Inside a working worm farm. Moist bedding is alive with composting worms, a sign that the system is active and the conditions are right.

Whether your space is big or small, and no matter the climate, these practical tips will help you set up and care for a thriving worm farm that suits your needs.

- **Hot and dry climates:** Choose a shaded, breezy spot for your worm farm. Insulate the sides with cardboard or timber cladding. Water the bedding lightly during heatwaves.
- **Cold and wet climates:** Lift the worm farm onto bricks for drainage. Add extra bedding so the mass holds warmth. Use a cover to protect from rainwater.
- **Small spaces:** A single-tiered farm fits under a bench. One or two worm tunnels can live in a large trough.
- **Larger plots:** Add more worm tunnels throughout long beds so each 1 metre (3 feet) of soil has a feed point. Pair these with a main worm farm near the compost area for bulk processing.
- **Safety and assurance:** Wash your hands after handling fresh feed or worm castings. Keep raw scraps and fresh leachate away from edible leaves. If anyone in your household is immune-compromised or pregnant, then it's extra important to use castings only as a soil top dressing and to ensure that any liquids (such as leachate or extracts) are well-diluted and applied to the soil, never to edible parts of plants.

Design integration and beauty

Keep your worm farm close to your kitchen and garden beds so feeding your worms becomes an easy habit.

Borrow the material palette of your garden. A timber screen, a painted cabinet or a neat bench housing will help the worm farm belong to the space.

Mark in-bed worm tunnels with subtle caps so they read as considered details rather than as afterthoughts. In highly visible beds with multiple worm tunnels, align the placement of the tunnels with planting rhythms so they create a relevant cadence. To get you started, try these two things this week:

'Keep your worm farm close to your kitchen and garden beds so feeding your worms becomes an easy habit.'

1. Install one worm tunnel in a productive bed. Use a single tunnel for 1–2 square metres (10–20 square feet) of gardening space. A good size for each tunnel is a pipe 10–15 centimetres (4–6 inches) in diameter and 30 centimetres (12 inches) long, with holes at least 5 millimetres (1/4 inch) wide drilled in the buried portion. Add about 5–10 centimetres (2–4 inches) of moist bedding plus a small handful of food scraps, and fit a secure cap on top.
2. Top-dress 1 square metre (10 square feet) of your garden with 1 kilogram (2 pounds) of worm castings. If you don't have your own castings yet, you can purchase ready-made castings from a nursery or garden centre. Sprinkle the castings evenly, and water lightly. Over the next fortnight, observe any changes in soil texture or plant growth.

Your fast guide to worm farms

Once you have these basics under control, your worm farm will work wonders for your garden.

Collect these materials:

- composting worms, such as red wigglers
- ventilated bin or tiered worm farm with drainage
- bedding mix of shredded cardboard, coir, leaf mould and a little finished compost
- cover layer of damp hessian or cardboard.

Set up your worm farm:

- Place the worm farm in bright shade with good airflow, close to the kitchen and garden beds; avoid full sun.
- Add the bedding mix, moisten it, and place the composting worms on top.
- Place the damp cover over the bedding mix and worms.
- Use a timber screen or bench housing to integrate the design with the garden.
- Ideally, keep the temperature between 15 and 25 degrees Celsius (59–77 degrees Fahrenheit).

Feed your worms:

- Chop food scraps to 2–3 centimetres (3/4–1 1/4 inches) in length.
- Remove the damp cover, and bury small amounts of the food scraps often.
- Replace the damp cover after each feed.

Use what the worms make:

- Collect leachate so it never sits in the base; if it smells clean and earthy, then dilute it with water (1:10) and apply to the soil.
- Harvest worm castings from the tray, avoiding fresh food and tiny white cocoons.
- Lightly top-dress the soil with worm castings every two to three months for potted plants, or two to three times per year for garden beds; aim for 0.5–1 kilogram (1–2 pounds) per 1 square metre (10 square feet).

Opposite page,
***Top left*_**Feeding my retro-fitted wheelie bin worm farm with kitchen scraps from the benchtop caddy. These small additions keep the system steady. ***Top right*_**Opening the inspection cap to collect worm castings. They contain rich biology for top dressing and planting holes. ***Bottom left*_**Collecting leachate from the tap at the base of the worm farm. It's a concentrated liquid that needs to be diluted before use on the garden. ***Bottom right*_**Diluting leachate with water at a ratio of roughly 1:10 before applying it to the soil.

Retro-Kit

GROWING ORGANICALLY AND REGENERATIVELY

This involves working with living systems so the garden becomes easier, not harder, over time. It protects soil life, reduces outside inputs, and invites biodiversity to share the work. As practical as it is beautiful, the result is planting that looks effortless yet carries deep resilience under the surface. Here are the core principles of growing organically and regeneratively:

- Feed the soil, then let the soil feed the plants.
- Keep roots in the ground through the year where the climate allows. Living roots support soil biology.
- Grow a diverse range of plants so pests have fewer easy targets, and beneficial insects have food and shelter.
- Disturb the soil as little as you can. Build fertility at the surface with compost and mulch.
- Use water carefully, and keep the surface covered to reduce evaporation.
- Observe first, then act. Small, regular adjustments are more powerful than big fixes.

Everyday practice

Discover what organic and regenerative gardening looks like day-to-day, and how simple routines create a resilient, thriving garden.

- **Fertility as a gentle, ongoing layer:** Top-dress beds with a 1–2-centimetre (1/2–3/4-inch) layer of mature compost, and repeat once or twice a year. Follow with a protective mulch that is suited to your climate. Avoid digging compost through the bed; soil life will do the mixing for you.
- **Planting for diversity and resilience:** Mix families and forms. Pair leafy crops with flowers that bring pollinators and predators. Tuck herbs among vegetables. Add shrubs and small trees at the edges where space allows so the garden has structure and year-round habitat. Aim for something in flower every month of the growing year.
- **Simple crop rotations:** Moving crops from bed to bed spreads demand and reduces disease pressure. Keep it basic so it's easy to follow. For example, a four-bed pattern might move in this sequence:
  1. fruit crops, such as tomato (*Solanum lycopersicum*) and capsicum (*Capsicum annuum*)
  2. leaf crops, such as lettuce (*Lactuca sativa*), broccoli (*Brassica oleracea* Italica Group), cabbage (*B. o.* Capitata Group) and kale (*B. o.* Acephala Group)
  3. root crops, such as carrot (*Daucus carota* subsp. *sativus*) and beetroot (*Beta vulgaris*)
  4. soil builders, such as sugar snap pea (*Pisum sativum*) and common bean (*Phaseolus vulgaris*).

  If a bed mixes families, then rotate the dominant crop family from that bed to a new bed next season.

— **Polycultures and companion planting:** Use small blocks or repeating clumps instead of long single rows. Plant beneficial-insect–attracting plantings through or alongside productive beds. Good options include dill (*Anethum graveolens*), fennel (*Foeniculum vulgare*), sweet alyssum (*Lobularia maritima*), pot marigold (*Calendula officinalis*), purple coneflower (*Echinacea purpurea*) and French marigold (*Tagetes patula*). These provide nectar, pollen and places for beneficial insects to live.

— **Integrated pest and disease management:** Start with healthy soil and plants. Check beds often, but learn how to differentiate between cosmetic damage and real threats. Encourage predators by keeping flowers and water in the garden. If you need a direct form of control, begin with physical methods such as hand-picking, barriers and covers. Use low-risk products sparingly, and always read the instructions first. The goal is balance rather than a pest-free garden. If absolutely necessary, spray an organically certified pesticide. I very rarely spray because my garden often finds its own balance; if it's unavoidable, then I favour eco-oil or neem-oil sprays. Or I give the bug-infested plants to my chickens, and enjoy their gift of eggs in return!

— **Seed and plant choice:** Choose varieties with known disease resistance that suit your climate. Favour open-pollinated plants when you plan to save seeds in future seasons. Source plants from growers who care for soil and avoid systemic chemicals where possible

Water, shade and shelter

Healthy soil holds moisture, yet the planting still needs help in heat or wind.

— Mulch to a depth that suits your climate. In hot regions, this may be 7–10 centimetres (2¾–4 inches). In cool regions, use lighter layers in spring so the soil can warm up.

— Create dappled shade for tender crops using climbers on frames or fruit trees pruned for light shade.

— Use windbreaks and living edges to slow and lift wind over beds.

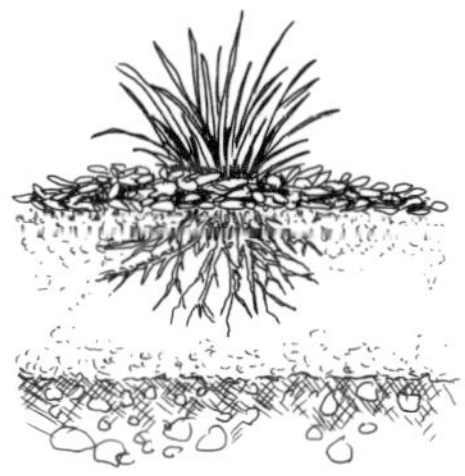

Herbicides in the productive garden

I don't use glyphosate or other chemical herbicides in my gardens. The reason is simple: they damage soil life and pose risks to human and animal health. Research continues to raise questions about links between glyphosate and health concerns. Some countries and councils have already restricted or banned its use in public spaces.

Here are some design-first alternatives:

— Mulch deeply to smother weeds and protect soil structure.

— Wherever possible, don't let weeds flower and go to seed. Even if you only have time to quickly pluck weed flowers rather than pulling out the whole plant, you will be saving the soil from weed seeds. As they say: 'One year's seeding is seven years' weeding.'

— Plant ground covers that outcompete weeds while adding beauty and habitat.

— Use flame weeding, boiling water or hand tools for small patches.

— Reimagine 'weeds' as soil indicators or temporary pioneer plants; often they're showing you what the soil needs.

Regeneration beyond the bed

Let parts of the garden rest with living covers between crops. Leave roots in place when you clear a bed. I just chop off spent plants at the base rather than pulling them out. The decaying roots become channels for air and water, and food for soil life.

Add 'bug hotels' and woody debris, and keep stick piles to host spiders and small reptiles where this is safe and appropriate for your location. These small yet generous ecosystem-affirming gestures build resilience without adding work.

Troubleshooting for growing organically

Every organic garden presents new opportunities to observe, learn and adapt. Here are some common situations you might encounter, and practical ways to guide your garden back to health:

- **Stalled growth despite compost additions:** Check the drainage and the soil pH. Consider the shade if the light is low. Review watering patterns.
- **Repeating disease on the same crop:** Increase the rotation interval, and choose a disease-resistant variety. Remove and bin affected plants rather than composting them if the disease is persistent.
- **Pests building despite interwoven flowering plantings:** Increase plant diversity, and reduce monoculture blocks. Review whether irrigation or fertilising is creating lush but weak growth.

Climate and scale adaptations

These quick notes will help you flourish no matter where you live or what kind of soil you have. Gardening is about observing, adapting and working with your local conditions. Every climate and space offers unique opportunities.

- **Hot and dry climates:** Choose heat-tolerant varieties. Increase organic mulch, and use deeper, less frequent watering so roots travel downwards. Add wind filters to protect plants from desiccating winds, and provide afternoon shade for tender crops. Consider wicking beds in places where water supply is limited or costly.
- **Cold and wet climates:** Raise beds a little to improve drainage and to warm soils sooner. Hold back on mulch in spring until the bed has warmed up. Use cloches, frost netting or small polytunnels to protect early plantings and to extend the season.
- **Heavy clay:** Avoid working the soil when it's wet. Keep adding compost and living roots. Plant deep-rooted species to open pathways for air and water over time.
- **Sandy soil:** Add compost often. Keep the surface mulched. Use windbreaks and living edges to reduce drying. Water lightly but more often to reduce leaching.
- **Small spaces and containers:** Your potting mix is your soil. Use the best-quality living mix with compost as a component that you can afford, top-dress lightly through the growing season, and keep the surface mulched with fine materials such as shredded leaves or mushroom compost. Mix productive plants with flowers and herbs so the whole container supports beneficial life. Pots can become tiny ecosystems in their own right.
- **Larger plots:** Repeat simple modules of beds and paths. Place perennial habitat plantings in well-thought-out locations so beneficial insects can move through the garden more easily.

Design integration and beauty

Regenerative planting can be elegant, especially if you think in layers. Ground covers soften edges and hold moisture. Perennials provide structure and rhythm. Annuals fill gaps, bring colour and extend the harvest. Repetition offers a gentle cadence.

A consistent edge detail frames productive beds so the space feels resolved. Flowering elements are part of the composition, not an afterthought. Plant forms, foliage, texture, tones and seasonal shifts should feel intentional, whether viewed from the verandah and the kitchen window or from within the beds. To get you started, try these two things this week:

1. Make a 'bug hotel' by drilling various-sized holes (3–10 millimetres; 1/8–1/2 inch) in a block of untreated wood, and placing it near your productive growing space to welcome native bees and beneficial insects. You can also bundle hollow stems, small sticks or bamboo canes together and set them horizontally to provide nesting spots for other garden helpers.
2. Map out a basic rotation for the next four edible plantings. Write your crop plan on a stake at the end of each bed so the sequence is easy to follow and adjust.

Above left_My potting shed and studio wall is a working nook, where sieves and tools are stored in plain sight. They become part of the garden's visual language.

Above right_These go-to hand tools are kept close and used often. Small, repeatable actions make the systems work.

ZUCCHINI

GROWING FROM SEED, AND OTHER PROPAGATION TECHNIQUES

Propagation is how you keep the garden moving. It's where ideas turn into plants, and where small daily actions set you up for abundance through the seasons. If done simply and well, it will save you money, preserve varieties you love and give you instant plants that are already suited to your conditions. Here are the essentials you'll need for propagating success:

'Propagation . . . will save you money, preserve varieties you love and give you instant plants.'

- **Seed-raising mix:** Aim for a fine, free-draining mix that holds moisture without staying wet. To make your own, sift mature compost with leaf mould and coarse sand or vermiculite in a ratio of 2:1:1 Otherwise, purchase a peat-free seed-raising blend from a garden centre or nursery. If the mix feels dry and dusty, or water runs off the surface at first (meaning it's hydrophobic), then pre-wet it in a tub before filling the seed trays. Gently fill trays without compacting; the mix should feel light and fluffy so fragile roots can grow through easily. Water after filling, then sow your seeds (see page 232).
- **Water and warmth:** Seeds need even moisture and the right temperature to sprout. Bottom watering keeps moisture steady. Place seed trays in a shallow tub of water for a few minutes, then drain. As a guide to temperature:
  1. Cool-season crops, such as lettuce (*Lactuca sativa*) and sugar snap pea (*Pisum sativum*), prefer 10–18 degrees Celsius (50–64 degrees Fahrenheit).
  2. Warm-season crops, such as tomato (*Solanum lycopersicum*), capsicum (*Capsicum annuum*) and basil (*Ocimum basilicum*), thrive at 18–24 degrees Celsius (64–75 degrees Fahrenheit).

  I've had great success using heat mats, which are readily available online. Alternatively, if you have a warm spot (such as near a hot-water service), then this can be a perfect cultivation location, as long as you move the plants into the light as soon as they emerge.
- **Light:** Most seedlings need bright light as soon as they emerge. A sunny window can work in mild seasons. In darker months or indoors, use LED grow lights for fourteen to sixteen hours each day, hung 10–15 centimetres (4–6 inches) above the leaves. Move the lights up as the seedlings grow.
- **Air and hygiene:** Good airflow prevents damping off (a common plant disease that affects seeds and seedlings, causing them to rot and collapse before or soon after emerging). Clean seed trays before using them, do not overwater, and remove any weak or mouldy seedlings promptly.
- **Labels:** Use a pencil or UV-stable marker on plastic, metal or timber labels, or on clean popsicle sticks. You can also repurpose old plastic pots by cutting them into strips for homemade labels. Place a duplicate label at the opposite end of each seed tray, just in case one fades or is lost.

Opposite page_Seed raising in the hybrid potting shed and greenhouse, using trays, pots and toilet-roll tubes, with a heat mat for bottom warmth and the chickens close by. Everything is compact and connected.

Sowing seeds

There are two methods: direct sowing into the garden bed, and sowing seeds into trays or soil blocks. Direct sowing suits crops that dislike root disturbance, such as carrot (*Daucus carota* subsp. *sativus*), parsnip (*Pastinaca sativa*), radish (*Raphanus sativus*), coriander (*Coriandrum sativum*), common bean (*Phaseolus vulgaris*) and sugar snap pea (*Pisum sativum*). Legumes (such as beans and peas) will often germinate quickly, and they don't cope well with transplant shock. They perform best when their roots grow undisturbed from the start.

Using seed trays or soil blocks suits crops that benefit from a head start or protection, such as broccoli (*Brassica oleracea* Italica Group), cabbage (*B. o.* Capitata Group), tomato (*Solanum lycopersicum*), lettuce (*Lactuca sativa*), onion (*Allium cepa*), capsicum (*Capsicum annuum*) and many flowers. This lets you control temperature, moisture and spacing.

Soil blocks are handy because they reduce plastic and encourage strong roots. Common sizes are 2.5-centimetre (1-inch) and 5-centimetre (2-inch) cubes. Start small, then transplant seedlings into larger blocks or pots.

Regardless of where you're sowing seeds, there's just one simple rule to follow: sow them at a depth of two to three times their diameter.

- For tiny seeds, such as those of lettuce: sprinkle them on the surface, gently press them in, then mist and cover lightly with sand or vermiculite.
- For medium seeds, such as those of cabbage: sow them about ½ centimetre (¼ inch) deep.
- For large seeds, such as those of beans and peas: sow them 2–4 centimetres (¾–1½ inches) deep.

Space seeds so that seedlings will not be crowded. For trays, two or three seeds per cell is usually enough. When seedlings appear, thin them out and only keep the strongest one.

Alternative seed starters

If you don't have access to seed trays or soil blocks, then here are some quick, easy-transplant, low-waste substitutes:

- **Toilet-roll centres:** Snugly place a number of cardboard toilet-roll centres upright in a shallow tub, and fill them with seed-raising mix. Sow one or two seeds per roll, and keep them evenly moist. When you're ready to plant out, cut a 1–2 centimetre (½–¾-inch) slit on either side of each roll base to help the roots to exit, then plant the whole roll. This method can be used instead of direct sowing for sugar snap pea (*Pisum sativum*), common bean (*Phaseolus vulgaris*), corn/maize (*Zea mays*), sunflowers (*Helianthus* spp.), sweet pea (*Lathyrus odoratus*), and pumpkins or squash (*Cucurbita* spp.) that you'll plant out young.
- **Egg-carton cells:** Use plain-pulp cartons (avoid glossy or heavily inked cartons). Puncture a drainage hole in each cell, fill the cell with seed-raising mix, then sow one seed per cell. When you're ready to plant out, tear off each cell and plant the entire plug. Transplant seedlings early, when you can see two or three true leaves (these are the first leaves that look like the adult

plant's foliage, which appear after the small, rounded seed leaves known as cotyledons). This method can be used for lettuce (*Lactuca sativa*), brassicas (*Brassica* spp.), onion (*Allium cepa*), pot marigold (*Calendula officinalis*) and marigolds (*Tagetes* spp.).

— **Seed snail (soil roll):** Spread a layer of pre-moistened seed-raising mix over a non-permeable liner. Roll it up snugly, stand it upright in a cup or pot, then sow seeds into the top surface. Keep them evenly moist. Once seedlings are sturdy (usually two to three weeks after sowing), unroll the snail, separate the seedlings and pot them on. This method can be used for sweet pea (*Lathyrus odoratus*), most salad greens, brassicas (*Brassica* spp.), onion (*Allium cepa*) and many annual flowers/herbs (small to medium seeds that you'll pot on promptly). Skip this method for plants with very large seeds, those that grow a taproot, and slow growers that can't be potted on quickly. (See the box on pages 234–5 for more detailed information on how to make a seed snail.)

Toilet-roll centres and egg-carton cells are brilliant for legumes and many flowers because they help to reduce transplant shock. Rather than transplanting the seedlings, you can plant the whole plug and let the fibre break down in the garden bed.

For all three methods, it's important to keep the seeds evenly moist (paper and cardboard will wick away water quickly). Water from the base where possible, label generously, and move to brighter light as soon as seedlings emerge.

Above left_Collecting globe thistle (*Echinops ritro*) seeds from the garden. I save what sets well and keep seeds on hand for the next season.
Above middle_A labelled jar of dried globe thistle seeds, ready for when sowing time next comes around.
Above right_My globe thistle threads through *Calamagrostis* 'Karl Foerster'. The thistle is a structural plant that holds its own in the drift and reliably provides seeds to gather.

How to make a seed snail (soil roll)

This is a compact way to start many seeds in one tidy, upright cylinder. The seedlings grow in little 'pockets' on top with minimal root tangling, so they can be easily potted on once the snail has been unrolled. For the liner, re-use something that you already have on hand; it's a great way to reduce waste.

You'll need:

- a non-permeable liner, such as a cut-open padded mailer, a plastic sheet or a piece of bubble wrap (bubbles facing upwards when laid out flat)
- fine, peat-free seed-raising mix that has been pre-moistened
- sticky tape or rubber bands
- a cup or old pot
- a mister or watering-can with a fine rose
- a bag, dome or clean soft-drink or milk bottle with the bottom cut off to use as a cover
- a label.

Method:

1. Cut the liner into a rectangle 15 centimetres (6 inches) high and 25–60 centimetres (10–24 inches) long (depending on how many seeds you want to start); medium to large seeds such as those of sweet pea (*Lathyrus odoratus*) appreciate a longer roll.
2. Lay the liner flat. Spread a 3–5-centimetre (1¼–2-inch) layer of pre-moistened seed-raising mix along the length, pressing it firmly so it forms a cohesive mat.
3. Roll it up (snug, not tight), and secure with sticky tape or rubber bands.
4. Stand the roll upright in the cup or old pot.
5. Add 1–2 centimetres (½– ¾ inch) of seed-raising mix to the top surface. Make 1-centimetre (½-inch) indents and insert one larger seed per hole, or press tiny seeds onto the surface and dust with mix.
6. Mist or gently water the top to settle. Add a loose cover to help maintain humidity for germination, as well as a label detailing the species.

Because the volume of seed-raising mix is small, check the moisture daily. Plan to water from the top; some growers stand rolls in a shallow tray for occasional bottom watering once seedlings have emerged (wicking depends on the roll's material). Ensure that the roll remains upright and supported.

Keep the roll indoors or in a sheltered spot until seedlings are sturdy. Many gardeners wait for two to three weeks before hardening off the plants (see page 235) and potting on.

To pot on, unroll patiently; seedlings separate along the coil with far less root damage than when pricking them out of a tight cell. Pot up each one or plant them in the garden as conditions allow.

Pros and cons:

- **Space-saving:** A windowsill can hold multiple rolls.
- **Gentle separations:** It's easy to undo the rolls and tease apart the seedlings.
- **Re-use first:** It gives packaging a second life, and you can clean and re-use the liner.
- **Moisture management:** Although the seed-raising mix is pre-moistened, the roll itself has a limited water 'reserve' so you can't let it dry out.
- **Stability:** Tall or thin rolls can topple over if they aren't nested snugly in the cup or pot.
- **Material choice:** Non-permeable liners reduce evaporation. Breathable liners dry faster and can encourage air-pruning of side roots, so they require closer attention.

Above left_Summer seedlings are raised in unbleached, unprinted toilet-roll tubes, labelled directly on the roll. When planted out, there is minimal root disturbance as the cardboard breaks down. ***Above right***_Potting on self-seeded plants from the garden. I use what appears naturally to fill gaps, to strengthen new beds and to share plants with others.

Transplanting seedlings

Prick out when the first two or three true leaves appear (for a definition of true leaves, see page 233). Hold the seedling by the leaves, not the stem, and move it into its own cell or a 5-centimetre (2-inch) pot. You can then pot on the seedling when its roots reach the container's holes but haven't yet started to circle.

Harden off for seven to ten days before planting the seedling into a garden bed. To do this, place the seedling outdoors for a few hours, out of direct midday sun and wind, then extend the time every couple of days. Reduce watering slightly towards the end of the hardening-off period, so the plant is not soft. This will minimise transplant shock.

The best time to transplant is late afternoon, once any heat has dissipated, or on an overcast day. Before transplanting, water the garden bed. Then plant the seedling at the same depth it grew in the pot, unless it's a crop that prefers otherwise.

For example, tomatoes (*Solanum lycopersicum*) can be planted deeper to encourage extra roots along the buried part of the stem. Firm the soil, and water in well. Provide shadecloth or a cloche for a few days if conditions become harsh.

Seed saving for resilience and joy

Saving seeds closes the loop and helps your garden to adapt to your local conditions over time. When choosing what to save, it really comes down to skill level:

- Beginners will find it easiest to gather seeds from self-pollinating crops, such as tomato (*Solanum lycopersicum*), sugar snap pea (*Pisum sativum*), common bean (*Phaseolus vulgaris*) and lettuce (*Lactuca sativa*).
- Those with more practice can try cross-pollinated crops, such as pumpkins (*Cucurbita* spp.), cucumber (*Cucumis sativus*), corn/maize (*Zea mays*) and broccoli (*Brassica oleracea* Italica Group). These require either spacing from related varieties or hand-pollination to ensure pure offspring.
- Open-pollinated seeds will grow like the parent. Seeds from F1 hybrids (these are often marked 'F1' on seed packets) can produce plants that look different from the parent and may not have the same flavour or vigour, because they don't 'come true' from seed.

How to save seeds:

- For dry-seeded crops, such as peas, beans and lettuce, allow the seeds to dry out on the plant. Harvest before rain. Finish drying the seeds indoors, then thresh and winnow.
- For wet-seeded crops, such as tomato and cucumber, scoop the seeds into a jar and add a little water. For tomato, ferment for two or three days, or until a light film forms (see page 339); for cucumber, ferment for up to three days or until the pulp floats and the seeds sink. Drain the jar, rinse the seeds, then place them on a plate to dry.
- For biennials, such as carrot (*Daucus carota* subsp. *sativus*) and beetroot (*Beta vulgaris*), save the seeds from strong plants.
  These need space or bagging to manage cross-pollination.

Ensure that seeds are thoroughly dry before storing them (they should snap rather than bend). Store them in airtight jars in a cool, dark place (a fridge works well for many species), and label each jar with the plant name and date. As an extra precaution, add a small packet of silica gel as a desiccant. Most seeds keep for one to five years if stored correctly, but carrot seeds tend to lose fertility with age. Test older batches by placing ten seeds on damp paper to see what percentage of them will germinate.

Other propagation methods

Beyond sowing seeds, you can also propagate plants from cuttings, by division and by layering:

- **Cuttings:** This method suits softwood and semi-hardwood plants such as herbs and many shrubs. Use sharp secateurs to cut healthy, non-flowering stems from the plant. Remove the lower leaves, and dip the cut ends in rooting powder/gel or raw honey (if you wish). Insert the cut ends into a free-draining potting mix, and cover the stems with a clear bag or cloche to hold in humidity. Keep the cuttings in bright shade. Many herb cuttings will also root in water and then can be potted on.

- **Division:** Clump-forming perennials such as chives (*Allium schoenoprasum*), rhubarb (*Rheum rhabarbarum*) and many ornamentals respond well to division. Lift the plant clump out of the ground, split it in half or quarters with a sharp spade or knife, and replant the sections with fresh compost.
- **Layering:** For plants that root where their stems touch the soil, such as blackberries (*Rubus fruticosus*), strawberries (*Fragaria × ananassa*) and rosemary (*Salvia rosmarinus*), peg a low branch to the ground, lightly nick the underside once or twice along its length, and cover with soil. Cut the stem free from the parent plant once it has rooted, usually after several weeks.

Troubleshooting for propagation

Sometimes, even with care, propagation presents a few common challenges. Here are quick solutions to help you succeed:

- **Poor seed germination:** Check the seed age, sow at the correct depth, and keep moisture even.
- **Damping off:** Improve airflow, water less often, and clean seed trays between batches.
- **Leggy seedlings:** Increase light, reduce heat, and brush your hand over the tops each day to strengthen stems.
- **Transplant shock:** Plant later in the day, water well, and provide temporary shade and shelter.

Climate and scale adaptations

Whatever your climate or growing space, these quick notes will help you adapt so your garden works for you and thrives, wherever you are.

- **Hot and dry climates:** Sow seeds in the cool of the morning. Provide shadecloth for seed trays. Water from below, and reduce heat stress with good airflow. Start warm-season crops earlier indoors so seedlings are robust before the heat arrives.
- **Cold and wet climates:** Use a cold frame or a small indoor set-up with lights to start seeds early. Raise seed trays on slats so air can move underneath. Delay mulch in spring until the soil has warmed up.
- **Small spaces and balconies:** Choose compact varieties, and sow fewer seeds more often. Use a clear lidded tub as a mini propagator. One tiered worm farm plus a few seed trays can live under a bench. Your wicking boxes can double as hardening-off zones if you add a hoop and a breathable cover.
- **Larger plots:** Scale up with soil blocks, sturdy benches and a nursery bed outdoors where young plants can grow on before planting out. Use a mesh cover, polytunnel or cloches to protect plants from wind, mice and pesky birds.

Cross-pollination isolation and simple workarounds

Managing cross-pollination depends on the plant, as distances required to prevent pollination vary by species and pollinators. In small gardens, use time and barriers. Grow only one variety of a cross-pollinating species at a time, bag flower heads, or hand-pollinate and tape the flower closed. For pumpkins (*Cucurbita* spp.), bag the flower before it opens, hand-pollinate, then re-bag or tape the flower closed and mark it with the variety that it has been pollinated with for the 'cross'.

Above left_Seedlings under a glass cloche. This is an easy way to maintain moisture and warmth around young plants, and it also brings a touch of beauty to the propagation bench.
Above right_A whittled stick plant label, written on with a permanent marker, is simple, re-usable and as beautiful as it is practical.

Design integration and beauty

A small propagation area can be one of the most beautiful parts of the garden, if the built elements match your material palette. Consider a timber slab bench with an old concrete wash trough, a compact cold frame glazed with salvaged glass, or a neat mini greenhouse constructed from the same metal as your fences.

Locate the propagation area where you will naturally pass each day, so watering and checking becomes a rhythm. Keep seed trays tidy and grouped by size, so the space feels resolved. I'm a big fan of order in beauty! Plant your favourite herbs or flowers beside the bench. It brings in beneficial insects and makes the work feel good. It will also encourage you to check on things as you make those incidental trips to pick flowers or harvest herbs. To get you started, try these two things this week:

1. Start one seed tray with seed-raising mix. Sow two easy crops, such as lettuce (*Lactuca sativa*) and basil (*Ocimum basilicum*). Water from below, and place in bright light.
2. Save seeds from one tomato (*Solanum lycopersicum*) plant you love. Ferment the fresh seeds briefly, rinse and dry thoroughly. Store them in a small jar with a desiccant packet, and make sure that you label the jar with the plant name and date.

WATERWISE GARDENING

Water is precious. The way you design and tend a garden can either waste water or make every drop count. Waterwise practice involves choosing to reduce demand, capture rain, move it gently through the site and deliver it to roots with care. When you integrate these choices from the beginning of your design, the garden becomes easier to live with and more resilient through heat, wind and storms. Here are the core principles of waterwise gardening:

'Water is precious. The way you design and tend a garden can either waste water or make every drop count.'

— Reduce demand first. Build living soil, keep the surface covered, choose plants that suit your climate, and group plants with similar watering needs.
— Slow, spread and sink rain wherever it falls. Let water infiltrate rather than rush away.
— Deliver water to the root zone. For example, install drip irrigation or soaker hoses beneath mulch, water slowly and deeply at the base of plants, or direct hose flow into small wells around each plant. For trees, water the soil beneath the outer edge of the canopy (the dripline), instead of near the trunk.
— Protect plants from weather extremes. Create shade, divert wind, and design for airflow.
— Make it beautiful. Tanks, rills, inlets and wicking beds can be both integral and elegant.

Wicking beds

A wicking bed is a self-watering container with a water reservoir at the base, a capillary layer, and a soil profile above, designed so moisture wicks upwards to keep roots evenly hydrated with far less evaporation than surface watering. This is ideal where water is limited, where summers are hot, or where you need a clean growing medium above poor or contaminated ground. For me, wicking beds also provide a way to create an extended watering buffer if I'm away from home. A few days between watering at the height of summer can be stretched out to a week. A regular wicking bed features:

— a sealed base with a reservoir depth of 150–200 millimetres (6–8 inches)
— washed scoria or gravel in the reservoir, with a particle size of 10–20 millimetres (1/2–3/4 inch)
— a geotextile or coarse fabric layer to separate the reservoir from the soil
— a soil layer that is 250–300 millimetres (10–12 inches) deep; treat this as living soil, and use no-dig principles (see pages 205–10)
— a vertical fill pipe that is 40–50 millimetres (1 1/2–2 inches) in diameter
— an overflow outlet (riser) set at the same level as the top of the reservoir, so the soil layer doesn't flood.

At Little Cottage on a Hill, I use intermediate bulk containers (IBCs) measuring 1 cubic metre (35 cubic feet), with the top cut off (see the box on pages 242–4). They are clad in timber and painted black for winter warmth and a refined finish. The height lifts the beds, which are set behind a fence, into the sun and away from the cold ground, and it also saves my back. Gardening while standing up is a true gift!

Many guides suggest replacing the soil every few years, but I don't. I top up with mature compost and keep the surface mulched. This wicking-bed system has been highly productive in my cold climate. In fact, from six wicking beds I was able to harvest over 160 kilograms (350 pounds) of produce in just eight weeks. Even as a lifelong gardener, I was utterly blown away!

How to use a wicking bed:

- Fill the reservoir until water runs from the overflow outlet (riser). In hot periods, refill when the top 5–10 centimetres (2–4 inches) of soil feel dry or when you see the water level drop in the riser; at other times, expect to have to fill it every one to four weeks (depending on crop size, heat and wind).
- Keep the surface mulched to reduce evaporative loss.
- Never feed scraps into the water layer. Keep worm tunnels in the soil layer above the fabric.
- Water freshly planted seeds and seedlings from above until their roots grow downwards.

Many different plants thrive in deep wicking beds, including:

- greedy fruiters and big roots, such as tomato (*Solanum lycopersicum*), capsicum (*Capsicum annuum*), eggplant (*Solanum melongena*), pumpkins (*Cucurbita* spp.), silverbeet (*Beta vulgaris* Cicla Group) and leek (*Allium ampeloprasum* Porrum Group); dwarf fruit trees (on suitable rootstock) and, in warm climates, citrus trees
- cut-and-come-again greens and herbs, such as lettuce (*Lactuca sativa*), Asian greens, parsley (*Petroselinum crispum*), basil (*Ocimum basilicum*), thyme (*Thymus vulgaris*) and oregano (*Origanum vulgare*)
- flowers for pollinators, such as pot marigold (*Calendula officinalis*), marigolds (*Tagetes* spp.), nasturtium (*Tropaeolum majus*), cosmos (*Cosmos* spp.) and climbing forms of sweet pea (*Lathyrus odoratus*)
- carrot (*Daucus carota* subsp. *sativus*) and parsnip (*Pastinaca sativa*), which can work if the top 100–150 millimetres (4–6 inches) of soil stays aerated and not overly rich; choose a sandy, open blend for true taproots.

Here are the most common wicking-bed problems and solutions:

- **Algae or mosquitoes:** Fit a tight cap on both the fill pipe and the overflow outlet (riser), and keep the openings shaded.
- **Sour (anaerobic) smell:** Reduce the water level, improve the overflow drainage, and ensure that the soil layer is not sitting in water. If you have worm tunnels in the wicking bed, then try adding more carbon.
- **Salt build-up in dry climates:** Once a season, let the reservoir run almost empty, then deeply water the wicking bed from the top to push salts from fertilisers or hard water downwards.
- **Water is visible but plants are wilting:** Stick your finger in the soil. If the soil feels dry, then give the wicking bed a deep water at the soil's surface.
- **Slow wicking when it's hot:** Top up with water; add 30–50 per cent more shade in summer, plus heavier mulch.

The wicking-bed garden between the house and the northern fence comprises eight 1 × 1 metre (3 × 3 foot) repurposed and timber-clad intermediate bulk container (IBC) beds lifted into the sun on a mulched 'chop and drop' ground plane, with integrated worm tunnels and vertical mesh making every face productive.

These quick climate and scale adaptations will help you have successful wicking beds no matter where you live:

- **Hot and dry climates:** Maximise mulch and summer shade. Ensure that the deep reservoir remains full in order to buffer water loss in heat spikes.
- **Cold and wet climates:** Keep beds slightly proud and ensure that the levelling pad (supportive base) drains; the external overflow outlet (riser) sets the water level so the soil doesn't get waterlogged.
- **Small or urban gardens:** One full-height intermediate bulk container (IBC) can replace two shallow halves and lets you grow vertically plus add a narrow bench edge.

Wicking beds are practical, but they can also add beauty to the garden. Clad them in battened timber, Corten steel slats or limewashed ply, leaving 'service windows' at the outlet valve and fill pipe for access.

Align the tops of the wicking beds at 'handrail' height for true 'stand-up' gardening and rhythm in the bed set-out grid. I love having my beds aligned in a perfect grid, as this is a repetitive spatial element in my wicking-bed garden. It turns a flat and narrow space into something three-dimensional and sculptural.

You can also use colours and planting palettes to your advantage. Repeat a compatible trio of species – such as rosemary (*Salvia rosmarinus*), thyme (*Thymus vulgaris*) and English lavender (*Lavandula angustifolia*) – as underplanting for height harmony and scent.

Evening light in the wicking-bed garden. Between my clad and painted intermediate bulk container (IBC) beds, there's a narrow walkway through which I pass daily in order to gather what I need for dinner and to see what has shifted.

Natasha's wicking-bed model

Since moving to Little Cottage On A Hill, and spurred on by our first $900 water bill, I've researched and refined my own full-height intermediate bulk container (IBC) model. It has a larger reservoir volume, greater soil depth and greater accessibility than other wicking beds.

Holding around 300 litres (80 gallons) of water and about 45 centimetres (18 inches) of wicking-active soil, it delivers moisture stability, plant resilience through heat and cold snaps, and the capacity to grow small trees. The height makes it accessible for those who can't bend over due to injury, while the design requires no holes in the liner, keeps the water level visible at a glance (no need to shine a torch down a dark stand pipe), and means you water less and grow more.

I run a standard inlet fill pipe (my 'stand pipe') and a separate external overflow riser connected to the IBC's base valve. The external riser is cut to the height of the reservoir top (where the scoria stops and the geotextile fabric starts). That single detail gives me instant water-level visibility, a passive overflow at the exact set point, and the option to divert water overflow to other beds with a click-on hose.

To build your own full-height IBC wicking bed, you'll need:

- base material: compacted gravel, road base or pavers
- a food-grade IBC: full height, with the cage retained (try sourcing it from Facebook Marketplace)
- a reservoir medium: enough 7–20-millimetre (3/8–3/4-inch) scoria or drainage gravel to fill the reservoir to a height of 250–300 millimetres (10–12 inches)
- an inlet fill pipe ('stand pipe'): 50-millimetre (2-inch) PVC pipe with a cap
- a soil–water separator: geotextile (puncture-resistant) fabric
- a growing medium: enough soil (a mix of screened compost, quality topsoil for water retention, and coarse minerals for structure) to fill the growing area to a height of 400–450 millimetres (16–18 inches)

Scan to download Natasha's wicking-bed garden guide.

- an external riser and valve kit: a 50-millimetre-wide (2-inch) PVC elbow plus a straight riser to set the water height; include a quick-connect hose fitting if you want to divert the overflow water
- silicone tape
- a worm tunnel comprising a 50-millimetre-wide (2-inch), 350-millimetre-long (14-inch) PVC pipe, perforated at the base, with a snug cap.
- live composting worms. Since a wicking bed is a closed system, composting worms cannot migrate from the surrounding garden. If you want your worm tunnel to break down organic matter and boost soil life, then add composting worms (such as red wigglers) to the tunnel along with moist bedding.

Follow these step-by-step instructions to build your wicking bed:

1. Create a level base for the wicking bed using compacted gravel, road base or pavers.
2. Cut off the top of the IBC, and retain it for use as a lid or shade. Keep the cage intact, and place the IBC on the level base.
3. Pour in the scoria or drainage gravel, and rake it level. Lightly compact the stones so the reservoir surface is flat and even. With the IBC's outside valve open, rinse the scoria or gravel to remove and flush out any dust or loose fine material.
4. Attach the PVC elbow and straight riser (external riser) to the outside base valve of the IBC with silicone tape to stop any minor drips at the valve threads, leaving the riser deliberately over-length so it sits at least 100 millimetres (4 inches) higher than the intended water level.
5. Fill the reservoir with water via the inlet fill pipe (stand pipe) until the water level sits about 5–10 millimetres (¼–½ inch) above the scoria or gravel. This settles the stones and allows you to confirm that the stone layer is level end to end. Check for any leaks.
6. Set the final height of the external riser. Look into the external riser to read the water level, then mark that height on the outside of the riser. Cut the riser to the exact height of the water level (the reservoir top, where the stones meet the geotextile fabric), so the overflow point sets the internal water-reservoir level precisely.
7. Drape the geotextile fabric over the scoria or drainage gravel, with generous upturns at the edges. Ensure that there are no gaps or rips.
8. Add the soil mix in 100-millimetre (4-inch) layers, giving each layer a gentle watering until damp but not sodden. Do not overcompact it. With time, the soil will settle by up to 10 per cent.
9. Bury the worm-tunnel pipe vertically so it sits in the soil profile (not in the reservoir), and ensure that the cap is just above the soil surface to stop soil from falling in when you open it.
10. Hose the surface to settle the soil, then check for steady drawdown over 24–48 hours by monitoring the water level in the external riser. Top up via the inlet fill pipe (stand pipe) as needed.

Watering during establishment

In wicking beds, seeds and young seedlings still need to be watered from above. The surface soil will always be drier than the wicking-active zone below, and roots need time to grow down before they can access stored moisture. Water newly sown seeds and seedlings from above until they are well established and their roots reach deeper into the soil profile. Once plants are settled, the wicking bed will do most of the work.

Operation and care

Always fill the wicking bed through the inlet fill pipe ('stand pipe'). The external riser is your level indicator, overflow pipe and diversion point. A simple glance at the riser will tell you the reservoir status: if water is visible near the top of the riser, then you know that the reservoir is full.

Occasionally, you may need to flush out and replace all of the water in the wicking-bed reservoir, for example if there is a build-up of salts (look for a white crust on the soil), or the water has become smelly or stagnant. Unscrew the riser, open the base valve, and drain the water. Refit the riser, and refill the water via the inlet fill pipe ('stand pipe').

To use the worm tunnel, add handfuls of chopped harvest trimmings plus a sprinkle of carbon (such as dry leaves or shredded cardboard). Cap snugly. (The worm tunnel turns the wicking bed into a little bioreactor where useful leachate is captured within the bed, and not wasted. That's the loop closing.)

Planting depth and spacing

The 400–450 millimetres (16–18 inches) of wicking-active soil supports deep-rooted crops and even small trees and shrubs with dwarf or compact rootstocks. This depth is the sweet spot for capillary lift from a 250–300-millimetre (10–12-inch) reservoir; it offers enough depth for roots to chase moisture without you having to saturate the soil's surface.

Here are some helpful guidelines:

- For heavy feeders, add slow compost top-ups, and maintain a 50–75-millimetre (2–3-inch) gap between the mulch and the stems.
- Grow one tree (dwarf citrus or stone fruit) per bed, underplanted with herbs.
- Cultivate two or three perennial staples, such as rhubarb (*Rheum rhabarbarum*) and artichoke (*Cynara cardunculus*), per bed, underplanted with salad greens or herbs.
- Utilise vertical planes for growing. Direct trailing plants down the face of the wicking-bed cladding. Growing frames extend the growing space upwards for climbing plants.

Drip irrigation

Drip irrigation is the most water-efficient option for many productive beds. It delivers a measured supply close to the roots (an emitter flow rate of 1–2 litres or $\frac{1}{4}$–$\frac{1}{2}$ gallon per hour is typical). A subsurface drip-irrigation system placed beneath mulch reduces water evaporation even further.

Water early in the morning so any drips on foliage dry quickly, and the soil has time to absorb the water before the heat rises. Aim to moisten the top 200–300 millimetres (8–12 inches) of soil. It can be difficult to know how far water is actually seeping into the ground, especially in dry times or hot climates with low rainfall, so check with a trowel.

In containers, use a dripper on a timer, or consider utilising a small olla (see the box below). An olla can moisten a radius of 30–45 centimetres (12–18 inches).

Keep the drip-irrigation system simple. Straight runs, accessible filters (I have an end cap that I can take off to flush the entire drip line), and one tidy manifold make maintenance easy. Bury lines shallowly beneath mulch, mark the runs neatly, and leave service loops at the ends for any future changes.

Olla: An ancient water wisdom

An olla is an unglazed, porous clay pot that you bury in the soil and fill with water. The water slowly seeps through the clay walls, delivering moisture directly to the surrounding soil at root level. Plants draw water as they need it, which makes the olla an efficient, low-waste irrigation method, especially in hot climates or for containers that dry out quickly.

Gardeners have used ollas for centuries in places such as North Africa, the Middle East, and Central and South America. Ollas are still valued today for:

- water efficiency (minimal evaporation or run-off)
- even soil moisture (this reduces stress on plants)
- low maintenance (you only refill them every few days, or even once a week, depending on their size and your climate).

Opposite page,
Top_Pea tendrils begin their climb on a wicking-bed frame.
Middle_Cutting coriander for the kitchen is just one small harvest from the garden bed.
Bottom_The wicking beds have a rain gauge, which allows me to measure how much water they receive during rainfall events.

Saving water

Saving water is about working with nature to make the most of every drop. Combining rainwater harvesting, mulching, suitable plant choices and microclimate creation helps you to maintain a healthy, resilient garden, no matter the weather. By adopting a mix of these strategies, you can dramatically reduce your garden's water demand.

Rainwater is a free resource that is helpful to keep on-site for those times when dry weather or drought threatens your garden. There are several ways to capture rain and use it well:

- **Roof catchment:** Fit clean gutters, leaf guards and a first-flush diverter. Just 1 millimetre (less than 1/16 inch) of rain on 1 square metre (10 square feet) of roof yields 1 litre (1/4 gallon) of water. So, when 10 millimetres (1/2 inch) of rain hits an average 100-square-metre (1000-square-foot) roof, about 1000 litres (260 gallons) can be collected.
- **Tank:** Choose a size and type that suits your space, budget and garden aesthetic. Place it where a short run of pipework is possible from the roof to the tank, and where it can become part of the garden composition. Screen the base with planting, or add cladding that matches fences or edges. Steel mesh can be used to train a climber for a green façade, making an unattractive tank visually disappear.
- **Distribution:** Gravity can send tank water to soaker hoses for small falls. For longer runs or drip irrigation, a small pump provides reliable pressure.
- **Overflow:** Send tank-water overflow to planted swales, rain gardens or infiltration trenches rather than to stormwater drains where this is safe and allowed by your local council. The aim is to slow, spread and sink water into the garden.

Mulch is a great water-saving tool. It shades the soil surface, reduces evaporation and protects soil life. The depth to use depends on your climate. In hot regions, 7–10 centimetres (2 3/4–4 inches) is common; in cool regions, use a lighter layer in spring so the soil can warm up.

Choose a mulch that suits your planting palette. Coarse chips are ideal for paths and under trees. Straw, mushroom compost or fine chips suit perennial or annual beds. Keep mulch clear of stems to avoid collar rot. Living ground covers such as thyme (*Thymus vulgaris*) and *Dichondra argentea* 'Silver Falls' work in a similar way to mulch while adding beauty and habitat.

Using plants that won't quickly become stressed in dry conditions will help to minimise demand for water in your garden. Shade, windbreaks and microclimates can all help with this:

- Use deciduous trees and climbers to cast summer shade and allow in winter light.
- During heatwaves, provide temporary shadecloth frames over tender plantings.
- Divert and buffer wind with hedging, greenery-covered fences and framed panels so air lifts over garden beds.
- Place tender crops on the more sheltered side of hardier plantings.
- Group plants by water needs, which is often called hydro-zoning. Grow thirsty plants together near taps and tanks, and drought-tolerant plants together elsewhere.

- In hot regions, favour plants with silvery or small leaves, aromatic foliage and deep roots – such as rosemary (*Salvia rosmarinus*), sage (*S. officinalis*), thyme (*Thymus vulgaris*) and olive (*Olea europaea*) – as they are adapted to hot conditions.
- Space plants to allow airflow. Overcrowding can increase humidity, disease pressure and water demand as plants compete in the root zone.

Adapted for extremes

Over millions of years, some plant species have adapted to cope with heat, cold, drought and wind. Many of these traits can be used to your advantage in a productive garden.

- Silvery or hairy leaves reflect sunlight and regulate water loss. Think olive (*Olea europaea*), sage (*Salvia officinalis*) and lamb's ear (*Stachys byzantina*).
- Small or narrow leaves reduce the surface area available for evaporation. Rosemary (*Salvia rosmarinus*), thyme (*Thymus vulgaris*) and English lavender (*Lavandula angustifolia*) are good examples.
- A thick, waxy cuticle creates a protective coating that slows water loss and shields leaves from heat and wind. It's found on plants such as cumquat (*Citrus japonica*), pineapple guava (*Feijoa sellowiana*) and many succulents.
- Deep roots reach water stored well below the soil's surface. Grape (*Vitis vinifera*) and fig (*Ficus carica*) thrive even in dry spells.

By mixing these survivors into your edible and ornamental plantings, you can create a garden that's beautiful, productive and resilient in all weather extremes.

***Far left*_**Pineapple guava (*Feijoa sellowiana*) is a dry-tolerant edible with thick, waxy leaves and deep roots that cope well in waterwise gardens.
***Left*_**English lavender (*Lavandula angustifolia*) has aromatic foliage and a fine structure that suits hot, dry conditions. Even when it is given minimal water, it supports pollinators.

The wicking-bed garden. This clever waterwise system holds moisture at the root zone, ensuring that the garden can carry on through summer with minimal top-ups of water.

Troubleshooting for watering

Here are common watering issues and quick tips for how to resolve them in any garden setting:

- **Plants are wilting despite regular watering:** Check root health and soil structure. Shallow daily watering can keep roots at the surface. Water less often but more deeply.
- **Water is pooling on beds:** Improve drainage, raise bed level slightly, and never water when the soil is already saturated.
- **Drip lines are clogging up:** Flush lines at the start of the growing season (end caps make this easy). If your water source carries sediment, then add a simple filter where practical.
- **Wicking beds are staying too wet:** Check that the overflow height is set correctly, and let the reservoir draw down before topping it up. Keep the surface open and aerated with a loose, coarse mulch layer; avoid compaction, and top up the mulch as it breaks down to maintain airflow.
- **Water runs off rather than infiltrating soil:** Keep soil covered with plants or mulch. Add compost often to improve structure. Use permeable paths such as gravel, woodchips and open pavers. Gently terrace steep slopes or stitch the slope with short contour paths (level paths that run across the slope to slow water and give it time to soak in).

Climate and scale adaptations

These quick notes will help you no matter where you live and what kind of soil you have.

— **Hot and dry climates:** Mulch deeply, ensure that there is afternoon shade for tender crops, and increase wind protection. Use wicking beds or install subsurface drip lines to deliver water to the root zone.

— **Cold and wet climates:** Improve drainage first. Raise beds slightly or use wicking beds to lift roots into warmer, aerated soil. Hold back on mulch in spring until the soil warms.

— **Heavy clay:** Avoid working wet soil. Keep adding compost. Over time, infiltration improves as roots and biology open pathways. Consider short contour paths or shallow swales to slow water.

— **Sandy soils:** Add compost often, mulch well, and shelter from the wind. Water more frequently in smaller doses to reduce nutrient leaching.

Small spaces and balconies: Use troughs, wicking boxes and compact tanks. A single neat downpipe diverter can fill a slimline tank for balcony watering. Keep systems tidy and close to hand.

— **Larger plots:** Repeat simple modules. Place taps and manifolds so every bed is within a short hose reach. Use planted swales and rain gardens to manage heavy rain.

Water triage in dry times

During drought, prioritise watering new plantings, young trees and crops that are central to your harvest. Established perennials with deep roots often cope with short dry spells. Accept that lawns and non-essential areas may become parched.

Design integration and beauty

Water systems can be beautiful. Tanks can frame a view or back a seating nook. A small rill can take overflow to a rain garden. Wicking beds can pick up the same cladding and edge details as fences and screens so the whole space reads as one visually resolved garden. Fill pipes and overflows can be neat details rather than eyesores. Choose a consistent material palette so the practical feels considered. To get you started, try these two things this week:

1. Calculate your next rain harvest. Multiply your roof area by the forecast rainfall to get the volume. As an example, 50 square metres (500 square feet) times 10 millimetres (½ inch) equals 500 litres (130 gallons). Decide how best to use this water.
2. Add one shade frame over a tender crop. Use stakes and a piece of shadecloth. Observe how leaf stress and water use change over a week.

Water shapes what's possible; structure multiplies it. With the soil hydrated and water needs understood, we can now stack the garden in three dimensions, opening up the harvest, beauty and access without expanding the footprint.

VERTICAL AND MULTIPLANE GROWING

On my steel-mesh structures out on the northern verge, I can run three pumpkins (including *Cucurbita maxima* 'Coventry') from a 30 × 60-centimetre (12 × 24-inch) planting pocket at the edge of one of the beds without surrendering the grassed paths; on the ground plane, those same vines would sprawl across 20–50 square metres (200–500 square feet). The lesson: when you treat limited space as horizontal, vertical and edge planes, you can multiply your growing area without increasing the footprint.

Vertical and multiplane growing means training plants to grow up, down and across structures – trellises, frames, fences, walls, arbours and the outside faces of raised beds – so light, airflow and harvest access improve while yield per square metre increases. It also provides an opportunity to create three-dimensional structures that are beautiful year-round. Here's a menu of simple, strong, repeatable structures:

- **Reinforcing-mesh panels (reo):** Stand a sheet at the bed edge or form an A-frame between beds; peg or bolt securely.
- **Arches/arbours:** Curve or frame two mesh panels to create a covered walkway; check head-height clearance (it should be greater than 2.1 metres; 7 feet).
- **Plant-support tripods:** Gather three or four hardwood stakes or metal rods and tie them firmly at the top for common bean (*Phaseolus vulgaris*) and cucumber (*Cucumis sativus*).
- **Wall wires:** Fix stainless-steel cables to masonry or timber posts for espaliered trees and berries; space wires 30–60 centimetres (12–24 inches) apart.
- **Garden-bed cladding:** Let nasturtium (*Tropaeolum majus*) and melon (*Cucumis melo*) trail down the outside face of raised or wicking beds to use the vertical drop.

What to grow vertically

Plenty of plants can be grown vertically, especially those with a climbing or trailing habit. Common bean (*Phaseolus vulgaris*) and sugar snap pea (*Pisum sativum*) are naturally twining climbers; guide the first few tendrils to the frame, then let them climb. For cucumber (*Cucumis sativus*), tie the main stem to mesh or strings so the fruits hang clean and straight. Zucchini (*Cucurbita pepo*) can be trained upright by staking and tying as a single stem; 'Costata Romanesco' and similar ribbed cultivars suit this approach.

Melon (*Cucumis melo*) and small pumpkins such as *Cucurbita maxima* 'Golden Nugget' grow well on sturdy mesh. When vines are guided and woven early in their growth, the plant will usually support its own fruits; use a soft net sling where wind or movement is an issue. For indeterminate/vining tomatoes (*Solanum lycopersicum*), train one or two main stems up a stake or string, removing small side shoots weekly.

Grow raspberry (*Rubus idaeus*) and thornless blackberries such as *Rubus ulmifolius* 'Waldo' on tensioned wires for neat rows and easy picking. With a bit of care and patience, many fruit trees can be trained as espaliers (grown flat against wires) or as cordons (a single stem on a wire or stake). Flowers and herbs such as nasturtium (*Tropaeolum majus*), sweet pea (*Lathyrus odoratus*) and common bean (*Phaseolus*

1

2

3

4

5

6

1_Lathyrus odoratus 'Almost Black' provides early summer scent and colour. This sweet pea cultivar turns a simple fence line into a wall of flowers.
2_Common beans (*Phaseolus vulgaris*) are grown in the hybrid potting shed and greenhouse. The pot-based trellis is made from fine metal mesh and string to extend the season upwards.
3_A black-painted timber fence clad with reinforcing mesh gives climbers a frame, and lets silver vein creeper (*Parthenocissus henryana*) and *Clematis* 'Huldine' soften the boundary and add visual depth.
4_Cucurbita maxima 'Coventry' is carried on an arbour made from curved reinforcing mesh. The heavy pumpkins are lifted into the air rather than being left to grow on the ground.
5_Huonville crabapple (*Malus* sp.) has been trained flat on reinforcing mesh against a steel fence. It is a compact vertical orchard on dwarfing rootstock.
6_Picking sugar snap peas (*Pisum sativum*). I use climbing crops to multiply the growing surface without expanding the garden's footprint.

***Above left*_**A simple bamboo-and-string frame guides sugar snap peas (*Pisum sativum*) that are growing in a repurposed copper boiler. It is a quick and beautiful vertical structure that lifts the crop and keeps the planting compact.
***Above right*_**Feathery asparagus (*Asparagus officinalis*) fronds are held upright within a timber-and-wire A-frame. This sculptural element supports growth while adding rhythm and repetition on the verge.

vulgaris) can be grown up trellises for pollinators; small-leaved creeping thyme (*Thymus serpyllum*) can be a useful living edge at the bed rim to soften hard lines. Here are some tips for training your plants:

- **Tomato:** Tie the stem loosely with soft ties every 20–30 centimetres (8–12 inches); keep one or two leaders, and remove any crowded foliage to improve airflow.
- **Cucumber:** Tie the stem to the mesh every 20–30 centimetres (8–12 inches); trim only what blocks paths or shades neighbours.
- **Melon/pumpkin:** Small- to medium-fruited varieties are easiest to grow on frames. Large-fruited types can be grown vertically with careful training and strong structures, but carry greater risk in windy or exposed conditions.
- **Fruit tree:** Train it flat against a fence or frame so it grows on one plane. The tree will produces fruits without taking up much three-dimensional space. Different fruit trees lend themselves to different forms, depending on how they fruit and the flexibility of their branches.
  - **Espalier:** In the first year, tie one vertical stem and two side branches to the lowest wire to make a 'T'. In the following years, train new side branches along higher wires to build tiers. (This is best suited to apples and pears.)
  - **Cordon:** Train a single-stemmed fruit tree (such as an apple or pear) vertically or at an angle, supported on wires. This allows you to grow it in a narrow strip where a full tree would never fit.

— **Fan:** Spread branches of a fruit tree out like a fan against a wall or trellis to capture sunlight and make fruits easy to reach. (This is ideal for stone fruits such as apricot, peach and plum).
— **Step-over:** This is a fruit tree (most often an apple or pear) grown as a knee-high single tier along a low wire, perfect along paths or as a low, productive edge.

Design considerations

Vertical elements add height, rhythm and structure to a garden. They can double as privacy screens, shade elements or sculptural features. Choose materials that suit your style – timber, recycled metal, painted frames – and think about how the layers will look through the seasons. Then consider the plane that your plants will occupy:

— **Overhead:** Think arches, pergolas and A-frames, and cables between posts.
— **Vertical:** These surfaces can be fences, wire-mesh panels, obelisks and wall cables.
— **Edge:** Plants can trail over bed rims and wicking-bed sides to reclaim otherwise lost growing territory.

When it comes to choosing plants, it's important to look at things such as spatial logic, palette and sensory cues:

— **Arches as portals:** Steel-mesh arches or arbours dripping with grape (*Vitis vinifera*), kiwifruit (*Actinidia chinensis* var. *deliciosa*) or passionfruit (*Passiflora edulis*), rather than the often-grown Chinese wisteria (*Wisteria sinensis*) or jasmine (*Jasminum officinale*), turn paths into foraging tunnels. Deciduous climbers offer shade in summer and admit light in winter.
— **Espalier as architecture:** Even leafless, the winter tracery reads as sculpture; use espaliered fruit trees along fences and as edible screens near busy areas for easy picking.
— **Edible hedges:** Swap ornamental evergreen shrubs for a line of edible species, such as blueberry (*Vaccinium corymbosum*), pineapple guava (*Feijoa sellowiana*) or rosemary (*Salvia rosmarinus*), for perfumed, harvestable edges.
— **Scented climbers:** Grow hops (*Humulus lupulus*) or star jasmine (*Trachelospermum jasminoides*) vertically at the back of non-edible zones to add aroma.
— **Edges that give back:** Let thyme (*Thymus vulgaris*), tarragon (*Artemisia dracunculus*) and strawberry (*Fragaria* × *ananassa*) trail over raised-bed edges for fragrance and softening.

Place vertically grown food species where people pass, such as near doors, paths and outdoor rooms. This will ensure that maintenance, checking and harvest become a part of everyday life and incidental garden walks. You can also use vertical growing to provide shade over benches plus filtered views that create depth.

With frames humming and fruits lifted to eye level, we can invite animals into the system without causing chaos, starting with the most generous workers of all: chickens.

Saffy's tip: Raising bonded chickens

If you want a calm, trusting flock, then start handling chicks from the day they arrive. Sit with them, speak softly, and let them get used to your hands. This regular, gentle contact makes them easier to manage as adults. Our early years with the flock showed me that these bonds enrich not just the garden system but the lives within it.

CHICKENS AS PART OF A PRODUCTIVE SYSTEM

Chickens became an integral part of our garden from the moment we moved to Oak & Monkey Puzzle. Like many tree changers, I wanted them for their eggs and their charm, but what I didn't expect was how profoundly they would shape our family life.

When our first two hens arrived, my daughter Saffron (known as Saffy) was barely three, and I had never seen her more calm or content than when she was in the orchard with them. Chickens became a bridge to the world for my autistic child. When she went to kindergarten, her teacher soon learned that if classmates wanted her to talk, all they had to do was ask about chickens. Then she would be off, reeling through fact after fact. From that point on, every nursery rhyme and playground song she knew was adapted with clucks and flaps.

Now that she's older, her human friendships have taken centrestage, but the chickens remain woven into our garden loop as:

— converters of kitchen scraps and garden waste into high-value fertiliser
— accelerators of compost when their manure is balanced with dry browns
— tidiers of weedy edges
— egg layers that turn even plant failures into protein.

Aphid-riddled brassicas, such as kale (*Brassica oleracea* Acephala Group) and cabbage (*B. o.* Capitata Group), don't feel like losses here; they are eggs in the making.

Backyard chickens have different lives from those in commercial systems. At home they can forage, dust bathe and live at a natural pace, which supports richer yolks, better-flavoured eggs and a standard of care that you can see. This is different from cage and barn systems, and even many free-range operations, where density and yard access vary widely.

Right_Saffron with Pearl, a Wyandotte raised from an egg. She carries the hen with the calm familiarity that comes from growing up alongside chickens. ***Far right***_Pearl in Saffron's arms. Chickens become part of both family life and the garden system, bringing companionship, care and daily rhythm.

Above_A small clutch of eggs from our mixed flock. Our Wyandottes lay creamy brown eggs, while our Araucanas lay soft blue eggs.
Far left_Saffron collecting eggs from the chicken housing. This is a small daily ritual that keeps the system ticking over.
Left_Handfuls of fresh eggs are proof that it doesn't take many chickens to bring another steady offering into the garden.

Be a good neighbour

Before installing a chicken coop, think about its impact on your neighbours, the wildlife and the surrounding area. Check your local council rules for acceptable bird numbers, building setbacks and rooster ownership before you build. When the coop is in place, keep odour and noise low through generous litter, good ventilation and timely cleaning.

Design the coop with local wildlife in mind. Net runs where foxes, snakes and other predators are present, and keep small creatures safe by limiting free ranging at sensitive times (such as late summer to autumn, when lizards are more active). Ecologist Tanya Loos reminds us to balance care for our birds with care for the local biology. Thoughtful siting and seasonal awareness protect both.

Opposite page,
Top left_Hens are not just egg layers; they are part of the garden and family life.
Top right_Eggs are the simplest daily harvest in my garden.
Bottom left_The flock in the coop will turn this caterpillar-riddled cabbage and spent straw into eggs, manure and a useful compost input.
Bottom right_The coop and run sit quietly in the garden, considered in design and fully enclosed for safety.

Why chickens belong in a sustainable garden

Chickens offer much more than just eggs or meat; they are active partners in a thriving, resilient garden system. By weaving chickens into your growing space, you introduce daily rhythms that enrich both the ecosystem and your own experience of home. Their movements respond to season and weather, tracing the living cycles that sustain both garden and gardener.

- They connect people, especially children, to the garden through daily interaction and observation.
- They turn kitchen and garden scraps, including pest-damaged plants, into fresh eggs and nutrient-rich manure.
- Their manure, when balanced with dry browns, accelerates the composting process.
- As they forage, scratch and dust bathe, chickens help to manage pests, aerate soil and recycle nutrients.
- They add resilience to the garden loop by transforming potential 'failures' into productive outputs.
- They invite a daily rhythm of care that deepens your awareness of the whole garden system.

If you are choosing breeds for longevity and health rather than maximum short-term laying, look to heritage birds. We prefer Araucanas, Wyandottes and Orpingtons for steady laying over many years and calmer temperaments, rather than commercial hybrids such as ISA Browns, which are bred to lay intensively and have shorter lifespans. Find a breed that suits your needs, your space and your climate.

Housing that works and looks good

Your chicken coop can be more than a shed tucked out of sight. Consider a small, well-made building that earns its place in the garden through beauty and function. These are the essentials for any coop:

- dry, draught-free shelter with generous cross-ventilation
- predator-proof construction (use hardware mesh rather than chicken wire)
- predator-proof latches and reliable night-time fastening
- easy access for cleaning
- a nearby sealed bin to store feed and bedding material.

When creating the coop, ensure that the interior is at least 0.4 square metres (4⅓ square feet) per standard hen; however, more space is always kinder and easier to manage. The chicken run should be 1–2 square metres (10–20 square feet) per hen. Increase the size in hot climates or when hens are confined to the run for long periods of time.

The design of the coop can be integrated into the landscape. Borrow materials used elsewhere so the coop reads as part of the garden language. Plant climbers or small shrubs on the run's sunny side for shade and to anchor the structure visually. Frame small views through and past the coop so it feels intentional, not tacked on.

When it comes to fitting out the interior of the chicken coop, follow these useful guidelines:

- Install perches that are 4–5 centimetres (1½–2 inches) wide, with rounded edges. Allow 20–30 centimetres (8–12 inches) of linear space per bird.
- Include one nesting box measuring 30 × 30 × 30 centimetres (12 × 12 × 12 inches) for every three to four hens (keep the nesting boxes dim, dry and lined with clean bedding material).
- Initially add 10–15 centimetres (4–6 inches) of clean, carbon-rich bedding material (also known as litter) – straw, dry leaves, wood shavings, or a blend, but avoid sawdust – to the floor of the coop, topped up little and often. Birds will mix it as they scratch.
- Allow a deep layer of litter to form on the floor so it becomes a tidy carbon sponge that traps odours and begins composting in place.
- Raise the run surface slightly, and add coarse woodchips, sand or straw, so good drainage keeps feet and feathers clean.

Fixed runs benefit from a second pen; alternate to allow plants and soil to recover. Where space allows, use a mobile coop and move birds through fallow beds or orchards; rest and reseed the ground as needed.

After clearing a crop, you can pen hens briefly in the resting bed to clean up caterpillars and aphids, scratch in debris, and add fertility before the next planting. However, protect irrigation systems before placing chickens in the bed, and remove the birds before they overwork the soil.

Feeding, water and health

The base diet of chickens is complete layer or grower feed. Supplement this with fresh kitchen and garden scraps free from sprays, toxins and contaminants. Also provide insoluble grit for digestion, and crushed eggshell for calcium. Scatter small amounts of whole grains as a treat, not as a staple. Avoid mouldy food, grapes, avocado skins and stones, chocolate, caffeine, very salty items, and raw or dried beans.

Chickens need fresh, cool water every day. Place the drinkers in the shade, and clean them often to prevent algae and slime.

For the health and comfort of your chickens, offer them a dry dust bath; clean sand with a little wood ash helps with mites and feather condition. Quarantine new birds before introducing them to the flock in order to avoid bringing in diseases. Keep feed in sealed bins and collect leftovers in the evening so as not to attract rodents.

Integrating chickens into compost and beds

Chicken litter and manure have much to offer the garden, especially when used wisely.

- **In compost:** Deep litter from the coop can be utilised as a high-nitrogen input for compost bays, but balance it with dry leaves, coarse woodchips or shredded cardboard.
- **Around growing plants:** Fresh chicken manure is nitrogen-rich and contains high levels of uric acid (which breaks down into ammonia) that can burn plants. It should be aged or composted for six to twelve months before use on garden beds where plants are growing.

— **On empty beds:** Fresh chicken manure can be applied directly to an empty garden bed, but do so at least four weeks before planting, and at least twelve weeks before harvesting any crop that has been in contact with the soil (such as root vegetables).

Troubleshooting for chickens

Here are the most common problems associated with chickens, and what you can do about them:

— **Smell building in the coop:** Add dry carbon, increase ventilation, and remove any wet bedding material.
— **Feather pecking:** Increase space, offer enrichment such as hanging greens, and review protein levels.
— **Red mites:** Clean the coop and nesting boxes thoroughly, refresh bedding, treat perches, and offer the chickens a dry dust bath. Given that red mites can severely impact chickens' health, treat your entire flock with an approved medicated treatment.
— **Rodents:** Elevate feeders, tidy spills, store feed securely, and use rodent-resistant construction materials.

Daily, weekly and seasonal rhythms

Chickens are a joy to have around, so it's not difficult to include them in the maintenance rhythms of the garden.

These are the daily tasks:

— Check water and feed; collect eggs; observe feet, eyes and behaviour for any changes.
— Add a handful of dry bedding material to freshen nesting boxes and ground litter if needed.
— Handle younger birds calmly to build trust and keep the flock easy to manage.

Here is your weekly to-do list:

— Turn or top up litter.
— Wash the drinkers.
— Tidy the feed storage.
— Do a quick predator-proofing check: coop/run mesh, latches and gaps.

These jobs are seasonal:

— **Summer heat:** Provide shade, extra water and more airflow. Freeze water bottles to float in drinkers during heat spikes.
— **Winter cold and wet:** Keep the litter deep and dry. Block prevailing winds while maintaining ventilation. Lift the drinkers off the floor.
— **Moulting time:** Expect a pause in egg production. Offer a little extra protein, and reduce chickens' stress by keeping routines predictable, avoiding overcrowding, providing shelter from weather and predators, handling birds calmly, and offering high-quality feed and access to favourite enrichment treats (such as greens, fresh bedding or scratch mix).

Chickens at any scale

Chickens can be integrated beautifully into a garden of any size. At Oak & Monkey Puzzle, our chooks lived within a 16 × 16-metre (52 × 52-foot) fenced orchard, a working flock that helped to keep woolly aphids and codling moths in check. Their home was an unapologetically extravagant structure, part coop and part folly, that we called the 'Taj Ma Fowl' or 'Chook Mahal'. It was a landmark in the landscape as much as a productive asset.

At Little Cottage on a Hill, space is precious, so their home tucks under the projected roofline of the studio and hybrid potting shed and greenhouse. The run and coop are fully integrated into the architecture; the house itself cantilevers off the back wall of the chicken run. It is small, elegant and meticulously detailed, and proof that in a productive garden, even the most functional structures can be designed with beauty in mind.

*Above left*_Pearl, our Wyandotte, perches on a birch-branch roost inside the coop.
*Above right*_Our coop features woven nesting baskets and a scalloped roofline.

To get you started, try these two things this week:

1. Add 5 centimetres (2 inches) of fresh, dry litter to your coop. Notice how quickly the odour drops and how active the birds become as they scratch.
2. Move a wheelbarrow load of spent litter to your compost bay or tower. Add an equal volume of dry leaves, turn the compost, then pour in water. Note the temperature rise over the next few days.

Animals are part of a living web; now we widen the lens to design for the birds, insects and soil life that share the work of a resilient garden.

CREATING FOR BIODIVERSITY AND BENEFICIAL PRESENCE

A biodiverse garden is resilient, generous and easy to care for because living systems share the work. Beneficial presence means designing for the creatures and processes that help you. Pollinators, predators, decomposers, soil fungi, birds, lizards, frogs and microbial life all belong here. Ecologist Tanya Loos calls this 'living with wildlife': reading the garden as habitat and stitching together corridors and connections so creatures can move, drink and shelter. Provide creatures with what they need, and you increase the likelihood of pollination, pest balance and nutrient cycling. Interest builds across the year, and the garden asks less of you while offering more back.

Lily Langham's night walks (see page 114) are a gentle reminder that half of the action occurs after dark, with hawkmoths often seen working Cleveland sage (*Salvia clevelandii*), lilies (*Lilium* spp.), carnations (*Dianthus* spp.) and giant hyssops (*Agastache* spp.) at twilight. A garden design that welcomes both day life and night life is one that works.

Biodiversity planting is the intentional layering of trees, shrubs, perennials, herbs and ground covers, with the addition of microhabitats such as leaf litter, wood, rock and water. The aim is to offer reliable sources of food and shelter as well as places of safe movement for wildlife all year round. A successful design includes a continuous sequence of nectar and pollen, clean shallow water, safe nesting and overwintering sites, minimal artificial light at night, careful chemical use, and a coherent structure that reads as part of the garden's design language. Here are the core principles of biodiversity planting:

- Feed the web rather than a single species. Flowers, woody structure, leaf litter and water build food chains.
- Continuity matters more than peaks. Keep something flowering or seeding every month of your growing year.
- Build porosity and safe passage. Hedges and layered borders that filter wind are better than solid barriers.
- Beauty is habitat. Repetition, rhythm and a focused material palette make biodiverse planting feel intentional.

Functional steps for biodiversity planting

This section guides you through the practical steps for designing biodiversity-rich gardens. You will map your garden's structure, learn to layer plants for habitat, and make specific choices that support wildlife in every season. By following these steps, you will create planting that will offer natural beauty and a haven for beneficial species.

Map your 'life' lines:

- Sketch paths, beds, hedges, fence lines, sheds and water points.
- Circle the edges where most life is likely to concentrate.
- Mark sun and wind.
- Note where water can safely linger after rain to form sippers and microhabitats.

Choose a simple layer stack:

- Structure using hedges, pleached plantings or open shrubs for wind filtering and perches.
- Create a middle layer of perennials and herbs for nectar and pollen.
- Add a ground plane of living cover and mulch for moisture and shelter.
- Make microhabitats using logs, stones, hollow stems and neat twig bundles for nesting and overwintering.
- Keep it legible by repeating materials and proportions used elsewhere on-site.

Plant a four-season nectar calendar:

— Aim for at least three species in flower in each season to provide reliable nectar across the year.
— In mild zones, plan for some blooms year-round; in colder areas, maximise diversity and overlap in spring and autumn so pollinators always find food, even outside the main summer flush.
— Plant in clumps and repeating drifts measuring ½–1 square metre (5–10 square feet) in area so insects can easily find them.

Build safe nesting and overwintering spots:

— After your autumn tidy-up, leave some hollow stems that are 10–30 centimetres (4–12 inches) in length, as these are ideal for cavity-nesting bees.
— Tuck a small brush pile or log into planting (where bushfire regulations allow).
— Net fruits only when needed using wildlife-safe netting with a small aperture, held off the foliage, and remove it promptly after harvest.

Use water and light effectively:

— Place a large shallow dish of water, about 30–40 centimetres (12–16 inches) in diameter and 3–5 centimetres (1¼–2 inches) deep, in a quiet and partly shaded spot near shrubs or low cover, and add pebbles for perches. Scrub it out weekly.
— Where space permits, build a lined pond with plants around the edge. During heatwaves, access to plenty of clean water can be lifesaving for birds and other wildlife.
— Keep night lighting warm in colour, low and shielded, and aim to turn it off by 10 pm. Position necessary access lighting away from nectar plants. I use small 'warm white' solar lights in strategic locations to illuminate paths and corners. These inexpensive yet reliable solar lights have small batteries that often only last until about midnight; the sun then recharges them the next day.

Design for safe passage and coexistence:

— Avoid large reflective panes or mirrors near planting to reduce bird strikes.
— Break up easy wildlife runways on continuous fences using trellis planes, and plant decoy shrubs for browsing animals away from valued garden beds.
— Place wildlife magnets such as ponds away from small children and pets (especially as snakes may be drawn to water).
— Provide refuge zones with long grass, stacked rocks and branches for reptiles and insects.
— Create stepping stones of cover from verge to beds to small trees to canopy.
— Use permeable or wildlife-friendly fencing, and avoid full enclosure that blocks movement.
— Keep dogs and cats managed during heat, fire or flood, when displaced wildlife may pass through.

*Above left*_A bee foraging in a nectar-rich flower is a small marker of a garden designed to feed pollinators.
*Above right*_A shallow birdbath with pebble perches gives insects a landing point and a way out.

Tread gently on chemistry:

— Start by improving soil health and biological diversity. Time any pest management to avoid harming beneficial insects. For example, prune or hand-pick pests early in the morning or late in the day when pollinators are less active.
— Use physical barriers and hand-picking to remove pests before considering chemical sprays.
— Follow local council guidance when any control is needed.

Uphold a maintenance rhythm:

— Every month during the growing season, deadhead flowers lightly to ensure continuous nectar. Leave some seed heads for the birds.
— Every three months, add 2–5 centimetres (3/4–2 inches) of new mulch. Refresh water and habitat points.
— In autumn, cut back only what flops onto paths. Leave sturdy stems as winter insect hotels, and rake leaves under shrubs for free mulch and insect cover.

High-performance and triple-value plants

These are plants in your garden that perform two or three roles, or provide two or three products or services, such as pollinator attractor, cut-flower value, edible yield, seasonal structure or microclimate service. Over the years, these high-performance plants have made significant contributions to my gardens:

- *Calamagrostis* 'Karl Foerster', *Miscanthus* 'Kleine Fontaine' and *Panicum virgatum* 'Heavy Metal': for wind filtering, nesting material and seeds, with modest inputs; check local invasive species lists for ornamental grasses in your region, and avoid these.
- *Echinops ritro* 'Veitch's Blue': for bees, sculptural seed heads and cut flowers
- *Eryngium bourgatii* 'Oxford Blue': for pollinators, architectural structure and cut flowers
- Lenten rose (*Helleborus* × *hybridus*): for winter pollen on mild days and quiet structure at ground level
- *Monarda* 'Jacob Cline': for nectar and cut-flower value through high summer
- purple coneflower (*Echinacea purpurea*), *E. p.* 'White Swan' and *E. p.* 'Double Scoop': for bees and butterflies, long vase life, and winter seed heads for birds
- *Salvia nemorosa* 'Ostfriesland' and *Agastache* 'Liquorice Blue': for bees and butterflies, aromatic foliage and drought tolerance
- *Sanguisorba officinalis* 'St Philibert': for long-season pollinator draw and cut flowers
- seaside daisy (*Erigeron karvinskianus*): for near continuous forage along path seams
- *Vaccinium corymbosum* 'Brigitta': for spring-blossom nectar, summer blueberries and autumn hedge colour
- white laceflower (*Orlaya grandiflora*): for early hoverflies and fine cut flowers.

Below left_Scots roses have a vivid autumn colour and hips that carry through the season. ***Below middle***_The pairing of ornamental grasses and avens (*Geum* spp.) creates high-performance movement, texture and seasonal interest. ***Below right***_White laceflower (*Orlaya grandiflora*) is a light, nectar-rich flower that draws in beneficial insects.

Innovative ways to welcome wildlife

These don't have to be grand gestures. Even the smallest action can make a big difference to your local wildlife.

- Consider homemade stem bundles rather than store-bought insect hotels. Cut 30-centimetre (12-inch) lengths of hollow or pithy stems, such as those of raspberry (*Rubus idaeus*), bamboos (*Bambusa* spp.) and teasels (*Dipsacus* spp.). Tie them in groups, and mount them under the eaves facing the morning sun. Replace them yearly as they decompose.
- Keep a warm, well-drained pocket of bare soil near a sunny wall for ground-nesting native bees.
- Add living mulch that both feeds and flowers. Plant thyme (*Thymus vulgaris*), Australian bugle (*Ajuga australis*) or German chamomile (*Matricaria chamomilla*) under shrubs, and clip the understorey high rather than close to preserve flowers and shelter for wildlife.
- Route your water-tank overflow to a planted basin edged with sedges and irises (*Iris* spp.) that are suited to your climate. This slows water, allowing it to sink into the soil, and creates a damp edge that supports insects, frogs and small birds.
- Train pollinator-attracting deciduous climbers, such as *Clematis* 'Huldine' and *C.* 'Rooguchi', through light screens for summer shade and winter light.

***Above left*_**This yellow form of yarrow (*Achillea millefolium*) is a generous plant for pollinators, structure and medicinal use.
***Above right*_**Braiding grass is Lily Langham's gentle way of shifting a plant off a path without cutting it back. It is a small yet practical gesture that becomes its own quiet installation.

'A productive garden is one that produces hope and life for you and all the other creatures.'

MARY REYNOLDS

We Are The ARK

Mary Reynolds is a self-confessed reformed landscape architect from Ireland whose career pivoted from award-winning artistry to ecological restoration. After becoming the youngest ever RHS Chelsea Flower Show gold medallist in 2002, she founded We Are The ARK (Acts of Restorative Kindness): a global invitation to return private and public green spaces to living sanctuary. Her work reframes the gardener's role: from consumer shaping land to guardian in service to it.

Mary resists the idea of 'surrender' as neglect; instead, she asks us to 'step into service to the natural world', actively holding integrity where invasive pressure and fragmentation now exist. For her, design is a key component of ecological restoration, because layered, legible ecotones* (from canopy to bare soil) multiply niches for life while weaving people through a place that still works as habitat. Beauty is not something imposed; it emerges from a relationship with the unique character of each patch of land and the native plant communities that feed the local web.

Productivity, through this lens, expands beyond harvest. A truly productive garden 'produces hope and life for you and all the other creatures', Mary tells me during our conversation, with food, water, cover and safe passage as the baseline. Windowsills, verges, small yards and big blocks each count when stitched together as a patchwork of 'ARKs' that form corridors across streets and suburbs. Start small (even cultivating local seeds in a window box counts), discover what arrives, and let that relationship guide the next move. Mary's invitation sits within a logic of function, systems and habitat: celebrate function, keep systems visible, and make habitat read as garden. These are the key takeaways from our conversation:

- Shift from consumer to cohabitant; act as a guardian in service to the land.
- Don't 'abandon' gardens, manage for integrity; use design to create layered ecotones* and to hold space against invasives.
- Native plant communities are the foundation stone of the food web, so start there.
- Redefine productivity: measure success by the return of life, not neatness.
- Build a patchwork of 'ARKs', from window boxes to community spaces, to reconnect corridors.
- Language matters: move from 'coloniser' impulses to guardian practice.

**An ecotone is a transition zone between two distinct ecosystems, where species from both environments mingle and interact. These areas are often rich in biodiversity, as they support organisms from each ecosystem as well as unique species adapted to the in-between conditions.*

Scan to hear my full conversation with Mary Reynolds, where we talk about ARKs and wildlife corridors, redefining 'productive' as restoration for all creatures, and moving from gardener to guardian in your own patch.

Start an ARK in any garden

When garden design unites with deliberate wildness, you have a space that offers perfect ARK coexistence.

- Give a patch of your garden or growing space (such as a pot, a verge or a bed) back to local native plants and the wildlife that depends on them. Source local seeds where possible.
- Build a number of ecotones, such as tree + shrub, herb + perennial, ground cover + pocket of bare soil (for ground-nesting bees).
- Construct porous boundaries and stepping-stone cover to link beds, verges and canopy.
- Manage invasive plants so natives can establish. If they're on your land, then they're your responsibility.
- Use repetition and simple edges so habitat reads as design.
- Add clean water sources with stones for perches, and refresh them often.
- Choose stem bundles/logs over fussy insect 'hotels', and replace them annually.
- Site wildlife magnets (ponds, dense cover) away from play areas and pets.
- Time cutbacks to protect dwellers; leave some seed heads and hollow stems.
- Keep night lighting low, warm and pointed away from nectar plants.
- Log the creatures that arrive, then tweak the garden design accordingly.

Here are some important garden guardian questions to ask yourself:

- Are your plant choices feeding the local web?
- Where can you add or widen an ecotone?
- What invasives are you currently tolerating?
- How does your site connect to a neighbouring corridor?
- What's one action you can take this month that adds habitat?

A blackbird in a meadow is just one small sign of life returning when we make space and step into service to the natural world.

Troubleshooting for biodiverse plantings

Here are some common situations that arise with biodiverse plantings, along with simple strategies to help your garden thrive and support wildlife year-round:

- **It looks messy:** Keep strong edges, repeat a short list of species in larger clumps, and stick to one material palette.
- **Pollinators arrived and so did pests:** Mix plant families, avoid over-fertilising, and add hoverfly hosts such as dill (*Anethum graveolens*) and yarrow (*Achillea millefolium*).
- **Birds are taking berries:** Plant a decoy row, pick earlier and more often, or use wildlife-safe netting for the brief harvest window.
- **Wasps and parasites in insect hotels:** Simplify your structures by using stems and logs, keep them small and in sunny/dry locations, and replace them annually.
- **Snails thriving in lush edges:** Add a dry gravel ribbon as a moat, and invite predators such as lizards with warm stones for basking. Alternatively, go out at night with a torch after rain, and collect snails as a morning treat for the chickens!

Climate and scale adaptations

These quick notes will help you no matter where you live.

Hot and dry climates:

- Use silver-leaved aromatics such as sages (*Salvia* spp.) and thyme (*Thymus vulgaris*).
- Ensure that mulch is 7–10 centimetres (2¾–4 inches) deep.
- Add afternoon shade screens and light wind filters.
- Keep water sources shallow and shaded.
- Grasses such as panicgrass (*Panicum* spp.) and silvergrass (*Miscanthus* spp.) offer seeds and structure with low inputs.

Cold and wet climates:

- Lift tree crowns slightly, and delay heavy spring mulch until the soil warms up.
- Use plants with strong winter structure, such as European hornbeam (*Carpinus betulus*) and oakleaf hydrangea (*Hydrangea quercifolia*).
- Cultivate plants with early blooms, such as Lenten rose (*Helleborus × hybridus*), for cold-season forage.

Small or urban spaces:

- Use slim hedges, trellis climbers and troughs that mix herbs and perennials with insect-supporting annuals.
- Grow blueberries (*Vaccinium corymbosum*) in large pots.
- Add a water dish on a stand for birds and bees.
- Choose one neat log or stem bundle rather than many scattered items. These can be design elements in their own right if considered as part of the repetitive material palette.

Rural or large plots:

- — Stitch beds with pollinator corridors by repeating contoured bands of shrubs and perennials.
- — Mow grass alleys and paths for access and structure.
- — Place compost bins close to chicken coops for ease of nutrient cycling and insect draw.
- — Pair pollinator corridors and perennial beds with lines of trees such as European hornbeam (*Carpinus betulus*) and orchard blocks to enhance microclimate, provide shelter, and create inviting routes for both wildlife and people throughout the landscape.

Design integration and beauty

Make habitat read as design by framing strips of insect-attracting plants with the same steel, timber or stone edging used elsewhere so they feel deliberate. Repeat two or three pollinator species along a path for rhythm.

Train light climbers such as *Clematis* 'Huldine' over wire frames for dappled shade and nectar at eye level. Echo fence or pergola tones in visible habitat features such as a log seat or stem-bundle ties. To get you started, try these two things this week:

1. Plant a small bed that offers a visual treat in every season. Consider plants such as:
   - — spring: white laceflower (*Orlaya grandiflora*)
   - — summer: *Monarda* 'Jacob Cline' and *Echinacea* 'Sombrero Baja'
   - — autumn: *Sanguisorba officinalis* 'St Philibert' and *Anemone* × *hybrida* 'Honorine Jobert'
   - — winter: leave seed heads of purple coneflowers (*Echinacea purpurea*) standing for small bird forage, and keep some hollow stems intact for overwintering insects.
2. Install a bundle of stems and twigs tucked into the edge of a bed, and set a shallow water dish with stones near a busy flower planting. Watch what arrives within a fortnight.

Diversity brings resilience; the next step is to wire that resilience into planning for hotter, drier, wilder seasons.

Water storage and movement

Store water in soil first through repeated additions of organic matter and mulch. Then add a tank that is the right size for your site and average rainfall (remembering that 1 millimetre [less than 1/16 inch] of rain on 1 square metre [10 square feet) of roof gives about 1 litre [34 fluid ounces] of water). Move the tank overflow to planted swales or rain gardens rather than the street (where it's safe and legal to do so). In dry regions, consider installing an extra reservoir bed or a second tank so you aren't reliant on one system.

CLIMATE RESILIENCE AND SEASONAL DISRUPTION

The weather is less predictable than it used to be. Heat arrives early, rain misses the month it used to claim, storms are sharper, frost can linger or vanish, and seasons slide. The most resilient gardens are designed and managed for these swings. Soil health comes first, then water management, protective structure, plant choice and a rhythm of observation and necessary adjustments. The aim is not to control the weather, but to help the garden continue to thrive despite uncertainty.

Resilience is easier when you have a simple way to move from noticing to action. This is the cycle of prompts I return to in my gardens. It turns an unsettled forecast into calm, visible steps:

— **Observe:** Read the real signals at your place, including soil moisture and temperature, wind direction, air humidity, cloud build-up and plant cues.

— **Anticipate:** Check the forecast and warnings, then name what is most at risk, for example young plants, pots, netting, irrigation, low points or access.

— **Prepare:** Reduce risk before it hits. Clear drains, secure loose items, add protective covers, move pots to shelter, and set priorities for watering and access.

— **Protect:** During the event, do the safest high-impact actions. Stabilise structures, keep water moving and shelter tender plants if possible.

— **Recover:** Once it passes, reset function. Clear debris, check irrigation and drainage, firm or stake plants, cover bare soil and top-dress with compost.

— **Record:** Write three lines about what happened, what you did and what you will change next time.

Spring light at the junction of the northern and western verges, where sun and frost sit side by side. Microclimate cues like this guide timing, plant choice and what is protected.

Core approach

Use the patterns below as a scaffold, and adapt them to your place and scale. They are the steady moves I lean on when the season will not sit still.

- — Build living soil that drains well yet holds moisture.
- — Reduce water demand before you add supply.
- — Protect plants from extremes with shade, wind barriers and airflow.
- — Choose diverse, climate-suited plantings with a backbone of perennials.
- — Plan for flexible timing. Follow natural phenomena rather than arbitrary dates.
- — Design with redundancy. Have more than one way to water, more than one nectar source, more than one windbreak. Plant a few extra seeds.

As weather and climate patterns become less certain, it's useful to swap fixed calendars for visible cues. Warm-season sowing is best done when the soil is consistently above 15 degrees Celsius (59 degrees Fahrenheit), depending on the crop. So check the soil temperature using a thermometer to a depth of 10 centimetres (4 inches).

Watch for local plant signals. When wattle (*Acacia* spp.) or lilac (*Syringa* spp.) flowers appear in your area, then review your next sowings. Map the first and last frosts not only by suburb but also by garden area or bed. A few metres of elevation or a hedge can change the date by days, sometimes weeks.

Design for the four main extremes

Gardens all over the country are likely to experience a number of weather extremes, including heat and drought, flooding and waterlogging, frost and cold snaps, and wind and storms. But there are things you can do to mitigate the damage.

To cope with heat and drought, it's important to reduce the stress on plants so they need less water:

- — Keep soil covered with organic mulch. In hot regions, 7–10 centimetres (2¾–4 inches) of mulch around established plantings works well.
- — Deliver water efficiently to roots using subsurface drip lines or wicking beds.
- — Provide afternoon shade for tender plants and crops with climber-clad frames. Small trees can be pruned to allow in dappled light.
- — Choose heat-tolerant, drought-wise plants with silver or small leaves and deep roots.
- — During heat spikes, erect temporary shadecloth and water early in the morning. One deep watering is often better than many shallow ones.

If your plants are subject to periodic flooding and waterlogging, then keep roots aerated and move water off the surface gently:

- — Lift beds a little so crowns sit above wet ground.
- — Improve surface drainage with shallow contour paths or discreet drains that lead to a rain garden or swale.
- — Use permeable paths so water can sink into the site.
- — In very wet positions, use wicking beds to lift the root zone into well-aerated soil, and set overflows carefully.
- — After a flood, rinse soil from leaves, remove silt from crowns, and add a light top dressing of mature compost to support recovery.

Planning for all possibilities

Write contingency plans (Plan A, Plan B and Plan C) for each season. If the first sowing fails because of heat, flood, pests or shifting seasons, then you may need to switch to a faster crop or a more resilient variety rather than repeating the same one. By having several options ready, you can respond flexibly and ensure that your garden remains productive. Keep a small reserve of seeds for repeat or substitute sowings.

Choose a mix of quick-growing and long-season crops so something is always on track. Protect a small nursery bed or a few trays under cover so replacements are ready to go.

Resilient planting design

Use a framework of perennials for structure and stability, and add edibles and ornamentals for colour, harvest and seasonal change. Consider placing deep-rooted perennials and shrubs at edges of beds to open soil and reduce wind at plant height. Include native or locally suited species for biodiversity that works with your climate. Mix plant families and forms so a single pest or disease does not remove a whole planting.

During frost and cold snaps, it's important to trap warmth and keep air moving past plants:

- Site tender plants on slight rises and away from frost pockets.
- Use cloches, row covers and cold frames. Remove covers on bright days for airflow.
- Delay spring mulching until the soil has warmed up.
- Add thermal mass close to tender plants. Water barrels and stone can moderate night lows.
- Choose hardy rootstocks and cold-tolerant varieties for edibles and ornamentals where needed.

For sites prone to wind and storms, slow and lift air currents over beds and protect structures:

- Plant layered windbreaks. A porous hedge restricts wind more effectively than a solid barrier.
- Use simple, wildlife-safe shade frames and cloche hoops that assemble quickly, and later store neatly, to protect tender plants from wind and hail.
- Stake new trees with flexible ties. Remove the stakes as soon as roots start to hold so trunks can strengthen. Trees need to be able to move to grow strong.
- Secure loose items and collect covers before storms blow them away.

During volatile seasons, walk through your garden daily and make small tweaks to prevent big losses. Water deeply and infrequently (where soil type allows) in the mornings to encourage roots to travel downwards and to build resilience. During times of great heat, harvest earlier in the day. Most of all, keep records because noticing patterns in your garden builds confidence faster than any chart or set of rules.

Troubleshooting for climate-resilient gardens

Here are some typical challenges that may arise even in climate-resilient gardens, with ways to turn each into an opportunity for thriving, adaptable planting:

- **Plants bolting in heat:** Choose bolt-resistant varieties, sow earlier or later, and provide afternoon shade.
- **Root rot in wet spells:** Improve drainage, and raise beds slightly. Reduce watering, and increase airflow.
- **Repeated pest outbreaks:** Increase diversity, add beneficial insect-attracting plants, and review watering and feeding that may be promoting soft and sappy growth.
- **Blossom drop in heat or cold snaps:** Protect plants with temporary covers, and water well the day before extreme conditions.

Climate and scale adaptations

These quick notes will help you no matter where you live.

- **Hot and dry climates:** Focus on deep mulch, afternoon shade for tender plants, gradual irrigation at the root zone, and wind protection. Choose hardy plants around the edges to shelter tender beds.

— **Cold and wet climates:** Lift beds, and improve drainage. Use covers and thermal mass for early and late shoulders of the season. Delay spring mulch until the soil has warmed up.
— **Small spaces and balconies:** Containers are mobile, so move them to shelter during times of high heat or wind. Use wicking boxes, small shade frames and timely covers to protect tender crops.

Design integration and beauty

Resilience can be elegant, and there's no need for it conform to any particular aesthetic. However, it's important to choose durable materials that weather well. Try repeating the same timber, steel or stone used elsewhere in your garden so protective structures feel intentional and visually aligned.

Shade frames can echo pergola proportions and materials. Netting can be neat and well tensioned. Tanks can be obscured by planting; alternatively, use them to frame a view or separate spaces. Rain gardens can carry the same planting language as your borders. When protective elements share your garden palette, the whole space reads as a resolved and cohesive whole, not temporary or improvised. To get you started, try these two things this week:

1. Check your soil temperature at a depth of 10 centimetres (4 inches) each morning for one week. Note how it changes, and use that information to time your next sowing.
2. Build one simple shade or frost frame suitable for a single bed, and find a place to store it neatly close to the bed so you can have it ready at short notice if the forecast weather shifts.

Resilience is a practice; circular design turns that practice into daily satisfaction and less waste.

*Far left*_The fire pit is ideal for embracing cold days and nights. *Left*_A useful task is saving the seeds of locally adapted plants.

CIRCULAR DESIGN AS SATISFACTION AND ETHICS

Circular design means designing so that as little as possible is wasted and everything is connected. It's practical because there are fewer inputs and fewer trips to the garden centre, and it's ethical because less waste is leaving your home and more life is supported in place. But it's also deeply satisfying. The garden becomes a living conversation that you're part of every day when scraps become soil; when water lands, slows and sinks; and when seeds you saved become next season's harvest. It's important to close the loops for a number of reasons:

- Fewer external inputs and more self-reliance when supply or weather is unreliable lead to a resilient garden.
- The richest, most stable soil fertility comes from cycling organic matter on-site.
- With less to buy, less to haul and fewer 'big fix' jobs, you save time and money.
- Systems that serve each other have less clutter and create a more considered and resolved garden with beauty and rhythm.

Find your flows: A quick garden audit

On a piece of paper, draw a table with three columns: inputs, processing sites and outputs. Walk through your space, and note what already flows from one category to the other.

Inputs include water, kitchen scraps, prunings, fallen leaves, bedding, seeds, sunlight, your time/energy.

Processing sites include compost bays, worm farms/tunnels, chickens and deep litter, wicking beds, rain tanks, shade/wind structures, propagation bench.

Outputs include worm castings, compost, mulch, clean greywater (where legal), eggs, seeds, leaf mould, heat from hot compost.

Circle any output that could be an input for another system. That's your first loop to build. Then mark 'leaks': places in your garden system where valuable resources are leaving instead of being re-used (in other words, a break in a closed-loop flow). Remedy these, and you will close your loops. You'll know this has happened if:

- your council rubbish bin is lighter
- you buy less bagged fertiliser/soil
- your garden beds hold moisture longer between waterings
- you can trace at least three outputs that have become inputs elsewhere
- the sustainable systems feel manageable, so there are fewer emergency fixes, there are more small and steady tasks, and incremental changes are making lasting impacts.

Scan to download a printable quick garden audit. It's a simple table that allows you to record what comes in, what happens and what leaves your garden.

Anchor loops

The three main anchor loops in any garden involve organic matter, water and seeds. Adapt the following loops to your own garden situation.

1 **Organic-matter loop (kitchen/garden → worms/compost → soil → harvest → kitchen/garden)**

- Kitchen scraps are placed in worm farms or in-bed worm tunnels.
- Dry leaves, shredded cardboard and straw go in the compost heap as 'browns'; harvest trimmings and spent crops as 'greens'.
- Worm castings and mature compost become a 1–2-centimetre (½–¾-inch) top dressing on garden beds.
- Mature compost can also be used as mulch to protect the soil and plant roots.
- Start the loop again with kitchen scraps, harvest trimmings and spent crops.

Design note: Give worm farms/tunnels and compost heaps the same material palette as edges and screens so they belong visually. Keep them within a short and convenient walk of the kitchen.

2 **Water loop (roof → tank → soil → plants → overflow to habitat)**

- Roof catchment can travel via a first-flush diverter to the tank.
- Water from the tank is delivered to root zones in the soil by drip lines or wicking beds.
- Mulch and ground covers keep moisture in the soil.
- Shade frames reduce plants' water demands during hot spells.
- Tank overflow is sent to a planted swale, rain garden or infiltration trench (where it's safe and legal to do so).

Design note: While the water loop doesn't return water to the roof, it's still considered a loop in the garden system because water flows sequentially through multiple uses – irrigating crops, sustaining soil life, then overflowing to nourish wildlife zones or recharge the water table – so nothing is wasted and the value of each drop is maximised.

Tanks can shape a courtyard or step down a slope as sculptural water stores. Thread rills through seating zones for appealing sound and cooling, or edge them with herbs to release scent. Overflows can feed citrus groves, spill into frog-friendly ponds or irrigate beds of edible water plants.

3 **Seed loop (save → sow → grow → save)**

- Choose one or two open-pollinated plants to save seeds from each season, such as sweet pea (*Lathyrus odoratus*), tomato (*Solanum lycopersicum*), sugar snap pea (*Pisum sativum*) or lettuce (*Lactuca sativa*).
- Dry seeds, label them, and store them in a cool, dark place.
- Sow the seeds during the next season; the plants may adapt progressively to your climate. Swap excess seeds with neighbours and friends to widen diversity.
- Start the loop again with the next season's seeds.

Design note: Small, beautiful seed drawers or artfully labelled jars on a shelf near your propagation bench turn the seed-saving practice into a pleasure.

Redundancy equals resilience

Redundancy prevents one weak link from breaking the whole circular loop. So it's helpful to design two ways to do any critical job. For example:

- two water sources (tank + mains, or two tanks)
- two fertility streams (compost + worms; worms + chicken litter matured in bays)
- two shade options (deciduous canopy + quick shadecloth frame).

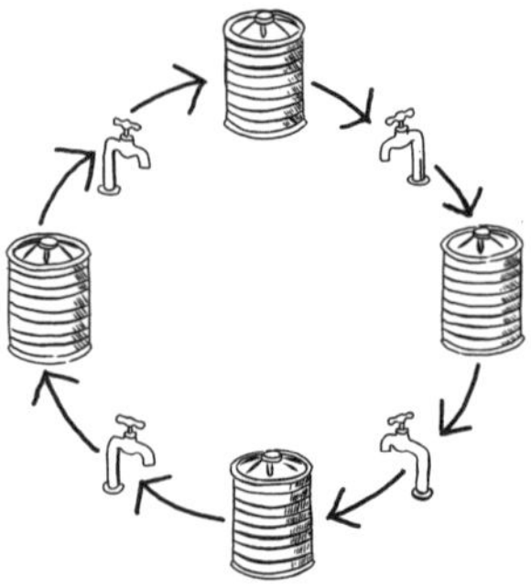

A simple loop map

If you're a visual person, try sketching a map of your space to see all of your loops at a glance.

1. Draw your house, taps, tanks, main paths and beds.
2. Add compost heaps, worm farm/tunnels, chicken coop and propagation bench.
3. With a green pen, mark the flow of scraps to worms/compost to garden beds to harvest.
4. With a blue pen, mark the flow of water from the roof to the tank to the drip lines/wicking beds to the garden beds, and the tank overflow.
5. With a red pen, mark the seed-saving practice, from seed-plant locations to seed storage to sowing/growing to seed saving.

Any long or awkward process or broken line offers you design prompts: shorten the path, move the element or add a missing link.

Troubleshooting for circular design

Here are some opportunities to refine and strengthen your circular design. With a few simple tweaks, you can keep resources cycling smoothly, reduce waste, and make your systems more beautiful and resilient:

- **Food scraps attracting pests:** Feed smaller amounts into the system, bury scraps in worm tunnels, or use a sealed tumbler. Add a secure lid to worm farms, and cap worm tunnels.
- **Too much 'green', smelly compost:** Add dry browns, mix for air, and cover with a dry layer of leaves.
- **Tank overflow eroding paths:** Plumb overflow to a planted basin. Use stones to dissipate flow.
- **Saved seeds not true to type:** Choose self-pollinators to start with, and only grow one variety at a time if you want seeds to stay true. Label seeds precisely.
- **Sustainable system looks 'tacked on':** Re-site or reclad using your garden's primary materials. Integrate with planting.

Climate and scale adaptations

These quick notes will help you no matter where you live.

- **Hot and dry climates:** Prioritise water and organic-matter loops first. Add deep mulch (7–10 centimetres; 2¾–4 inches) to garden beds, provide afternoon shade for tender crops, and install subsurface drip lines or wicking beds. Site tanks in shade, and insulate or clad exposed intermediate bulk containers (IBCs).
- **Cold and wet climates:** Lift root zones using raised or wicking beds, manage tank overflows to rain gardens, and delay heavy spring mulch until the soil warms up. Keep compost covered, and use leaf-mould cages for gentle, slow carbon.
- **Small spaces/balconies:** Keep your loops compact: countertop caddy → worm farm under a bench → castings into troughs; downpipe diverter → slimline tank → watering-can; one or two seed jars that you refresh each season.

The wicking-bed garden at Little Cottage on a Hill sits between the house and the northern verge, with the gates opened to extend the kitchen threshold into the beds. Short, permeable paths and repeated materials help the whole space to read as one connected loop, ready for a future deck connection.

— **Larger plots:** Repeat modules. Consider a cadence and rhythm of repeatable or complementary bed/path units; a central compost and leaf-mould yard beside a chicken run; tanks feeding simple manifolds; planted swales stitching the site.

Design integration and beauty

Circular systems work best when they're enjoyable to use. Paths should be short between the kitchen, worms/compost and garden beds, and made from a permeable, comfortable footing.

Repeat any timber/steel/stone details consistently across bays, tanks and edges so the eye sees one cohesive garden. Create quiet structure by aligning worm tunnels with plant rows, cladding intermediate bulk container (IBC) wicking beds to match fences, and screening bins with planting that also feeds local pollinators. To get you started, try these two things this week:

1. Close one loop: route your tank overflow to a planted basin or rain garden, or install a single worm tunnel in a high-use bed and feed it twice this week.
2. Do a fifteen-minute flow audit, and list your top three leaks (for example, green waste leaving the site, overwatering, buying bagged compost). Choose one small fix that you can implement in the next seven days.

SEASONAL PLANTING AND SOWING GUIDE

This guide is written from lived practice in a cold temperate garden. To serve readers across Australia and beyond, it also includes warm temperate, arid or semi-arid, subtropical and tropical climates. Find the table that matches your climate, then search by the current season in your own hemisphere. The action key will tell you how to sow or propagate during that season. Use the tables as a compass, and adapt them to your place. Start small. Observe. Adjust. There are no failures here. Only lessons.

Useful information

Keep these things in mind when working in the garden. In general, these are the soil-temperature planting cues to follow, with the temperature taken at a depth of 10 centimetres (4 inches):

— warm-season fruiting vegetables: at or above 18 degrees Celsius (64 degrees Fahrenheit)
— beans, corn/maize, pumpkins: at or above 16 degrees Celsius (60 degrees Fahrenheit)
— cool-season greens and root vegetables: 10–15 degrees Celsius (50–59 degrees Fahrenheit).

If you want to grow poppy species, then check your country and state rules first. Growing the opium poppy (*Papaver somniferum*) or the great scarlet poppy (*P. bracteatum*) without a licence is restricted in many places, while other species are generally permitted for ornamental use. Always confirm your local regulations before planting.

In many countries and states, netting for backyard fruit trees must be wildlife-safe. Choose mesh with holes that are 5 × 5 millimetres (1/4 × 1/4 inch) or smaller at full stretch, and keep the mesh taut over fully supported frames.

Index by crop family or type

This section groups edible, medicinal, ornamental and other garden plants by their family or use, and provides quick practical pointers for sowing, planting and ongoing care. Use these lists as a guide to plan and rotate your plantings for a productive, resilient garden year-round.

— **Edible and/or cutting flowers:** bishop's weed (*Ammi majus*), borage (*Borago officinalis*), buttercups (*Ranunculus* spp.), cornflower (*Centaurea cyanus*), cosmos (*Cosmos bipinnatus*), daffodils (*Narcissus* spp.), dahlias (*Dahlia* spp.), love-in-a-mist (*Nigella damascena*), marigolds (*Tagetes* spp.), nasturtium (*Tropaeolum majus*), poppies (such as Iceland poppy [*Oreomecon nudicaulis*] and oriental poppy [*Papaver orientale*]), Siberian larkspur (*Delphinium grandiflorum*), sunflowers (*Helianthus* spp.), sweet alyssum (*Lobularia maritima*), sweet pea (*Lathyrus odoratus*), tulips (*Tulipa* spp.), windflowers (*Anemone* spp.), woolflowers (*Celosia* spp.), zinnia (*Zinnia elegans*) – S or T as per season.

Action key

BR = plant bare-rooted trees and canes
C = take cuttings
D = divide clumps or runners
P = plant out seedlings or plant perennials
S = direct sow
SI = sow indoors or under cover
T = plant tubers, corms, bulbs

- **Fruits and berries:** apples (*Malus* spp.), cherry (*Prunus avium*), pears (*Pyrus* spp.), plum (*Prunus domestica*), quince (*Cydonia oblonga*), raspberry (*Rubus idaeus*), grape (*Vitis vinifera*) – BR during dormancy; bananas (*Musa* spp.), blueberry (*Vaccinium corymbosum*), fig (*Ficus carica*), olive (*Olea europaea*), papaya (*Carica papaya*), passionfruit (*Passiflora edulis*) – P in spring (or autumn in mild climates); citrus trees – P in spring or autumn in frost-free windows; strawberry (*Fragaria × ananassa*) – P or D in spring or autumn by climate.
- **Fruiting vegetables:** broad bean (*Vicia faba*), corn/maize (*Zea mays*), cowpea (*Vigna unguiculata*), okra (*Abelmoschus esculentus*), snake bean (*Vigna unguiculata* subsp. *sesquipedalis*), sugar snap pea (*Pisum sativum*), sweet potato (*Ipomoea batatas*) – plant at the recommended time for your region; chilli/capsicum (*Capsicum annuum*), eggplant (*Solanum melongena*), tomato (*Solanum lycopersicum*) – SI or P when soil reaches 18 degrees Celsius (64 degrees Fahrenheit); common bean (*Phaseolus vulgaris*) – S when soil reaches 16 degrees Celsius (60 degrees Fahrenheit); cucumber (*Cucumis sativus*), melon (*Cucumis melo*), pumpkins (*Cucurbita* spp.), zucchini (*Cucurbita pepo*) – S or P in warm soil.
- **Leafy greens and brassicas:** kale and cabbage (forms of *Brassica oleracea*) – SI or P to avoid pest pressure; lettuce (*Lactuca sativa*) – S or SI most seasons except peak heat; radicchio (*Cichorium intybus*)– S in autumn in warm climates; silverbeet (*Beta vulgaris* Cicla Group) – S in mild seasons or as conditions allow; spinach (*Spinacia oleracea*) – S in spring and autumn in warm climates, and winter in subtropics.
- **Medicinals:** aloe (*Aloe vera*), comfrey (*Symphytum officinale*), feverfew (*Tanacetum parthenium*), German chamomile (*Matricaria chamomilla*), gotu kola (*Centella asiatica*), holy basil (*Ocimum tenuiflorum*), lemon balm (*Melissa officinalis*), pot marigold (*Calendula officinalis*), purple coneflower (*Echinacea purpurea*), rosella (*Hibiscus sabdariffa*), valerian (*Valeriana officinalis*), yarrow (*Achillea millefolium*) – S or P according to the climate.
- **Herbs and aromatics:** basil (*Ocimum basilicum*), bay tree (*Laurus nobilis*), chives (*Allium schoenoprasum*), coriander (*Coriandrum sativum*), dill (*Anethum graveolens*), lavenders (*Lavandula* spp.), lemongrass (*Cymbopogon citratus*), mints (*Mentha* spp.), oregano (*Origanum vulgare*), parsley (*Petroselinum crispum*), rosemary (*Salvia rosmarinus*), sage (*Salvia officinalis*), Thai basil (*Ocimum basilicum* var. *thyrsiflora*), Thai mint (*Mentha arvensis*) thyme (*Thymus vulgaris*), Vietnamese mint (*Persicaria odorata*) – P or C, in spring and autumn in well-drained soil.
- **Roots, tubers and bulbs:** asparagus (*Asparagus officinalis*), galangal (*Alpinia galanga*), potato (*Solanum tuberosum*), rhubarb (*Rheum rhabarbarum*), shallot (*Allium cepa* Aggregatum Group), turmeric (*Curcuma longa*) – plant at the recommended time for your region; beetroot (*Beta vulgaris*) – S across a wide window; carrot (*Daucus carota* subsp. *sativus*) – S in cool shoulder seasons; garlic (*Allium sativum*), onion (*Allium cepa*) – P as sets or cloves in autumn in cool climates, and winter in warm climates; radish (*Raphanus sativus*) – S in succession.

Cold temperate seasonal guidance

This table provides information on sowing, planting, propagating and maintaining key crops in cold temperate regions. Adjust the timings to suit your local conditions, and use the guide to help keep your beds consistently productive throughout the year.

Plant type	Spring	Summer	Autumn	Winter
Vegetables	tomato, chilli, eggplant – SI or P; sugar snap pea, spinach, lettuce, Asian greens, beetroot, carrot, radish – S; potato – T; onion sets and shallots – P	lettuce, common bean, beetroot, carrot, radish – succession S; zucchini, cucumber, melon – P if season is long enough	spinach, Asian greens, broad bean – S; garlic cloves and onion sets – P; potato – T in mild areas	protect crops; start early brassicas and lettuce under cover – S; asparagus crowns – P
Herbs	basil, parsley, dill – SI or P; thyme, oregano, sage, rosemary, mints – P or C; lavenders – C	basil and coriander – S or P in part-shade; thyme, rosemary, lavenders – C	chives, mints, oregano – P or D; rosemary and sage – C	currants and rosemary – C; bay tree and thyme – P in mild spells
Medicinals	pot marigold and German chamomile – S; purple coneflower, yarrow, lemon balm – P; comfrey – D from root sections	holy basil – S or P; harvest and dry German chamomile, yarrow, pot marigold	pot marigold – S; valerian – P; purple coneflower and yarrow – D if crowded	prepare comfrey roots for spring; German chamomile – S under cover
Flowers	sweet pea early; cosmos, cornflower, Siberian larkspur, pot marigold, nasturtium, sweet alyssum – S; dahlias – T after frost risk	zinnias, sunflowers, marigolds, bishop's weed – S; deadhead for continuous cutting	sweet pea, cornflower, Siberian larkspur – S; windflowers and buttercups – T; poppies where legal – P	tulips and daffodils – T for structure where necessary; sweet pea – S under cover
Fruits	rhubarb – D; strawberry – P or D; blueberry and raspberry – P; late BR for trees and canes if ground is workable	citrus trees in containers – P; summer prune pome and stone fruit trees; wildlife-safe netting as needed	apples, pears, quince, plum, cherry – BR in late autumn to winter; strawberry – P	rhubarb – D; deciduous trees and canes – BR; prune pome and stone fruit trees on dry days; graft in late winter

Action key

BR = plant bare-rooted trees and canes
C = take cuttings
D = divide clumps or runners
P = plant out seedlings or plant perennials
S = direct sow
SI = sow indoors or under cover
T = plant tubers, corms, bulbs

1_**Cucumber:** Plant out in summer.
2_**Oriental poppy:** Plant out in autumn.
3_**Beetroot:** Direct sow in spring and summer.
4_**Carrot:** Direct sow in spring and summer.
5_**Quince:** Plant bare-rooted trees in autumn.
6_**Rhubarb:** Divide in winter or spring.
7_**Melon:** Plant out in summer, if the season is long enough.
8_**Nasturtium:** Direct sow in spring.
9_**Potato:** Plant tubers in spring. In mild areas, plant tubers in autumn.

1

2

3

4

6

7

8

9

Warm temperate seasonal guidance

This table provides information on sowing, planting, propagating and maintaining key crops in warm temperate regions. Adjust the timings to suit your local conditions, and use the guide to help keep your beds consistently productive throughout the year.

Plant type	Spring	Summer	Autumn	Winter
Vegetables	carrot, beetroot, radish, silverbeet – S; tomato, capsicum, eggplant – SI then P; pumpkins – P once warm	beans, cucumber, zucchini, lettuce – P in shade; corn/maize – S or P, depending on season length	spinach, Asian greens, broad bean – S; garlic and onion sets – P	brassicas and onion – P; asparagus crowns – P
Herbs	basil and dill – S or P; thyme, oregano, rosemary, sage, lavenders – P or C	basil and Vietnamese mint – S or P; lavenders and rosemary – C	chives and mints – P or D; oregano – P	rosemary – semi-hardwood C; bay tree and thyme – P on mild days
Medicinals	pot marigold and German chamomile – S; purple coneflower and feverfew – P	harvest and dry German chamomile, pot marigold, yarrow; holy basil – S or Pl	pot marigold – S; valerian – P; all crowded perennials – D	German chamomile – S under cover; comfrey – D
Flowers	cosmos, zinnias, sunflowers, bishop's weed, nasturtium, borage – S; dahlias – T	sunflowers, zinnias, marigolds – S; deadhead faded flowers	sweet pea, cornflower, Siberian larkspur – S; windflowers and buttercups – T	spring corms (e.g., *Anemone, Ranunculus*) in mild zones – T; sweet pea – S under cover
Fruits	finish BR planting early; strawberry – P; thin blossoms on heavily set trees	summer prune stone fruit trees; net as needed; layer grape shoots	deciduous trees and canes – BR; strawberry – P	prune pome fruit trees and vines; graft late winter; BR continues until buds swell

Action key

BR = plant bare-rooted trees and canes
C = take cuttings
D = divide clumps or runners
P = plant out seedlings or plant perennials
S = direct sow
SI = sow indoors or under cover
T = plant tubers, corms, bulbs

1_**Capsicum:** Start under cover, then plant out once the weather is warm in spring.
2_**Cucumber:** Plant out in summer.
3_**Quince:** Thin blossoms on heavily set trees in spring.
4_**Zucchini:** Plant out in a shaded place in summer.
5_**Purple coneflower:** Plant out in spring.
6_**Carrot:** Direct sow in spring.
7_**Borage:** Direct sow in spring.
8_**Lavenders:** Take cuttings in spring and summer.
9_**Beans:** Plant out in a shaded place in summer.

1

2

3

4

6

7

8

9

Subtropical seasonal guidance

This table provides information on sowing, planting, propagating and maintaining key crops in subtropical regions. Adjust the timings to suit your local conditions, and use the guide to help keep your beds consistently productive throughout the year.

Plant type	Spring	Summer	Autumn	Winter
Vegetables	common bean, corn/ maize, cucumber, pumpkins, okra – S; tomato, chilli, eggplant – SI or P	snake bean and tropical greens – S; sweet potato slips – P	leafy greens, Asian greens, beetroot, carrot – S; early garlic and onion – P; broad bean – S in cooler pockets	brassicas, sugar snap pea, lettuce, spinach – S or P with light frost protection if needed
Herbs	basil and Thai basil – S or P; lemongrass – P; rosemary and lavenders – C while nights are still cool	basil – succession S; lemongrass – D, P; mints and oregano – C in shade	coriander and parsley – S or P; rosemary and sage – C as nights cool	dill, parsley, coriander – P
Medicinals	holy basil – S or P; gotu kola and aloe – P where suited	harvest and dry holy basil; rosella – S where suited	German chamomile and pot marigold – S; purple coneflower – P as nights cool	pot marigold and poppies where legal – S; sweet pea – S in frost-light zones
Flowers	zinnias, cosmos, marigolds, sunflowers, bishop's weed – S; dahlias – T	sunflowers and woolflowers – S with airflow for humidity	sweet pea, cornflower, Siberian larkspur – S where winters are mild	pot marigold and poppies where legal – S; sweet pea – S in frost-light zones
Fruits	citrus trees and passionfruit – P in sheltered positions	prune after fruiting for airflow; layer and tip prune vigorous vines	strawberry – P for winter and spring cropping	light pruning of deciduous fruit trees due to short dormancy; strawberry and low-chill cane fruits – P in mild pockets

Action key

BR = plant bare-rooted trees and canes
C = take cuttings
D = divide clumps or runners
P = plant out seedlings or plant perennials
S = direct sow
SI = sow indoors or under cover
T = plant tubers, corms, bulbs

1_**Onion:** Plant out in autumn.
2_**Asian greens:** Direct sow in autumn.
3_**Purple broccoli:** Plant out in winter.
4_**Radicchio:** Direct sow in autumn.
5_**Tomato:** Sow indoors or under cover in spring, then plant out once the soil is warm.
6_**Cabbage:** Plant out in winter.
7_**Iceland poppy:** Plant out in winter, in frost-light zones.
8_**Sage:** Take cuttings in autumn, as nights cool.
9_**Cucumber:** Direct sow in spring.

1

2

3

4

6

7

8

9

Tropical seasonal guidance

This table provides information on sowing, planting, propagating and maintaining key crops in tropical regions. Anchor sowing windows to the beginning and end of your wet and dry seasons. Prioritise airflow, shade design and water quality.

Plant type	Spring	Summer	Autumn	Winter
Vegetables	snake bean – S; okra – S; cucumber and pumpkins – S; tomato – S with strong airflow or SI then P; sweet potato slips – P	tropical greens – succession S; provide salad greens with shade; water in the early morning	leafy greens – S; common bean and quick roots – S as heat moderates	sugar snap pea, lettuce, Asian greens – S; protect from rare cold snaps
Herbs	tropical basils – S; lemongrass – P; Thai mint – P; turmeric and galangal – T or P where available	lemongrass – D; mints – C in shade	coriander and dill – S; chives – D	coriander and parsley thrive
Medicinals	gotu kola – P; aloe – P; holy basil – S	harvest and dry when humidity is low; renew sowings after heavy rain	renew sowings after wet season; harvest and dry during low-humidity windows	aloe and gotu kola – harvest as needed
Flowers	woolflowers, zinnias, marigolds – S; sunflowers – S with wide spacing	harvest and dry when humidity is low; renew sowings after heavy rain	sweet pea – S only where winters are very mild and dry	pause sowing; focus on airflow and disease control in dense plantings
Fruits	banana pups, papaya, passionfruit – P in prepared ground with wind protection	prune and train for airflow; use exclusion where fruit fly is a pressure	strawberry – P for winter and early spring cropping in milder tropical zones	light prune and tip prune; dormancy is short

Action key

BR = plant bare-rooted trees and canes
C = take cuttings
D = divide clumps or runners
P = plant out seedlings or plant perennials
S = direct sow
SI = sow indoors or under cover
T = plant tubers, corms, bulbs

*1*_**Silverbeet:** Succession sow in summer as part of tropical greens.
*2*_**Strawberry:** Plant out in autumn for winter and early spring cropping in milder tropical zones.
*3*_**Cucumber:** Direct sow in spring.
*4*_**Sugar snap pea:** Direct sow in winter. Protect from rare cold snaps.
*5*_**Tomato:** Sow indoors or under cover in spring. Plant out where there is strong airflow.
*6*_**Asian greens:** Direct sow in winter.
*7*_**Lettuce:** Direct sow in winter. Protect from rare cold snaps.
*8*_**Pumpkins:** Direct sow in spring.
*9*_**Sweet pea:** Direct sow in autumn, only where winters are very mild and dry.

1

2

3

4

6

7

8

9

Arid or semi-arid seasonal guidance

This table provides information on sowing, planting, propagating and maintaining key crops in arid or semi-arid regions. Adjust the timings to suit your local conditions, and use the guide to help keep your beds consistently productive throughout the year.

Plant type	Spring	Summer	Autumn	Winter
Vegetables	early sugar snap pea and spinach – S; common bean, corn/maize, pumpkins – S as soil warms, with windbreaks and deep mulch	cowpea and okra – S; sweet potato – P; provide shade for leafy greens or pause sowing	carrot, beetroot, radish, leafy greens – S; garlic – P; broad bean – S as heat drops	sugar snap pea and leafy greens – S where frost is light; use low polytunnels for cold snaps
Herbs	basil – S or P; rosemary, thyme, sage – P with very sharp drainage	basil under shadecloth; tough annuals only; water deeply and infrequently where soil type allows	coriander and parsley – S or P; rosemary and sage – C while nights are warm	sow cool-season types in frost-light pockets or under cover
Medicinals	pot marigold, yarrow, cosmos, zinnias, sunflowers, bishop's weed – S; purple coneflower – P	pause sowing and planting; focus on harvest and heat protection	German chamomile – S; valerian – P; pot marigold – S	sow cool-season types in frost-light pockets or under cover
Flowers	pot marigold, yarrow, cosmos, zinnias, sunflowers, bishop's weed – S	tough annuals only; water deeply and infrequently where soil type allows	sweet pea, cornflower, Siberian larkspur – S	sow cool-season types in frost-light pockets or under over
Fruits	grape, fig, olive – P; mulch deeply	irrigate deeply; whitewash trunks; provide reflective or dappled shade	strawberry – P; prune vines after harvest	deciduous trees and canes – BR; graft in late winter

Action key

BR = plant bare-rooted trees and canes
C = take cuttings
D = divide clumps or runners
P = plant out seedlings or plant perennials
S = direct sow
SI = sow indoors or under cover
T = plant tubers, corms, bulbs

*1*_**Sugar snap pea:** Direct sow in early spring. In winter, direct sow where frost is light, and use low polytunnels for cold snaps.
*2*_**Spinach:** Direct sow in early spring.
*3*_**Grape:** Plant out in spring and mulch deeply.
*4*_**Common bean:** Direct sow as soil warms in spring, with windbreaks and deep mulch.
*5*_**Pumpkins:** Direct sow as soil warms in spring, with windbreaks and deep mulch.
*6*_**Carrot:** Direct sow in autumn.
*7*_**Fig:** Plant out in spring, and mulch deeply.
*8*_**Beetroot:** Direct sow in autumn.
*9*_**Purple coneflower:** Plant out in spring.

1

2

3

4

6

7

8

9

THE RHYTHM OF SUSTAINABILITY

Sustainability in the garden isn't a style you apply, it's a rhythm you live. It's the soft thud of kitchen scraps emptied into a worm farm before you've had your second sip of tea. It's the raised bed that stays crumbly even after rain because you fed the soil and left the fungi to stitch it together. It's the overflow from a rain tank that trickles silently into a planted basin, humming with life long after the storm has passed. It's the satisfaction of placing just-picked flowers on the table, knowing they fed bees before they filled a vase.

I didn't discover this all at once, and I'm still learning. I gleaned it the gradual and satisfying way across two very different gardens. At Oak & Monkey Puzzle, the scale asked for bold and expansive gestures: compost bays you could walk into; formal terraces carved from the slope to mitigate, catch and hold water; trees as filters for the hot western sun. Even the pathways were designed to slow moisture and allow it to sink into the ground. At Little Cottage on a Hill, the work has been distilled and reimagined. I've tucked worm tunnels through the growing layer. Raised intermediate bulk container (IBC) wicking beds that lift soil into the winter sun. Built compost towers that read like vertical punctuation marks across the garden. Smaller moves; same intent. I've always asked how each element can do more than one thing. Let it belong to the place. Let it be functional and practical. Let it be beautiful enough so that I'll keep using it, and each and every time it makes my heart sing.

Below left_I find that a watering-can is best for small irrigation jobs. ***Below right***_My simple garden toolkit is ready for daily tending.

Because beauty matters. It nourishes the mind. It keeps systems alive. The most efficient set-up will fail if it's misaligned with how you live. A rainwater tank can be reimagined as a backrest that frames a view. A chicken coop can echo the aesthetics and materiality of your home. Mulch that looks deliberate will be topped up happily. An eyesore will be ignored, yet it will still be the white elephant in the garden room, no matter how small. There's no single aesthetic for sustainability. It can be minimalist or romantic, wild or formal. What matters is that it's considered. When function and form are inseparable, maintenance becomes a rhythm, not a burden. The utilitarian brings joy.

We don't control the seasons. Bulbs flower early. Fungi don't arrive. Rain slips into the 'wrong' month entirely. The answer is not to garden harder, it's to garden wiser. Build soil that holds moisture within a living matrix. Reduce demand before adding supply. Choose diverse plantings. Protect with shade and wind filters. Watch for the seasonal signals: sap rising, soil warming, hoverflies returning. Redundancy is not waste, it's resilience. Two ways to water. Two sources of fertility. Two forms of shelter. Whether you're growing on a balcony or across an acreage, the intent is the same.

Essential takeaways

If there's one thing I want you to carry from this chapter, it's permission to begin. Try one wicking bed. Tuck a worm tunnel into a pot. Plant for insects and pollinators, and see which ones your garden loves. Save seeds from your best (open-pollinated) tomato. Sketch a loop of how you move through your garden, and reconsider one path so a daily task becomes easier. Small moves compound. Loops close. New habits lead to lasting change. The garden grows steadier under your feet. Be brave enough to try and to fail.

***Above left*_**There are always small tasks to complete in the wicking-bed garden, regardless of the season.
***Above right*_**Wire cloches are perfect protective structures for tender plants. They keep large pests such as possums away from the leaves.

When something doesn't work, that's the opportunity for refining and learning. I always say that design is an iterative process, and so is learning. A soggy bed will tell you where the overflow needs to go. A sluggish compost tower will remind you that it needs more carbon. A sulking plant might point to wind you hadn't noticed at knee height. This certainly isn't failure, it's information. Adjust. Try again. Keep systems visible so you can read them at a glance. Celebrate them so you'll return to them. Over time, the garden won't just produce, it will hum. And your life will grow richer in all the little ways that money can't buy.

Across these pages, we've returned again and again to the things that matter most: living soil, no-dig practice, compost and worms, regenerative growing, water capture, seed saving, climate resilience, and circular systems that turn waste into resource. Together they form a garden that is as beautiful as it is sustaining.

Sustainability isn't a finish line, it's a relationship. One that is nurtured when you arrive with a wheelbarrow of leaves in autumn. When you offer shade in summer. When you plant something not for yourself, but for the birds that share their morning song with you. It's a way of existing that, with every small change and contribution, feels more and more like a life lived ethically, ecologically, aesthetically. When your scraps become soil, when rain stays, when you eat the first strawberry while standing where it grew, there's a contentment and quiet voice that beckons you to keep going. This is worth sustaining. This truly is a life lived well.

If you're just starting, then begin small. If you're refining, then finesse a single loop or skill. If you're already deep in, then ask where beauty might turn a chore into a ritual. These aren't perfect systems. They're evolving practices shaped by observation, consideration and creativity. And they hold true at every scale. Whether you're growing in pots on a balcony or stewarding an expansive block, the principles remain the same: design with purpose, adapt with care, and let each element serve more than one role. Take what serves. Adapt the rest. Make it yours. Close one loop today, and the garden will show you the next one.

Inspirational sustainability

The pages of this book are written from my studio in a cold temperate garden. Short summers. Long light at the edges of the day. The systems hold. They make sense of weather and work, and they invite beauty to do some of the lifting.

I've included a feature on Jerry Coleby-Williams' garden, Bellis, because the same principles breathe in a tropical language. Water and shade are designed. Food and habitat sit close to the kitchen door. It is suburban in scale and rigorous in practice. That matters to me because good systems should fit an ordinary day.

I've been watching the evolution of Bellis for the past twenty years, following along remotely as Jerry has shared his garden's journey through the much-loved ABC TV show *Gardening Australia*. I was fortunate enough to meet Jerry in person when we were both keynote speakers at the Ballarat Begonia Festival. He is as fascinating as he is forthright, and it was then that I gained a deeper insight into Bellis, not just as a garden but as an evolving model of abundance, resilience and ecological thinking.

As you step into this feature, look for the constants. Closed loops. Right plant, right place. Beauty held to purpose. Then meet me in Chapter 11, where we gather what the garden offers and carry it into the kitchen and into the week.

Bellis in Brisbane, Queensland. Jerry Coleby-Williams' suburban subtropical garden has been shaped over two decades to build living soil, capture water and grow food within a small footprint.

BELLIS

Twenty years of sustainable abundance in subtropical Australia by Jerry Coleby-Williams

This project has highlighted the value of a small plot of land and how intensive food production can help a household live more affordably and sustainably. The intent has always been that what I do in Brisbane can be replicated by an ordinary family on an ordinary income anywhere in Australia.

In 2003, I found a semi-original 1914 Queenslander house on gently sloping grass. The extremely acidic, impoverished, compacted, ancient acid sulphate soil that greeted me took years to transform into the fertile, crumbly tilth I wanted.

The more you depend on homegrown food, the greater the importance of eliminating soil nutritional deficiencies. Soil laboratory testing revealed precisely what needed addressing. Re-testing five years later confirmed that improvements had been achieved.

I started by rotary hoeing, mixing the two layers (sand over clay) together and incorporating plenty of organic matter. I sowed and dug in three successive green manures before setting out the garden. Within two years, my garden was providing a surplus of food, seeds, plants and preserves.

A 21,000-litre (5500-gallon) rainwater tank was installed for drinking and household use. Rainfall in the subtropics has always been fickle, and no season exactly repeats. Over the years, I've become used to erratic rainfall, and flooding rain of increased volume and frequency.

'The most political act of your life is the food you eat. We get three votes (meals) a day that determine the food systems we support.'

'Level beds prevent run-off, while raising them encourages drainage.'

I minimised water-shedding hardscape with porous surfaces that slow the movement of stormwater and encourage it to move vertically into the soil. Mulched footpaths, lawn and garden beds hinder run-off, encouraging water to soak in.

Level beds prevent run-off, while raising them encourages drainage. Soil is enriched by digging in 2 kilograms (4 pounds) of compost or rotted manure per square metre twice every year. Growing conditions improve while atmospheric CO_2 is sequestered.

When the rainwater tank overflows, surplus enters a drainage system installed 700 millimetres (28 inches) below the soil's surface, deeply watering the soil. If the subsoil becomes saturated, then the drainage system directs water into a stormwater-infiltration well in the front garden at the lowest point of the property. This porous well captures nutrients and sediment, and passively waters the front garden that otherwise depends on natural rainfall.

Solar panels generate more energy than we require. Instead of heating the house during winter, we wear appropriate clothes. For summer cooling, we have fans and external blinds.

The sewerage system digests human waste, processing all black and grey-water before sterilising it, and this water is then used to flush the toilet in a closed loop. If your local authority will not allow this, then install a greywater-recycling system. We use green cleaners because surplus, nutrient-enriched wastewater is used for irrigation. During watering bans, I sustain my orchard and a few crops using wastewater.

Climate resilience and seasonal disruption

Our warming climate is having a similar effect to that of putting my Brisbane garden on a trailer and slowly dragging it north. By mid-century, when the urban heat island effect will have doubled, we'll have conditions similar to Townsville in 2000.

I wanted an ornamental front garden with architectural evergreen foliage to provide structure, with flowers for seasonal interest. I planted different species already thriving in Townsville, so they could grow into Brisbane's emerging new climate: palms, cycads, pandanus, shrubs, ferns, bromeliads, succulents and other perennials. Unlike the food garden, it is low maintenance.

The food garden provides ingredients for meals I want to eat. I listed every ingredient from my favourite cookbook that can be grown in Brisbane. I can't grow wheat (*Triticum aestivum*), but I can make polenta from cornmeal. Instead of rice (*Oryza sativa*), I grow cocoyam (*Xanthosoma sagittifolium*), cassava (*Manihot esculenta*) and bananas (*Musa* spp.). I eat all edible parts of a plant, which means if I grow pumpkins (*Cucurbita* spp.) I eat the flowers, leaves and fruits.

The annual cropping cycle involves growing tropical annuals in the warm seasons and cool-climate annuals in winter. As Brisbane's climate has warmed, cultural hangovers such as potato (*Solanum tuberosum*) have been quickly abandoned. Crops must justify the space, effort, time and water used to produce them. Instead, I grow resilient and dependable staples: bananas (*Musa* spp.), sweet potato (*Ipomoea batatas*), yam (*Dioscorea alata*), elephant foot yam (*Amorphophallus paeoniifolius*) and *Carica papaya* 'Southern Red'.

One of my best decisions was to use the dry spring weather to produce seeds from winter crops. Rather than battling drying weather, I use it to my advantage, directing unused wastewater to my orchard, not thirsty annuals.

If there are losses or failures, then I upgrade. I planted sugar palm (*Arenga pinnata*) to produce my own palm sugar. This palm grows well, but the erratic wet season never provided the consistent moisture necessary to get enough sap flow for harvesting and conversion into sugar. When it died of old age, I upgraded to a soursop (*Annona muricata*), which fruits all year round.

As a director of the Seed Savers' Network, I advise gardeners to grow non-hybrid crops and to save seeds from their best plants. By saving seeds of certain cool-climate crops, such as perennial Chinese celery (*Apium graveolens* var. *secalinum*), we gradually adapt these crops to local soils and conditions. My first success was subtropical-adapted Chinese celery. It took five years to become localised and provide celery all year round.

Subtropical winters are too short and warm to grow broad bean (*Vicia faba*). Winter minimum temperatures are rising quickly, so I put this to good use. I sow zucchini/marrow (*Cucurbita pepo*) and cucumber (*Cucumis sativus*) in autumn to crop into winter. Ten years ago, I demonstrated that I can sow a crop of corn/maize (*Zea mays*) every month of the year. In my garden, corn is no longer seasonal.

The garden as legacy and model

The most valuable aspect of this project is that much has been measured. I never have fewer than 70 edible things on the menu, and sometimes more than 150.

My garden uses a fraction of the 5000 litres (1300 gallons) of water required by irrigated farming to produce a day's supply of food for a person. In drought, 21,000 litres (5500 gallons) of recycled wastewater keeps the 300-square-metre (3200-square-foot) food garden in production all year.

Originally earthworm free, the soil now hosts an average of ten worms per square metre. I have raised the soil organic carbon content by 4 per cent, increasing the water-holding capacity of the soil by around 140,000 litres (37,000 gallons).

This household produces zero food waste, and we live carbon positive lives. Solar panels keep me in credit, while the soil sequesters more atmospheric CO_2 than the household and my old petrol car generate.

My advice to gardeners is to start small and simple. Gradually increase the scale and variety of what you grow as you gain confidence. Sprouting seeds takes little time and just a windowsill. With containers, you can grow food on a balcony. Plant a fruit tree. At ten years old, my Tahitian lime (*Citrus* × *latifolia*) occupied the space of a king-size bed and provided enough fruits for marmalade to pay my mortgage for six weeks.

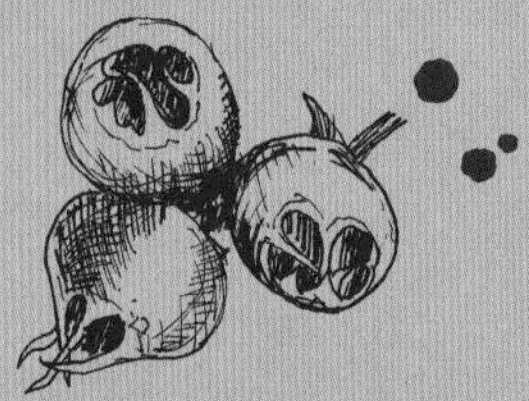

11
HARVESTING THE REWARDS

Harvesting and preserving are acts of offering. Whether it's a jar of syrup, a bowl of tomatoes or a string of garlic, it's one of the simplest and most powerful ways we can say, 'I thought of you.'

THE WISDOM OF NONNA CARMELA

When people ask me why I'm so passionate about harvesting and preserving, I often find myself thinking back to my early twenties when I was living in Reservoir, Melbourne, with my Italian boyfriend. Not far from us lived my boyfriend's grandparents. We'd often visit, and without fail I would ask Nonna Carmela what she had growing in her garden. She'd always wave her hand and say, 'Ah, nothing, nothing in the garden.' But I'd persist, asking if I could just have a look. And I'd wander outside, knowing full well that her 'nothing' would be a treasure trove.

Nonna Carmela always pretended that she had no secrets in the kitchen, but when you'd ask her for a recipe, she'd brush it off with the same answer every time. 'Twelve eggs,' she'd say in a Sicilian accent, whether you were asking about pasta or focaccia or pastasciutta. It was her way of keeping it close and also maybe her way of saying, 'You just need to watch.'

So I watched. She showed me how to prepare pickled eggplant: slicing it just so, layering it with vinegar and oil, pressing it down firmly. I saw how the seasons turned in her garden and noticed how much it meant to her when I brought over something I'd grown. 'Did you buy this at the supermarket?' she'd ask, narrowing her eyes. When I told her I grew it, she'd call out to whoever was there: 'Look at this! She grew this! Natasha, you should be a farmer!' And maybe that was the first time I saw clearly how gardening could be an act of pride and love.

WHAT HARVESTING MEANS IN MY PRACTICE

Harvest, for me, is not the finale; it's a conversation between garden, kitchen and community. I grow for our table, for the neighbours' tables and for the jars on the shelf that hold memories of summer past when the days are short and harvests are harder to find in the garden. I grow with preserving outcomes in mind, planting varieties that bottle, dry or ferment beautifully. I harvest with presence: a slow walk at first light or in that soft hour before dark, basket on arm, mind softened.

I've learned to pick by feel and by sound: the snap of a bean, the bloom on a plum, the gentle give of a tomato that's ready to be picked now, not tomorrow. I try to harvest little and often, do a quick back-door stocktake: what we eat fresh, what goes into jars, what gets shared. This is how I avoid overwhelm and waste. It's also how I stay in relationship with the garden rather than just extracting from it.

I'm unapologetic about 'imperfect' produce. Small garlic? I ferment the cloves in their skins rather than fuss with peeling. A run of cool days that stalls ripening? I lean into green-tomato chutney instead of waiting for red. Way too many herbs at once? I dry them for winter teas or crumble them into salts.

'I lean into green-tomato chutney instead of waiting for red. Way too many herbs at once? I dry them for winter teas or crumble them into salts.'

Dehydrating has become a true love: thin orange slices laid on trays, gradually turning translucent and flame-bright; apple rings for lunchboxes; sometimes it's tomato skins left over from passata making, dried and blitzed into a ruby dust for the pantry.

And because I want drinks that carry the season, I make apple-cider-vinegar shrubs (syrups) to hold the flavour, most often rhubarb (because that's what I have in the garden in abundance) with orange zest and ginger. They're fast, forgiving and endlessly useful. I serve them with mineral water and a sprig of lemon verbena, or fold a splash into the dressing when a salad needs a little lift. This is the thread that runs through my practice: grow it, notice it, translate it, share it. Here's how to build ritual into the year:

— **Keep harvest pathways clear and short:** My most-picked beds sit closest to the kitchen door; the preserving bench is just inside, with knives, weights, clean jars, labels and a laundry basket for surplus produce.

— **Use small, stackable containers:** Have crates for fruits; shallow trays for herbs; lidded tubs for brining and salting. Make it light and portable, and you will reach for it.

— **Set 'windows' rather than dates:** I block out loose preserving windows on the family calendar – flowers from European elder (*Sambucus nigra*) in early summer; stone fruits in mid-to-late summer; tomatoes (*Solanum lycopersicum*) in late summer; quinces (*Cydonia oblonga*) in autumn; citrus and dehydrating through winter; berries whenever the birds allow – and respond to what the weather brings.

— **Build weekly check-ins:** A ten-minute harvest stocktake at the back door will tell you what must be used, what can be bottled, and what should be gifted.

— **Dry the light, bottle the heavy, freeze the fragile:** Herbs and citrus slices dehydrate; tomatoes and stone fruits preserve well; peas and berries freeze beautifully on trays before bagging.

— **Make drinks part of the preserving plan:** Keep a running list of shrub (syrup) ideas tied to produce gluts (for example, rhubarb + orange zest + ginger; strawberry + basil; blackberry + bay leaves). Mix the syrups with mineral water or swirl into yoghurt, cakes and puddings.

— **Design for generosity:** Keep a crate, brown paper bags and string by the door. When abundance arrives, it's easy to make up a bundle and drop it to a neighbour.

Ferments and preserves on the kitchen bench. They are a practical way to turn gluts, seconds and excess into something that keeps, stretching what the garden offers well beyond the day it was picked.

Why it matters

I come back to Nonna Carmela's hand in the air as she says 'nothing in the garden' and the unassuming abundance that was there when you bothered to look. Harvesting, preserving and sharing are how I stay tethered to that way of being: grounded, practical, generous. They're how I stitch memory into daily life so my children know where flavour comes from, and that 'enough' grows when we share what we have.

When seasons surprise us with too much rain or not enough sun, these practices turn setbacks into something prized. They turn what could be a disappointment into chutney, a small harvest into a gathered table. Most of all, they keep me attentive: to timing, to place, to people. The jars on the shelf are not trophies. They're letters to our future selves that say, 'We paid attention.'

Makes 1 kg (2 lb 4 oz)

Nonna Carmela's pickled eggplant (melanzane sott'olio)

- 6 medium eggplants (aubergines), about 1.8 kg (4 lb) total
- 4–6 garlic cloves
- 1 small bunch fresh mint
- 3 tablespoons coarse salt
- 4 cups (1 litre) water
- 8 cups (2 litres) white vinegar
- 1 tablespoon whole black peppercorns
- 2 tablespoons salted capers
- 600 ml (21 fl oz) extra-virgin olive oil

I learned this method with my sleeves rolled up at Nonna Carmela's sink, and I still hear her 'twelve eggs' whenever I reach for the vinegar (see page 297). It's a pressed pickle that's salty, tangy and deeply Sicilian. For Australians used to cooked eggplant, this will feel surprising, which is exactly the point. For this recipe, you will need a few sterilised glass jars that can hold 1–2 cups (250–500 millilitres) each.

Slice the eggplants lengthways into slices 1 centimetre (1/2 inch) thick. Slice the garlic cloves, finely shred the fresh mint leaves, and rinse the capers.

In a colander, layer the eggplant slices, sprinkling salt on each layer. Place a weight on top. Leave overnight (about twelve hours) to draw out excess liquid.

The next morning, squeeze the eggplant slices to remove any remaining liquid. Place the water and white vinegar in a saucepan, and bring to a boil. Drop the squeezed eggplant slices into the boiling mixture to blanch. When the mixture returns to a boil, remove from the heat.

Strain the eggplant slices in a clean colander. Wrap the slices in a clean tea towel, layer by layer, and press to draw out more liquid. Leave wrapped until all the liquid has been extracted (overnight is best).

When the eggplant is cold and fairly dry, layer it in the glass jars with garlic slices, shredded mint, whole black peppercorns and capers. Press down firmly on each layer. Cover completely with olive oil, ensuring that no air pockets remain, and place the lid on tightly. Store the sealed jars in the fridge.

Let the flavours infuse for at least three days before eating. The pickled eggplant is best after a week. Always ensure that the pickled eggplant remains fully submerged in oil, and use it within one month. To make the most of your pickled eggplant, eat it:

—on crusty bread with a drizzle of oil from the jar
—as part of an antipasto plate with olives, salami and cheese
—paired with pecorino or mozzarella
—as a side to grilled meats such as pork or lamb
—in a panino with fresh tomato, basil and prosciutto
—chopped and tossed through hot pasta with its oil and parsley
—mixed into a warm bean salad.

Sterilising bottles and jars

Many of the recipes in this chapter call for sterilised bottles or jars. First wash the bottles or jars and their lids in hot soapy water, or run them through the dishwasher. Rinse them well, then place them, lying on their sides, in a low oven (100 degrees Celsius; 200 degrees Fahrenheit) for about 15 minutes or until completely dry.

200

CHERIE HAUSLER

Edible abundance and the generous table

On a wind-polished hill in the Barossa, Cherie Hausler cooks like a gardener and gardens like a cook. She lets the season lead, makes beauty useful and turns sun-warm tomatoes into meals that feel like home.

Cherie lives where food and place braid together. After chapters in Sydney, London and Bangkok (co-owning the acclaimed Eat Me restaurant with her brother), she came home to South Australia and a weathered 150-year-old rectory farmhouse on Koonunga Hill. There, with her husband Damien, she's been restoring both the house and the grounds in the slow, salvage-first way that matches her ethos: use what's at hand, honour what already exists, cook what the garden gives. The result is not just a kitchen garden, it's a lived system: glasshouse tomatoes and orchard fruits, ferments on the bench, teas and steeped tonics from the land outside her door.

She works across different spheres – from her cookbook *A Plant-Based Farmhouse* and her podcast *All The Things* to in-person workshops and an SBS TV series – yet the thread is constant: essential, plant-based, seasonal, generous nourishment. In the Barossa's Mediterranean light, Cherie and Damien have learned to make micro-climates using straw bales and a greenhouse, and to ride the edges of abundance and lean years with preserves, breads and transformative staples. She talks about seasons as if they're life chapters: spring as a soft opening, summer as the grand parade, autumn as the reckoning, winter as the time for teas and repair. And she cooks accordingly.

Cherie anchors the edible abundance theme well with her glasshouse tomato sourdough panzanella recipe (which appears in her book, *A Plant-Based Farmhouse*, and has been reproduced on page 304). It's a salad that makes a virtue of day-old bread and celebrates tomatoes the way her family always has. The headnote is a portrait of inheritance: a father who refused to compromise on flavour, siblings growing tomatoes in improbable places, and the satisfaction of handing over a paper bag full of warm fruits to keep a cycle alive. It's food as memory, and memory as method, which is precisely the spirit of this chapter.

I've been lucky enough to enjoy the fruits of Cherie's labour, and the way a meal prepared by her can transform into a generous table, and rich and warm conversation.

These are the key takeaways from our conversation:

- If the desire is there, then growing can start anywhere and with almost nothing: balconies, rooftops, car parks.
- Seasonal living requires constant adaptation; working with nature's flux builds resilience rather than control.
- Food is a personal relationship formed by experience; noticing that relationship (without judgement) lets you choose what you want it to become.
- Mindfulness with regard to the everyday 'miracles' of natural systems keeps Cherie's practice grounded and generous.
- Plant-based, nutrient-dense, waste-aware lived ethics flow into practical kitchen moves: ferments, vinegars, breads and recipes led by the harvest.

Tiny-space growing ideas

Choose one edible that you love and one small container, and grow the plant on a sunny ledge. Scavenge polystyrene boxes, and punch drainage holes in them before turning them into mini garden beds; use community compost where possible. Share or borrow growing space: back lanes, car parks, rooftops or a neighbour's nature strip.

Scan to watch my full conversation with Cherie, where we talk about letting the season lead, making beauty useful, and turning home-grown produce into meals that feel like home.

Serves 2–4

Cherie's glasshouse tomato sourdough panzanella

- 300 g ($10^1/_2$ oz) day-old sourdough
- 350 g (12 oz) mixed tomatoes (for example, Roma, Cherry, Oxheart, Mortgage Lifter)
- 50 g ($1^3/_4$ oz) Kalamata olives
- 20 g ($^3/_4$ oz) fresh basil
- 5 g ($^1/_8$ oz) fresh marjoram
- 30 g (1 oz) capers
- 60 ml (2 fl oz) balsamic vinegar
- 50 ml ($1^3/_4$ fl oz) extra-virgin olive oil
- pinch of freshly ground black pepper
- salt, to taste

Cherie says: My dad was a master tomato grower when we were kids; he took tomato growing very seriously, mostly because he is one of the fussiest people I know when it comes to tomatoes and refused to eat anything that wasn't up to his standard. He'd rather go without than compromise on flavour. My brother inherited the same tomato fixation; when we lived together as adults in North Melbourne many years later, we dedicated the only space in the tiny yard of our rented terrace house to tomato growing. It's almost impossible to replicate that sun-drenched, dry heat that gives so much flavour to South Australian tomatoes, but he never gave up. He even grew tomatoes on his apartment balcony in Bangkok, and we made a vegie garden in the parking lot at Eat Me, trying in vain to bring the Mediterranean flavour of our childhood to the tropical climate of Thailand. Tomatoes hold a disproportionately important place in our family is what I'm getting at, so when we finally built the glasshouse on our hill in the Barossa, the first thing that went in were tomatoes.

We planted as many different kinds of tomatoes as we could in that debut season so we could see what would work best. Turns out they all liked it here and so each year we now end up with an array of tomatoes in different colours and sizes, all with that unmistakable fragrance that envelops you when you brush past their leaves hunting for ripe fruits. I love sharing them with my mum and dad, especially now they no longer have a vegie garden. My dad doesn't say much when I hand over a paper bag of still-warm fruits, he just brings a tomato to his nose and gives a bit of a nod, but I know the master's cycle has been successfully completed!

Panzanella is one of the best ways I know to really let good tomatoes shine, and it's also one of my favourite uses for sourdough that has just gone past the point of sandwiches and into toast territory.

Tear the sourdough into 2–3-centimetre ($^3/_4$–$1^1/_4$-inch) pieces. Slice the tomatoes into quarters. Remove the pips from the Kalamata olives.

Combine the torn pieces of bread and the sliced tomatoes in a large bowl. Stir to release some of the juices of the tomatoes for the bread to soak up.

Add all of the remaining ingredients, and stir again to ensure that the balsamic vinegar and extra-virgin olive oil have been taken up by the bread. I usually let this sit for a couple of minutes before serving so the flavours can meld.

The smell of the ripe tomatoes with the fragrance of the herbs is the signature scent of summer for me.

Natasha's spiced green-tomato chutney

Makes about 1 kg (2 lb 4 oz)

- 3–4 cm ($1\frac{1}{4}$–$1\frac{1}{2}$ in) piece of fresh ginger
- 15 garlic cloves
- 1 kg (2 lb 4 oz) green tomatoes
- ½ teaspoon chilli powder, or to taste
- 500 g (1 lb 2 oz) light brown sugar or coconut sugar
- 350 ml (12 fl oz) malt vinegar or apple cider vinegar

I respond to a glut or seasonal oddity with curiosity: do I trade it, brine it, blitz it or gift it? Imperfect fruits can be turned into jam, syrup or shrub. Tiny garlic is perfect for fermenting in its skin (see page 326). I grow green tomatoes on purpose now for chutney. This recipe found me at Oak & Monkey Puzzle during a run of short seasons. In Spargo Creek, we'd hold off planting tomatoes until the second week of November (Melbourne Cup Day was our frost-safe marker), and cool temperatures often meant that many fruits stayed stubbornly green. When this chutney joined my repertoire, it was a spoon-worthy revelation!

I often make triple-quantity batches. If you do the same, then allow extra time, and use a broad, shallow pan or jam pan to speed up the reduction. Any green tomato works. I've used every type I can get my hands on , but the less juicy or pulpy varieties will reduce faster. For this recipe, you will need about four sterilised glass jars that can hold 1 cup (250 millilitres) each.

Grate the fresh ginger. Finely chop or mince the garlic cloves. Dice the tomatoes.

Place all of the ingredients into a wide, heavy pan. Stir over medium heat until the sugar has dissolved, then bring to a steady boil over high heat.

Lower to a lively simmer over medium heat. Cook, stirring often and scraping the base, until the mixture is thick and glossy. (You want the chutney to part like a 'jam trail' when you drag a spoon through the pan.) For a single batch, this will take 45–60 minutes; if the tomatoes are very juicy, then it will take longer.

Taste, and adjust the heat with extra chilli powder if desired. (You could also add a little cumin or smoked paprika if you like those flavours.)

Ladle the chutney into hot sterilised jars, and seal while the chutney is still hot. Unopened jars have kept for years in my cool, dark pantry; once opened, store the chutney in the fridge and use it within about three months. To use the tomato chutney, you can:

- eat it by the spoonful
- pop it onto really good pork sausages
- serve it alongside curry
- plop it on a ploughman's board
- spoon it alongside sharp cheddar and oatcakes
- swirl it through yoghurt for a quick grill sauce
- use it to glaze halloumi in the last two minutes of frying
- fold a spoonful into lentils or beans to wake them up
- spread it under cheese in toasted sandwiches.

Elderberry safety and botany

Cook elderberries thoroughly; raw berries, leaves, stems and unripe fruits all contain cyanogenic glycosides, which can release cyanide in the body and cause nausea, vomiting, diarrhoea or worse. Cooking makes elderberries safe to eat. Always remove stems when stripping fruits. The berries follow the flowers; if you pick the blossoms, then you'll have fewer berries later when they're meant to form from the pollinated flowers in summer.

Opposite page_Oak & Monkey Puzzle and its surrounds, 2016. Photographs by Meg Travis. Four snapshots from our season of foraging country lanes, gathering hawthorn, and turning what we found into syrups and preserves, with Meg's self-portrait holding the story of that time.

Scan to watch my full conversation with Meg Travis, where we talk about life before, during and after Oak & Monkey Puzzle.

MEG TRAVIS

Syrups as seasonal anchors

I met Meg in the season of hedgerows shimmering with shiny black and deep purple berries, days spent down lanes, hands stained maroon for weeks, evenings turning what we gathered into syrups and preserves. We set up camp at the Oak & Monkey Puzzle kitchen bench with a stack of old recipe books, an apothecary's collection of spices, and a great deal of experimentation and patience. I'd never made elderberry syrup before, but for Meg it was deeply ingrained in her English way of life. Together we thought we would put our own twist on it with a heady spiced version that filled the kitchen with aroma for days.

Elderberries can either dominate or disappear, depending on what you pair them with. Meg's instinct was to let the berry sit centrestage and edit anything that tried to upstage it, while also tuning the muskiness for which the berry is known, and adding cinnamon as a background note, clove for a little lift, and cardamom for brightness, with restraint. We tasted from small spoons, then in hot water, then with a splash of mineral water, maybe even a dash of whisky, because I believe a syrup needs to perform across contexts if it's to earn pantry space.

What I loved about our syrup-making collaborations was the process and restraint. We chased purity and balance until the result felt inevitable, as if the garden wrote the recipe first. That is what our spiced elderberry syrup (see page 312) is: a friendly, repeatable anchor for a year of drinks and desserts, tuned so the berry stays true without tipping into anything muddy or medicinal. It's a treat when winter asks for warming spice and when summer asks for fizz.

I'm always careful with process. I sterilise bottles, gently filter the fruit-laden liquid for clarity, and date every bottle because in winter that date on the label is a small pleasure in itself, a reminder of the day we bottled the syrup. Every time I pull a bottle of this syrup from the shelf, I remember those late nights, a quiet house of sleeping children, two women in a kitchen filled with giggles and a simple aim: to hold a season in a bottle without losing its light, but make it something that's utterly extraordinary, one small purposeful ingredient at a time.

Notes from our kitchen collaboration

Keep these things in mind when making syrups:

— Start with the aroma, then balance the supporting flavours so the fruit remains the lead voice.
— Build structure with a bright acid finish that keeps the fruit notes clean, not cloying.
— Keep it versatile, and aim for a syrup that can be enjoyed hot, cold and in baking.
— Taste in hot, cold and bubbly drinks before you lock in a batch.
— Keep ratios stable, and change only one variable per trial.
— Make a small test batch, then scale up the amount.
— Hygiene matters! Fill the sterilised bottles with hot syrup, cool them quickly, then store them in a cool, dark place until opened.
— Label and date every bottle, so you can track what you loved and repeat it.

10
RHUBARB
FIZZ

Makes about 8 cups (2 litres)

Oak & Monkey Puzzle spiced elderberry syrup

- 500 g (1 lb 2 oz) fresh elderberries, or 120 g ($4^1/_4$ oz) dried elderberries
- 6 cups (1.5 litres) water
- 75 g ($2^3/_4$ oz) citric acid
- 2.5 kg (5 lb 8 oz) white (granulated) sugar
- 3 teaspoons mixed spices of your choice (for example, cloves, cinnamon, ginger, allspice, cardamom, nutmeg)

Meg and I tuned this syrup at the old Oak & Monkey Puzzle kitchen bench, tasting and retasting until the spice felt right. The kitchen became our anchor during those months together, the place we eagerly returned to after many afternoons spent foraging. For this recipe, you will need a fine-mesh strainer or muslin (cheesecloth) and three or four sterilised glass bottles that can hold 2–3 cups (500–750 millilitres) each.

If you're using fresh elderberries, then remove any stems and rinse the berries well. However, if you're using dried elderberries, then skip this step.

Combine the elderberries and water in a large saucepan. Bring to a boil over medium–high heat. Once boiling, reduce the heat to low and let the mixture simmer uncovered for 45–60 minutes, or until the berries have burst and the liquid has reduced slightly and is darkly coloured. Stir occasionally.

Remove the saucepan from the heat, and let the mixture cool. Using a fine-mesh strainer or muslin (cheesecloth), strain the syrup into a clean large saucepan. Press down on the berries to extract all the liquid.

Bring the strained liquid to a boil over medium–high heat. Once boiling, reduce the heat to low and add the citric acid, sugar and your chosen spices. Stir until the citric acid and sugar have fully dissolved and the spices have been distributed through the liquid.

While the liquid is hot, use a funnel and a ladle to pour it into the sterilised glass bottles, and secure the lids. Let the bottles cool, then store them in a cool, dark place. Allow the syrup to mature for at least three days before drinking; the flavours will meld and deepen. Once opened, the syrup will keep in the fridge for up to six weeks.

Enjoy your homemade spiced elderberry syrup by adding it to cocktails or hot toddies. You can also:

- drizzle it over pancakes or your favourite sweet treat
- pour it warm over semolina cake or butter cake
- stir it into hot water with lemon during winter (a splash of whisky wouldn't go astray)
- mix it with sparkling water, gin and a squeeze of lemon in summer
- drizzle it over grilled stone fruits or poached pears
- shake it into an elderberry and ginger mocktail (syrup, ginger beer, lime).

Tips: Adjust the amount of sugar and the spice level according to your preferences. Try using other berries in this recipe, and experiment with different spices.

cultivate · forage · preserve
NATASHA MORGAN
RHUBARB
VANILLA SYRUP

Natasha's rhubarb, orange zest and ginger shrub

- 2 parts fresh rhubarb (or replace it with unblemished fruits, such as strawberries, raspberries or destoned and chopped plums)
- a few strips of orange zest for every 500 g (1 lb 2 oz) of rhubarb (avoid the bitter white pith)
- a few thin slices of fresh ginger for every 500 g (1 lb 2 oz) of rhubarb (more if you want a punchy warmth)
- 1 part white (granulated) sugar (white sugar provides a clean flavour; raw sugar adds depth)
- 1 part apple cider vinegar

In drinks, a shrub is a sweet-tart syrup made by combining fruits (or herbs), sugar and vinegar (traditionally apple cider vinegar). The vinegar draws out the flavour of the fruits and gives the syrup a bright and tangy note, while the sweetness of the sugar balances that acidity. Shrubs have their roots in seventeenth- and eighteenth-century preservation, when vinegar was used to keep fruits fresh long after harvest. Today, they're valued for their complexity and refreshing bite. They can be mixed with still or sparkling water for a non-alcoholic drink, or shaken into cocktails for depth and lift.

This shrub recipe is my last-minute salvation for fruits picked right on the edge of their peak; it's bright, bracing and endlessly versatile. I haven't given fixed ingredient amounts here, just a ratio of tartness, sweetness and bright spice that you can adjust to your taste. For this recipe, you will need a few sterilised glass bottles.

Cut the rhubarb into small pieces so it releases flavour easily.

Combine the rhubarb pieces, orange zest strips, ginger slices and sugar in a bowl. Toss well, cover, and leave covered for 24–48 hours or until the sugar has drawn out the juices into a vivid syrup. (If the weather is hot, then place the bowl in the fridge to prevent the mix from fermenting.)

Strain the syrup, pressing gently to capture all the liquid, and discard (or compost) the solids or use them in baking.

Stir in 1 part apple cider vinegar to 1 part syrup, adjusting to taste.

Pour the shrub into the bottles, and store it in the fridge. It will keep for a few weeks, and the flavour will mellow over time. (If the syrup starts to smell bad, then no longer use it.)

To serve, mix a splash of shrub with sparkling water for a bright and tangy refresher, or use it in cocktails for complexity; add a sprig of rosemary or lemon verbena for an extra flourish. You can also:

- splash it into vinaigrettes for bitter leaves
- add a dash to a pan sauce for pork (or roasted carrots, if you're cooking plant-based dishes)
- stir it into tonic water with a thumb of fresh ginger
- fold a spoonful through whipped yoghurt to serve over poached fruits.

A note on vinegar choice

I like to use raw apple cider vinegar that still contains the mother. This means it's a live culture, and over time it can continue to ferment, which may make your shrub taste more vinegary as the natural bacteria consume any remaining sugars. If you prefer the flavour to stay stable, then you can either use pasteurised apple cider vinegar, or briefly heat your raw vinegar to above 70 degrees Celsius (160 degrees Fahrenheit) to pasteurise it. Heating will stop the live culture from continuing to ferment.

'[*Fermentation is*] *the magic on the bench.*'

SHARON FLYNN

Aliveness as a preserving method

When seasons lurch – too wet, too sudden, too much – fermentation gives us back control without fighting nature. It meets the harvest where it is, then gently carries it forwards. The founder of The Fermentary, Sharon Flynn, invites us to preserve with trust: to let the garden keep changing, softly, on the bench.

I've known Sharon for many years. She hosted fermenting workshops at Oak & Monkey Puzzle, we've revelled in the magic that's made when my spiced elderberry syrup meets her milk kefir, and she even photographed her book *Ferment for Good* at Oak & Monkey Puzzle. Our collaborations and conversations continue to this day.

Sharon has helped thousands of home cooks turn excess into something alive, bubbling, bright and deeply nourishing. Her practice is wild fermentation: small-batch, sensory, and grounded in tradition rather than trend. The why behind it is personal. Years of living and learning abroad collided with a family health crisis at home, and fermentation moved from useful to vital. It was a way to care for bodies and to steady a household rhythm. Today, Sharon's work is internationally recognised, but it stays local in feeling: fermentation crocks on the bench, bottles in a crate, eyes reading bubbles rather than timers.

Sharon's voice lands perfectly in this chapter because she reframes 'saving' food as transformation: surplus becoming flavour, fizz and future memory. She also hands readers a sturdy kind of confidence, plus permission to begin without knowing everything, to taste as you go, and to lean on the garden's microbes in the same way that you lean on good soil.

What I love most is how Sharon folds care into method. She asks us to pack jars with intention: to imagine the table months from now, the people to whom we'll hand a bottle, the moment we'll open a crock that 'sings back'. It's practical magic: brine, salt, fruit, time, plus a little faith. In a year that rarely runs in a straight line, this is a preserving practice that meets real life: forgiving of gluts, friendly to imperfect produce, and generous in return.

These are the key takeaways from our conversation:

- Preserving abundance saves nutrition, adds flavour and stores a season without electricity.
- Start with fresh, not mushy produce; adding salt plus excluding oxygen steers the microbes you want; trim small surface mould, but discard hairy/foul ferments.
- To 'read' a ferment, look for bubbles, colour shifts and a 'fizz' on the tongue; open and taste often with clean hands.
- The fermentation process works better in cold climates; if you live in a hot climate, you may need to use a cooler/esky or even bury the crock.
- If you have a glut of fruits, then freeze whole pieces or blend (with skins on) into a paste and create portions for later sodas.
- Fermentation teaches trust and patience; pack jars with intention for the future table.

Scan to watch my full conversation with Sharon Flynn, where we talk about fermentation and the story behind her passion.

KILNER

ging.
mum

Sharon's ginger bug

Makes 2 cups (500 ml)

Also known as a ginger beer mother, a ginger bug is a living starter made purely with ginger, sugar, water and time. You feed this every day until it starts to bubble and come alive, the same way you start a sourdough mother. This excellent and reliable starter can be used to boost drinks such as kvass or wild soda (a naturally fermented soft drink made using wild, airborne yeasts and bacteria rather than added commercial yeast cultures or carbonation). For this recipe, you will need a 2-cup (500-millilitre) jar, a piece of muslin (cheesecloth) and a rubber band.

- 2.5 cm (1 in) piece of fresh ginger, plus 5 pieces extra for feeding
- 2 teaspoons raw sugar, plus 10 teaspoons extra for feeding
- 1 cup (250 ml) unchlorinated water, plus 10 tablespoons extra for feeding

Rinse the ginger well under running water to remove any dirt; do not peel it.

Grate or finely chop the first piece of ginger into the jar, and add the sugar and water. Stir well. Cover with the piece of muslin (cheesecloth), secure with the rubber band, and place the jar in a warm spot in your kitchen.

On days two to six, feed it the same amount of ginger and sugar, plus 2 tablespoons of water. Stir well each time, and cover with the muslin (cheesecloth) between feedings. The mix will start to bubble. By the seventh day, your culture should be smelling yeasty and fresh. If so, then it's ready to use as a starter culture; if it has developed a foul, musty or rotten odour, then discard it and begin a new batch.

Like a sourdough mother, a ginger bug can be kept in the fridge. Make sure to feed it the same menu once a week, leaving it out each time to warm up enough to start eating. A couple of hours is good, then put it back into the fridge.

Whenever you use any of the ginger bug, remember to replace it with the same quantity of fresh ingredients. To use the ginger bug, you can:

- splash it into any seasonal soda (rhubarb, quince, plum, elderflower, feijoa)
- add a spoonful of it to fruit soda for a faster, finer fizz
- fold it into pancake batter for a lift
- swirl it through dressings for mild heat and complexity.

Other sodas from a ginger beer mother

Once your ginger bug is well established, strain off ¼ cup (60 millilitres) of the liquid and mix it into 4 cups (1 litre) of flavoured or infused water. You'll also need some form of sugar in there to feed the yeasts and get some happy fizz. So add either 1–3 tablespoons of your favourite syrup, or 1 cup of chopped fruits and herbs. Combine well, place the mixture in a plastic bottle with the lid on, and let sit for two to five days. Ginger bug yeasts are very active, and these drinks are notorious exploders, so plastic bottles and prompt refrigeration are both recommended.

Sharon's wild ginger beer

Makes about 8 cups (2 litres)

- 400 g (14 oz) unpeeled fresh ginger
- 8 cups (2 litres) water
- juice of 4 lemons
- 100–150 g ($3^1/_2$–$5^1/_2$ oz) honey, to taste
- $^1/_2$ cup (125 ml) strained ginger bug liquid

This naturally fermented ginger beer uses a ginger bug starter to produce a lively, tangy and refreshing drink, perfect for hot days or for sharing with friends and family. For this recipe, you will need an 8-cup (2-litre) jar, muslin (cheesecloth) and sterilised glass bottles.

Thinly slice the ginger, and place it into a saucepan with the water and lemon juice. Bring to a simmer over medium heat, allowing the flavours to infuse for 20 minutes. Remove from the heat, stir in the honey, and allow the mixture to cool.

Strain the mixture through the muslin (cheesecloth) and into a jug. Add the strained liquid from the ginger bug, and mix in well. Pour the mixture into the bottles, place the lids on, and store them on a kitchen bench out of direct sunlight, or in a pantry or cupboard. This is a very fizzy brew, so make sure to store it carefully. Perhaps attach a balloon to the top of one bottle to keep an eye on the carbonation level.

Depending on the room temperature, the fermentation will take anywhere from four to ten days. Once the ginger beer is fizzy, place the bottles into the fridge to slow down the ferment. It's important that you don't just leave the bottles out, otherwise the pressure inside will continue to build and the ginger beer may either gush out uncontrollably or lose its pleasant flavour. Refrigerate for a couple of days, and then enjoy it. But always open the bottles with care.

Choosing a cloth for fermentation

Muslin (cheesecloth) is often recommended to cover fermenting jars, but you can actually use any clean, breathable cloth made of natural fibres. Linen, cotton, an old tea towel, a cut-up sheet or even a Chux cloth all work well. The goal is to let air circulate while keeping out dust and insects. Sharon Flynn of The Fermentary recommends practicality; there's no need for specialty cheesecloth unless you have it on hand. Just choose something clean and easy to secure with a rubber band or string.

22/10
ging
beer
ging
mum

Sharon's rhubarb fizz

Makes 4 cups (1 litre)

- 1 bunch rhubarb
- 250 g (9 oz) caster (superfine) sugar
- splash of vinegar (white wine, apple cider or kombucha vinegar)
- juice of 1/2 lemon
- 8 cups (2 litres) water

This jewel-pink tonic has a sweet-tart fizz that can get slightly boozy. Rhubarb is great for your gut and has been used medicinally for thousands of years. I craved it in all its forms throughout my pregnancies and beyond. For this recipe, you will need a 12-cup (3-litre) jar, a piece of muslin (cheesecloth) and sterilised glass bottles.

Freeze the rhubarb if you have time because it will bring out the flavour a little more. When you're ready to make the fizz, thaw the rhubarb, cut off the ends, and chop up the rest so you end up with about 300 g (10½ oz) of rhubarb.

Place the chopped rhubarb into the jar, add the sugar, vinegar and lemon juice, and leave to macerate for an hour.

Pour in the water, stir well, and cover with the muslin (cheesecloth). Leave it on the kitchen bench (out of direct sunlight) for three to five days, making sure to stir it occasionally and check on the flavour. It's ready when it's no longer too sweet (but not too sour) and is slightly effervescent.

Strain the mixture through the muslin (cheesecloth) over a sieve, gathering the rhubarb and squeezing it to get as much liquid out as possible. (Keep this rhubarb and store in a 2 per cent brine to eat like a pickle, or cook it up with some sugar and apples until soft to enjoy with yoghurt or in a pie.)

Pour the liquid into the glass bottles and place the lids on properly. Sit the bottles out of the fridge for a day, and then check for fizziness. Depending on your brew, it might take a week to get really fizzy. If keeping an eye on the bottles is inconvenient, then let the brew age in the fridge. You can add another taste layer to this drink by throwing in a handful of rose petals. To use the rhubarb fizz, you can:

- pour it into a tall glass over ice with a sprig of lemon verbena
- serve it half-and-half with mineral water as a garden soda
- use it to deglaze roasted rhubarb or strawberries.

A citrus note for your rhubarb fizz

If you'd like to add another layer of flavour, then slip some dehydrated orange slices (see page 330) into the jar with the rhubarb. They bring a soft citrus bitterness, a gentle perfume and a beautiful visual note without overwhelming the rhubarb. Only add a few orange slices, though, so the delightful, sherbet-like flavour of the rhubarb fizz still shines.

22/10
JERUSALEM ARTICHOKES

Sharon's simple brined vegetables

Makes 1 kg (2 lb 4 oz)

Wild brine ferments are the real deal (or 'dill', as we like to say). The sour comes from lactic acid (not vinegar), and the vegetables stay raw but are transformed by fermentation, making the flavours complex and earthy. They feel amazing as they hit your belly and feed your gut with good living bacteria, so it's particularly satisfying to see a whole jar of carrots or beans eaten in one sitting. Also, you can drink the brine as it is or in a cocktail, or use it in salad dressings or as the vinegar in mustard. The brine is as wonderful as the actual vegetables you're fermenting.

In this case we're fermenting cherry tomatoes, which will fizz as you bite them open, but you can also use this recipe for Jerusalem artichokes (see the photos on the opposite page), beans, carrots, onions, celery, cauliflower and more. Just avoid anything with too much chlorophyll, such as kale. Zucchini doesn't do well in this recipe, nor do broccoli florets, but the stems do.

Regardless of the vegetable you choose, it will take on the flavour of whatever you add to the brine. I like a bit of garlic; black pepper and mustard seeds are also great. Fresh basil or oregano are amazing with tomatoes.

After the initial fermentation time, place the brined vegetables into the fridge for another week or two to get even more flavour into them. For this recipe, you will need a 4-cup (1-litre) jar.

- About 500 g (1 lb 2 oz) cherry tomatoes (enough to pack the jar tightly)
- a few sprigs of oregano
- handful of basil leaves
- 1/2 teaspoon peppercorns
- 1–2 garlic cloves
- 30 g (1 oz) fine salt
- 4 cups (1 litre) water

Cut the tops off the cherry tomatoes, and pack them tightly into the jar. Add the oregano, basil leaves, peppercorns and garlic cloves.

Dissolve the fine salt in the water to make a 3 per cent brine, and pour it into the jar, leaving a little headroom. Seal the jar. If you're making cucumber pickles, then use the knobbly style and increase the brine ratio to 5 per cent (50 grams or 1 3/4 ounces of salt per 4 cups of water). The key to crunchy cucumber pickles is adding a tannin (such as a vine leaf or a bit of black tea).

This is a fast ferment. It will only take about five days at room temperature. It can go longer, but check first by taking out one cherry tomato to taste and to make sure that it hasn't become mushy. Put your jar on a plate to protect your bench from any bubbling brine that may overflow. If you're using a normal jar with a lid, then make sure to 'burp' the gas from the jar every couple of days; a specialist fermentation jar with an airlock won't need to be 'burped'.

Refrigerate when the cherry tomatoes are lively, flavourful and fizzy when you bite into them. They can be kept in the fridge for eight weeks or more (sometimes even years, if no mould grows), but you'll most likely eat them before then! To use the brined vegetables, you can:

- keep them as everyday pickles for the fridge
- chop them and add them to grain bowls
- fold them into an egg salad for tang
- dice them finely and sprinkle them into winter soups.

Brining Jerusalem artichokes

Jerusalem artichokes are an excellent source of prebiotic fibre. When they're in season, there are usually a lot of them, so this recipe is a fabulous way to preserve the glut. Add a few bay leaves, some lemon rind and a sprig of thyme to the jar. The fermentation process breaks down the inulin in Jerusalem artichokes, making them more digestible. You'll be less prone to bloating and gas after eating them. (They don't call them farty-chokes for nothing!)

Natasha's fermented garlic in its skins

- fresh, unpeeled garlic heads or loose cloves
- non-iodised sea or rock salt
- cool, dechlorinated water

Sharon Flynn has long shaped how I think about the plants I grow and the harvests I glean from them. Her ferments don't just stretch a season – days into weeks, weeks into months – they also offer gut-healing, body-nourishing transformations.

Years ago, a friend at her wits' end with a disappointing garlic crop gifted me a box of tiny leftover bulbs. I racked my brain for a way to use them that didn't involve peeling hundreds of fiddly cloves; the skins glue themselves to your fingers, you end up smelling like a lamb roast, and you look tarred and feathered for your trouble. That's when I turned to Sharon's simple brine and thought: why not ferment the cloves in their skins? There's no fiddly peeling or prep at all.

The result was a revelation: deeply savoury, probiotic garlic, and tiny cloves that pop cleanly from their jackets. It's been my go-to ever since for less-than-ideal harvests: bulbs that are too small, or threatening to sprout before I can use them all. It's a neat example of my layered approach: turning what might feel like a chore into a high-performance outcome. Often the problems that the garden hands me are the most exciting invitations to turn 'lemons into lemonade'.

For this recipe, you will need a sterilised glass jar (about 25 per cent bigger than the quantity of garlic) with either a fermentation lid/airlock or a standard lid, as well as something to keep the cloves submerged (such as a glass paperweight, a small jar or a zip-lock bag filled with 3–4 per cent brine).

Brush any soil off garlic heads, remove any tough outer wrappers, and trim off the dried root tuft. Separate garlic heads into cloves (there's no need to peel the cloves).

Place the cloves into the jar, leaving 4 centimetres (1½ inches) headspace.

Dissolve the salt in the water so it creates a 3–4 per cent brine (remembering that 1 per cent is 10 grams or ⅓ ounce salt in 1 litre or ¼ gallon water). I reach for 3 per cent when I want a softer lactic tang; 4 per cent when it's warm or I want the garlic to stay firmer.

Cover the cloves with the brine, ensuring that the liquid reaches 1–2 centimetres (½–¾ inches) above the cloves. Add the weight so the garlic cloves stay under the surface.

If your jar has an airlock lid, then fit it and you're set. If your jar has a regular lid, then loosen it daily during the first week to 'burp' it (release CO_2), then once every few days. Set the jar on a saucer to catch 'happy bubbles' that might cause a little to overflow.

Keep the jar on the kitchen bench at a cool room temperature (18–22 degrees Celsius; 64–71 degrees Fahrenheit), out of direct sun. Expect cloudiness and bubbles; these are good signs.

In my experience, it usually takes two to three weeks for the garlic to ferment. Taste from day ten. Move the jar to the fridge when the bubbling stops, the flavour is rounded and saline–tart, and the cloves slip easily from their skins. Fermented garlic will keep for many months (effectively 'indefinitely', with beautiful flavour).

To use the fermented garlic, pop a clove from its skin into dressings, sauces, soups or braises. The brine is liquid gold. Splash it into vinaigrettes or a pan sauce, or use it as a brightening dash in mayonnaise. You can also:

- pop a clove from its skin, and rub it onto toast with olive oil
- mash fermented garlic into butter, aioli or pan juices
- slice the garlic into warm lentils with lemon and herbs.

Notes and variations

If you see a white film on the brine surface, don't worry, as this is harmless. It's known as kahm yeast, and it can simply be skimmed off. Cloudiness in the liquid is also fine. However, fuzzy and/or coloured mould or rotten smells in the jar mean that you need to discard the ferment and start again.

Sprouting or tiny garlic cloves ferment beautifully; this recipe exists for them. It can also be used for ginger and turmeric. Wash well with their skins on, and pack them into 3–4 per cent brine (exactly as for garlic). Ferment for seven to fourteen days to taste, then refrigerate.

'For me, a productive garden is having something at all times . . . even if it's just a handful of salad greens.'

EMMA GALLOWAY

Turning flops into flavours

Emma Galloway (of My Darling Lemon Thyme fame) gardens and cooks with an intuitive steadiness: small daily walks, seasonal observation, and the courage to transform mistakes into flavourful opportunities.

Emma grew up with a massive vegie patch and citrus orchard in Raglan, New Zealand; her dad even ran a weekly vegie-box service back in the 1980s, well ahead of the times. That early saturation in growing and preserving became a kind of osmosis: food and garden braided into one steady thread of life. Now a chef and a writer, Emma has a disarmingly simple lens: start small, grow what you love, learn by doing. She doesn't romanticise the work. Most seasons, at least one crop humbles her. Recently, a whole bed of onions refused to form bulbs. Instead of despairing, she reached for the dehydrator, sliced the onions (tops and all), dried them to glassy shards, and blitzed a year's worth of onion powder. The result was so good she would do it again, on purpose.

Her anchor isn't a rigid ritual so much as a short, quiet walk three or four times a week through beds and borders, noting pests, new growth and what has changed since her last visit. It's a walking meditation and a reminder that the garden answers to place, not to a planting calendar.

Emma's definition of a productive garden is gentle and exacting at once: there's always something to pick, even just a handful of parsley, while bigger crops ebb and flow through the year. She trusts seasonal cues over strict calendar dates, adjusting to climate shifts and paying attention to moon phases, liquid-feeding in the week before the full moon, for example. And she keeps the seed cycle turning, fermenting tomato seeds to clean and store them for next time (see page 339). Her work in print and online has coaxed thousands to try, fail, try again, and finally taste their own crops.

These are the key takeaways from our conversation:

- Failure is normal. One crop a season will likely flop, so treat it as problem-solving practice.
- Intuitive gardening involves observing, adjusting, keeping notes and resisting rigid dates.
- Productive gardening means that there is always something to pick, even if it's small.
- Seasonal/Indigenous cues plus moon phases can guide timing.
- Maintain seed-to-seed cycles, such as fermenting tomato seeds for easy storage.

Scan to watch my full conversation with Emma Galloway, where we talk about making the most of every harvest.

Emma's dehydrated onion powder

Emma's generosity lives in the way she reframes failure, like the season her onions didn't produce bulbs. She chopped the lot (greens and all), dehydrated them, and blitzed the shards into onion powder. For this recipe, you will need a dehydrator or oven, a food processor and an airtight glass jar.

any onions that failed to produce bulbs

Trim off damaged parts of the onions, but try to keep most of the tops. Finely slice the onions and tops.

Spread the sliced onions and tops in a single layer on dehydrator or oven trays (baking paper or mesh liners will help to stop the onion pieces falling through the gaps of dehydrator trays).

Dry the sliced onions and tops at a low heat (about 50 degrees Celsius; 120 degrees Fahrenheit) until they are crisp/brittle (with no tackiness when cooled).

Place the sliced onions and tops in the food processor, and pulse to a fine powder. Sieve the powder if you love it smooth; keep a little texture if you prefer it more rustic.

Store the onion powder in an airtight glass jar in a dark cupboard. If it's humid, then add a few grains of dry rice in a paper sachet. The onion powder will last for up to 12 months; have a smaller jar on the kitchen bench for day-to-day use, and keep the rest sealed away. To use the onion powder, you can:

- dust it over roasted vegies straight from the oven for instant depth
- mix it with flaky salt to make 'onion salt'
- whisk it into vinaigrettes or yoghurt dressings for a soft, savoury base note
- fold it through labneh, butter or soft cheese for quick spreads
- stir it into soups, stews or curries when you want onion flavour without the bulk
- sprinkle it over scrambled eggs or avocado toast for a quick lift
- add it to bread or cracker dough for umami flavour running through the bake.

Natasha's dehydrated orange slices

whole fresh oranges
(the recipe also works with lemons, limes or cumquats)

I dry citrus fruits all season, in a cadence that turns zesty winter goodness into stored brightness. Thin rounds laid on dehydrator trays become little gems; their translucent, ambered edges catch the light. They move easily between uses: a garnish on a cake, slipped into tea, dropped into a winter simmer pot, or tucked into jars for gifts. It's a way of holding on to the season, of making sure that no orange is wasted, and of weaving small care rituals into the pantry. For this recipe, you will need:

- *a sharp knife or mandolin for clean, even rounds*
- *a tea towel for blotting away excess juice*
- *a dehydrator or oven*
- *airtight jars to store the dried fruits in a dark, dry place.*

Wash, dry and slice the oranges in rounds that are 3–4 millimetres (less than 3/16 inch) thick. Place them onto dehydrator or oven trays, and blot them with the tea towel to reduce excess juice.

Place the trays into the dehydrator or oven set to a low heat (50–60 degrees Celsius; 120–140 degrees Fahrenheit) for six to twelve hours or until the flesh is dry and the pith is no longer tacky (the time will depend on the juiciness of the oranges and the quality of the dehydrator/oven).

Let the trays cool. Return any soft slices to the dehydrator or oven.

Stack the dry slices in airtight jars. Store the jars in a dark, dry place for up to a year.

A note on waxed citrus

A thin layer of food-grade wax is often applied to commercially grown fruits, including citrus and apples, in order to slow moisture loss, extend shelf life and improve appearance. When dehydrating citrus, this wax can slow down the process, cause uneven drying and remain on the peel as moisture is removed.

I prefer to use fruits in their most natural state whenever possible. While food-grade waxes may be considered safe, choosing unwaxed fruits means fewer treatments and less interference with the fruits. This is one reason why I love buying direct from growers at farmers' markets, where I can ask questions, find out how recently produce was harvested, and buy what is truly seasonal.

If you're unsure whether your citrus has been waxed, then it's best to wash and scrub the skin before use. Fortunately, homegrown fruits are naturally unwaxed.

PETRINA BURRILL

Flowers as food for the soul

Petrina Burrill (known online as Petrina Blooms) grows beauty at scale so she can give it away. This is proof that generosity, not perfection, is the true engine of an abundant garden. Her suburban garden makes abundance public: tens of thousands of bulbs rising in waves, a wisteria-like curtain at the door, bouquets carried through the house as if they're company. Cutting and sharing are her daily joy.

Petrina traces her love of flowers to her great-grandmother's cottage garden, where at four and a half she was handed the snips and invited to 'pick the flowers'; nothing was off limits. Her great-grandmother believed that children should be trusted with beauty. That early permission became a practice of generosity: grow widely, give freely, and let beauty be ordinary, not rare. A florist by training, Petrina has spent sixteen years re-creating that permission for others; first on balconies and rental thresholds, then later in soil that she could finally call her own.

When she moved into her current place, she kept the bones of the garden and flattened the rest, designing a space that could hold tens of thousands of bulbs, succession-planted for a near-continuous chorus. In 2020, her 'private' passion turned outwards when a spring bouquet posted online led to a flood of requests. She switched her account to public and realised that what she'd been doing for years wasn't 'normal', but it was needed.

Today her work sits squarely in the slow-flower movement: grow local and in season, as chemical-light as possible, and be mindful of footprint. 'It's the opposite to fast flowers . . . no chemicals and no nasties,' she says. If a client asks for peonies

Scan to watch my full conversation with Petrina Burrill, where we talk about seasonal rhythm, generosity and home-bunch conditioning.

out of season, then she reframes the brief towards what the garden is truly offering that week.

The work is seasonal choreography: late autumn is cutting back and getting bulbs in; winter is 'sticks and bones', an eerie beauty thrumming with energy; sixteen weeks later, spring erupts; seedlings for summer wait on the balcony before being planted out. The harvest is not only the bouquet, but also the ritual of flowers joining her wherever she is at home, or, in lean seasons, floating camellias in a bowl so the house still holds bloom.

Petrina's practice widens our definition of 'harvest' beyond food to a daily rituals of giving, where flowers become nourishment for rooms, relationships and seasons. She moves arrangements through the house, from study to kitchen to cool step at night, so the flowers are lived with, not just looked at. In lean moments, she gathers what falls and makes a small altar devoted to the ordinary. Giving is the throughline: to teachers, friends, strangers who need a lift. The garden is not an exhibition; it's a way of restoring meaning. What Petrina models is not extravagance but accessible abundance. Start small, plant what you love, observe what thrives, and let joy and generosity ripple out into the world.

These are the key takeaways from our conversation:

- Beauty is necessity, not luxury; you can create it from seeds without great expense.
- The slow-flower approach prioritises local, seasonal growing and no chemicals; it avoids hothouse imports.
- Succession is choreography: cut back and plant in late autumn, savour winter structure, expect spring about sixteen weeks later (depending on your climate), raise summer annuals on a balcony before planting out.
- Harvest is a living practice, so move bouquets through the house to be enjoyed wherever home finds you.
- Start small and plant what you love; observe local gardens and learn by doing.

Home-bunch harvest

Here are Petrina's top tips for harvesting and displaying beautiful flowers:

- Cut flowers in the cool of the morning, and place them in fresh water in the cleanest buckets you own.
- Strip any leaves that will sit below the waterline, and recut the stems on a slant.
- Arrange the flowers in a vase, and refresh the water daily.
- Give the blooms a 'night rest' somewhere cool overnight; during the day, move them with you from room to room.
- In sparse seasons, gather what falls – flower heads, seed heads and foliage – and stage small moments.

'I feel like a millionaire in raspberry season.'

CAROLINE PARKER

Medicine and care

Known to many as The Cottage Herbalist, Caroline Parker practises a generous, everyday form of herbalism that fits inside a home kitchen as easily as it does a garden. She is a degree-qualified Western herbalist and lifelong grower who teaches people to begin with what they have: a handful of rosehips, a pot of raw honey, a windowsill of herbs. Her work is about accessibility and rhythm: listening to seasons, gathering simply, and making remedies that are beautiful, useful and repeatable.

Caroline marks time by what the garden is doing rather than by the wall calendar: elderflowers opening, rosehips colouring, the quiet turn towards winter. That attention becomes practice. An oxymel (apple-cider vinegar and honey infused with plant material) is one such practice. It's a bright, soothing tonic that preserves a moment in the year and brings it to the table: sipped in hot water, whisked into dressings, drizzled over roasted vegetables.

What I love most in Caroline's approach is her refusal to make herbal knowledge precious. She invites people to start small: grow medicinal flowers, dry rosehips whole for tea, keep a notebook, trade what you have for what you can't grow. Beauty matters in her making: teas should look as lovely as they taste; jars on the pantry shelf should feel like a promise. Her message is steadying in a time of abundance and overwhelm: you don't have to do everything to do something meaningful. Begin with one plant, one recipe, one shared jar. Let the seasons teach you the rest.

These are the key takeaways from our conversation:

- Seasonal cues, not dates, drive her making; she 'lives by the outside calendar'.
- Start with easy, generous herbs (such as kitchen aromatics), and build from there.
- Abundance grows through sharing; trading gluts with neighbours builds resilience.
- Use the whole plant where possible (for example, parsley roots in stock) to close loops.
- Everyday use matters: remedies belong in ordinary meals (dressings, teas); they shouldn't be reserved for when you're sick.

Scan to watch my full conversation with Caroline Parker, where we talk about oxymels, living by the outside calendar, and everyday remedies.

Caroline's rosehip oxymel

- fresh rosehips
- raw apple cider vinegar
- raw local honey

A garden can be a home pharmacy if we let it. Inspired by a long afternoon Caroline and I spent in autumn foraging for wild rosehips, her oxymel is vinegar-and-honey wisdom: tart, throat-kind and batch-friendly. This recipe is proof that everyday medicine can be seasonal, beautiful and generous, and a harvest translated into care. For this recipe, you will need a sterilised glass jar and glass bottle, a fine sieve, muslin (cheesecloth) and a funnel.

Wash the rosehips gently, and remove any stems and sepals (the small, leafy parts at the blossom end of the rosehip). Cut the rosehips in half.

Fill the jar three-quarters full with rosehips.

Pour in the apple cider vinegar so it covers the rosehips, then top up the remaining quarter of the jar with honey. If the honey is a little thick, warm the honey jar in a bowl of hot water until the honey has a runnier consistency, then pour it into your jar of rosehips.

Stir the jar's contents using the blade of a butter knife or a chopstick, and push out any air bubbles. Make sure that the rosehips are completely covered by the liquid, adding a little more apple cider vinegar if needed.

Place the lid on securely, then give the jar a good shake. (If you're using a metal lid, then place a square of baking paper between the lid and the jar before securing the lid; this prevents corrosion from the vinegar.) Label the jar with the ingredients and the date.

Let the rosehips macerate in a cool, dark spot for four to six weeks.

Strain the rosehips through the fine sieve lined with muslin (cheesecloth). Gather up the edges of the fabric, twist tightly and squeeze out the excess liquid from the rosehips. Pop the spent rosehips into your compost or feed them to your chickens as a treat.

Decant the rosehip oxymel into the glass bottle using the funnel, secure the lid, and label with the ingredients and the date. Keep the rosehip oxymel in the fridge for up to six months. To use the rosehip oxymel, you can:

— take it by the teaspoonful as is
— make it into a salad dressing
— drizzle it over roasted vegetables
— splash it into soda water for a refreshing drink.

What is an oxymel?

An oxymel is a traditional herbal preparation made with vinegar and honey. The name comes from the Greek *oxys*, meaning sharp, and *meli*, meaning honey. This is a clue to both its flavour and its function.

Vinegar draws out minerals and certain medicinal constituents from plants, while honey softens the acidity, preserves the mixture, and adds its own soothing, antimicrobial qualities.

Oxymels have long been used as gentle, everyday preparations, sitting somewhere between food and medicine. Their strength lies in being seasonal and accessible, something to reach for regularly rather than only when unwell.

An oxymel with rosehips captures their vitamin-rich, immune-supporting qualities in a form that can be taken by the spoonful, added to warm water or woven into daily ritual.

'All the things' basic balm

Makes 30 ml (1 fl oz)

This is a simple, adaptable recipe I return to in every season; it's made to live by the sink as much as in the bathroom cabinet. It was first created during a workshop I hosted with Cherie Hausler of All The Things *podcast fame, hence the name, and it was so good that I kept making it! You can adjust this plant-based recipe to suit your needs by including your favourite essential oils. The base balm can become a lip salve, gardener's hand rescue, silky moisturiser, muscle rub, pulse-point soother and more, depending on the aromatic(s) you choose. For this recipe, you will need a sterilised 30-millilitre (1-fl-oz) jar.*

- 1 tablespoon cocoa butter
- 1/2 tablespoon shea butter
- 1/2 tablespoon coconut oil
- 4–6 drops essential oil(s) of your choice

Place the cocoa butter, shea butter and coconut oil in a small double boiler. Slowly melt the ingredients, mixing them together gently with a metal spoon, and ensuring that no steam or water enters the liquid.

Once the mixture has completely melted into a clear liquid, carefully remove the double boiler from the heat and allow the mixture to cool slightly (until it's warm but cool enough to touch). I place the double boiler on a tea towel to remove any moisture from the underside.

Add your choice of essential oil(s), one drop at a time, to the mixture. (Note that the completely cool balm will have a slightly stronger scent once it has been applied to the skin.) Stir well. Pour the balm into the small jar. If you wish to add dried lavender or other medicinal flowers or herbs to your balm, then allow the liquid to cool a little more first so that they don't float or sink to the bottom of the jar.

Place the jar in the refrigerator for 30 minutes or until the balm has completely cooled and solidified. Store it in a cool, dry spot out of direct sunlight for up to twelve months. Always use a clean spoon or spatula (or freshly washed hands) to remove balm from the jar. This helps to avoid contamination and keeps your balm fresher for longer. To adapt the balm, you can add:

- eucalyptus oil for an invigorating cold-and-flu chest rub
- rose and cedarwood oils for grounding and steadying before big days
- lemon verbena and peppermint oils for fresh, clear-headed mornings
- lavender and chamomile oils for a wind-down ritual before bedtime.

Herb steam bundle for the shower or bath

This is a simple and fragrant way to turn fresh harvests into everyday care. Gather together a handful of aromatic stems, such as eucalyptus, rosemary, thyme, peppermint, lemon verbena or chamomile. Tie up the bundle with twine, and hang it under the shower head or from the bath tap; let hot water pass through the bundle. Steam will release the essential oils, which will help to clear the head, soften the skin and perfume the room. Compost the bundle after use.

Caution: Avoid direct contact with the bundles if you have sensitive skin. Ventilate the bathroom well, and check for allergic reactions.

SEEDS AS STORY: SOVEREIGNTY, GENEROSITY, CONTINUITY

Seeds carry the harvest forwards. I keep the best fruits for their seeds because each season of saved seeds holds a little more knowledge of my place; plants are earlier to set, steadier in wind and more at home in our short, cool season.

Others save seeds for sovereignty, for lineage, for the small miracle of beginning again next season. A paper envelope with a date and a name is a portable memory, proof that generosity can travel across fences and kitchens, and still arrive alive. Seeds are the part of the harvest that I don't eat; I bank them. This is how flavour, resilience and memory move forwards.

Save seeds from the plant species and varieties that you love in your climate, then swap locally to widen your garden's resilience. Collect a 'farewell bouquet' of seed heads before the first frost; dry and strip them ready for next year's planting.

'Collect a "farewell bouquet" of seed heads before the first frost; dry and strip them ready for next year's planting.'

Emma Galloway's simple tomato-seed ferment

Fermenting frees Emma's tomato seeds from their gel, helps them to store better, and keeps her local-climate-adapted seed line going. It turns one tomato into seasons of continuity. This is how she does it:

1. Scoop out the ripe tomato pulp and seeds, and place it into a small jar. Add just enough water to loosen the gel.
2. Cover the jar with muslin (cheesecloth). Leave the jar on the bench at room temperature for two or three days or until a light film forms and most of the seeds sink to the bottom of the jar. Skim the film.
3. Tip the jar contents into a fine sieve, and rinse until the clinging gel is gone.
4. Spread the seeds thinly on a plate, a piece of baking paper or some mesh to dry completely.
5. Place the dry seeds into a jar, and label with the variety and year. Store the jar in a cool, dry place.
6. Swap the seeds with friends, or grow the same plant again next season.

Emma still loves saving tomato seeds directly onto paper towel, but fermentation is now her favourite way to obtain clean, easy-to-store tomato seeds.

Opposite page,
Top left_End-of-season tomatoes are hung upside down so they keep ripening off the vine.
Top right_Bean pods are left to dry on the plant, creating seeds for the next growing season.
Bottom left_Saving seeds is a yearly ritual in the garden.
Bottom right_Picking ripened tomatoes from hanging vines. This extends the harvest through the first frosts.

'Beauty is not a luxury; it's an everyday need. Spreading seeds is spreading a tiny part of beauty, and it helps my family survive.'

ALLA OLKHOVSKA

Seeds as livelihood

One seed can hold a household. In Kharkiv, Ukraine, Alla Olkhovska collects and cleans the seeds of rare clematis (*Clematis* spp.) and peonies (*Paeonia* spp.) by hand each autumn, selling packets of hope that now travel the world.

Alla tends a small, inherited garden made by her great-grandfather and still entered through his weathered wooden gate. In peony season, she walks beside plants rescued from her great-grandmother's clumps; in autumn, she gathers seeds by hand, feeling for ripeness, then dries, cleans and parcels them. When the full-scale war began and evacuation wasn't possible, seeds became both lifeline and language. 'My family survives due to the seed orders,' she says. It's not an exaggeration. Selling seeds gives her money for groceries, medicine and generator fuel. Her photographs and catalogues travel first; then the seeds themselves go out into the world. Each packet offers quiet continuity, biodiversity and survival.

Alla is a clematis devotee, growing unusual species and saving what might otherwise be lost in a country where seed propagation hasn't always been common practice. In her hands, clematis, peonies and phlox (*Phlox* spp.) become a way to look past sirens and towards seasons. She speaks plainly about the work: cold fingers, tiny seeds, sorting out the bad, labelling late into the night by candlelight; she also speaks of the ritual in spring sowing, summer deadheading and autumn gathering, anchoring time when time is so unpredictable. 'Sometimes . . . I say to myself, do not think about war. Think about flowers.' The envelope is her measure of resistance.

Alla Olkhovska in her inherited family garden in Kharkiv, Ukraine. It is a special place of beauty and continuity across generations.

I admire how a single garden can become a community – orders, notes, kindness flowing back across borders – so that one person's seed line threads into thousands of beds. This is why Alla belongs here, in a chapter about harvest as story: because saving seeds is saving meaning.

Seeds are gathered, cleaned and packed by Alla. Each small bag sent out into the world represents not only her livelihood but also a quiet act of resilience.

Making a living from seeds

Alla's seed-selling business has a clear circular model:

- **Start small:** Alla posts online photos of seed heads from her family garden in Kharkiv.
- **Make it legible:** She lists varieties and timing, then builds a simple catalogue.
- **Invite connection:** Orders begin; each packet includes a note about the plant and her growing tips.
- **Scale by trust:** Gardeners share their results, and requests for seeds increase; the income is a lifeline.
- **Keep the loop alive:** Alla saves seeds again each season, adding species that might otherwise disappear.

Scan to watch my full conversation with Alla Olkhovska, where we talk about gardening in a war zone, clematis and peony seeds, and her family garden in Kharkiv.

HARVEST AS A WAY OF LIVING

Harvest isn't an end point. It's the choreography between garden, kitchen, memory and care, made visible in jars, bottles, bunches and balms.

I can't help but come back to Nonna Carmela. To her 'nothing in the garden' that turned out to be everything. To the pride in her eyes when told her that I grew something from seed. Her pickled eggplant, which was salted, weighted and packed just so, showed me what care and ritual looks like in a jar. You grow a little more than you need because generosity is the point. You offer a jar to someone just because you're thinking of them.

This chapter has been a ledger of those small, decisive gestures that turn 'not perfect' into pantry gold. When onions refuse to form bulbs, Emma Galloway dries and blitzes them to season a winter's worth of cooking. When my garlic runs to tiny cloves, I brine-ferment them whole with their skins on. Green tomatoes become chutney on purpose now, not as a consolation. It's the same logic everywhere: trade a glut, ferment a surplus, dehydrate a citrus gem for later. The work is practical, yes, but it's also an ethic of care.

Preserving, too, is how we mark time. Meg Travis and I tuned a spiced elderberry syrup at the old bench, tasting until the balance sang; that bottle is a late summer memory you can pour. My rhubarb, orange zest and ginger shrub rides the edge between sweet and sharp, especially when poured over ice with a sprig of lemon verbena. Sharon Flynn's ginger bug and rhubarb fizz remind me that aliveness – microbial life, such as yeasts, bacteria and enzymes – is the preservative, not the enemy. On the shelf with the rosehip oxymel and the little tin of 'all the things' basic balm, I can see a year, held.

*Far left*_A tomato worthy of a prize, sliced and eaten as it is. When a fruit tastes this good, you enjoy it fresh and then save the seeds for a future harvest.
*Left*_A precious asparagus haul, picked in its prime. After the last harvest, the patch is left to rest until the next growing season.

***Above left*_*Capsicum* 'Courtyard', harvested in early June. More than dinner, it's a late-season reward that comes from growing to my conditions and saving seeds from the survivors, so the plants I grow are gradually shaped to my garden.
***Above right*_A summer harvest. Some things are eaten fresh, some go into jars, and some are placed into a bag and delivered to a neighbour's doorstep, to be repaid later in a generous exchange of winter citrus.

More than food

The garden's gifts aren't only edible. Petrina Burrill's armfuls of slow flowers, grown spray-free and cut with joy, teach me to move bouquets through the house like companions, to float a single bloom in a bowl when the season runs lean, and to accept that beauty is a human necessity, not a luxury.

And then there are seeds, the smallest harvest with the longest reach. Emma Galloway's tomato seeds, fermented clean and stored for next year's hands, keep a lineage alive on a plate. Alla Olkhovska's clematis and peony seeds carry a household's survival and a public story; one seed as sovereignty, livelihood, continuity. The circle tightens and widens at once: what we have can be shared, and what we share comes back to us.

If Chapter 10 was the systems and scaffolding that make abundance possible, then Chapter 11 has been the translation: how that abundance becomes food, medicine, fragrance and connection. It's the lived practice: a tray in the dehydrator while dinner simmers; a ferment burbling on the bench; a child shelling peas; a bouquet cut for a neighbour; a warm winter syrup drunk from a favourite mug. The satisfaction is stored, but it's also immediate. You feel it in the steadying rhythm, in the way the kitchen picks up where the garden leaves off.

Next, we turn to space and applying design to any place. The habits you've met here – saving seeds, drying citrus, brewing fizz, arranging flowers, bottling a season – become our design brief. How do we shape paths, benches, shelves and beds so these rituals have a home whether you garden on a balcony, on a verge, in a courtyard or in a paddock? How do we make room for a preserving day, a seed-drying tray, a bouquet station, a shady chair? Design, at any scale, is simply making it easier to live the way you mean to.

Nonna Carmela would have waved her hand and called it 'nothing'. We know better. It's garden and kitchen, people and place, all looped together season by season in the ordinary magic of a well-lived harvest.

PART -IV-

From garden to legacy

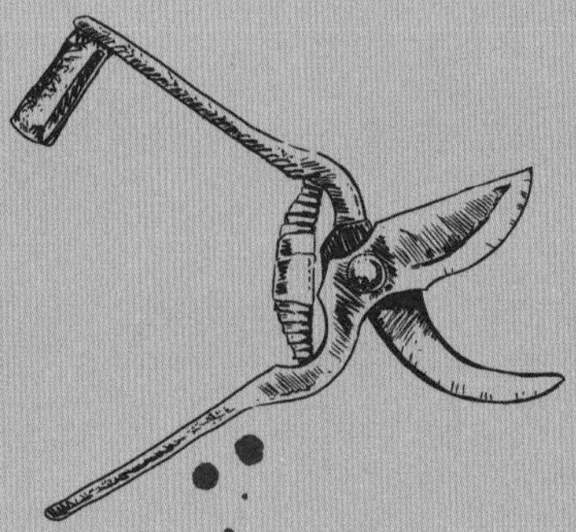

12 SCALABLE GARDEN DESIGNS

In both of my gardens, the design asks the same questions. What and who is this garden for? Where will bodies stop and move? What wants to grow here? This chapter demonstrates that you can build systems which suit your reality today and then adjust them as life changes tomorrow.

A PATTERN LANGUAGE FOR ANY SCALE

Scale is never the boundary or the confines within which you operate. It's a way of perceiving not just time but space and life in a garden. For me, design principles and philosophies don't change at different scales; they simply translate differently. Whether it's soil health, water cycles, microclimates or planting patterns, the principles are universal regardless of the scale.

When I think in terms of scale, I'm not asking: can this be done here? Rather, I'm considering how it will be expressed. For example, I'm not wondering whether or not I can have an orchard. I'm thinking about how I have the orchard. If I don't have space for a full orchard, then can I espalier the fruit trees? There is a process of constant reimagining and reinterpreting, depending on the scale at which you are operating.

Thinking about scale in this way frees us from the idea that gardens must be a certain size or type in order to be substantive, fruitful and important. It reminds us that gardening and creating productive spaces are not just about the area of ground under our feet, but the relationships between soil, plants, cycles of life and seasonality. By shifting our view, we can see that even the smallest act of gardening operates in a much bigger framework. A tiny plot is still part of the broader context and contributes to the landscape as a whole.

Scale is temporal as well as spatial. It's the time it takes a seed to sprout. It's the seasonal rhythms and cycles: sap rising in the very first buds of spring, through to atrophy, decline and rest from autumn into winter. And it's the shifting climate over centuries. All of these scales overlap.

Diverse scales and decisions

Every garden I have ever created has existed at multiple scales at once. At Oak & Monkey Puzzle, the design was one huge garden made of many smaller precincts, or rooms. At Little Cottage on a Hill, the scale has been reduced to verges and wicking beds, but if you shift the scale down even more, then each wicking bed can be considered its own element.

Oak & Monkey Puzzle was a canvas on which I could paint almost everything I could imagine. When I first moved to Little Cottage on a Hill, I could not have known that it would be equally productive and giving, in just a fraction of the area. The difference is that instead of gardening being unencumbered by the vastness of space, every element here has to earn its keep.

A large garden can do many things, and each part does not have to work very hard. At Little Cottage on a Hill, I soon worked out that every square centimetre relies on a well-thought-out decision. What I commit to in one place is equally a decision about what I can't have elsewhere. To plant something that I will have to nurse along means taking my attention away from the abundant wicking beds. In other words, the care I might put into one ill-suited plant would be better given to a wicking bed that offers me tens of kilos of produce.

If we ground ourselves in the foundations of design, then we can navigate various scales without being overwhelmed. Remember: the same principles apply at any scale. We need to learn to design with scale and not be defined by it.

CLARITY OF PURPOSE

A design brief allows a garden to really hold its centre, its anchor, its clarity of purpose. Without it, a space risks becoming a patchwork of haphazard ideas and good intentions that lack cohesion. Every decision, from the start of a path to the placement of a tree, needs to be measured against that explicit purpose.

At Oak & Monkey Puzzle, the landscape brought to life all of the things that were on my chalkboards at the old scout hall in inner-city Melbourne, when I was first imagining a vocation shaped by my passions. That was its purpose. I could easily see how the landscape could be designed, lived in, interacted with, and inhabited to meet that intent.

Little Cottage on a Hill maintains the productive heart of Oak & Monkey Puzzle, but it's expressed in a smaller scale. I still have a kitchen garden, as well as cut flowers and berries. I still have views and thresholds, rooms and edges. There is rhythm and space to rest; a sense of immersion, of a garden enveloping you. It still does all of the things I wanted Oak & Monkey Puzzle to do, but it does them in a more concentrated way.

Late summer on the western verge at Little Cottage on a Hill. An abundant drift of anise hyssop (*Agastache foeniculum*) and stonecrops (*Sedum* spp.) holds the garden's clarity of purpose: layered planting that is beautiful, productive and generous to biodiversity within a small footprint.

At Oak & Monkey Puzzle, the primary axis – the one that lined up perfectly with the front door and the window in the library, transporting you into the landscape and terminating at the forest backdrop – was pivotal. Equally so was the vista from the master bedroom all the way down to the paddocks and the bushland beyond.

At Little Cottage on a Hill, the sightline from the gravel circle – the seat facing west to capture and revel in the end-of-day sun and the long view of the rolling hills in the distance – is just as important. This is what clarity of purpose brings: an understanding of how you want to inhabit a space, and which landscapes resonate with you.

Clarity of purpose is also about defining how you want your garden to be productive. I needed to be able to cut flowers, and I can do this in both my western and northern verge gardens. But my cut flowers are not confined to designated spaces at Little Cottage on a Hill, they are embedded across the garden. Instead of one area with a singular purpose, the spaces here are multilayered and multifunctional.

Where the mown lawn spines of Oak & Monkey Puzzle created negative space between precincts of the landscape, at Little Cottage on a Hill the grassed areas provide that respite between garden beds. Out on the verge, the lawn itself has become the planting canvas. In the wicking-bed garden, mulched paths have become the cohesive plane on which the beds sit.

Clarity of purpose is ultimately about setting a design brief for yourself. It involves understanding and articulating how you want to live, what motivates you, what brings you joy, and what it means for you to live well.

Glossary of clarity of purpose terms

You'll encounter these terms throughout the chapter, so let's take a moment to get familiar with what they mean.

- **Design intent** is the overarching idea that guides decisions.
- **Conceptual framework** is the scaffolding of ideas that hold the design together.
- **Guiding principle** is the core value or idea that directs choices.
- **Legibility** is how easily the design communicates its logic and order.
- **Hierarchy of spaces** recognises which areas hold prominence and which support.
- **Functional coherence** ensures that all elements work together without contradiction.

Scale as a lens

Keep these ideas in mind:

- Design principles stay constant. Scale simply changes their expression.
- Shrink size, not purpose (for example, orchards become espaliers; compost bays become worm tunnels).
- Read both space and time, from a seed's sprouting days to a tree canopy's decades.
- Hold the structure and design brief close so scale does not overwhelm.
- Every garden, no matter the size, operates at multiple scales at once.

RHYTHMS AND PAUSES

Every garden is experienced in both movement and stillness. It's like the inhale and exhale of breathing. Paths set you in a direction; they carry you forwards. Beds create a rhythm or a tempo, a staccato or a softness, depending on the way in which they are formed. And open spaces, benches and the widening of a path ensure that you slow down and stop.

A pause can also be a lookout from a hilltop, the sound of a babbling water feature or a glimpse of a statue that helps the eyes to rest. But it doesn't have to be about space: it can be about experience. Rhythm, too, can be about experience. The way light flashes through a canopy of trees, or wind moves across an embankment of grasses. Or, as at Little Cottage on a Hill, the way Lebanese crabapples (*Malus trilobata*) line a driveway courtyard like sentinels, leading you towards the studio space for a workshop.

'Without rhythms, a garden can feel restless, confused; without pauses, it can be overwhelming.'

Without rhythms, a garden can feel restless, confused; without pauses, it can be overwhelming. It's like wandering through IKEA and not knowing which way to look because there's just so much to see. One space leads into another, further and further, until you're completely overstimulated and unable to focus.

Good design knows when to draw you onwards and quicken the pace, and also when to create a quiet interlude. Just as for the composition in an artwork, the negative space is as important as the positive space. In a garden, the negative space is the pause and the positive space is the activity: the planting, the intensity.

Repetition of elements, such as fencing material, bed edges, gravel types and hedge species, builds rhythm. English box (*Buxus sempervirens*) balls are measured sculptural forms throughout the landscape at Little Cottage on a Hill, while the choice of European hornbeam (*Carpinus betulus*) as a core structural planting repeated across spaces at Oak & Monkey Puzzle offered visual harmony. Together, rhythms and pauses reveal the cadence at which to inhabit the space, and they create calm, even in gardens alive with activity.

There are many ways to think about rhythms and pauses. Don't be confined by normative ideas, such as a row of standard *Rosa* 'Iceberg' plants at the front of a cottage. Think instead about experience and ephemerality, about how garden movement and stillness shift across a day, a month, a year, as well as through the physicality of space. Most importantly, rhythms and pauses are always shaped through materiality: the grade of gravel, the softness of mulch, the texture or flow of repeated plants, the sensation underfoot. All of it matters.

Opposite page_Late autumn, looking from the western verge to the northern verge at Little Cottage on a Hill. A ground plane of grass carries the garden beds, while repeated verticals – the ornamental grasses and the timber-and-wire A-frame growing structures – set the rhythm. The glowing late-season textural planting creates a pause that slows you down and holds you in place.

Glossary of rhythm and pause terms

These words are associated with rhythm:

- **Repetition** is the deliberate recurrence of forms, materials or plantings.
- **Cadence** is the beat or pacing created by design elements.
- **Sequence** is the ordered progression of experiences or views.
- **Pattern** is a repeated arrangement that provides structure.
- **Continuity** is the sense of flow across spaces.
- **Modulation** is the variation within repetition that adds interest.
- **Progression** is a gradation or movement in size, spacing or intensity.
- **Order** is the underlying structure that makes repetition legible.

These words are associated with pause:

- **Resting point** is a place where movement naturally slows.
- **Terminus** is the deliberate end of a path or view.
- **Threshold** is the in-between space where transition invites stillness.
- **Focal point** is an element that holds the gaze and halts motion.
- **Compression and release** are a narrowing followed by an expansion to create a pause.
- **Interruption** is the deliberate break in repetition to create emphasis.
- **Void or clearing** is the absence of form that gives space to breathe.
- **Interval** is the spacing between elements, which determines pacing.

Other important words to know:

- **Spatial tempo** is the balance of speed and rest in how a garden is moved through.
- **Pacing** is the measured progression that guides the body and the eye.
- **Articulation** is how rhythm and pause together give clarity to form.
- **Choreography** is the orchestrated movement through a space.
- **Balance of repetition and contrast** is the dual force that creates both rhythm and rest.

***Top*_**A cup of tea on a fence post is a small pause in the garden. ***Above*_**This pretty barrenwort (*Epimedium* sp.) offers delicate flowers on fine stems that dance in the breeze.

ROOMS AND EDGES

Gardens are made legible by their rooms and edges, or spatial structure. A room in a garden is not always walled, but it is always defined as a space that is held, gathered or contained. Garden rooms might be broad lawns framed by planting, secluded courtyards enclosed by hedges, or borders that invite you to linger.

Edges mark where one experience gives way to another: the shade of trees to the brightness of an open lawn, the ordered bed to the looseness of a meadow. They also work hard: a hedge or fence line keeps stock out, while a low wall or steel edge holds in mulch. A woven divider can separate the plants that are precious from those that can be more wild.

The concept of rooms carries intimacy, whereas edges bring clear definition. Together, they shape the way we move, linger and care for what grows. Rooms allow you to put down jobs and pick them up again without confusion. They give purpose in a more considered manner than the overarching garden themes.

If we think of rooms as rhythms and edges as pauses, then it becomes apparent that the relationship between the two is like positive space and negative space: one cannot exist without the other. In tandem, they create legibility, sequence and cadence in the garden.

Late spring on the western verge at Little Cottage on a Hill. A gravel circle and steel edge form a clear room and threshold, with a monolithic seat as the resting point. Around it, repeated drifts and rounded forms create pattern and cadence, so the planting reads as a legible edge even as it grows more enveloping through the season.

*Top*_Avens (*Geum* spp.) and asters (*Symphyotrichum* spp.) make for a long-flowering mix that softens edges and keeps the garden moving.
*Above*_The garden bed on the long boundary is edged with red-barked dogwoods (*Cornus alba*), daffodils (*Narcissus* spp.) and jonquils (*N. jonquilla*). This defines both street and garden.
*Opposite page*_Little Cottage on a Hill from across the road. The verge is a threshold that shapes privacy at the boundary while holding the wider view to the hills beyond.

Glossary of room and edge terms

These words are associated with room:

- **Space** is an area defined by atmosphere, qualities or experiences, not just boundaries.
- **Enclosure** is the sense of being held by garden elements, whether or not there are physical barriers.
- **Compartment** is a distinct pocket within the garden, shaped for clarity, pause or uniqueness.
- **Outdoor room** is a garden space created to welcome, comfort and nurture experiences as an indoor room would.
- **Zone** is a garden section defined experientially rather than by hard dividers.
- **Court or courtyard** is an open, often sunlit gathering space, shaped by surrounding elements that foster invitation and interaction.
- **Cell** is a small, intimate garden pocket for quiet reflection or a response to surrounding activities.
- **Volume** is the quality of space as felt by height, depth, light and movement.

These words are associated with edge:

- **Boundary** is the soft or sharp transition in feeling, view or activity in the garden.
- **Margin** is the nuanced edge between garden moments.
- **Interface** is the meeting zone where two garden areas connect and invite movement, interaction or curiosity.
- **Transition** is the designed passage between spaces that guides, prepares or holds the body or senses.
- **Perimeter** is the outer reach of a space that defines its extent.
- **Frame** is the device that highlights, contains or foregrounds a view or experience.

Other important words to know:

- **Spatial structure** is the underlying logic, rhythm and connection between spaces.
- **Figure and ground** are the interplay between focus and backdrop in the garden.
- **Mosaic** is the rich patchwork of garden spaces or plantings as a whole.
- **Hierarchy of spaces** is the result of ranking them according to the roles they play as prominent features or support acts.
- **Domain** is a distinct sphere that has a particular use, mood or connection in the garden.

THRESHOLDS AND VIEWS

Thresholds mark the moments of crossing: the shift from one space into another, the halt at a gate, the narrowing of a path before it opens up again, the canopy of trees as you move through a forest and into open spacc. Thcy hcightcn awarcncss and stall the body, asking us to notice the change. Most importantly, a good threshold is both practical and symbolic. It tells you that you are arriving, departing or entering something distinct.

Views are the counterpoint. They extend your sight, carry you forwards and anchor the wider landscape to the garden. Views frame experience, whether it's borrowing a distant tree line, glimpsing something interesting through plantings, or seeing the sky from a small walled courtyard.

Together, thresholds and views orchestrate movement and attention, much like rhythms and pauses. One slows and marks transition, while the other carries and expands your perception and your experience.

What thresholds and views look like on a garden plan

Establish at least one primary axis or sightline that carries the eye through the garden. Incorporate a borrowed view from beyond the boundary to expand the garden's scale. Balance this with a contained internal focal point, such as a specimen tree, a framed bed or a water feature. Define thresholds by shifting the surface, material or enclosure to signal a transition, and articulate the thresholds before layering details so the sequence of movement remains clear.

What structure and layering look like on a garden plan

Establish primary structural elements first – canopy trees, major paths, walls, hedges – then introduce secondary structures to reinforce the garden, such as smaller trees, low hedges and edging materials. Fix the structure before adding the layers, so the order remains consistent and anchored even as planting shifts across time and seasons.

Layer vertically, from the canopy and shrub tiers to the understorey and ground cover, then layer temporally. Include early-, mid- and late-season succession plantings for continuous presence.

Thresholds and views don't need to be grand. They can be as simple as a small garden bed at the end of a mown lawn pathway, or a bench angled to catch the western afternoon sun. At Little Cottage on a Hill, it's the gate that leads from the verge into the private garden space, and the arbour that marks the shift between the kitchen garden and the driveway. It's these quiet, considered gestures that matter as much as sweeping axes or a borrowed mountain.

Glossary of threshold and view terms

These words are associated with threshold:

- **Transition zone** is the space where one garden feeling or function gently gives way to another.
- **Interface** is the meeting point or overlap between different materials, spaces or experiences.
- **Gateway** is a physical or inferred entry feature that signals a physical or emotional shift between two places.
- **Portal** is a special opening that invites passage and marks a moment of arrival.
- **Node** is a place where pathways, ideas or energies converge, sparking choice or pause.
- **Compression and release** are the paired sensations of moving through tight, contained spaces into more open, expansive ones.

These words are associated with view:

- **Sightline** is a clear line of vision connecting one point to another.
- **Vista** is a broad, often distant garden view revealed from a certain point.
- **Prospect** is a promising or inviting view that draws you onwards.
- **Outlook** is a position designed for surveying the garden or wider landscape.
- **Framed view** is an aspect intentionally bordered by plants or structures to focus attention.
- **Borrowed view** is a garden scene extended by including distant or adjacent features in its composition.
- **Visual axis** is an imaginary or physical straight line that guides the eye through the garden.
- **Terminated view** is an aspect purposefully ended by a feature, such as a tree, wall or sculpture.
- **Panorama** is a sweeping, wide-angle garden scene that unfolds before you.

STRUCTURE AND LAYERING

Gardens are held together and made cohesive through their structure, but they come to life through their layers. Structure is the backbone or framework formed by paths, walls, trees, hedges, clipped elements and fence lines. Without it, a garden drifts; with too much, a garden feels stiff, oppressed and constrained.

At Oak & Monkey Puzzle, the forest backdrop, the clearing, the axes, the European hornbeam (*Carpinus betulus*) plantings and the mown paths all provided structure. So did the areas between the kitchen garden, the berry terrace and the cut-flower garden. The gradient of spaces from the formal garden to the meadows to the bushland setting was another form of structure. The ground plane and its materiality supplied structure, too.

At Little Cottage on a Hill, the gridded matrix of the wicking-bed garden provides structure, as does the reinforcing mesh on the walls and the timber-and-wire fencing. The rhythm and pattern of the smaller garden beds on the northern verge, and their relationship with the grassed areas, offer structure. Pineapple guava (*Feijoa sellowiana*) hedges and climbers along fence lines are also structural.

Layering brings depth from canopy to understorey, shrub to ground cover, annual to perennial, ephemeral to enduring. Each layer adds complexity and resilience. But layering is not just vertical. It's also seasonal and temporal: a bulb that flowers in spring, a perennial that fills a space in summer, a tree that matures over decades. Rich layers create continuity across time.

Planting patterns – the mixture of perennials, edibles, herbs and medicinal plants – offer layering opportunities. Not just in three dimensions, but across the seasons: from verdant growth in spring and floriferous colour in summer to seed heads in autumn and stark but beautiful stems right through winter. Layering is the way light moves across the garden from early morning to late afternoon, bringing some things into focus while others recede into shadow. It's also the relationship between the height of plants and the light, and the way that one plant can serve many roles: cut flower, medicinal, ecological, biodiverse.

Good design balances both the clarity of structure and the softness of layering. When used in combination, they enrich the garden with order and abundance, they allow a garden to feel whole yet alive, and they add vital multifunctionality.

***Below left*_**The gravel circle on the western verge at Little Cottage on a Hill. A path draws you between the house and gate, while *Geum* 'Totally Tangerine' and oriental poppies (*Papaver orientale*) stitch the verge beds together so structure and season read as one.
***Below middle*_**Clipped English box (*Buxus sempervirens*) balls are the backbone of the western verge garden. Around that repeated form, a drift of *Geum* 'Totally Tangerine' softens the edges and carries early-summer colour through the planting.
Below right*_Geum* 'Totally Tangerine' in early summer. This single colour becomes structure, repeated in small notes across the verge so the layered planting feels cohesive rather than busy.

Opposite page,
Top_At Little Cottage on a Hill, lawn and gravel set the framework and spatial order, with spade-cut bed edges and steel edging holding the geometry. Within that structure, layered planting adds depth, texture and density.
Bottom_Little Cottage on a Hill from the north, looking south. Layered planting and vertical structures create depth, while the sightline holds the distant Great Dividing Range.

Glossary of structure and layering terms

These words are associated with structure:

- **Framework** is the underlying skeleton that shapes and supports the garden's spaces.
- **Spatial order** is the deliberate arrangement of spaces to guide movement and experience.
- **Armature** is a supportive backbone that holds elements together, often invisible but essential.
- **Backbone** is the main structural feature giving coherence and clarity to the design.
- **Geometry** is the pattern of shapes and lines that organise the garden.
- **Infrastructure** is the set of built systems, such as paths, irrigation and boundaries, that sustains the garden.
- **Hierarchy** is the system of ranking spaces or elements according to their importance or role.
- **Form-giving elements** are the features that define the shape and character of the garden.

These words are associated with layering:

- **Stratification** is the arrangement of plants or materials in vertical layers, offering depth and complexity.
- **Succession** is the changing sequence of planting or growth over time.
- **Overlay** is the placement of one element atop another, creating richness and meaning.
- **Texture** is the feel and appearance of garden materials, from smooth leaves to rough bark.
- **Depth** is the sense of distance or layering that creates spatial richness.
- **Density or opacity** is how tightly plants or elements are grouped, affecting visibility and atmosphere.
- **Multivalence** is the ability of a space or element to express several meanings or functions at once.

Other important words to know:

- **Matrix** is a background network of plants or forms that knits the garden together.
- **Spatial hierarchy** is the arrangement of spaces in order of prominence or intimacy.
- **Framework planting** is the key planting that establishes structure and lasting presence.
- **Compositional depth** is the layered arrangement of forms, colours and textures to create visual and experiential richness.

MULTIFUNCTIONAL INFRASTRUCTURE

The best gardens work hard. This means that their elements are doing two or more things at the same time. When every element contributes more than one service, the whole system is stronger, more dynamic, more efficient and more giving. Therefore multifunctionality makes gardens resilient.

Paths can be both circulation spaces and permeable water soaks. They can define areas, create gathering spaces and reflect light in a shaded part of the garden. A wall is an enclosure, but it can also be a windbreak, a habitat, a vertical garden and an orchard. In this way it serves multiple functional and experiential roles while also offering visual delight. A water tank is storage, but it can also be a threshold or a separating element that obscures an undesirable view. A pergola or an arbour offers shade, but it can also be a structure for climbing plants and an invitation to gather.

This kind of layering of purpose means that no part of the garden is redundant. Every investment earns its keep. Multifunctional infrastructure also ties human use to ecological functions. Compost bins become nutrient cycles. Swales become habitat corridors. Beehives become both a source of pollination and productivity. What looks like practicality is also philosophy: designing in ways where a garden holds people, place and ecology all at once.

At Oak & Monkey Puzzle, even the ground plane was multifunctional. The gravel between the beds in the cut-flower garden offered the opportunity to display a sculpture, to rest a wheelbarrow when clearing out a bed at the end of winter, to lay out a harvest and even to dry the fruits of my labour. The deck in front of the converted shipping container became a place for morning tea, a pruning bench in winter, and a space for a micro wedding ceremony. At other times, it was simply somewhere to sit and take in the afternoon sun.

*Right*_The driveway courtyard as the studio forecourt. It is a multifunctional space that works as arrival, circulation and a place to sit and take in the light.
*Far right*_Ivy sits on an antique campaign chair, a small pause within the working garden.

Above _A driveway that behaves like a courtyard. At Little Cottage on a Hill, the gravel forecourt outside my studio is a circulation space, an outdoor room and a place to pause. Willow and Ivy are often beside me while I read in the afternoon sun.
Far left _Old copper boilers repurposed as large planters. Utilitarian objects can become generous herb beds and working containers.
Left _Gravel as a canvas. Large pots and movable elements let the studio forecourt expand and contract, turning a practical access space into an extra growing zone and a working courtyard, depending on what the day needs.

What multifunctional infrastructure looks like on a garden plan

Use walls, pergolas and trellises for both enclosure and microclimate. Design the circulation – your network of garden paths and routes for movement – to also manage water, drainage, infiltration and collection. Let tanks, ponds and swales act as water storage and habitat. Treat compost, beehives and wicking beds as human utilities and ecological services. Seek at least two functions for every element before you draw the detail.

Versatility on a smaller scale

I would argue that multifunctional infrastructure is even more important in smaller spaces because the constraints of size amplify the need for each element to work harder.

At Little Cottage on a Hill, the driveway is a courtyard, a forecourt and an access way. It's an invitation into the property, but also a space where I can pull in my caravan. Fence lines are boundaries between property titles, but they have also become vertical gardens and backdrops to sightlines. They create depth by lifting the garden from the ground plane into the vertical.

The growing frames on the northern verge provide thresholds and arbours between the beds, but they also carry all manner of productive climbers that would not otherwise have a place in such a small site.

The wicking beds are little gardens in their own right, but together the modules do so much more. They combine waterwise gardening with ergonomic design, helping to reduce my water bill while also eliminating the need for me to bend over while working. As well as being sculptural, they create microclimates and produce an incredible harvest. Cohesion is achieved through their materiality, their colour and their connection with the broader extent of the garden.

Glossary of multifunctional infrastructure terms

You'll encounter these terms throughout the chapter, so let's take a moment to get familiar with what they mean.

- **Programmed space** is an area shaped for a specific use, but open to adaptation.
- **Adaptive design** is design that responds and evolves in step with climate, community and daily rhythms.
- **Layered infrastructure** is the stacking of networks, such as water, soil, access and shelter, to support life in many ways at once.
- **Performative landscape** is a garden that gives more than it takes, offering beauty, yield and habitat.
- **Working landscape** is a space where productivity and purpose shape the design.
- **Green infrastructure** is the living system of plants, soil and water in the garden.
- **Hybrid system** is a mix of built and living elements that work together for human and ecological benefit.
- **Multi-benefit design** is when each part of the garden serves at least two roles.
- **Ecosystem service** is a garden function, such as pollination, water filtration or cooling shade, that sustains living things.
- **Resilient system** is a garden design that can adapt, bounce back and keep functioning through change and challenge.
- **Productive landscape** is any space shaped to yield food, resources or wellbeing.

RESTRAINT AND BREATH

A garden needs discipline as much as it needs generosity. Restraint holds back the impulse to add more, more, more. It allows certain elements to stand clear and be read without distraction. A limited palette of plants combined with repeated materials ensures that restraint creates clarity.

Breath is the counterpoint. It's the openness between gestures, the spaces left unplanted, the intervals that let the eyes and body rest. Breath gives proportion. It allows the garden to feel spacious, even in tight ground. Where restraint edits, breath releases.

Together, restraint and breath create balance while preventing clutter, suffocation and overstimulation. This design principle is not about austerity, but self-control.

A hedge reads more strongly when it's not competing with ten other forms. A bed of Lenten roses (*Helleborus × hybridus*) is more powerful when it's given some space around it. A highly detailed perennial garden sings with a clean edge and a surrounding materiality that contrasts with the flower colours.

By knowing when to contract and when to expand, you'll ensure that your garden gains coherence and calm. It's that moment in a painter's journey when they know to put the brush down because if they don't, the art becomes a muddy, overworked mess. It's the place between order and tangle, between chaos and legibility. It's the difference between having a home that's lived in and purposeful, and one that feels like a hoarder's paradise.

What restraint and breath look like on a garden plan

Limit planting palettes to a coherent set of species, textures or tones that are repeated for effect. Use material continuity to unify zones across the site. Leave negative space to provide proportion. Balance voids and solids, built mass and open areas. Decide what to omit before choosing what to add.

TIME AS A MATERIAL

A garden is never fixed; it's always in flux, always in the process of becoming. Consequently, time can be treated as a material in the same way as soil, stone or water. It shapes what can be seen and what is yet to come, what is anticipated and what is revealed.

Designing with time means thinking within the scales of growth and change. Seeds sprout in days. Perennials fill in over seasons. An espalier takes form over years. Trees unfold their presence across decades.

A path can remain constant, but the plantings around it may envelop and narrow the edge. The canopy above will close in, altering light and temperature. A bare bed in winter will be abundant by midsummer. Patience and prospect become part of the design language. The gardener learns to read what is present while holding what is still to come.

Time also gives texture. Eroding stone, moss on timber or leaves composting into soil enrich the garden as much as any planting plan. To work with time as a material is to accept impermanence and to design for succession, renewal and adaptation.

The true structure of a garden includes years, seasons and cycles. It's the way a maturing hedge frames a view, or equally impedes one. It's the emergence of ephemeral layers, as at Little Cottage on a Hill, where bulbs rise just as the winter growth is decaying. It's designing for patina and weathering, the forces of nature that improve hard surfaces with age.

What access and comfort look like on a garden plan

Design the circulation first, then place comfort elements at the pauses. Maintain suitable path widths and gradients for ease of walking, planned activities, tools, wheelchairs and wheelbarrows. Choose surfaces that are stable underfoot and appropriate for all seasons. Orientate seating and gathering areas towards winter sun and summer shade. Use windbreaks, hedges and walls to create protected microclimates.

Opposite page,
Top left_A crisp interface between lawn and bed makes circulation legible on the northern verge, clearly signalling where you walk and where planting begins.
Top right_At the western verge entry, the antique steel gate and the visually permeable timber-and-wire fence share the same rhythm of solid and void, offering physical access and a clear line of sight between street and garden.
Bottom left_The fence's open weave lets grasses and perennials move through, softening the boundary and creating a living threshold between public verge and private garden.
Bottom right_Gravel underfoot, English box (*Buxus sempervirens*) balls in the ground plane and a fastigiate Lebanese crabapple (*Malus trilobata*) selected for its narrow footprint keep door-swing space clear and access comfortable in the driveway courtyard.

ACCESS AND COMFORT

Successful garden design considers how people enter, move through and utilise the space. Access is the framework of circulation: paths, thresholds, steps, and the surfaces that make a garden legible and usable. It's about the practical elements, such as alignment, slope, width and surface texture, that ensure everyone can reach the places where life and function occur.

Comfort is what happens once you arrive. It's the ergonomics of seating, the orientation of benches, the balance of sun and shade. It's the way a hedge shields you from wind, or a wall stores and radiates warmth into the evening. Comfort is designed as much as access. It depends on microclimate and proportions, as well as material choices that make a space feel settled and welcoming.

Without access, a garden is a folly. Without comfort, it's only a corridor. Together, access and comfort transform gardens from visual settings into inhabited environments. Access ensures continuity of movement, while comfort offers quality of rest and experience. One promotes flow. The other supports sojourn. They both create a space in which it's possible to live well.

Glossary of access and comfort terms

These words are associated with access:

- **Circulation** is the movement of people, water, wind, animals or energy through a garden, shaped by paths, openings and plantings to support ecological flows, sensory experience and everyday access.
- **Spatial legibility** is how clearly and intuitively a garden reveals its structure and the relationships between places, making navigation effortless.

These words are associated with comfort:

- **Inhabitation** is the feeling of being welcomed and settled in a garden space.
- **Amenity** is the presence of features, such as shade, seating, water and beauty, that enhance everyday ease and enjoyment.
- **Ergonomics** is the thoughtful shaping of spaces and elements for fit, comfort and graceful use.
- **Microclimate** is a unique local garden atmosphere created by sun, shade, wind and shelter.
- **Refuge** is a space designed to feel safe, sheltered and restorative.
- **Dwelling** is a deeper, lingering presence within a space.

Nº 1

What generosity and exchange look like on a garden plan

Plant with surplus in mind: one for you, one for pollinators, one to share. Include exchange systems such as compost, seed saving, cuttings and water cycling. Provide habitat layers, from a single birdbath to a full hedgerow. Design for scale of giving, from a pot on a balcony and a border in a backyard to a grove on a hillside. Build generosity into the plan before you count what the garden offers.

GENEROSITY AND EXCHANGE

A garden is not only what it holds, but also what it gives. Generosity is built into the very nature of plants. One seed becomes hundreds. One flower draws in pollinating insects from far away. One tree can shade a family, house birds and feed ladybirds. Exchange follows naturally. Soil trades nutrients for leaf litter. Flowers swap nectar for pollination. Gardeners share cuttings and harvests across fences.

Generosity in design doesn't depend on size. A balcony pot of basil (*Ocimum basilicum*) can flavour a meal and scent the air just as surely as a field of herbs can feed a community. A small wildlife corner offers as much ecological service as a hedgerow across a paddock. Scale shifts the form, but never the principle.

When generosity and exchange are part of a garden's design, the space becomes more than a private area. It becomes a participant in the wider web: feeding, sheltering, sharing, connecting, building community. The return is not only harvest, but belonging.

A verge planted with a few edible species and herbs, containing a little sign that says, 'Feel free to pick me', creates a neighbourhood. A chair placed on the nature strip, laden with extra produce in the height of summer's glut, creates relationships. And bunches of flowers, at a time when a community is in mourning, foster shared empathy and a sense of grieving.

A few years ago, there was a tragic accident in the centre of Daylesford where five people were killed by a runaway car (the driver had had a hypoglycaemic episode). Not knowing how to contribute in any meaningful way given the gravity of the incident, I did what I often do when I feel lost: I made bouquets from flowers in my garden. This time, I put them out on the street with an urn of hot water, some cups and tea. I sent an invitation to my community: if you're struggling, grab a posy and share it with someone in need, such as a first responder or a neighbour. This gave me a sense of purpose, and a way to navigate through the discomfort of big feelings. And it allowed me to connect with my community in a time of need.

I have done this before. At Oak & Monkey Puzzle, in the middle of my court battles and my most difficult times, there was one night at Christmas when I was deep in crippling anxiety and I couldn't sleep. So I got up and made floral arrangements from gathered garden cuttings. I placed them on the roadside with a sign inviting people to take them, to share them with others who might also be struggling.

Gardens allow connection like nothing else does. They are my love language, how I express generosity. Oak & Monkey Puzzle was also a place where collaborations, skills, stories, produce and experiences were exchanged. At a fraction of the size, Little Cottage on a Hill is still able to offer and share in the same way. Generosity and exchange can occur at any scale.

VALUABLE VOICES OF SCALE

In the following features, we step into a handful of gardens and projects to look closely at the devices that make scale legible: the way a seat holds the body, how a fence becomes an orchard, how a path also carries service and season. Each contributor shows a clear move that works in a large or small way, and why it holds.

For each, I've pointed out something to watch for: their scale lens, one move that can be adjusted up or down, or a small thing that you can try. The language remains the same as that used in the first half of the chapter: clarity of purpose, rhythms and pauses, rooms and edges, thresholds and views, structure and layering, multifunctional infrastructure, restraint and breath, time, access and comfort, generosity and exchange. However, it's just viewed through different sites and climates.

CONNIE CAO

An abundant city plot

Connie Cao is a Melbourne-based urban gardener and author whose modest backyard proves that intention, rhythm and cultural awareness can transform a compact site into a place of plenty: what she calls 'a farm in suburbia'. In 2024, she published *Your Asian Veggie Patch*, a beginner-friendly guide that marries cultivation with family recipes and seasonal cooking. The book's premise is simple and generous: grow what you love to eat, and let the garden carry meaning as well as yield. The

Connie Cao's 'farm in suburbia', a compact city garden where every corner is used. Netting, greenhouse structure and dense planting support abundance.

Connie Cao's suburban plot layers flowers, edibles and protected growing spaces into one productive and beautiful garden.

beauty here is not a set piece; it's the pleasure of tending a place that gives back, week after week.

The garden that anchors her work measures around 170 square metres (1830 square feet), including a 20-square-metre (215-square-foot) patio. When Connie and her husband moved in eight years ago, the yard was 'pretty much weeds and mulch that soon turned into weeds'. Rather than rushing to plant, she spent a year watching light and shadow, growing seeds in pots to test different positions, and 'resting and thinking' until the logic of the place revealed itself.

From there, she worked on one project at a time. The first big step was soil and structure: raised beds for annual vegetables to get above heavy clay, in a pattern of four rectangles with two horseshoe beds to maximise reach and flow. Losing crops to wildlife forced a quick revision. She enclosed the productive core with a DIY aviary-mesh frame and overhead netting, a family build led by her engineer father that turned frustration into resilience.

The following years layered function and delight. A small greenhouse for seed raising. Vertical frames to soften fences and lift fruiting canes. Arches for beans and berries. A chicken run and coop to fold scraps and manure into soil. A quiet rhythm of compost, worm farms and rainwater on tap. Flowers arrived both as habitat and as joy. 'I always thought I needed to live on a farm to grow all the food I wanted, but I keep amazing myself at how much I can squeeze into a backyard . . . growing in a small space makes you more creative.'

'Year by year, we tackled one big project at a time.'

Connie's design voice is shaped by family heritage. The Australian-born daughter of Chinese parents, she grew up eating an array of Chinese vegetables – many without knowing their English names – and learned to grow them while working in the garden alongside her dad. Culture is part of her brief. She grows Asian greens from family seeds, trades seedlings with friends, and gifts harvests over the fence. Plants become a language, a way to share stories, recipes and memories across a street, a city, a country. Her garden now holds winter melon (*Benincasa hispida*), amaranth greens (*Amaranthus tricolor*) and more, as much for reminiscence and cuisine as for showing what's possible on a small suburban block.

'I always thought I needed to live on a farm to grow all the food I wanted, but I keep amazing myself at how much I can squeeze into a backyard . . . growing in a small space makes you more creative.'

Tips for designing at a small scale

If you're standing at a balcony rail or a bare courtyard and wondering where to begin, Connie's lens is clear: picture the plan in rooms and edges, from the kitchen to a compact axis of beds, each within easy reach. Then pick one project, make it beautiful enough that you will visit it every day, and let the garden teach you the rest.

Cadence is incremental in Connie's garden, with time in between projects to live with the change. Beds first, then netting, then a greenhouse, then chickens. That rhythm keeps labour realistic and the design responsive. 'Starting with fewer beds let me build confidence and time management before expanding.' The effect she is eventually seeking is 'magical jungle' or 'secret garden', layered and alive and still legible. Gardening has taught her patience, proportion and care.

Connie's garden is practical, but its ease matters as much as its yield. She tucks seats where the body would rest anyway. Paths invite slow loops. Taller plantings are sited behind seating in such a way that visitors feel held, with glimpses outward to keep orientation. These are scalable safety cues that in Connie's compact setting have become the difference between a yard you cross and a garden you inhabit.

What the work has taught her

Connie describes gardening as a life skill that builds food security and steadies the mind. She learned to begin modestly, to experiment, to enjoy the 'making' as much as the harvest. She discovered that smallness sharpens creativity, that cultural plants carry belonging, and that community multiplies the reach of a tiny plot. The result is a place that feeds her kitchen and her practice: a garden grown by seasons, not spectacle, and a public body of work that gives others the courage to begin.

How Connie's garden teaches scale

Connie's compact garden is a vibrant classroom for design at a small scale. Every corner is shaped by intention: watching, revising and letting beauty grow out of what the site, culture and family make possible. Her lessons are simple and lived. They remind us that creativity and abundance aren't measured in square metres, but in how deeply you notice, adapt and share.

— **Start with appetite:** Plant for the way you cook and share; keep the productive heart within arm's reach of the house.
— **Use rooms and names:** Small plots feel considered and grounding when edges hold space and each pocket has a purpose ('raspberry lane', 'flower aisle').
— **Lift vertically without clutter:** Arches, trellises and mesh soften fences and turn boundaries into fruiting larders.
— **Protect the core:** A simple, well-built enclosure returns time and harvest by reducing heartbreak caused by wildlife.

Scan to watch my full conversation with Connie Cao, where we talk about designing for abundance in small spaces, cultural connections through growing food, and how patience and iteration shape resilient, beautiful gardens.

— **Water slow, soil first:** Have compost and worms on a loop. Use drippers so water can soak; 'a slow drip lets the soil actually drink'.
— **Let flowers work:** Pollinators, beneficial insects and people all respond to blooms. Beauty is a tool here, not a garnish.
— **Build in layers, gradually:** One significant project each season allows the garden to grow into comfort and capacity.

CHRISTIAN DOUGLAS

Food-forward blend of botanicals

Christian Douglas is a British-born Californian designer whose work seamlessly integrates food, ecology and beauty as one harmonious garden. He places productive planting where life already happens, and uses structure and proportion so that edible and ornamental are not at odds. His practice meets people where they are and provides a clear path from interest to action.

Christian dissolves the old divide between ornamental and productive. He cultivates food plants near doors, along paths and beside seating, ensuring that there is adequate sunlight for the elements that need it most. He uses perennial edibles as structure, so the garden reads as composed across the year. Annual crops are concentrated where water and attention are abundant, and their frames are designed so that the space still looks good when the beds are resting. A shallow rill invites children and pollinators. A line of fruiting species along a fence turns an edge into a harvest. His stance is generous and practical: make the path from interest to practice short and joyful. 'My hope is that we remove the term edible, and just call them "landscapes".'

'My hope is that we remove the term edible, and just call them "landscapes".'

Design principles across scale

Christian's practice bridges conventional landscape design and permaculture so that food, ecology and beauty read as one garden, not as separate zones. This is how he incorporates other design principles:

— **Clarity of purpose:** Being 'food forward' means growing edibles where hands already work and where life happens. Keep the productive heart beside doors, paths and seats so it's used daily.
— **Rhythms and pauses:** Rills and meadows create a soft, repeating tempo that also offers clear places to rest.
— **Rooms and edges:** Fruiting fences and espaliered lines transform boundaries into abundant edges of yield.
— **Structure and layering:** Perennial edibles (trees, berries, herbs) are year-round structure; annuals are seasonal layers concentrated where water and attention are available.
— **Multifunctional infrastructure:** Crafted frames and beds look good even at rest; retaining walls, pool edges and paths can carry crops.
— **Access and comfort:** Paths and thresholds double as reach and routine.
— **Generosity and exchange:** 'Meet people where they are,' and make the journey from interest to practice simple and enjoyable.

Scan to watch my full conversation with Christian Douglas, where we talk about bridging conventional and permaculture design, the food-forward philosophy, and designing gardens that are abundant, ecological and beautiful at any scale.

A habitat-rich garden by Christian Douglas, designed for reduced water demand and shaped around orchard trees, productive terraces, native planting and places for rest, including a camp-fire seating area and a cedar sauna above. Purposefully conceived as a residential wellness retreat for an athletic family, the garden reflects Christian's food-forward approach. Beauty, ecology and daily life are designed as one considered whole.

Christian's tips for garden organisation can work at any scale:

- **Share the sun:** Map the sunlight first. Give the sunniest spot to food plants, then 'share' what's left of the light across ornamentals and play areas.
- **Lift verticals without heavy shade:** Arches and trellises along paths and fence lines add yield and enclosure without darkening small sites.
- **Concentrate care:** Keep high-input annuals where water and tools are within a few steps; let perennials carry the year-round composition elsewhere.
- **Design for the off-season:** Make frames, edging and bed geometry beautiful so the garden reads well when vegie beds are resting.
- **Invite play and pollinators:** A shallow rill with mini-bridges is safe for children and holds their attention for hours, and it draws insects; habitat, learning and delight in one gesture.

'When you grow food close to the house, people garden more, they learn quicker, they eat healthier.'

Ways to garden with others

If your space is limited or non-existent, then consider collaborative tending. You may have an elderly neighbour who has rich soil but needs a hand to keep things safe and orderly. Join a small group that takes on an allotment together. Borrow a friend's verge that can carry herbs and flowers for the street. Ensure that you have clear agreements that keep generosity at the centre. Share skills, share the harvest, and share small costs that make the garden workable.

Set up a shelf or table with seedlings and cuttings to share. Host a seasonal working bee and eat together at the end. Keep a short list of jobs that suit different bodies and various ages. Community multiplies the effect of a small garden and softens the labour of a large one.

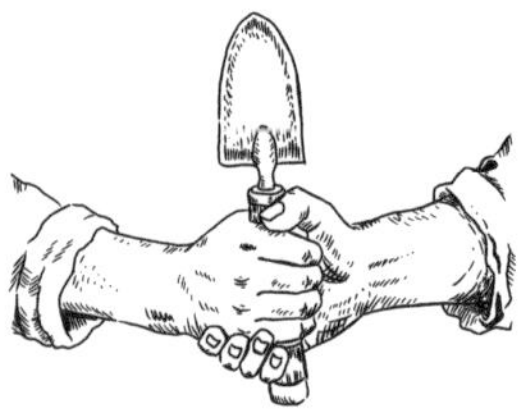

TRANSLATING DESIGN DEVICES FOR DIFFERENT SPACES

With the scale lenses in mind, the devices that follow read as invitations, not rules. They're ways to make scale feel human wherever you begin. Here's how I translate the same principles when space is tight:

— **Vertical lift with light touch:** Use slim frames, basic arches and airy trellises that give height without casting heavy shade. Train climbers where they can cool a window or frame a view. Keep the geometry and materiality consistent so the space reads as clearly connected.

— **Negative space as generosity:** Leave a strip of open ground or gravel inside a tight layout. It becomes a workspace, a place to sit, and a respite that allows the planting to be seen. In a small garden, this single act can transform the space's ambience for the better.

— **Borrowed landscape without clutter:** Frame a distant tree, a sky window or a nearby hillside. Use a narrow opening to guide the eye. Keep plant heights graded so the view is readable from the spot where you sit most often.

— **Storage and reach:** Position a small tool rail or a lidded box within easy reach of the main bed. Keep a bucket near the tap. Put a hook for a hose where your hand already passes. Design for how you work, tend and enjoy. Ease is the goal.

And here is how I hold clarity when scale is generous:

— **Rooms with long views:** Use hedges, tree lines, low walls and changes in ground to shape garden rooms. Keep a few long views clean so the garden feels generous rather than busy or constrained. Use repetition of form to stitch rooms together.

— **Axes and pauses:** Strengthen one or two main lines through the garden. Give them places to pause that are simple and generous: a gravel circle with a tree; a bench or seat at a crossing. This makes a large place legible to new visitors and restful for the people who tend it.

— **Multipurpose platforms:** Identify surfaces that can be utilised in different ways throughout the year. A deck that can host teaching. A lawn that can hold a table. A broad step that also serves as a place to sit while pruning or harvesting herbs. Plan the access, lighting and power points early so that shifts in use are easy to accommodate.

TRANSLATING SCALE FOR VARIED CLIMATES AND SPACES

The following ideas demonstrate how clarity of purpose, rhythms, rooms, edges and multifunctional structure can be adapted to different levels of heat, cold, wind or urban glare, and how a balcony, courtyard, verge, backyard or acreage translates that intelligence into everyday movements. Think of them as small rehearsals for bigger seasons: design tuned to place so that care, experience and habitation can scale with your life.

Hot and dry

Design for maintaining shade, slowing water and covering soil. Keep planting where you can reach it with ease. Use light verticals for climbers so shade arrives without heavy structure. Choose surfaces that don't radiate heat back into the garden. Hold water where roots can drink rather than letting it run across the ground surface.

Cold and wet

Lift roots out of saturated ground. Keep paths permeable and sure underfoot. Offer shelter from wind near the places you work. Use structure to hold form through winter so the garden looks composed while seasonal plants rest. Place compost and tools where you can reach them without crossing boggy ground.

Windy conditions

Work with the wind rather than fight it at every edge. Rooms can be created with hedges that filter rather than block air movement. Use planting and built elements to make lees. Keep taller planting on the windward side, and on the leeward side, provide a clear place to sit and work. Secure loose items, and keep surfaces stable.

Urban heat and glare

First shade the part of the garden that receives harsh afternoon sun. Lighten the colour of hard surfaces where you can, and add vertical greenery to cool walls. Choose pale, matt mulches that don't hold heat (such as straw or sugarcane mulch). Bring water close to plant roots, and give it time to soak in. Use permeable frames so air can move. Make a small place to sit where a passing breeze can cool the skin.

Late spring on the verge. Repurposed timber-and-wire fence panels are leaned to create simple A-frames through the beds that give rhythm and vertical lift while the planting grows back after its spring cut. It is a repeatable device I use at any scale, supported here by cloche hoops for seasonal protection.

Things to try this week

Now it's time to take scalable design principles and bring them into practice in your own garden, regardless of its size.

If you have a balcony:

- Place three deep containers close to the doorway so tending becomes easy.
- Intermingle species in the containers or keep one pot for flowers to bring pollinators and to lift your mood.
- Add one light trellis for a climber that provides verticality and late-afternoon shade.
- Use a slow watering method so the soil is moist but not saturated.
- Set a small hook for tools where you often work so that you can reach them easily and keep them tidy.

If you have a courtyard:

- Establish one clear axis from the door to a seat where the body wants to rest.
- Keep the material used underfoot light and generous.
- Use a pair of slim arches to form a room and to carry productive climbers.
- Select one hedge or a cluster of clipped shrubs to maintain structure in winter.
- Keep storage near a tap so cleaning and packing up at day's end is easy.

If you have a verge:

- — Plant tough herbs and flowers that invite conversation and help pollinators.
- — Design verge edges with open fencing, slats, mesh or spaced plants that let neighbours see in and encourage easy conversation.
- — Use an uncomplicated rhythm of repeated plants so the verge reads as considered and cohesive.
- — Choose mulch that stays put and doesn't wash into the street.
- — Add a small sign that invites seedling swaps and seasonal sharing.

If you have a backyard:

- — Build a workspace near the house with a bench, a tap and tool hooks.
- — Concentrate annuals or higher-maintenance plants where water and attention are readily available.
- — Use hedges, step-over espaliers or low walls to form clear garden rooms aligned with your design brief's functions.
- — Grow a fruiting species up a fence to turn an edge into a larder.
- — Leave a gravelled area or threshold as a multifunctional recess and workspace.

If you have an acreage:

- — Strengthen one or two long views, and protect them from visual clutter.
- — Use hedgerows and tree lines to create garden rooms, temper the wind and establish microclimates.
- — Keep paths permeable and sized for movement, gathering and the equipment you use.
- — Place the water and compost so that the wheelbarrow route is short, dry and strategically accessible.
- — Plan one multipurpose platform, deck or gravel/lawn expanse that can shift from workspace to play area with ease.

Across a balcony, a courtyard, a verge, a backyard or an acreage, the same intelligence holds: design allows care to scale. Begin with what matters, then set rhythms, rooms and edges that hold those priorities in place. Keep structures simple and layer with restraint so the garden reads well in all seasons. Place systems where they're easy to use, and ensure that paths and access routes follow the natural ways people and water move through the garden. Stay attuned to climate and place. Let the garden teach you, and adjust it as your life changes. When these ideas are present, any space can hold a productive, beautiful and well-lived life. And you'll have the capacity to invite others into the making and the harvest, which we'll do in Chapter 13.

CASS HOOKE

Shade, slow water, calm abundance

Cass Hooke is a grower and educator working through hot, dry summers and limited rainfall on the Hay Plains of New South Wales. Her gardens demonstrate what abundance can mean when heat and dryness are constants: healthy soil, a resilient structure, and planting that earns its keep. Summers routinely climb into the high 40s Celsius (110s Fahrenheit); winters are cold with regular frosts. Annual rain is sparse (about 360 millimetres; 14 inches). In this climate, winter and the shoulder seasons are the most productive times; summer is when the garden goes into survival mode.

Climate rhythm: A winter gardener by necessity

Cass's most productive window is autumn through to spring. In the summer, she pares back her activities, keeps living plants shaded and watered on a drip system, and focuses on planning, repairs and small, achievable tasks. 'My motivation peaks from autumn to spring . . . in summer it's about keeping things alive.' This is time as a material: winter for making, summer for survival, with shoulder seasons for adjustment.

The borrowed landscape can be brown and severely parched, so she has planted hedges and trees to create enclosure and a green view. In this climate of extremes, garden rooms and edges are wind-filtered and shade-held, with views edited for calm.

Water logic: Drip placement and bore realities

The garden relies on bore water, which is delivered by drip line to let roots drink slowly; overhead watering is avoided because bore water is sulphurous and saline, so it can mark or burn foliage. During rare periods of rainfall, there is always a visible boost in growth; Cass collects rainwater for the house. Garden beds and projects are placed where water and tools are close to hand, so care remains realistic when heat arrives.

Soil strategy: Build structure, keep it covered

Cass is frank about being 'impatient' and practical with soil. She brought in soil to break up heavy clay and improve drainage, and has continued to build the soil with compost (including bulk deliveries when viable), blood and bone, worm castings and mulch.

For isolated gardeners, she suggests buying compost in bulk and mixing it with available loam/topsoil, using whatever machinery is on hand. It's a realistic way to start when inputs are scarce. Woodchips from arborists are gold if you have space to store them. Cass's ground is never left bare.

Shade by design (not improvisation)

Shade is planned into the layout. Arbours, pergolas, light frames and climbers are used to cool paths and gathering spaces; hedges and trees establish long-term protection and a sense of enclosure in vast, open landscapes. Projects are scaled to fit the season's energy and the demands of farm and family.

Scaling Cass's approach

Here's how to bring Cass's ideas into your own green space:

- For a balcony or small garden, begin with one raised container or a short bed that you'll visit daily. Run a slow drip line, and mulch so the water holds. Add a light screen for afternoon shade.
- For a suburban yard, add a shade line (such as a light arbour, hedge or screen) where the afternoon sun bites. Concentrate planting close to your water source. Keep soil covered all year.
- For an acreage, consider shelter belts and shade trees. Choose plants that tolerate bore water and seasonal extremes. Carefully site compost, water and other care systems so the route between them and the garden beds is as short as possible.

Scan to watch my full conversation with Cass Hooke, where we talk about gardening in extreme heat and drought, practical water and soil strategies, and building resilient, beautiful gardens with what's available.

Cass Hooke's garden on the Hay Plains in New South Wales, an oasis built by design. Shade, slow water and resilient planting create a sense of verdant respite within a demanding, semi-arid landscape.

Planting: Resilient anchors that do more than one job

Plant choices are frost-hardy and heat-tolerant, suited to poor rainfall and bore water. Cass favours plants that support birds and beneficial insects (and reduce pests) alongside edibles. 'Productivity for me is having a healthy garden.' Abundance here is not showiness, it's a living system that holds together under stress.

How Cass's garden teaches scale

Cass's approach to scale is shaped by a demanding climate: she adapts through careful observation, incremental projects and practical choices tailored to what's possible each season. Her garden demonstrates that real abundance comes from starting small, working with what you have, and building resilience through sharing and flexibility. These are the lessons that guide her, no matter the site or challenge.

- **Start small, then extend:** Each garden is unique; discover your microclimates before scaling.
- **Locate vegies close to the house:** Proximity wins, especially when heat reduces bandwidth.
- **Design for the year you'll get:** Some years are harsher; restraint protects calm. Summer heat demands pragmatic choices.
- **Let community lighten the load:** Share tips, seedlings, materials.

The constant is viable, considered design that makes dry seasons survivable for both plants and people: observation first, small steps, then build what works in that climate.

'My motivation peaks from autumn to spring . . . in summer it's about keeping things alive.'

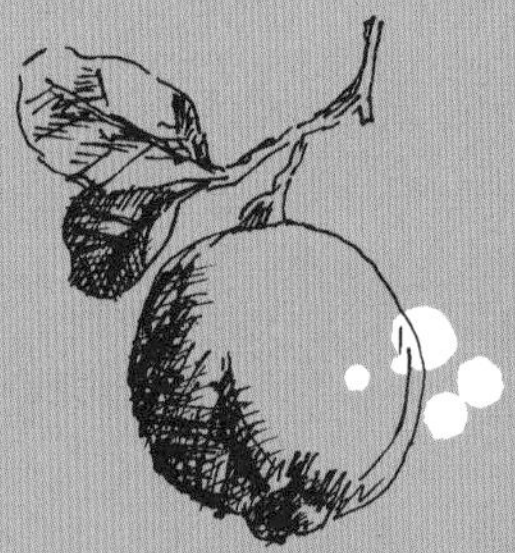

13
BUILDING COMMUNITY THROUGH GARDENING

I've never planned community, but I do make space for it in my garden. My foxgloves (Digitalis purpurea) *tower on the verge. Someone stops, smiles, asks if I'll save the seeds. Weeks later, I text them: 'Packet's in the letterbox.'*

CULTIVATING CONNECTION

I've joked for years that I built a life by accident from the end of the long bench at Cliffy's, a café that I call my other home and my office. In fact, I wrote most of this book there, cup of English breakfast tea beside my laptop, glancing over my screen occasionally at the customers as they walked in, the same parade of familiar faces.

I go there because I'm a creature of habit, a solo parent and an introvert who needs a soft entry point into the world each morning after parenting two extraordinary and neurodiverse young people and seeing them off to school. My daily morning-cuppa routine at Cliffy's is where I regroup, where I connect without a prearranged diary entry. Here, conversation finds me. And it's where all of my collaborations start, too. Since moving to the country, this café 'habit' has serendipitously rooted me deeply in community.

Growing and giving

People sometimes think I'm a social butterfly, a host-everything type. I'm definitely not. I've run fundraisers and long-table lunches when it mattered, but most of my community is built in the between spaces: over a fence, at the café, through a DM after I share on my socials what's flowering and why. Workshops help, of course; I've never had a room of gardeners who weren't big-hearted. Doing what I love, what I'm passionate about, this self-selects for generosity. Soil and season do, too.

What I've learned is this: grow a little more than you need, and you'll meet the people you were meant to feed. Grow visibly, and someone will find their way in. Share the surplus – seedlings, jars, cut flowers, the odd 'free to take' – and a web forms without a plan or a strategy. That's what I love. And it constantly reminds me that what you offer in time, attention and care comes back as connection. Community is what we give and what returns.

I also know that community isn't just a gate left open and a kettle flicked on. It's asynchronous. It's the bag of lemons on the doorstep; the comment from someone who has been learning alongside me online for years; the person who tries my cockatoo-deterrent hack (see page 148) because their mangoes have been ravaged season after season, then messages back with their own possum-deterrent tips. It's a thousand small recognitions adding up to belonging.

I come from the world of design, so thresholds matter to me. How you arrive, where you pause, what you notice first, how it feels. The same thinking applies here. Community can be fostered through small design gestures. You can shape for it: a seat where people naturally stop, a verge that says welcome, a path wide enough for a gathering at dusk. You can also shape for quiet: a nook where a friend can sit among billowing grasses and confide that a loved one has just passed.

This chapter gathers the ways these things happen at my place, at yours, online, in shared soil, and reveals the people who make them tangible. All prove the same point: generosity is a practice, and gardens are very good at teaching it.

Finding your people (without forcing it)

Start where you already are. The café bench you sit at anyway. The verge you walk past daily. Put something there that signals 'yes': a pot of lemon balm (*Melissa officinalis*) with a handwritten tag; a tray of spare seedlings; a small sign that says 'ask me about the unusual beans'.

Keep some growing space for 'community overflow'. Plant those few extra seeds, and plan to give the produce away: parcels for neighbours, a swap box at the gate, posies for the corner shop.

Join and volunteer with local groups, such as the friends of your nearest botanic garden, the community garden's monthly swap, the school plot on Saturdays. You don't need to be in charge to belong; you only have to show up.

Check out the digital places built for gardeners. The Gardenstead online community is aimed at gardeners of all skill levels. It's designed for the questions you think are 'too basic', the small victories you worry aren't 'worthy' and the seasons when you need someone to say, 'That's normal.' It's gentle on purpose.

Host without hosting, by sharing the work you'd be doing anyway: 'I'm pruning on Sunday 10–12, secateurs on the table, tea's on.' People will come, help, ask.

Make room for quiet belonging. A seat with a view of a favourite bed. A path wide enough for two (or three or four!). A nook among the flowers where a hand can be held without the need for eye contact. Connection doesn't need to be organised, but if you make space for it, serendipity will find its way.

Western verge at Little Cottage on a Hill. The gravel circle sits on an overscaled path that offers a place to pause and catch up with neighbours. It is the kind of connection that grows when you make space for people.

THE KIND OF COMMUNITY A GARDEN MAKES

Daylesford has taught me how community stretches over fences, through letter-boxes, across wi-fi. I learned how it forms by doing, by showing up to the same seat at the same café, by answering the odd message about keeping gravel tidy and free from weeds, by leaving small and seemingly insignificant things on doorsteps with notes that say, 'For you.'

Most mornings, I go to Cliffy's because it connects me back into the world in a way that provides structure but also allows serendipity and trust to fill the gaps and shape the day from there. People find me there, but I don't have to be 'on'. I can talk about the black ice on the south side of the hill or how the 'Cambridge Rival' strawberry runners (which Lizzie the barista gifted me last season) are producing, and I can duck out when the words run thin or a different kind of focus calls.

That is how it has always unfolded for me, through side doors and in-between spaces. It's ironic that my work keeps bringing me, an introvert, back to people, to shared effort, to the kind of exchange that feels ordinary and generous at the same time. Generosity has been the only currency that's never left me feeling broke. I have given to a fault, and I have also received more than I knew how to ask for. When I say, 'The garden gave me that,' I mean it. It gave me a way to connect where I can truly be me, and so much more. It still does.

Holding me, and holding others

I grew up with the weight of expectation: be capable, be excellent, achieve, never rely on anyone. That script worked . . . until it didn't. I faced a difficult relationship, the slow admission of anxiety I could no longer out-organise, and then years as a solo parent of two neurodiverse kids, largely without family close by. I don't talk about this because I need sympathy, but because this is my truth and the situation that taught me how much a garden can hold me while I learned to hold other people.

When the kids were small and the house was loud, and there was no one coming at 6 pm to take over the chaos, I could step outside and do one useful thing. Tie in a cane. Water the beans. Pick enough for dinner, and a posy for the roadside stall. If a neighbour called past, I didn't have to find a script. We could stand side-by-side and talk about the barrage of millipedes that had come inside after the rain. It sounds small, and it was. But it was also everything. The garden made calm company possible when I didn't have the energy for more.

Now, I can see it clearly: the garden is where connection comes easiest for me because it's where I am most myself. Not because it's beautiful (although this helps), not because it's productive (although a harvest is always welcome), but because the pace makes sense. A bed will give if you tend it. A plant will sulk if you coax it into submission out of season. People aren't so different. The more I tuned my days to cycles and seasonal rituals instead of dates and accolades, the more steady, generous and unforced connection turned up.

In the years when I felt most alone, the garden grounded me, then sowed the seeds for other people to steady me, too. Parents at school asked what I was growing.

People out in the ether, who had read a post and then turned up at a workshop, nervous to step inside, left hours later with the joy and inspiration of learning and sharing etched across their faces. We almost always parted as friends. Community, for me, is a rhizome that grows more roots, burgeoning into new earth and unknown territory every time someone makes the choice to be authentic, generous, curious, warm . . . even for a minute.

Most days it looks small. I talk to someone at the café. I reply to a message late at night when the kids are asleep. I put spare zucchinis out on the verge and trust that they will walk themselves down the street. Some days it's bigger: a long-lunch table, a full workshop, a kitchen covered in autumn's harvest, a conveyor belt of bottles and sticky hands covered in syrup. The throughline is the same. I don't build community by making bigger asks. I build it by paying attention to what is already here, and by recognising that I need it, especially as a parent, especially when energy is thin, especially when the season asks more of me than I planned to give.

Inspirational connections

This chapter follows those threads, the quiet connectors, the impulse to give, the way knowledge moves through hands and seasons. It helps to see how other people do it, too.

Madeleine Gasparinatos and Emily Allen turned a friendship into a garden catch-up that you can join. Their *Avant Gardeners* podcast began at a friend's place in Cygnet, Tasmania, recorded so the talk could continue when life shifted, and it remains deliberately welcoming rather than credentialled. That welcome now extends to conversations with remarkable gardeners and thinkers from around the world, and it was through *Avant Gardeners* that I first connected with Charles Dowding, one of the most generous garden figures I've met. Tasmania sets Madeleine and Emily's tempo. What is sprouting now, what failed last week, what to savour because it's in season. Their community links are small yet powerful: an Instagram profile, a knowledgeable grocer, a walking group. The lesson is about permission: start small, share the misses and keep showing up together.

Patrick Vernuccio, aka The Frenchie Gardener, demonstrates what radical public visibility can achieve when it's held with a generous intention. By sowing seeds on a balcony in Amsterdam, he found a practice that steadied a racing work life. He began The Frenchie Gardener as a diary for friends, and strangers arrived; he co-founded Gardenstead, a gardening social-media app, so gardeners could ask real questions, talk in growing zones, and meet offline without the pressure of an ad-optimised algorithm. He demystifies gardening, from dividing supermarket basil to investing in good soil, expecting failure and learning by doing. His information is ordinary, warm and precise enough to be useful. That tone invites participation, which is exactly how community grows.

Opposite page_Cliffy's in Daylesford, Victoria. This corner of the produce counter is where I wrote this book, cup of tea in hand, perched at the communal bench. It is where neighbours drop in, conversations begin easily, strangers become friends, and one familiar seat can hold an entire web of care, generosity and belonging.

PEANUT BUTTER
CRISPY CHILLI OIL
RELISH
FANCY HANK'S
KETCHUP

'We thought: we'll get ten listeners or whatever.'

AVANT GARDENERS

A friendship on the air

I met Madeleine Gasparinatos and Emily Allen in a very modern way: via social-media posts, DMs, then a proper chat. I quickly realised that what they were making wasn't 'a gardening podcast' so much as a table to which you could pull up a chair. *Avant Gardeners* began the way all good projects do: with a group of friends – including Phyllida ('Pip') Steele-Wareham (see pages 166–7), whom I also now call a friend – sitting outside, swapping tips and stories while kids orbited, wine replacing coffee, and the talk never quite ending. When Pip moved away, the friends pressed record. Not to perform, just to keep the conversation going. They figured that ten people might listen. The point was fun, warmth and learning out loud. That tone is the community.

Tasmania shapes their voice. Seasonality is on loudspeaker there. You feel the hunkering down of winter, the market rush when Dave-the-seedling-guy is in, the group text when fruit trees land or the Woodbridge Fruit Tree Nursery sale counts down its final year. You eat what's best now because out-of-season tastes terrible once you've had a carrot dug an hour ago. That rhythm makes its way into every episode: what people are planting, what failed, what to savour, how the year rearranges your social life. It's not nostalgia; it's logistics, insights and joy intertwined.

Madeleine and Emily designed *Avant Gardeners* for welcome, not expertise. Questions are accessible by intent. Failures are shared first. Episodes open with a glass of something to warm things up, then gardening memories, and they often return to the same comfort: everyone starts somewhere, everyone kills plants, and

Madeleine Gasparinatos (left) and Emily Allen of *Avant Gardeners*. Through conversation that is warm, funny and grounded in real life, their podcast has become a generous meeting place for gardeners where curiosity, seasonal learning and community are given room to grow.

learning sticks when it's tethered to a story. Someone's son once ate Pip's apricots and said they tasted like 'sunshine'. That's their level: precise, human and unforgettable.

Their checks and balances are simple: are we still having fun? If the answer's yes, then they keep going. If something lands badly, then they edit for tone; not to polish the reality out of it, but to keep the space kind. Listeners write to say that they feel like they're in on a chat with friends, which is precisely the point. The social life of gardening matters as much as soil pH here. You're allowed to ask 'silly' questions. You're also allowed to not know what a blueberry grows on. (It's a bush, by the way; you'll never forget once you've picked them sun-warmed.)

'I've kind of got this buzz after we chat to every single person . . . "Oh my gosh, I need to do that tomorrow."'

Community, for them, looks like small bridges: a Facebook page where raspberry canes change hands; a grocer who labels provenance so kids start choosing by place; a walking group that becomes a gardening group if you're new in town and need to meet people. It's crop swaps, wicking-bed experiments promised for 'one day soon', and that feeling after a guest signs off when the podcast hosts have the buzz to try something tomorrow. The legacy they're building isn't numbers, it's permission to start small, to fail publicly, to treat silliness and approachability as teaching tools.

Madeleine and Emily have made a tender, durable doorway for people who want in to gardening but don't yet have the confidence or the language. They're proof that friendship is a viable infrastructure for a global community, that laughter is a vehicle for learning, and that visibility done with generosity can reduce intimidation instead of inflating it. I came to them as a guest and left feeling like a neighbour. That's the work done right.

Scan to hear my full conversation with Madeleine Gasparinatos and Emily Allen, where we talk about how a friendship became a community, how Tasmanian seasonality shapes everything, and why starting small and sharing failures builds confidence.

PATRICK VERNUCCIO

Radical visibility, gentle invitation

The first time Patrick tells you his balcony story, you can hear the moment his life tipped. He was in his mid-thirties, living in an Amsterdam apartment with a balcony. He bought packets of lettuce (*Lactuca sativa*) and radish (*Raphanus sativus*) seeds at the garden centre because they reminded him of his grandparents. Back at home, he had no idea what to do with them, so he threw the lot into potting mix and hoped for the best. Sprouts appeared. Wonder followed. A small domestic decision became a turning point: the Netflix corporate marketing strategist with a restless mind found something that grounded him. He didn't yet have the language for it beyond 'this makes me feel good', but he knew it would change his life.

What moved alongside that feeling was a shift in tempo. Gardening cushioned the anxiety that had been humming under his days: the need to be on, delivering, producing for 60+ hours a week. He started composting. He bought less, noticed more. The garden reframed value: time in cycles, not tasks; satisfaction in tending, not acquiring. He describes it as becoming more rooted. Not in a mystical way, just the precise sensation of being held by a practice that asks for presence.

The public part began almost as a joke. Back at the office, his colleagues teased him – 'Make an Instagram account for the balcony!' – so he did, using the nickname they'd given him for his accent. 'The Frenchie Gardener' wasn't a brand, but people soon became curious, then grateful, then brave enough to try for themselves.

'I don't take my phone at all. I just go in my garden and I enjoy.'

The balcony became a commons across cities, a thread between windowsills. That early intimacy never entirely left, even as the follower numbers climbed past a million.

Patrick doesn't trade in perfection. He shares the bit where he squints at a seed and can't imagine greenery coming from it; the part where he learns the hard way that not every herb is doomed (sometimes it's just overcrowded and needs dividing); the admission that the pull of a global followership can eat the pleasure out of the garden if he lets it. He has built guardrails: there are blocks of space and time where the phone stays inside; moments he keeps for himself so the practice remains his sanctuary, not only his stage. When the radical visibility of notoriety on public platforms surges, he steps back to protect the joy. He intentionally models that quiet and authentic leadership so newcomers learn not to burn the thing they love by broadcasting it excessively.

Enriching online community

I had long admired Patrick's work, but I first met him properly through Gardenstead; I now work alongside him as the Global Community Manager on the platform he co-founded to give gardeners a kinder and more authentic and connected place to gather. The idea behind Gardenstead is simple: it's a social space designed around genuine questions: what's sprouting now, what's eating the kale, where do I find a seed swap near me. You open the app, and the feed contains plants, people, small wins, honest messes. Not numbers, not performance. The long game is connection that spills off-screen: meet-ups, crop swaps, neighbours introducing themselves because a digital thread gave them a reason. That's city-scale intimacy: a million gardeners, a kitchen-table tone.

When we talk about legacy, he doesn't claim expertise as a credential; he insists that the idea of ordinariness invites people into gardening. 'It's easier than you think,' he tells people who feel excluded by the myth of the green thumb. Start small. Buy decent organic potting mix. Expect failure; you'll learn faster. This is demystification as a public service, and it's profoundly community-building: the more people who feel 'this is for me', the more gardens appear where there were none.

It would be disingenuous not to name what made his pivot possible. Patrick is clear-eyed about privilege; he had the option to leave a secure career and try a year of something new. He's also frank about the courage it still took, and about wishing that more people who can afford this leap would take it for work with purpose. I value that honesty. It locates his story in the world as it is, not the world some pretend it to be.

What I see while watching him and working with him is a form of hospitality. The door is open, the tone is warm, the laughter is frequent, the instruction is precise enough to be useful but never out of reach. That's why families send him messages about children who started sowing seeds, and people who've never grown anything report first harvests with a pride. The account isn't a pedestal; it's a chair pulled out for you. That's what initially drew me to Gardenstead. It was the place I had been waiting for, and I was happy to put my bum on that seat.

On the internet, that tone matters. He'll tell you that 'likes' can deliver dopamine and that content creators don't always admit that. He'll also tell you the metric that now counts most to him is the quality of attention: conversations that lead to real-world action, people who meet because a post gave them a common

Scan to hear my full conversation with Patrick Vernuccio, where we talk about demystifying gardening, building guardrails that protect joy, and turning online connection into real-world meet-ups.

language, the patient accumulation of gardeners who keep going. Gardenstead is built for that ethos: healthier communities, not bigger ones.

He dreams in networks, not nodes: balconies grown into corridors of green; school plots; verge gardens; shared compost habits that interrupt the waste stream; micro-forests stitched between apartments. None of it is heroic. All of it is possible. You don't need to move to the country; you can tweak your city life and let the practice reshape what you notice. He is living proof that just a few seeds grown on a lonely balcony can be the impetus to nurture and re-create the self, and in time the world.

'Without a great soil, no healthy plants.'

Patrick's endeavours show that community isn't always a table in the local playground or a chair at a café. Sometimes it's a person online who makes the first step feel small enough to try. Sometimes it's a platform that lowers the volume so we can hear each other. Sometimes it's a boundary that protects a practice so it stays generous. Patrick's work makes space for all three. If you're starting online and want it to lead somewhere real:

- Share what failed and what you'd do differently next time. It keeps the work real and generous.
- Protect your joy by scheduling device-free gardening windows so the practice doesn't become content-orientated.
- Start small and specific, perhaps with one herb that can teach you success. Invest in good soil, and learn about your sunlight.
- Ask one genuine gardening question, and answer two from someone who's newer at it than you. Reciprocity builds culture.
- Use the digital world to cultivate the local one. Join an online planting-zone group, or list a spare seed packet on Gardenstead and arrange a place to meet.

Patrick Vernuccio's balcony garden, where it began. A small, daily gardening practice turned a few pots into a way of living, and then into a wider invitation for others to start where they are.

TIME TO FIND YOUR TRIBE

If you've read from the beginning of this book, then you'll know that I talk a lot about living well. Not as a slogan, but as the currency for what 'success' now means to me. It's a measure that can't be quantified, but I feel it to my core in a deep sense of contentment and internal alignment. And, again and again, in authentic connection: quiet, ordinary, cumulative, across a bench, a path, a letterbox, a verge.

If there's one thing I want you to carry from this chapter, then it's permission. Allow yourself to be the person who leaves a jar on a step or a tray of seedlings under a handwritten sign. To design for experience as much as for harvest, to choose a path that means two people can walk abreast, to keep your fences legible but equally permeable so your garden can talk to the street. Let yourself start small, stay consistent, witness seasons through their rituals, give more than you think you can and accept more than you're used to receiving. That last one is hard. I'm still learning to sit with it.

For me, community looks like this now. The kids and I move through a town that knows us. The garden feeds us and other people, in food and in pace. There is a constant, low-humming exchange of tools, jars, tips, cuttings. I teach and I learn. I host and I show up. I overcome the gravity of putting myself out into the world with my feet on the ground, and I write like no one is listening until someone says, 'That helped,' then I write again. There is far less performance in my life and more practice. Less proving, more sharing. The garden made that possible, and it keeps me honest about the kind of neighbour, parent and collaborator I want to be.

If you're standing at the edge of your own version of this, unsure of where to begin, then start where your heart and feet already want to go. Put something out there that says, 'You're welcome.' Grow slightly more than you need. Let go of the hesitation, and say yes to the conversation. Leave a packet in a letterbox. Make the first gesture small enough to easily repeat. Pass it on. You don't have to gather a crowd. You only have to be open enough to let the garden guide you and to be your truest self.

That is the kind of community a garden makes. And it's the one I choose, time and time again. It's local, lived-in, generous, and held together by the simplest acts that we are willing to keep doing and sharing, over and over again.

Maybe I'm finally brave enough to say it plainly: I adore this life. Not the tidy social-media pictures of it, but the actual hands-in-the-dirt moments. I love that my children are growing up with a sense that dinner comes out of soil and that help comes from people, not from some abstract idea of 'support'. I love that the last red-fleshed fig on my tree tastes even sweeter because I've given the rest away. I love that, somewhere far from here, someone will save seeds because I said it was worth it, and I will never know their name. That's enough.

What comes next, in Chapter 14, is legacy. For me, that's not a standing ovation as the curtain closes; it's what gets passed along in the doing and being. A seed folded into a square of newspaper. A habit of roasting tomatoes in March so August still tastes like sunshine. A platform that makes a beginner feel brave. A field dinner that teaches a child the price and pleasure of good bread.

Opposite page,
Top_Kaiya: good neighbour, free spirit, talented creative. A candid moment on the verge from the book's photo shoot, boots borrowed on the spot when your shoes don't quite cut the mustard, because this is how community works here. It is practical, generous and immediate.
Bottom left_My dear friend Alison at her home-based Two Fold Bakehouse, a slow-food sourdough bakery built from community-supported weekly subscriptions. My verge-grown spinach is swapped for bread, a small exchange that keeps the currency of living well in constant circulation.
Bottom right_A cutting passed from hand to hand. The verge becomes a place for seedlings, stories and new connections, where generosity travels quietly through the neighbourhood.

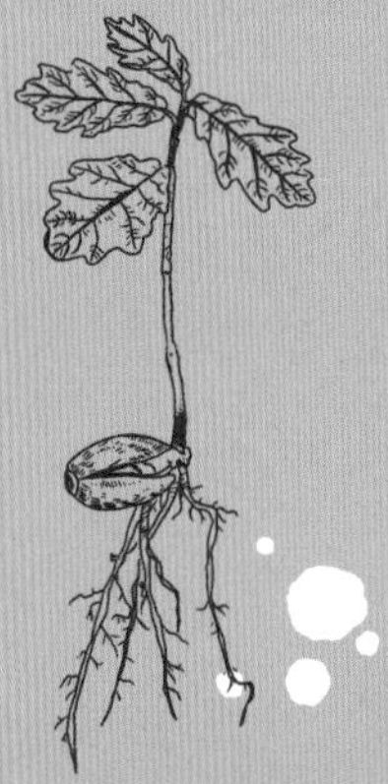

14 YOUR PRODUCTIVE GARDEN LEGACY

For me, legacy lives in the way a garden reshapes a life from the inside out and then ripples into the lives around it. The question at the heart of this chapter is: what are you cultivating that might last?

WHERE LEGACY BEGINS

At Oak & Monkey Puzzle, there were evenings when the light fell so softly that I'd stop whatever I was doing and run outside to catch it, borage (*Borago officinalis*) lit from behind, bees making their final flight, the whole garden briefly glowing. In those moments, the garden steadied me. It made me a better parent and a calmer person, and it gave our home a rhythm that felt more truthful.

Those evenings taught me that what we make in a garden is never only material. The things we tend, repeat and return to begin shaping how a place holds us, and how that way of living extends into the lives around us.

WHAT WE LEAVE BEHIND

Gardens don't hold their shape because we drafted up a concept plan; they hold their shape because, season after season, someone chose to tend them. Those choices are accumulative:

- — the way we build soil: leaving it more vibrant and dynamic than we found it
- — the notes we leave in a diary: when the rain fell, when the ground dried out, when the first spring blossom opened
- — the decision to make room: a damp patch for frogs, a stacked stone nook for lizards, a tangled thorny hedge for wrens
- — the way we share: seeds with a friend, the surprise of a bag of pink-fleshed crabapples hanging on the gate, the garden's successes and failures teased out over a pot of tea.

Years from now, someone will open that diary and think about when to net the berries, and a child will recognise a tomato in their hands before they've learned its name. Every one of those choices teaches someone else how to grow. Even if they never meet us.

LEGACY AS A PRACTICE, NOT A PROJECT

Legacy is not a finale. It's the rhythm of small, recurring acts that become part of a place. When energy dips or time is thin, practice carries you forwards.

Choose two or three seasonal rituals that hold the garden steady, such as a passata day, an afternoon hanging garlic plaits under cover, the autumn pack-up when tools are cleaned and oiled. These rituals keep the work and the people moving when motivation wavers.

Design for city-scale intimacy, and make the welcome to your place structural so it happens without a plan. A backed seat with a view, a bench near herbs, a clear path to water. These small intentions invite company, conversation and teaching.

Seasonal rituals and good design only become legacy when they travel through people. Welcome is the conduit; it's how a practice is picked up, copied and passed on.

LEGACY THROUGH PEOPLE

I've come to learn that teaching others is one of the most durable forms of gardening. Not as an encyclopaedia of facts, but as an invitation to a way of moving: noticing, tending, allowing. I see it in families like mine who garden together, in the generosity of mentors such as Patrick Vernuccio, in community workshops where a compost bin becomes a conversation about the local café's coffee grounds. What we share is one layer of the design iteration, but it's the kind that you feel in your heart: community as a verb.

Family lines

I have watched my children regulate their biggest and most uncomfortable feelings in the garden. A chicken scratching for bugs and worms locks in otherwise haphazard attention. Raking autumn leaves and topping up compost bays has filled my boy with a sense of achievement and pride. Golden hour settles the house. Daily rounds anchor us.

The garden teaches me to be less frantic, which teaches them that there is another pace available to human life. They know that I always come back inside with softer shoulders and a smile. They may never remember a plant list, but they'll definitely recall the smell of tomato leaves, the taste of the season's first podded pea and the crunch of frost under their feet.

I have watched children grow their sense of self in dirt, small hands on the hose, muddy knees, the brave first bite of a bitter green. No matter the scale, from a pot to a plot, gardens teach children how to belong to something greater.

If you're gardening with children, then I invite you to make the tasks real. Give them the worm farm. Ask them to top up the bird feeder. Let them choose the carnivorous plant that catches the flies. Teach them how to harvest gently. Give them the names for what they see. To provide this language is to grant them belonging. It will mark their minds and hearts long after all of the dirt has been washed off.

Patrick Vernuccio: Community and inheritance

Patrick Vernuccio is living proof that you don't need formal training to pass something on; his one balcony and two packets of seeds in Amsterdam taught thousands to begin (see pages 385–7). The garden softened his anxiety, giving him somewhere to put his hands and his attention. He began sharing what he was learning online. What grew was not just vegies, it was a community.

His advice to new growers is simple: start small, invest in good soil, and let success build your curiosity. It matters that people hear this from someone who didn't begin as a horticulturist, that children learn the word 'soil' instead of 'dirt'. It's legacy made visible in everyday life.

He is building digital spaces for that legacy to gather and develop, where gardeners can meet by growing zone, swap seeds and trade courage. When he describes his proudest moments, they are mornings in the garden with his young son, naming plants and harvesting cape gooseberries. Impact and inheritance are measured in time together.

LEGACY THROUGH SYSTEMS

The next generation in the garden, my children at the driveway courtyard table. Daily time outside becomes its own inheritance: steadier rhythms, shared attention and a place that holds family life.

The systems we set in motion go far beyond our single actions. A worm farm someone keeps feeding. A seed jar labelled and passed on. These are quiet infrastructures of generosity.

I think often of Alla Olkhovska in Kharkiv, Ukraine, who tends a family garden under bombardment (see pages 398–400). In the terror of blackouts and drone strikes, she keeps returning to the plants. The garden is an inheritance in more ways than one: apple trees (*Malus* spp.) her great-grandfather planted, peonies (*Paeonia* spp.) from her great-grandmother, a wooden gate made by a relative's hands. She cared for the failing peonies, revived them, and added her own loves, clematises (*Clematis* spp.) climbing through the old bones of the orchard.

It's a living thread through four generations that Alla has chosen to strengthen by teaching, photographing, writing and sending seeds into the world. The garden has become a lifeline for her family and a bridge to peace beyond the war.

Ecologist Tanya Loos reminds me that a garden can double as a small field station. Learn to read tracks and calls, to notice who is using what you built. Leave leaf litter through winter, keep one log for insects and small creatures, add shallow water, shield a corner from lights at night. Keep a species list on the fridge that anyone in your family can add to. Take the same photo from the same spot each season. Those notes and observations are a time machine. They help the next person in the garden to learn faster. They turn care into evidence the whole family can see for years to come.

In my own garden beds, I've tried to follow Tanya's idea of 'reading the life you made'. Possums decimated my kale (*Brassica oleracea* Acephala Group) and roses; the fence became their runway. Lifting the productive core into raised wicking beds changed the story. The height and smooth cladding eliminated access and losses, and the steady water reduced plant stress. It was a happy accident in future-proofing! My daily surveys and photos show it clearly: fewer bite marks, better growth, a calmer gardener (yes, that's me!).

Top left_A summer collection from my garden, arranged as a seasonal stocktake. It's a small ritual of attention and making that offers a way to read what is flowering now and what this small but bountiful place is giving back.
Top right_A handful of fruits from the Lebanese crabapple (*Malus trilobata*). A species introduced to me by Lily Langham, it carries her voice into my garden. It's a triple-value tree because it provides beauty, yield and the quiet reminder that so much of what we grow arrives through friendship.
Bottom left_Harvesting spears from asparagus (*Asparagus officinalis*). It is a brief ritual that occurs once a year, in spring.
Bottom right_A bucketful of seasonal flowers, gathered for an arrangement, marks what is abundant in spring.

A workshop in motion on the verge at Little Cottage on a Hill. This is how the garden travels, not as a finished thing but as a shared practice. One person learns a small way of seeing, a soil habit, a design move, a seasonal cue, then carries it home and passes it on. The same ripple that brought a Lebanese crabapple (*Malus trilobata*) into my garden now moves outwards again, from this patch of ground into other places, other hands, other lives.

CULTURAL CONTINUITY AND MEMORY

Gardens carry culture. They hold memory, and they are passed on. When I think of legacy and gardens, instead of seminal works or exemplars, or even vegies and compost, I see the way that gardens give people a reason to get up, to notice, to share

Alla Olkhovska's seed envelopes (see page 399) bring strangers into kinship. Supporters abroad buy her ebooks and seeds. She, in turn, passes on some of that help to neighbours to pay for medicine. The web is widened. That is social and emotional capital you cannot tally but you can feel, the kind that keeps communities upright during impossible winters and protracted wars.

I have watched friendships form over a wheelbarrow. I have seen my children steady themselves among the garden beds, their nervous systems finding rhythm in daily rounds. We don't talk about that often when we say 'productive garden', but it belongs here. A life lived well is part of the harvest.

If culture is memory carried forwards, then Mary Reynolds (see page 396) offers a framework for it: ARKs and corridors that stitch our small patches into a wider quilt.

MARY REYNOLDS

Corridors, ARKs and intergenerational thinking

I first came across Mary Reynolds through friend and landscape architect Mark McDowall, an office colleague now running his own practice in Ireland. He sent me and Mary an email that brought disparate parts of the world closer than I could have imagined. We recognised each other quickly, two designers who had learned, sometimes the hard way, that neatness and control don't always equal care. We compared notes from different hemispheres, and our affinity was immediate; we both saw the garden as teacher, not showroom, and design as a way to serve what is living, not to stage it.

There is a moment in Mary's story that will never leave me. On a winter morning in Wexford, she witnessed a fox, then two hares, then a hedgehog, all running from an area where a dense thicket had been replaced with a house and a lawn. She followed them down the lane and understood, viscerally, what her design drawings could erase and what they could repair. That was the hinge. She founded We Are The ARK (Acts of Restorative Kindness), and the work turned towards sanctuary, corridors and the long labour of stitching life back in. When Mary says we must step into service, she is not being poetic. She is precise about our role now.

Mary offers us a brave widening of the word 'productive'. Yes, we grow food, flowers and medicine. We also grow passage, shelter and time. In Mary's language, a good garden should produce restoration for pollinators, soil, fungi, birds . . . and the people learning to notice them. She is clear that letting go is not walking away. We still design, but we do it for edges, layers and continuity. We line a hedge with the neighbour's hedge. We leave an ARK patch wild and defend it through the awkward seasons. We think in decades and hand over systems that can be kept, not just admired. Here, in a chapter about legacy, Mary helps us to think beyond our fence line so we can see how a verge becomes a doorway, how a small wild patch becomes part of a neighbourhood quilt of life. That is the thread she pulls through this book: courage to intervene wisely, humility to stand back, and an invitation to leave something the next steward can keep growing.

Mary asks us to widen the frame: gardens as ARKs, corridors, acts of restorative kindness that outlast our lifetimes. That call to action resonates deeply and compels me to keep asking more of how my gardens grow, live and work.

Neighbourhood legacy

Your courtyard, garden or verge is a chance to extend habitat beyond your fence line. When your planting lines up with a neighbour's, a hedge becomes a corridor. A small Acts of Restorative Kindness (ARK) patch along the footpath adds shelter, nectar, seeds and cover, and it gives wildlife somewhere to move through. If you want to invite people in, then make it easy. A simple note in the letterbox can open a conversation about cuttings, seeds and what you are both growing for. This is Mary Reynolds' legacy at street and neighbourhood scale: intentional, significant and achievable.

'We're just plants without roots.'

***Opposite page*_**The view from Little Cottage on A Hill's entry garden to the verge, a planted threshold that carries habitat beyond the fence line. The bird feeder is a small marker of intent: a productive garden must give more than it takes, and allow space for all creatures.

Scan to hear my full conversation with Mary Reynolds, where we talk about ARKs and wildlife corridors, redefining 'productive' as restoration for all creatures, and moving from gardener to guardian in your own patch.

ALLA OLKHOVSKA

Gardening in a war zone

I first found Alla through her plant photographs and then through her words, plain, steady, unsentimental, about keeping a garden going while the grid failed and the air-raid sirens wailed across Kharkiv, Ukraine. She writes ebooks on clematis (*Clematis* spp.), not from a quiet studio but from the cold, damp patience of a basement while living through blackouts. When the power drops, she keeps cleaning seeds by hand. When fear surges, she tells herself to think about flowers. I hand the page to Alla now. Listen to her as you would a friend across the fence. Then decide which small act you will carry forwards.

What does it mean to care for something while surrounded by destruction?

Caring for something alive when everything around is being destroyed becomes an act of resistance, a fight against chaos. It's about choosing to grow life when there's death, finding hope when there's despair, and showing that beauty can still exist even during war. It turns gardening into a powerful message of strength. It's a way to feel in control and connected when everything else is falling apart.

The war makes taking care of things so much harder. Finding what you need is difficult, and staying safe is a constant worry. Even though it takes so much courage and effort, it makes caring for something even more meaningful, proving that life and beauty can still grow, even in the worst times. It's a decision to focus on growth, beauty and the future, even when things are hard, and that's a powerful act of resistance.

How important is it to you to tend the same land that your forebears once did?

I received the garden from my granny, but she wasn't the first owner. My great-grandfather was given this piece of land in Kharkiv as a military service award because he was a hero of World War II. He built the house with his own hands, and he planned an orchard and planted many apple trees (*Malus* spp.).

'To tend the same land that they once did is deeply meaningful; it's about continuing a tradition and honouring the legacy of those who came before. It's very important for me to carry on what they started.'

To tend the same land that they once did is deeply meaningful; it's about continuing a tradition and honouring the legacy of those who came before. It's very important for me to carry on what they started.

Though my passion leans more towards flowers, and I had to cut down most of the apple trees due to old age, I still have some apple trees that my great-grandfather planted. I treasure these trees, and I do everything I can to integrate them into my garden design. I cherish their amazing spring blossoms. Nothing compares to the beauty of flowering apple trees, to my mind, and I still eat the fruits they produce each year.

In doing so, I'm not just tending to the land, but tending to the deep connection between the generations, preserving their story and keeping their memory alive through the fruits of their labour. It helps me to remain grateful and enjoy the world's beauty.

Kharkiv, Ukraine. Photograph by Alla Olkhovska. The reality of gardening in a war zone: tending to life continues alongside visible destruction.

How did your seed shop begin, and how has it helped to support your family?

As my collection of rare plants grew, especially clematises (*Clematis* spp.) and peonies (*Paeonia* spp.), and my social media developed, I started getting more requests from other gardeners for seeds. One day, I decided to create a small catalogue with just a few varieties to share. This was several years before the war. The catalogue became very popular among local gardeners, and gradually I added more varieties. I never imagined how important my catalogue and seeds would become during the war. They are helping us survive; the money enables us to buy necessary food and medicines for my family.

What does it mean to send your seeds to gardeners around the world?

Sending seeds to gardeners around the world is a deeply meaningful act because it represents connection and hope. It's a way to participate in a global community, fostering a network of shared passion and appreciation for nature.

Each tiny seed carries the potential for growth, resilience and transformation, symbolising the power of individuals to cultivate positive change in their own spaces and beyond. It's about nurturing not only gardens, but also relationships, and contributing to a better world. It's a testament to the enduring human spirit and the belief that even in the face of challenges, beauty and life can flourish.

'I couldn't imagine that [my garden] would play such an important role during the war for me and for my family.'

Do you see this work as a form of legacy building?

Absolutely! Beyond the immediate benefits of providing a lifeline to my family and a source of beauty to gardens worldwide, I think that I'm also creating a lasting impact on several levels:

— **Preservation of rare plants:** I have lots of rare species, and by sharing their seeds I'm helping to preserve biodiversity and prevent the loss of unique plant varieties for future generations.

— **Symbol of resilience:** The act of cultivating beauty and life in a war zone sends a powerful message of hope and resilience. This message becomes part of the story of my plants, inspiring others to persevere and create even in the face of adversity.

— **Contribution to knowledge:** By meticulously observing and documenting my plants, as demonstrated in my ebooks, I'm contributing to the collective knowledge of horticulture, leaving a valuable resource for other gardeners.

— **Inspiration and hope:** Very often my followers write to me that my story inspires them to find beauty and create meaning in their lives, regardless of their circumstances. This inspiration is a lasting legacy that extends far beyond the borders of my garden.

Are there seasonal rituals that help you to feel connected to time or memory?

I have an old tradition to create a farewell arrangement, which means the last arrangement of the garden season. I usually try to make it before the first frosts, or if they are too early then right after the first slight frosts.

The first farewell arrangement was made many years ago. At that time I didn't have a professional camera and I didn't even have an Instagram account. But my photo taken on the simplest and cheapest point-and shoot-camera became so popular on Facebook that I decided to continue the tradition. So every year I have a very different farewell arrangement. I always take photos of them and enjoy them throughout the whole year.

If someone were to ask you why you still garden, how would you answer?

I'd say it's because it's a way to fight back, a source of hope, and a way to connect with others. But it's also because the garden is how my family survives. Gardening is my job and my passion, and that helps us to continue.

Through seed orders, ebook sales and the ability to connect with my Patreon supporters, the garden provides a tangible source of income that enables us to meet our most basic needs. Knowing that my work directly helps my family to eat and stay healthy makes me keep going, no matter how hard it gets. That responsibility is what drives me.

When I take care of those plants, I'm not just gardening; I'm showing that I believe in life, beauty and the future. I'm refusing to give up. By sharing the beauty of my garden and what I've learned, I can connect with people, offer a little comfort and inspire them to find their own hope, wherever they are. The garden proves that people can grow and thrive, no matter what problems they face.

Scan to read the unabridged piece and to hear my full conversation with Alla Olkhovska, where we talk about seed saving as a lifeline during war, the farewell bouquet tradition and other seasonal rituals, and how shared seeds carry connection and legacy worldwide.

PRACTICE NOTES THAT YOU CAN USE

Take a breath. What follows turns back to practice, not to minimise what you've just read in Alla's story, but because the right response to witnessing is tending. These are small, doable moves that keep hope in our hands. Think of them as legacy-making actions that you can take this week, this month, this year.

Create a legacy notebook by recording:

- — the first blossom, first bee and first frost each year
- — what you left standing over winter, and who used it: insect, animal or human.
- — what thrived without attention, and what needed watching
- — seeds you saved, and where they went
- — a simple map of nesting sites, water sources and wildlife-feeding shrubs.

Designate a small neighbourhood bowl with:

- — a place for it on the step each week during harvesting season
- — a note listing the name of what is inside and how you like to cook it
- — an invitation to swap, even if it's just herbs or a lemon.

Cultivate an ARK corner comprising:

- — one garden patch you stop tidying
- — one log you keep for beetles and lizards
- — one shallow dish you refill with fresh water
- — one native plant you add each season.

***Far left*_Harvesting rainbow chard (*Beta vulgaris* Cicla Group). Tending becomes food and record.**
***Left*_A seasonal garden arrangement. It is gathered, noticed and shared as a marker of the year.**

SUCCESSION AND STEWARDSHIP

After a lifetime of designing gardens and public spaces, I think about handover as an important and generous act. Not as a grand bequest, but as a practical kindness. If I had to leave tomorrow, what would let the next person step in and keep this place thriving, quickly and confidently? What would help them hear the garden?

This is the handover pack I would leave for Little Cottage on a Hill. Use it, adapt it, make it yours.

— a site plan, marked with the truth of the place: water paths and pooling points, wind lanes, frost pockets and the line of winter sun
— a soil log, bed by bed: what the soil is like now, what has been added, what drains fast, what holds, what performs
— a seasonal running sheet: what happens when, what to net and when, the peak berry weeks, sowing windows, and what stays standing for structure and habitat
— a water-system map: taps, tanks and pump notes, shut-offs, where the drip lines run, and the simple routine that keeps them clear
— a living-loops guide: compost, worm farm and worm tunnels, what to feed, how often, what not to add, and the early signs that something is off
— a plant register: fruit trees, shrubs, perennials and the core annual rotations, with pruning windows, plants that dislike hard cuts, and plants that flower on new wood
— a seed index: what is worth saving here, dates saved, germination notes and what cross-pollinates with what
— habitat notes: places to deliberately leave messy through winter, why those tangles matter, who shelters here, and where shallow water sits for birds, insects and other small creatures
— a short welcome letter so the garden feels like a companion, not a project.

WHAT IS MY LEGACY, AND WHY?

Oak & Monkey Puzzle gave me scale and bravery. It taught me that I could shape land, then, in time, that I didn't need to shape all of it. Little Cottage on a Hill taught me restraint, attention and how to teach from a place that feels like home. The designer in me still loves good lines and long views, but I have let a little wildness in, left seed heads standing, watched who arrives.

The thread through both places is the same: the garden keeps returning me to myself. It asks me to live at the pace of seasons. It corrects me when I reach for too much. It shows my children there is another way to build a day. When I share that journey through writing, teaching, kitchens, verges and the QR-linked conversations on these pages, I see sparks catch.

***Opposite page*_**A workshop on the verge at Little Cottage on a Hill, where the garden is visible and shared. This is what everyday courage looks like in practice: skills passed on, neighbours in conversation, and a strip of land that gives more than it takes.

'If I could name my legacy, I would want it to be everyday courage: turn a lawn into a garden, grow enough to share, give a strip of land back to the insects, talk to a neighbour over a fence about worms.'

If I could name my legacy, I would want it to be everyday courage: turn a lawn into a garden, grow enough to share, give a strip of land back to the insects, talk to a neighbour over a fence about worms. I would want it to be a long habit of paying attention and passing things on.

GROW ONE THING

Imagine, for a moment, that you are the only person in the world who decides to grow one thing. Just one.

Not a garden overhaul. Not a reinvention of your life. Not a perfectly orchestrated project. Just one small act that fits inside the life you already have.

A single pot on a windowsill. A strip of verge that used to be bare. A seed tucked into soil beside the back step, or a cutting taken from a neighbour's plant with their blessing and a smile. That one small act might not look like much from a distance. But up close, it's a decision to live differently. It's you saying, quietly but clearly, I'm here. I'm paying attention and choosing to participate. That's the beginning of agency.

Because this book was never really about gardening as a hobby. It has always been about how you live. How you move through a year. How you make meaning in the middle of ordinary days. It has been about soil under your nails and soup on the stove, community at the letterbox and conversations over a fence. It has been about building a life that feels aligned and generous, one small seasonal act at a time.

Growing one thing is where all of that comes into focus.

Grow one thing, and you begin to notice light. You see where the sun lands in winter and where it lingers in summer. You start to understand wind and shade, frost and heat, not as abstract concepts but as the conditions that shape a living being you have chosen to care for. Grow one thing, and you begin to sense your own seasons, too: the days when you have energy to tend, and the days when simply stepping outside to look and breathe is enough.

Grow one thing, and you remember that beauty is not an extra. It's what draws you back to the work when you're tired, what makes tending feel instinctive rather than forced. A single pot of lemon balm (*Melissa officinalis*) by the back door, brushed each time you walk past. The first zucchini sliced into a pan, more precious than its size suggests. A handful of flowers cut from a garden that is still finding its shape. None of these things solves the world. But they steady you inside it.

Grow one thing, and you're no longer separate from the systems that feed people. You see that good soil is not a given; it's a relationship. You start to understand that compost is transformation made visible. That water is not just what comes from a tap, but what moves through a landscape. That food is not a commodity, but a conversation between place, weather, time and care.

Grow one thing, and community has a soft place to land. A pot of parsley (*Petroselinum crispum*) outside the front gate with a small note that says, 'Take some.' A tray of spare seedlings left at the café or on a neighbour's step. A jar of jam made from fruits you grew, gifted with no expectation of return. None of this requires a grand gesture. It only asks that you grow a little more than you need and trust that what you offer will find its way. There is no performance here. Only participation.

Grow one thing, and your garden – no matter how small – becomes part of a larger living fabric. Pollinators arrive. Birds notice. Children ask questions. Friends who swore they had black thumbs see your pot of herbs or your climbing beans and think, *Maybe I could do that*. They start with a single plant of their own, and suddenly it's not just you. A balcony changes. A street shifts. A schoolyard begins to sprout. These are tiny acts, but they accumulate. They always have.

This is how change actually happens. Not in perfectly orchestrated campaigns or flawless garden plans, but in the quiet decision to repeatedly show up for something living. To keep watering. To learn from failure. To start again next season with information that you didn't have before. A single seed planted in good soil doesn't stay that way for long. It becomes food. Then knowledge. Then confidence. Then generosity. Then culture.

So, this is your invitation. Not to overhaul your whole life. Not to wait until you have more time, more space, more certainty. Not to build the perfect garden, or to feed an entire town, or to save the planet single-handedly. But to simply grow one thing. Choose one plant that calls to you. One herb you long to cook with. One flower whose scent makes your shoulders drop. One fruit you dream about eating warm from the sun. Commit to that. Find a pot, a patch, a borrowed corner of soil. Learn what it needs. Pay attention to how it responds. Let it teach you about patience, about observation, about care that is not rushed or performative, but woven into your days.

Opposite page_A seasonal garden arrangement, gathered from what was on offer in the moment. Grow one thing, then another, and the garden becomes generous: beauty, abundance and a sense of legacy are built one stem at a time.

'Grow one thing, and your garden – no matter how small – becomes part of a larger living fabric.'

Scan to keep growing one thing. You'll find seasonal guides, simple how-tos and shared stories to support you, one plant at a time.

And then, when the moment is right, let it move outwards in one simple way. Share a handful with a neighbour, or swap it for something else. Cook it, and feed someone you love. Save seeds or take cuttings and tuck them into someone else's hands. Or simply notice what it taught you, and carry that forwards. There is nothing to prove here. Only something to begin.

If everyone who held this book in their hands chose to grow only one thing, then the world wouldn't look different overnight. But it would *feel* different almost immediately. There would be more noticing. More sharing. More small, steady acts of care stitched into the fabric of ordinary days. And that is where real legacy lives: not in monuments, but in habits. Not in declarations, but in what we quietly keep doing.

So, picture the one thing you will grow. Name it. See where it might live. Imagine yourself, three or maybe six months from now, reaching out to touch it, to harvest from it, to share it. Think about the person you will have become in the process, someone who chose to participate, to tend, to learn, to give. That person is not hypothetical. That person is you, beginning now.

And when you close this book, whether that is later today or many seasons from now, let it be a companion in action, not just an object on a shelf. Step outside into whatever space you have – a balcony, a verge, a courtyard, a farm or a single sunny windowsill – and make one honest promise to yourself and to the world around you: I will grow one thing. And from that so much more will grow, quietly and generously.

A NOTE FROM DUSK

In 2015, at the nexus of embarking on sharing my journey through pictures, words and workshops, and a family life that was slowly imploding, a wise woman said to me, 'Write like no one's listening.' To put myself in the public eye was daunting, but I was compelled to share what brings me joy and meaning, and a lifetime of being anchored in the garden for every high and low.

I wrote this book for the person who thinks they don't have enough time, enough space, enough knowledge. You don't need to change the world this year. Just change the metre in front of you. Put your hands in the soil. Learn the name of the bird that visits in the afternoon. Teach someone what you learned. That is how we pass it on, one season, one note, one act of generosity at a time.

The garden keeps teaching. Quietly. Constantly. Season after season, it invites us back into rhythm. Not to control it, but to participate.

What it offers in beauty, in care, in impact, that's the legacy we leave behind. Not in grand gestures, but in small acts of tending: compost turned, seeds passed between hands, the way a child learns to pick herbs by scent.

This kind of legacy is lived, not declared. You see it in the paths we shape through our days, in the gardens we grow for others as much as for ourselves, in the way we make room for kindness, place and pause. It's in the lives we create with our hands and our hearts. It's in the worlds we shape in soil, in conversation, in care. It's in the communities and collaborations we foster, not to prove what we've done, but to pass something on. Because long after the last harvest has been gathered, what remains is not just what we grew but what we made possible.

Opposite page_Wild rosehips foraged in the last light, a small harvest carried forwards into winter. This is my closing note to you: start where you are, notice what your place offers, and let one honest act of tending lead to the next.

CONCLUSION

I've just come inside from a lap of the wicking-bed garden. It's winter, but there's a warmth among the beds. Purple sprouting broccoli (*Brassica oleracea* Italica Group) is holding. Sweet peas (*Lathyrus odoratus*) are on the brink of popping. Borage (*Borago officinalis*) has its very first blue stars. Carrots (*Daucus carota* subsp. *sativus*) are finger thick. Sugar snap peas (*Pisum sativum*) with curly tendrils make a web that reaches for the sky. Soft fronds of fennel (*Foeniculum vulgare*) wave gently. And beyond the fence line, this sense of protection: the weak sun hits the dark cladding, and it throws a little heat back into the space. Just enough to take the edge off the cold.

A productive garden does that for me: it throws solace, joy and nourishment my way. I used to think that 'productive' was a way of being – well doing, actually – and also what I picked and preserved; now I know that it's also a measure of what the place restores in me. Simone Bliss talks about spaces as healing, and it's helped me name what I already knew in my bones. And then there's Alla Olkhovska. For her, beauty is not a luxury; it's a human necessity. In my life, beauty is not decoration; it's survival of a different kind.

The psychology of productive gardening

I've come back again and again to Austrian psychiatrist Viktor Frankl while making this book. His 1946 book *Man's Search for Meaning* has stayed with me since I read it many years ago during some of my most difficult times. Shaped by the worst of human experience, Frankl's words keep pointing to meaning as the thing that allows us to endure. He borrows a line from Friedrich Nietzsche that has followed me around the garden for years when he says, 'Those who have a "why" to live for can bear almost any "how".' Frankl is clear-eyed about it: happiness isn't something you chase, it arrives as the side effect of giving yourself to a cause beyond yourself.

That lands for me like a spade being plunged deep into soil. When I'm in the garden, I know that I'm contributing to something bigger than my own life. Soil that will outlast me. A season that doesn't care for my schedule but accepts my hands anyway. A bowl of soup made from what we grew that anchors the end of a long day. The meaning is in the tending. The 'why' is in the work itself. And then the happiness shows up, not as a prize, but as a consequence: contentment for which I didn't have to prove myself.

It's why I joined and agreed to grow Gardenstead during those earliest start-up days, in a radical leap of faith: to be part of something bigger than my own fence line. I don't think there's ever been a time in the world when these ideas mattered more: pace, presence, generosity, participation, care. The garden is honest about those things. You can manipulate small parts, but you can't force the whole. You can intercede, but you can't control. That's where my meaning lives.

From productivity to pages

Making this book has changed me. Talking to other people about their places and their practices has deepened my own knowledge. The process has felt like something underground and connective: rhizome-like in its persistence, mycelial in the way it has linked unlikely things. Emailing gardeners I've admired for years took courage. But not one person said no to participating in the book, which tells you everything about gardeners and designers who love the living world. The door is open if you knock with a generous tone.

From the beginning, I knew that this book had to weave other people's voices with mine. I'm not an oracle. I don't know it all. My life has been shaped by teachers and neighbours, by failures, by seasons that made me change my mind, by brave emails and side-door conversations. Who am I to pretend otherwise? I'm one step along my own path. And that's where the invitation lives: just give it a go. You are on your path, too. That is more than okay. We're all learning. It's a continuum.

My own continuum stretches from a child pottering in a garden, to student, landscape architect, lecturer, public-realm designer. Then Oak & Monkey Puzzle – my tree change with a purpose – arrived, and I could never have predicted how profound that season would be. I don't think I could have gone through that time without the garden holding my hand. Now I'm at Little Cottage on a Hill, smaller and reimagined, living my largest life. Teaching. Sharing. Happier than I've ever been.

There was a day at Oak & Monkey Puzzle, amid the pandemic, when I realised that soil, sky, air and water are my currency for living well. If those are steady, then I can find my footing. My belly will be full. My mind will quiet. My heart can repair. No therapist, no relationship, no accolade could give me what the garden has given me: unconditional contentment. I say that as someone who carries privilege and acknowledges it. I've had choices, even when they were hard. At the forks in the road, there were still options. There were times when life was on the brink, but I knew that I wouldn't be destitute. I don't take that for granted for a moment. It's an incredible opportunity to do what I love.

Helping hands

My father once told me: 'You don't need to be perfect.' And it's true. In the garden I can be perfectly imperfect because everything around me is. My father also said, 'If you do what you love, then you'll be good at it. And if you're good at it, then you'll always be okay.' The garden has been that for me, something to come home to, over and over. Some days are hard, but it never feels like work.

Other people have also guided me. One of Mum's oldest friends, Susie, let me potter in her garden, sent me home with a cutting or a few seeds, and never asked me to be anyone but myself. She sowed something in me that has never stopped growing. Dr Lee Ariav named something in me before I could see it. That kind of generosity is a model I try to carry forwards in workshops, in writing, in how I inhabit the world. Lily Langham, to whose garden I continue to return, has a shared passion for plants. And there are so many more. Every single contributor in this book.

My children teach me most of all. I remember Saffron one day yelling, 'Mum, stop!' as if it were urgent. She bent down and picked up a mottled yellow, green, orange, red and brown leaf with craggy edges, and looked at it like it was a jewel. 'Isn't it beautiful?' Her eyes were as big as saucers. The smallest thing can hold a world.

So here is my invitation. Make a cup of tea. If you're in your pyjamas, so be it. If you only have a minute, that's fine. Go for a tiny wander. See if one thing in your garden has changed. A seed pushing the surface. A bird finding a puddle. A web that wasn't there yesterday. A ladybird on a post making a meal of an aphid. Notice just one living thing. That's all you need to do today. Tomorrow, you can do something more.

Grow garlic (*Allium sativum*), and share it with a neighbour. Say yes to a bag of lemons on the step. Answer a question from the person who's just starting, even if you're only one step ahead. Plant one thing. Let your kid come inside with grubby hands and a grin so wide you'll never forget it. Pay attention to how plants change shape after rain. Slow for winter. Feel the sap rise in spring.

Don't be afraid to try . . . or to fail. Every tiny moment is a lesson. Design is iterative. So is life. So is gardening. So is learning.

I hope this book lives on your coffee table or your potting bench. I hope Emily Weaving's images pull you back in when words can't. I hope the contributors' voices sit beside you when you're unsure. I hope my voice feels like a hand on your shoulder when I say, 'Start where your feet are. Change the metre in front of you.'

Let happiness be your guide

Writing this book has reminded me that a 'productive garden' is not a fixed definition, it's a living one. It's expanded as I've listened to people growing in heat and in frost; to those who host under one huge roof; to a woman cleaning seeds by candlelight while sirens sound; to a man who turned a balcony into a classroom; to gardeners with verges that became invitations. This book is here to grow this knowledge.

I've discovered that my garden keeps teaching me how to live well, how to be more present, more benevolent, more myself. Whether it's 5 acres or 515 square metres (5545 square feet), I've always had what I've needed. My cautious hope, without presumption, is that your place can offer you some version of that, too.

I'm aware of my privilege. I've also worked my guts out. And I'm grateful for the people who gave me chances, who taught me, who opened their gardens and their notebooks, who said yes to my nervous emails, who showed up to workshops, who left cherries at the door, who trusted me with their stories. Community, kindness and generosity are my other currencies, equal to soil and sky and water and air.

If there is a single thing I want to place in your hands at the end, it's this: you don't need to change the world this year. Attend to the tiny patch of earth in front of you. Look closely. Participate. Let beauty be necessary. Let meaning emerge from what you tend. Let happiness ensue.

I don't know exactly where I'll go from here. I do know, though, that I won't stop being curious. I won't stop learning, sharing and creating. The seasons keep turning, the work keeps teaching, and the garden keeps returning me to myself.

I hope that you find what it is that truly makes your life feel well-lived, too.

***Opposite page*_**A long table in the garden at Little Cottage on a Hill, with friends and family gathered close. This is the point of all the tending: a well-lived life shaped by seasons, generosity and shared meals, and the garden's offerings.

AFTERWORD

In 2003, having taken on landscape architecture as a double degree to bookend my architecture studies, I found myself in Dr Lee Ariav's design studio at RMIT, drawn into a way of working where reflection wasn't just a technique, but a way of understanding the world. We were encouraged to think with our hands and hearts, to observe deeply, to let time and memory reveal the shape of things. That experience – those conversations, those wrestles with ideas – still echo through my work and how I inhabit the world today.

What I came to understand in that studio, and again while writing this book, is that design doesn't always move in a straight line. You begin with an idea or a quiet intuition, then test it from every angle. And sometimes, after all the exploration, you return to where you started. Only now, you know why it matters. That process of deepening something you sensed early on is what this book has been for me.

A 'productive' garden is about what it yields and what it holds. It's about rhythm, presence, memory and generosity. Lee helped me to see that. In many ways, this book is the continuation of a conversation that began more than twenty years ago. One that's still evolving. One that stretches across oceans, seasons and years.

I've included Lee's words here not to shift the tone, but to honour its roots. His semester-long design studio was one of the first places I realised that designing a garden wasn't only about solving problems. It was about listening to place, reading its layers and learning to work with what time leaves behind. I share Lee's reflection with gratitude for what was taught, what was received and what continues.

Reflection by Dr Lee Ariav

Architectural 'problems' are by nature ill-defined and therefore have multiple solutions, with no guaranteed procedure for obtaining a solution. This is why designers and architects 'play around' with ideas in a seemingly erratic process of trial and error, building up a repertoire of experiences that help them develop an intuition for what will work in the problematic situation. Thus, the studio is often compared to a playground that allows students to hone their design thinking and skills through learning by doing, while collaborating with the studio master (coach). The coach accompanies and guides the students in their architectural problem-solving endeavours; however, they cannot 'teach' exactly how this is accomplished.

The student–coach team is therefore required to develop a rapport in order to produce a common basis for formulation and acquisition of complex declarative and procedural knowledge. Interestingly and crucially, the learning process is not unilateral, as the coach has to react, adapt, augment and reflect the student's moves. In this sense, each meeting between coach and student resembles a wrestling session, in which the goal is not submission but rather a close-range exchange in which the knowledge shared is tacit more often than not. With the passage of time, as the learner's skills and awareness increase, the coach's role is assumed by the student themself.

Formal architectural knowledge and skills may be ingrained by means of apprenticeship and practice; although, architectural thinking – the ability to conceptualise and identify valuable architectural solutions – is produced by knowing in action (the skilled doing that flows without pause), reflection in action (thinking on your feet while doing) and reflection on reflection in action (the later pause to analyse what happened and why, in order to improve practice).

My time at RMIT

During 2003, together with my wife and three-month-old daughter, I travelled to Melbourne to teach a landscape architecture studio at RMIT. The studio began with a series of short-term tasks intended to increase the team's awareness of the unplanned or unintended, so students would learn to turn unexpected findings into productive directions while honing the skill of reflection.

The students were an enthusiastic and diverse young group, and they accepted the unfamiliar style of teaching offered by this foreign coach. The productive energy that developed was great, with one student standing out from the start. Unlike her classmates, Natasha Morgan was already trained as an architect, with a clear talent, a keen mind and an openness to developing further in the field of landscape architecture.

Our project site was located within the boundaries of the RMIT campus, enabling the team to rediscover the familiar, and where, as in any studio, the underlying objective was actually to enable each participant to gain some insight into their own developing identities as architects. Thus, the various project stages were designed to develop awareness and interdependency of the two thinking systems as outlined by the late Daniel Kahneman: System 1, which employs quick intuition to contend with the stream of sensory input (producer of considerable tacit and subsidiary knowledge); and System 2, which uses slower, more rational thought and reasoning (producer of declarative knowledge). The project was named The Me Park.

With her unique dexterity, Natasha committed herself fully to the search, taking on the idea of reflection literally and conceptually. Her rigorous site analysis revealed layers of history, plans and time. The history of Melbourne and the site were interpreted by Natasha as a palimpsest of architectural moves and intentions. She acutely identified that the site strata would seep through each other, like the colours in the works of American abstract expressionist Mark Rothko. The design began to emerge, as did the landscape master in the designer. The final work bears a resemblance to – however preceded – Peter Eisenman's The Garden of Lost Footsteps.

The playground studio was greatly successful, and naturally Natasha's work was awarded first prize as 'Best Project' of the semester. After I returned home, our fruitful collaboration continued in the framework of Natasha's nationally acclaimed and award-winning final dissertation and project. The oceans and time differences between Australia and Israel were met with mutual dedication, Natasha in Melbourne, and me responding late at night from my desk in our tiny domestic bomb shelter.

When I arrived in Melbourne, I was hopeful that I would have something to tell the students that they had to know. To my great fortune, I couldn't imagine being trusted to such an extent. I am grateful for this opportunity to be part of this work. Being remembered as a positive influence on your students' work is a teacher's greatest achievement, especially when the student happens to be Natasha Morgan.

ABOUT THE AUTHOR

Natasha Morgan is an award-winning landscape architect, lifelong gardener, educator and writer based in Australia. She is known for making productive gardens feel achievable and beautiful, and for helping people build gardens that support real lives, across every scale and season.

Natasha's relationship with the garden began in childhood, and it has remained her most reliable place of return. When life shifts shape, the garden is where she finds her centre. It is where the noise of the world softens, where attention becomes practical, and where change is measured in small, steady acts.

Formally trained in architecture and landscape architecture, Natasha worked for many years on major public projects, including six years on the Australian Garden (Stage 2), Royal Botanic Gardens Cranbourne, and she held senior roles in practice and research. An educator for more than 25 years, she spent over a decade lecturing in landscape architecture, from first-year to postgraduate level.

In 2014, Natasha left the inner city for country Victoria with a clear intention: to live her values in real time. On five acres at Spargo Creek, she created Oak & Monkey Puzzle, an internationally recognised experiment in beauty, productivity and community. Today, her work continues at Little Cottage on a Hill in Daylesford, where 515 square metres hold a whole philosophy: that any space, at any scale, can become a generous, life-giving garden.

Through her writing, teaching, public speaking and workshops, Natasha invites people into this world. Her purpose is simple and expansive: to help people grow one thing, then another, then a life that feels more grounded, connected and alive.

Find Natasha and step into her world:
Website: www.natashamorgan.com.au
Instagram: @natasha_morgan_
Facebook: @NatashaMorgan.com.au
YouTube: @Natasha_Morgan_
Gardenstead: @natasha_morgan_

Scan for a curated list of references, resources, further reading and practical links so you can keep learning.

ACKNOWLEDGEMENTS

Before anything else, there is the land. The hill in Daylesford, the fall of light, the breath of the forest. Here, I am most at home. When I keep close to this place, I fill my cup and begin again. In hard seasons, I return and it meets me. This landscape is the ground from which I write, and the place this book grew.

To my children, Saffron and Oliver. Without question, you are my greatest pride and reason for being; not for having come from me, but for the light you bring as your own remarkable selves. You are my sharpest critics, my truest allies and my daily inspiration. Thank you for teaching me to see the world with new eyes, to notice beauty in the everyday, to find understanding through complexity rather than conformity, and for guiding me always back to my most authentic self.

To my mother, for your tenacity, fierce love and unwavering belief in my capacity.

To my dad, for encouraging me to do what I love, to do it well and to keep my cup filled with what is true.

To my other dad, Pops, for opening doors to wonder and giving me ways to navigate each new chapter.

To my sister, Rebecca, my rock.

To Susie, who gave me the gift of pottering, for every cutting, seed and quiet permission to simply be.

To all the contributors – your generosity is the thread that binds these pages. Thank you to those near and far who opened hearts, minds and diaries, making space and time for conversations and contributions.

With gratitude to Jane Willson for the invitation to write, and to Melissa Kayser, Andrea O'Connor and Sarah Odgers at Murdoch Books for your steadfast support. Who knew that this would become one of the biggest projects of my life, expanding far beyond what I could have imagined? Warmest thanks to my editor, Dannielle Viera, whose insight, patience and weekend work made it possible to bring this book to the finish line.

Thank you also to Klarissa Pfisterer. You brought my world, with its imagery and design, into every page, creating a companion that readers can return to, grounded in lived experience and landscape, and reflecting the vision I hoped this book would hold.

To Emily Weaving, whose photographic journey has travelled with me from the very first days of Oak & Monkey Puzzle. Your extraordinary gift is to capture that mysterious meeting point between vision and what grows beyond it. Through your lens, each landscape's fleeting shifts of light, shade and season become images that hold both what I imagine and all that unfolds far beyond me. I could not wish for a more fitting companion to document this journey and help tell its story in pictures.

CONTRIBUTORS AND GARDENS

Dr Lee Ariav

Dr Lee Ariav has been a lecturer in the fields of landscape, architecture and design for over 25 years, mainly with the Technion in Haifa, Israel. Trained as a landscape architect with the Technion, he earned his MA (Architecture & Urban Culture) from the CCCB+UPC in Barcelona, Spain. While teaching in Israel and as a visiting academic in many other countries, he completed his PhD in the field of shared mental models in learning and teaching architecture. He specialises in the formative stages of education and applying Lev Vygotsky's Zone of Proximal Development (ZPD) in the studio, and focuses on the concepts of sharedness levels and scaffolding space.

Avant Gardeners

Madeleine Gasparinatos and Emily Allen are the creators and hosts of *Avant Gardeners*, a candid gardening podcast recorded from their homes and gardens on Melukerdee Country in Tasmania's Huon Valley. Self-described gardening beginners with 'lots of enthusiasm but very little know-how', they met and bonded over maternity-leave catch-ups in a friend's garden, and now interview experienced growers and designers over drinks to uncover practical tips and honest stories of success and failure.

Their episodes feature chats about their own messy, ever-evolving orchards, vegie patches, chickens and pest battles, alongside conversations with guests such as Kirsten Bradley from Milkwood, Charles Dowding and Phyllida Steele-Wareham, making gardening feel accessible, social and unpolished. *Avant Gardeners* is available on Apple Podcasts, Spotify and other major platforms.

Website: www.avant-gardeners.com
Instagram: @avantgardeners.podcast

Bank House, Newlyn, Victoria

Andrew Lowth and Nigel Smith are the owners and hands-on creators of Bank House, a 6070-square-metre (1½-acre) country garden in Newlyn, in Victoria's Central Highlands.

Behind the nineteenth-century former Bank of Australasia building, the garden is arranged as a sequence of rooms. Influenced by classic English gardens such as Hidcote, yet grounded in Central Victoria's seasons, Bank House is mostly private but occasionally opens to visitors, and has been featured in *Country Style* and *Australian House & Garden*.

Website: www.bankhousenewlyn.com

Simone Bliss

Simone Bliss is an Australian landscape architect and the founder and Creative Director of SBLA Studio, an award-winning landscape architecture and urban design practice with offices in Melbourne and Launceston. She established SBLA Studio in 2016 with a focus on creating socially responsive, environmentally sensitive landscapes that connect people with place. Her work spans a wide range of scales, from masterplanning and urban design to detailed public spaces and custom play environments. She is known for combining ecological thinking, artistic expression and technical expertise to transform conceptual ideas into functional and engaging environments.

Simone is an active contributor to the design profession and has served on the City of Melbourne Design Review Panel and other advisory bodies. Her work emphasises connection to landscape and respect for Country, with a strong commitment to collaborative and inclusive design practices. She is widely recognised for her creativity, innovation and advocacy for socially and environmentally responsible landscape architecture.

Website: www.sbla.net.au

Petrina Burrill

Petrina Burrill transforms the world of floriculture with an infectious passion that radiates through every bloom she grows and arranges. Her enchanting garden has captivated a global audience of more than half a million followers across TikTok and Instagram, where she shares vibrant floral artistry and practical gardening wisdom with boundless enthusiasm.

With international experience as a florist, Petrina has honed her craft across diverse landscapes and cultures, growing distinctive varieties that allow her to create truly original arrangements, each piece telling a story from soil to celebration. Through workshops around the world, she collaborates with renowned florists who share her commitment to sustainable practices and the transformative power of nature's beauty.

Her garden and work have been featured on *Gardening Australia*, *Better Homes and Gardens*, *The Design Files* and in the acclaimed floral publication *Bloom*, among other outlets, and she is a sought-after speaker at the Melbourne International Flower & Garden Show. Currently working on a book slated for release in 2027, Petrina continues to nurture both flowers and a flourishing community of garden enthusiasts who follow her journey online.

Instagram: @petrinablooms

Connie Cao

Connie Cao is a passionate urban permaculture gardener and author of *Your Asian Veggie Patch*. Based in Melbourne, she's spent the past eight years transforming a backyard full of weeds into an abundant garden filled with vegies, berries, fruits and flowers. She believes that spaces of all sizes can become productive, thriving gardens, and would love to inspire more people to grow food and flowers in backyards and small areas.

Websites: www.connieandluna.com
www.gardenwithconnie.com
Instagram: @connieandluna

Jerry Coleby-Williams

Jerry Coleby-Williams is an internationally renowned horticulturist, conservationist and pioneer of sustainability and organic best practice, initially trained at the Royal Botanic Gardens, Kew, and the Royal Horticultural Society in the United Kingdom.

He has managed nurseries, urban forests, heritage parks and one of London's busiest garden centres, and he helped to establish the Australian Botanic Garden Mount Annan. For twelve years he managed the Royal Botanic Garden Sydney, where his Rare & Threatened Plants Garden launched a long career in radio, television, writing and public speaking, including ABC Radio's *Talkback Gardening* since 1995 and ABC TV's *Gardening Australia* since 1999.

Jerry is a pioneer of sustainable, low-carbon living. In 2003, he created Bellis, a retrofitted Queenslander house and garden in Brisbane that exports surplus solar power, recycles all wastewater, grows over 500 kinds of plants and supports more than 580 animal species, while generating zero food waste.

Bellis functions as a community seed bank and nursery, supplying diverse seeds and plants. The project's success has led to international recognition, including an invitation for Jerry to speak on sustainable food production at the United Nations in Geneva and the archiving of his widely followed website by the Australian National Library.

Website: www.jerry-coleby-williams.net

Daylesford Longhouse

Conceived and created by co-owners Ronnen Goren and Trace Streeter with architecture practice Partners Hill, Daylesford Longhouse is a mixed-use property that combines home, working farm, garden, cooking school and reception space within a single greenhouse-like structure that stretches for 110 metres (360 feet) along a ridgeline in the Central Victorian highlands. The expansive roof moderates winter frosts and summer heat, creating a protected interior climate for growing, cooking and gathering. The 8-hectare (20-acre) hilltop site weaves productive gardens, animal yards and communal spaces into one linear sequence for daily life and shared meals.

Website: www.daylesfordlonghouse.com.au
Instagram: @dlonghouse

Christian Douglas

Christian Douglas is a landscape architect and garden designer whose practice, Christian Douglas Design, creates ecologically informed, food-productive lush landscapes in the San Francisco Bay area. Drawing on formal training in classical design and work in regenerative agriculture, he is known for gardens where orchard, kitchen bed and habitat are woven into terraces, courtyards and pools so that foraging, wildlife and everyday life occupy the same ground. Christian has spent more than 30 years creating landscapes across England, Jordan and the United States, alongside working and teaching on farms and at education centres. That experience underpins his conviction that contemporary garden design has a responsibility to repair our relationship with land and food; in his work, clipped structure and crafted stone sit with espaliered fruit trees, beehives, chickens and 'wild wonderland' plantings that invite people and pollinators to graze through a space.

His projects have received awards and wide coverage in titles such as *Architectural Digest*, *The Wall Street Journal*, *The Financial Times* and *House Beautiful*, and the Gardenista website. His edible–ornamental gardens are profiled for their mix of structure, wildness and invitation to harvest.

Christian's design philosophy is distilled in his book *The Food Forward Garden*, a guide to integrating herbs, vegetables, fruits and berries into landscapes without sacrificing style. Alongside design practice, he writes, teaches and appears in interviews and workshops, encouraging gardeners to make 'edible swaps', see soil and biodiversity as primary design materials, and treat productive gardens not as add-ons but as the living heart of resilient outdoor spaces.

Website: www.christian-douglas.com

Charles Dowding

Charles Dowding is an English horticulturist, market gardener and author who has pioneered modern no-dig organic gardening in the United Kingdom since the early 1980s. At his Somerset garden, Homeacres, he has spent more than a decade running side-by-side trials comparing dug and undug beds, documenting how undisturbed, compost-mulched soil produces fewer weeds, higher yields and better resilience with far less labour.

A self-taught gardener who questioned conventional cultivation from the outset, Charles has developed a clear, accessible growing and teaching approach that focuses on feeding soil life rather than plants, minimising disturbance and trusting structure built by roots, fungi and organisms. At Homeacres, he grows intensively on a relatively small footprint, supplying vegetables to local shops and restaurants, and showing visitors how continuous cropping, surface compost and simple bed preparation can replace spade-digging, double-digging and heavy machinery.

He shares his methods through books, articles, an extensive video library and online courses that have helped to popularise no-dig gardening well beyond the United Kingdom, and influenced home gardeners, community gardens and small farms worldwide. In recognition of his work as the 'guru of no-dig', his approach has been showcased at events such as the RHS Hampton Court Palace Garden Festival and acknowledged with awards including the RHS Elizabeth Medal of Honour.

Website: www.charlesdowding.co.uk
Instagram: @charles_dowding
YouTube: @CharlesDowding1nodig

Matthew Evans

Matthew Evans is an Australian food writer, former chef and restaurateur, and farmer based in southern Tasmania, where he runs Fat Pig Farm and writes and presents on soil, food systems and ethical eating. His shift from restaurants to farming was documented in the television series *Gourmet Farmer* and its follow-up programs. He raises pigs, cattle and poultry, grows mixed crops, and runs paddock-to-plate cooking classes, long lunches and workshops. His recent work has focused on soil as the foundation of flavour and planetary health, culminating in his book *Soil*.

Website: www.fatpig.farm
Instagram: @fat_pig_farm

Kate Flood

Known as Compostable Kate online, Kate Flood is an Australian sustainability educator and author who shows that composting is practical, science-backed and genuinely approachable. A former high-school food-technology teacher, she turned her frustration at classroom food waste during the Covid years into resources that place composting at the heart of successful home gardening and that build soil literacy for all ages. She works with councils, schools, community programs and local businesses, and appears in media and podcasts, revealing how everyday scraps can become 'garden gold' that feeds plants and soil life while reducing landfill. Her bestselling book *The Compost Coach* offers step-by-step guidance for people living in apartments and houses, covering soil ecology, carbon to nitrogen balance, and troubleshooting. Through Instagram, TikTok and workshops, she demystifies hot composting, worm farms and Bokashi with playfulness and scientific clarity. Based in Sydney in a small semi, she proves that impact does not require scale.

Instagram: @compostable.kate

Sharon Flynn

Sharon Flynn is an inspiring and consistent advocate for wild and naturally fermented foods. Her lifelong passion for fermented foods as well as her desire to support the gut health of her daughters led her to establish The Fermentary in 2012. The Fermentary supplies a variety of wild fermented food and drinks to stores and restaurants both within Australia and internationally.

Sharon is the bestselling author of *Ferment for Good* (2017), and her second book, *Wild Drinks* (2022), continues to inspire and engage readers with her compelling enthusiasm for fermentation and food sovereignty. Sharon and her ferments have received numerous accolades: in 2016 she was named *Delicious Magazine*'s Outstanding Artisan, and in 2021 she was awarded 'legend status' by the Melbourne Food and Wine Festival for her advocacy and production in the food industry. Her mission is to encourage everyone to consume at least one mouthful of living food daily.

Website: www.thefermentary.com.au
Instagram: @thefermentary, @sharon__flynn

Emma Galloway

Emma Galloway is the bestselling author of three cookbooks, with a fourth soon to be released. She's also a chef, photographer, aspiring potter and keen gardener, and the creator of the award-winning food blog *My Darling Lemon Thyme*. She lives in Raglan, New Zealand.

Website: www.mydarlinglemonthyme.com
Instagram: @mydarlinglemonthyme

Cherie Hausler

Cherie Hausler is a Barossa Valley-based food writer, stylist, product and recipe developer, tea blender, restaurateur, presenter and cookbook author. After early years in Sydney television and food media, including a long-running vegetarian column in *Delicious* magazine, she returned to the Barossa, created vegan products for the local

farmers' market, ran pop-up events, opened a plant-based retail store, and spent thirteen years consulting to Maggie Beer on writing, styling and brand development. She later founded All The Things, pioneering artisan vegan white-mould cheeses and other plant-based products now stocked through independent retailers and national supermarkets. She is the creator of the TV series *All The Things* and the author of *A Plant-Based Farmhouse*.
Instagram: @allthethings_au, @cherie_hausler

Cass Hooke

Cassandra (Cass) Hooke is an arid-zone gardener, botanist and founder of Outback Gardens, growing on a working sheep property near Hay, New South Wales, where summer temperatures can exceed 45 degrees Celsius (113 degrees Fahrenheit) and rainfall is scarce. With a science degree majoring in botany and conservation, she pairs strong plant knowledge with lived experience of gardening in one of Australia's toughest climates. Through Outback Gardens and as arid-climate columnist for *ABC Organic Gardener*, Cass shares practical, design-led approaches to dryland planting for gardeners facing extreme conditions.
Instagram: @outbackgardens

Lily Langham

Lily Langham is a plant-life artist and gardener whose Three Chimneys property at Basalt, near Daylesford, is a richly layered country garden shaped by the Central Victorian seasons. Working with volcanic soil, heavy frosts and long summers, she has created intimate spaces where grasses, perennials, fruit trees and self-sown plants are arranged to capture light and invite wildlife. Three Chimneys is also Lily's working studio, where she gathers plant material and found objects to create installations, wreaths and arrangements that blur the line between gardening and sculpture. Through open days, workshops and writing, she shares this observation-led approach to making gardens.
Instagram: @lilylangham_gardens

Tanya Loos

Living in Central Victoria, Tanya Loos is a field naturalist, educator and science communicator, and she is also the Avian Influenza Response Coordinator for BirdLife Australia. Not surprisingly, she is passionate about nature. Via writing, radio and giving presentations, Tanya loves drawing from ecological science to educate and inspire people to care about wildlife and habitat.

In 2023, she published *Daylesford Nature Diary: Six seasons in the foothill forests*, and in 2024 she launched a book about fostering coexistence with our earthmates here in Australia: *Living with Wildlife: A guide for our homes and backyards*.

Tanya loves taking people out into the forest and local bush for slow nature rambles, looking for scats and signs left by our elusive fauna, and enjoying the behaviour of some of our more well-known species.
Website: www.tanyaloos.com
Instagram: @tansnaturediary

Joanna Maclennan

Joanna Maclennan is a freelance photographer based in France. She was the photographer and creator of *Living Wild: New beginnings in the great outdoors*, which was written by her brother, Oliver Maclennan.

Specialising in interiors, lifestyle and environmental stories, Joanna has contributed work to publications including *The World of Interiors*, *Cabana*, *Milieu*, *House & Garden*, *Elle Decoration* and *The New York Times*, where her images often explore slow, place-based ways of living. She is also the photographer behind *The Foraged Home* and its French edition, *Esprit récup'*, both of which celebrate sustainable design and homes created from salvaged and foraged materials.

Alongside commercial and editorial assignments, she runs photography workshops in Provence and shares fine-art prints and books through her online shop. She continues to document people and spaces that embody creativity, resourcefulness and life close to the land.
Website: www.joannamaclennan.com
Instagram: @joannamaclennanphotography

Oliver Maclennan

Oliver Maclennan is currently based in Romania, and the author of *Living Wild: New beginnings in the great outdoors*, created by his sister, photographer Joanna Maclennan. He previously collaborated with Joanna on *The Foraged Home*, which profiles homes built using salvaged and foraged materials, and has contributed to magazines and publications focused on design, landscape and alternative ways of living.

A lifelong outdoors enthusiast, he often writes about people who have reshaped their lives around nature, simple living and time spent outside, weaving reportage with reflective storytelling. Through his books and articles, he explores how everyday environments – cabins, cottages, caravans and wild places – can contribute to more connected, creative and environmentally attuned lives.
Instagram: @olivermaclennan

Mark McDowall

Mark McDowall is a landscape architect originally from Australia, now residing in Ireland. He is a member of both the Garden & Landscape Designers Association and the Irish Landscape Institute, and is the Co-founder and Director of Cooney McDowall Design Studio, a landscape architecture and garden design practice established in 2023 to craft innovative outdoor spaces that reveal each site's inherent story.

Before founding his own practice, he held senior roles including Regional Director at ParkHood Landscape Architects in Belfast and Senior Landscape Architect at Taylor Cullity Lethlean, Australia's most highly awarded landscape architecture firm, where he contributed to internationally recognised projects such as the Australian Garden at the Royal Botanic Gardens Cranbourne, Elizabeth Quay in Perth and public works for The University of Sydney.

Mark's portfolio spans residential gardens, botanic gardens, waterfronts, public parks, educational campuses and urban streetscapes, and several of his projects have received national and international design awards.

Website: www.cmdstudio.ie

Instagram: @markmcdowall, @c.m.d.studio

Alla Olkhovska

Alla Olkhovska is a gardener, seed saver, photographer and writer living in Kharkiv, Ukraine, where she tends her family's multigenerational garden during ongoing missile attacks, drone strikes and winter blackouts. Inherited from her grandmother and rooted in an apple orchard planted by her great-grandfather in the 1950s, the garden has become both sanctuary and livelihood as she fills it with rare clematis, peonies and other unusual plants, while still cherishing a few of the original apple trees.

Through her Linden Grove seed catalogue, Alla sends hand-collected seeds to gardeners across Europe, North America, Asia and Oceania, providing her with crucial income for essentials. She is the author of the ebooks *Clematis* (published by Floret Flowers and reviewed by the International Clematis Society) and *Clematis Passports*, and she shares her work through Patreon, photography, webinars and the film *Gardening in a War Zone*.

Website: www.zaap.bio/allaolkhovska

Instagram: @allaolkhovska

Caroline Parker

Caroline Parker is a BHSc-qualified Western herbalist, gardener, forager and author of *The Medicinal Garden*. She is the founder of The Cottage Herbalist in the Wombat State Forest on Dja Dja Wurrung and Wadawurrung Country in Central Victoria. From her home studio, she hand-blends award-winning teas and tisanes in small batches using certified organic ingredients alongside seasonally wildcrafted or homegrown botanicals, and teaches practical workshops that make herbal medicine part of everyday life. Caroline is a member of the Naturopaths & Herbalists Association of Australia and The Herb Society in the United Kingdom, and contributes through talks, podcasts and publications including *Pip* and *Lost*.

Website: www.thecottageherbalist.com.au

Instagram: @thecottageherbalist

Tim Pilgrim

Based on Dja Dja Wurrung Country in Central Victoria, Tim Pilgrim is renowned for naturalistic, plant-driven gardens that are diverse, seasonal and climate-proof. With formal horticultural training and nearly two decades of experience, he blends traditional and contemporary approaches to create sustainable, climate-appropriate plantings grounded in the Australian landscape. His studio designs with a strong sense of place, balancing the site with the adjoining landscape, and considering both the experience of people and the habitat for other creatures. A true plantsman, Tim brings deep plant knowledge and a refined design eye, with experience on iconic gardens including The Garden of St Erth, Blackwood, and Paul Bangay's Stonefields. His work has been featured in *Country Style*, *The Design Files* and *Gardens Illustrated*.

Website: www.tpgardens.com.au

Instagram: @t.p_gardens

Mary Reynolds

Mary Reynolds is a reformed landscape designer who launched her international career by winning a gold medal for garden design at the 2002 Chelsea Flower Show in London – a story later told in the movie, *Dare to be Wild*. She is trying to rewild the concept of landscape design into a positive-impact profession that puts nature into the role of lead designer. A bestselling author, activist, speaker, writer, columnist and occasional television presenter, Mary is the founder of the global movement We Are The ARK (Acts of Restorative Kindness). Her mission is to decolonise our patches of this planet, garden by garden, park by park. She believes that it is past time to restore Earth's native plant and animal communities, and reminds people that our role here on this beautiful planet is one of guardian, not gardener.

Websites: www.marymary.ie, www.wearetheark.org

Instagram: @wildmarymary

Jac Semmler

Based in Australia but working internationally, Jac Semmler is a widely recognised horticulturist and innovator in dry-summer plantings, and the director of the award-winning Super Bloom plant practice. With a mission of 'plants for the people' in a changing climate, she brings beauty, diversity and delight through planting designs, skilled horticulture and plant art projects. Jac is the author of *Super Bloom*, *The Super Bloom Handbook* and *Flower Power*.
Website: www.thesuperbloom.com.au
Instagram: @jac.semmler, @superbloomau

Phyllida Steele-Wareham

Phyllida (Pip) Steele-Wareham is a trained designer, horticulturist, writer and organic gardener. She spent her childhood in the bush in Arnhem Land and the rainforests of Far North Queensland. Later, she overhauled a run-down farm in Tasmania, which led to her leaving a corporate career for a life in horticulture. Through online avenues, she is currently sharing her journey of reinstating the food and flower gardens at Moorfield, an 1860s former sheep station on Dja Dja Wurrung Country in the Goldfields region of Central Victoria. She has been promoting her love of gardens and their impact on people for over ten years.
Website: thegardenatmoorfield.substack.com
Instagram: @the_garden_at_moorfield

The Stones, Clydesdale, Victoria

Jeremy Valentine and Grant Francis are the custodians of The Stones, a historic 1850s stone farmhouse and 1.2-hectare (3-acre) garden on Dja Dja Wurrung Country in Central Victoria, between Daylesford and Castlemaine.

Over more than a decade, they have transformed its rocky, drought-prone, volcanic paddocks into an ever-evolving, plant-rich landscape of architectural succulents, silvers and greens, stone walls and whimsical structures that respond closely to the site's extremes rather than to decorative fashions. Their garden has been profiled by outlets such as *The Design Files*, *Better Homes and Gardens*, *Gardening Australia* and Open Gardens Victoria, and it is celebrated as a tough-climate garden that feels deeply at ease in its historical setting.

Jeremy also writes about The Stones and regional life, penning monthly newsletters and essays that explore climate, place and the evolving character of the garden.
Instagram: @thestonescentralvictoria

Paul Thompson

Paul Thompson is an Australian landscape architect renowned since 1970 for his designs using Australian native plants. He was responsible for the planting of many landmark projects, such as the Australian Garden at the Royal Botanic Gardens Cranbourne (1995–2012) and the Forest Gallery at Museums Victoria (2000). He was involved with all scales of public gardens, parks and private landscapes across Australia. His work shows how richly layered native plantings can create resilient, biodiverse, climate-responsive places, and it has influenced more than one generation of designers and gardeners.

His designs have been included and described in many books and publications, and he is the author of *Australian Planting Design*, which is widely regarded as one of the country's most authoritative texts on designing with plants. It continues to sell in digital form. After 55 years, Paul recently stepped into retirement, leaving an enduring legacy in both designed landscapes and the way Australians think about planting with their own flora.

Meg Travis

Meg Travis is a grower, cook and writer based in Cornwall, England. She tends One Field Farm, a small windswept field in Crantock that has long fed her family and shaped her seasonal rhythm, even as life has shifted in recent years. Her path into food and farming began with her money-free Girl Friday year when she travelled between households and small creative businesses, swapping skills for meals, a place at the table and the chance to learn. That journey brought her to Oak & Monkey Puzzle in 2016, a season of shared work and preserving that helped to set the course for the field-based, community-rooted life she has built since. She now works at the organic farm Nancarrow, growing, preserving and writing, and her work often centres on simple seasonal cooking and bottles of hedgerow cordial and syrup.
Instagram: @girlfridays_notes

Patrick Vernuccio

Known as The Frenchie Gardener, Patrick Vernuccio is a French author, facilitator and content creator who promotes urban gardening. He regularly shares his deep passion for growing food in small urban spaces and educates more than two million gardening enthusiasts on his social-media accounts. Patrick would like us to welcome nature back into our cities and our lives by re-creating an essential connection with food, seasons and biodiversity. A certified permaculturist, he is adapting its philosophy and techniques for a more urban regenerative lifestyle. He is also the co-founder of Gardenstead, a free gardening social-media app.
Website: www.thefrenchiegardener.com
Instagram: @thefrenchiegardener

INDEX

Published in 2026 by Murdoch Books,
an imprint of Allen & Unwin

Murdoch Books Australia
Cammeraygal Country
83 Alexander Street
Crows Nest NSW 2065
Phone: +61 (0)2 8425 0100
murdochbooks.com.au
info@murdochbooks.com.au

Murdoch Books UK
Ormond House
26–27 Boswell Street
London WC1N 3JZ
Phone: +44 (0) 20 8785 5995
murdochbooks.co.uk
info@murdochbooks.co.uk

For corporate orders and custom publishing,
contact our business development team at
salesenquiries@murdochbooks.com.au

Publisher: Melissa Kayser
Editorial manager: Andrea O'Connor
Design manager: Sarah Odgers
Editor: Dannielle Viera
Photographer: Emily Weaving
Illustrators: Saffron Howard and Natasha Morgan
Production manager: Natalie Crouch

MIX
Paper | Supporting responsible forestry
FSC www.fsc.org FSC® C008047

Murdoch Books acknowledges the Traditional Owners of the Country on which we live and work. We pay our respects to all Aboriginal and Torres Strait Islander Elders, past and present.

ISBN 9 781 76150 1333

NATIONAL LIBRARY OF AUSTRALIA
A catalogue record for this book is available from the National Library of Australia

A catalogue record for this book is available from the British Library

Colour reproduction by Megan Ellis

Printed in China by C&C Offset Printing Co., Ltd.

OVEN GUIDE: You may find cooking times vary depending on the oven and oven setting you are using. For fan-forced (convection) ovens, as a general rule, set the oven temperature to 20°C (25–50°F) lower than indicated in the recipe.

We have used 20 ml (4 teaspoon) tablespoon measures. If you are using a 15 ml (3 teaspoon) tablespoon add an extra teaspoon of the ingredient for each tablespoon specified.

10 9 8 7 6 5 4 3 2 1